D1714025

A Pugwash Monograph

Nuclear Weapons

The Road to Zero

EDITED BY

Joseph Rotblat
1995 Nobel Laureate for Peace

EXECUTIVE EDITOR

Frank Blackaby

WestviewPress
A Division of HarperCollinsPublishers

Copyright © 1998 by Westview Press, A Division of HarperCollins Publishers, Inc.

Published in 1998 in the United States of America by Westview Press, 5500 Central Avenue, Boulder, Colorado 80301-2877, and in the United Kingdom by Westview Press, 12 Hid's Copse Road, Cumnor Hill, Oxford OX2 9JJ

A CIP catalog record for this book is available from the Library of Congress.
ISBN 0-8133-3517-5

The paper used in this publication meets the requirements of the American National Standard for Permanence of Paper for Printed Library Materials Z39.48-1984.

10   9   8   7   6   5   4   3   2   1

Contents

Preface

The Pugwash Monograph *A Nuclear-Weapon-Free World: Desirable? Feasible?* edited by Joseph Rotblat, Jack Steinberger and Bhalchandra Udgaonkar, published in 1993, was the outcome of a comprehensive study carried out by Pugwash on the need to eliminate nuclear weapons, and on the ways to achieve this. The book has since been translated into seven languages – Arabic, Chinese, French, Japanese, Russian, Spanish and Swedish. In 1995 (after the award of the Nobel Peace Prize to Pugwash) the book was published by Westview Press in a paperback edition.

The publication of the Pugwash Monograph can be seen as the start of serious studies on the concept of a nuclear-weapon-free world. These include several reports from the Henry L. Stimson Center in the United States, the INESAP group in Germany, the International Association of Lawyers Against Nuclear Arms, and the Committee on International Security and Arms Control (CISAC) of the US National Academy of Sciences. As a direct outcome of the Pugwash Monograph, the Australian Government set up the Canberra Commission. The Report of the Commission, published in 1996, is a powerful exposition of the urgent need to rid the world of nuclear weapons.

In addition to these studies there have been important pronouncements, both by individuals – high ranking military and political leaders – and by groups. These include the statement from the International Generals and Admirals, 60 of them from 17 countries, and the clear opinion from the International Court of Justice on the obligation of the nuclear powers to proceed to nuclear disarmament. The result of all this is that the notion of a nuclear-weapon-free world is no longer the fanciful dream of a fringe group, but a sound and practical objective, which could be realized in the foreseeable future.

There is also a growing mass movement centred around the "Abolition 2000" network.

Despite all this, the basic policy of the nuclear weapon states (or at least four of them) remains unaltered: nuclear weapons are needed for their security.

While the present situation can be described as a stalemate, there have been a number of events since 1993, some marking progress towards an NWFW but others moving away from the goal. On the positive side, the Nuclear Non-Proliferation Treaty is now practically universal, leaving the three threshold states, India, Pakistan, and Israel, as notorious exceptions. On the other hand, the indefinite extension of the NPT in 1995 is viewed by some in the nuclear weapon states as a licence for the indefinite retention of nuclear weapons.

The Comprehensive Test Ban Treaty, though not yet in force, has been adopted by a very large number of states, including all five nuclear powers, and it seems very unlikely that any of these will resume testing. On the other hand, the USA is carrying out sub-critical testing, apparently allowed under the CTBT, but causing unease to many other parties to the Treaty. The US stewardship programme provides for nuclear weapon "modernization," which is difficult to distinguish from new weapon development.

In the bilateral negotiations on the reduction of nuclear arsenals some progress has been made at the summit meeting between Presidents Clinton and Yeltsin in Helsinki, March 1997 – a further stage of dismantlement of strategic weapons in START III is planned. On the other hand, START II has not yet been ratified by the Duma, and this is unlikely to happen in view of the enlargement of NATO, strongly opposed by all parties in Russia.

A Malaysian-sponsored resolution, calling for a Nuclear Weapons Convention, was passed by a large majority of the UN General Assembly in December 1996, but the Conference on Disarmament in Geneva, the body that needs to implement it, is completely stymied. The nuclear weapon powers are clearly in no hurry. They are planning to keep their nuclear weapons until well into the next century. An NWFW is still beyond their horizon.

A continued stalemate is dangerous. It may close the window of opportunity that opened after the end of the Cold War, and lead to a new nuclear arms race.

It was for these reasons that Pugwash decided to revisit the problem, bring it up-to-date, and put forward suggestions for progress. The results of this study, discussed at a Pugwash Workshop held in London in October 1996, are presented in this volume.

The book is in two parts. The first part is an up-to-date argument for an NWFW. After an analysis of the fundamental issues involved in the first chapter, the following five chapters discuss the main difficulties that have emerged in the debate on the issue: the several stages that may be required; the various aspects of verifying agreements on the elimination of nuclear weapons – technological verification, societal verification; the problem of theft of weapons and materials; and finally the motivation for, and effects of, attempts to violate the Convention.

The second part is an assessment of the current situation, a review of the forward and backward steps on the way to an NWFW. In seven chapters, three aspects are discussed: nuclear weapon deployments, doctrines, and treaties.

As usual in Pugwash, the views expressed in the chapters are the views of the authors: they do not necessarily coincide with the views of the institutions to which the contributors are affiliated.

The same applies to the "Introduction and Summary," which precedes the main text and includes a brief history of the subject. It was written by Frank Blackaby, the Executive Editor.

The bulk of the editorial work was done by Blackaby and by Tom Milne. To both of them, I want to express my profound gratitude.

Joseph Rotblat

Abbreviations and Acronyms

ABM	anti-ballistic missile
ACDA	(US) Arms Control and Disarmament Agency
ASMP	Air-Sol Moyenne Portée
BMD	ballistic missile defence
BMDP	Ballistic Missile Defense Program
BWC	Biological Weapons Convention
C3I	command, control, communications, and intelligence
CBM	confidence building measure
CBO	(US) Congressional Budget Office
CD	Conference on Disarmament
CFE	Conventional Forces in Europe
CINC	Commander in Chief
CIS	Commonwealth of Independent States
CISAC	Committee on International Security and Arms Control (of the US Academy of Sciences)
CTB(T)	Comprehensive Test Ban (Treaty)
CWC	Chemical Weapons Convention
DOD	(US) Department of Defense
DOE	(US) Department of Energy
EURATOM	European Atomic Energy Agency
FSU	former Soviet Union
G-7	Group of Seven industrialized nations
G-21	Group of 21
GAN	Gosatomnadzor (Russia's civilian oversight nuclear agency)
HE	high explosive
HEU	highly-enriched uranium
IAEA	International Atomic Energy Agency
ICBM	intercontinental ballistic missile
ICJ	International Court of Justice
INF	Intermediate-range Nuclear Forces (Treaty)
LEU	low-enriched uranium
LWR	light water reactor
MBFR	mutual and balanced force reductions
MINATOM	(Russian) Ministry of Atomic Energy
MIRV	multiple independently-targetable re-entry vehicles
MOA	Memorandum of Agreement
MOX	mixed oxide (fuel)
MPC&A	materials, protection, control and accounting
MTCR	Missile Technology Control Regime

NAM	Non-aligned Movement
NAS	(US) National Academy of Sciences
NASA	North American Space Agency
NATO	North Atlantic Treaty Organization
NCA	national command authorities
NFU	no first use
NGO	non-governmental organization
NIF	National Ignition Facility
NMD	national missile defence
(N)NWS	(non-) nuclear weapon state
NPR	Nuclear Posture Review
NPT	Non-Proliferation Treaty
NRDC	Natural Resources Defense Council
NSA	negative security assurance
NWC	Nuclear Weapons Convention
NWF(W)	nuclear-weapon-free (world)
OSCE	Organization for Security and Cooperation in Europe
OTA	Office of Technology Assessment
P-5	Permanent Five members of the UN Security Council
PCAST	President's Committee of Advisers on Science and Technology
PNE	peaceful nuclear explosion
PTBT	Partial Test Ban Treaty
REACT	rapid executions and combat targeting
RERTR	Reduced Enrichment for Research and Test Reactors
RFAF	Russian Federation Air Force
SALT	Strategic Arms Limitation Talks
SBIRS	Space-based Infra-red System
SBSS	Science-based Stockpile Stewardship programme
SDI	Strategic Defense Initiative
SLBM	submarine-launched ballistic missile
SSBN	nuclear powered ballistic missile submarine
START	Strategic Arms Reduction Talks/Treaty
STRATCOM	Strategic Command
STS	stockpile-to-target sequence
SV	societal verification
T-3	threshold nuclear states (India, Israel, Pakistan)
TASM	Tactical Air-to-surface Missile
THAAD	Theatre High Altitude Area Defense
TMD	theatre missile defence
TNW	tactical nuclear weapon
UN(SC)	United Nations (Security Council)
WMD	weapons of mass destruction

About the Contributors

Frank Blackaby, UK, is president of Abolition 2000 UK and vice-president of the National Peace Council. Previously he has been director of the Stockholm International Peace Research Institute, and deputy director of the National Institute of Economic and Social Research, London.

Matthew Bunn, USA, is assistant director of the Program on Science, Technology, and Public Policy at the John F. Kennedy School of Government. Previously he has worked on nuclear materials issues at the National Academy of Sciences and the Office of Science and Technology Policy in the Executive Office of the President of the United States.

Thomas Cochran, USA, is senior scientist and director of the Nuclear Program at the Natural Resources Defense Council, Washington D.C.

Steve Fetter, USA, is an associate professor in the School of Public Affairs at the University of Maryland, College Park, and a member of the National Academy of Sciences' Committee on International Security and Arms Control. Previously he has been special assistant to the Assistant Secretary of Defense for International Security Policy; Council on Foreign Relations fellow at the State Department; and a research fellow at Stanford and Harvard Universities, and the Lawrence Livermore National Laboratory.

Cathleen Fisher, USA, is a senior associate at the Henry L. Stimson Center, Washington D.C., where she directs the Center's project on Eliminating Weapons of Mass Destruction. Previously she was assistant professor in the Department of Political Science, Emory University.

Richard L. Garwin, USA, is an emeritus Fellow at IBM's Thomas J. Watson Research Center, senior fellow for Science and Technology at the Council on Foreign Relations in New York, and adjunct professor of physics at Columbia University, New York. Previously he has been a nuclear weapons designer, and a member of the President's Science Advisory Committee.

John P. Holdren, USA, is Teresa and John Heinz Professor of Environmental Policy and director of the Program on Science, Technology and Public Policy in the John F. Kennedy School of Government, and professor of environmental science and public policy in the Department of Earth and Planetary Sciences at Harvard University. He is also chair of the Committee on International Security and Arms Control of the US National Academy of Sciences and a member of President Clinton's Committee of Advisors on Science and Technology.

Rebecca Johnson, UK, is director of The Acronym Institute, London, and has monitored disarmament negotiations in Geneva and New York for several years.

Michael MccGwire, UK, is an honorary fellow in the Faculty of Social and Political Sciences, Cambridge University, and honorary professor of international politics at the University of Wales, Aberystwyth. Previously he has been a British naval officer (1942-67) and a senior fellow at the Brookings Institution (1979-90).

Tom Milne, UK, is a researcher at the London Office of the Pugwash Conferences on Science and World Affairs.

Alexander Nikitin, Russia, is director of the Centre for Political and International Studies, Moscow. He is also professor of political science at the Moscow State Institute of International Relations under the Ministry of Foreign Affairs and vice-chairman of the Russian Pugwash Committee of Scientists for Disarmament.

Robert S. Norris, USA, is a senior scientist with the Natural Resources Defense Council Nuclear Program, Washington D.C., and director of the Council's Nuclear Weapons Databook Project.

Christopher E. Paine, USA, is a senior research associate with the Natural Resources Defense Council Nuclear Program, Washington D.C. Previously he was a Congressional Staff Member involved in nuclear arms control and non-proliferation issues.

John Pike, USA, is director of the Space Policy Project at the Federation of American Scientists, Washington D.C.

Daniel Plesch, UK, is director of the British American Security Information Council.

Jan Prawitz, Sweden, is a visiting scholar at the Swedish Institute for International Affairs, Stockholm. Previously he has been a senior fellow at the National Defence Research Establishment, and special assistant for disarmament at the Ministry of Defence, Sweden.

Joseph Rotblat, UK, is emeritus professor of physics at the University of London. A participant in the Manhattan Project during World War II, he is a signatory of the Russell-Einstein Manifesto, and recipient, with Pugwash, of the 1995 Nobel Peace Prize. The first secretary-general of Pugwash, he was later its president, and is now a member of its executive committee.

Vadim Simonenko, Russia, is deputy scientific director, Russian Federal Nuclear Centre - Institute of Technical Physics, Chelyabinsk.

Introduction and Summary

Frank Blackaby

The State of the Argument

The idea of a nuclear-weapon-free world has come in from the cold. Twelve years ago it was still beyond the fringes of serious political discussion – seen as wholly fanciful, part of some far-distant Utopia. In the last twelve years, the idea has worked its way through to a position on the map of political possibility. It could actually happen. How has this change come about? Here is a brief description of a succession of steps that changed the nature of the argument.

In March 1985 Konstantin Chernenko, General Secretary of the Communist Party of the Soviet Union, died, and was succeeded by Mikhail Gorbachev. At Gorbachev's first summit meeting with President Reagan in November of that year, the joint communiqué said: "A nuclear war cannot be won and must never be fought." The nuclear weapon experts, certainly in the West, clearly regarded this as a pious statement of no particular significance – for instance, Paul Nitze's record of the meeting does not mention it. It was in fact a step which rejected the battlefield use of nuclear weapons: a step towards the conclusion that the sole possible use of nuclear weapons was to deter their use by another nuclear power. Then, of course, if there were no other nuclear weapon powers, that function, too, would lapse.

In January 1986 Gorbachev wrote to Reagan proposing a broad timetable for the elimination of all nuclear weapons by the end of the century. Reagan's advisers dismissed this as a propaganda ploy. Reagan himself, however, reacted rather differently, asking: "Why wait until the year 2000?" At Reykjavik in October 1986, to the horror of his advisers, Reagan might well have agreed to a joint statement endorsing the objective of eliminating nuclear weapons; he, too, wanted to get rid of them. However, he was determined to press ahead with his Strategic Defense Initiative; this Gorbachev could not accept.

The idea emerged again, in a rather different form, in 1992. Les Aspin, later to become President Clinton's first Secretary of Defense, circulated a working paper on nuclear weapon policy. He argued that the dominant need was for the USA to prevent the further spread of nuclear weapons:

> During the Cold War, if an opportunity had somehow arisen to rid the world of nuclear weapons, the United States would have declined ...
> If we now had the opportunity to ban all nuclear weapons, we would. That is how profound the change is that we have undergone.

Aspin was suggesting that the USA's main objective must be to prevent the proliferation of nuclear weapons. If a worldwide ban was feasible, that would be one way of doing it. The United States could safely rely on its superiority in conventional military capability.

Also in the early 1990s, Robert McNamara, former US Secretary of Defense, re-examined the Cuban missile crisis of 1962, together with others – Russians and Cubans – who had been parties to the decisions taken. It became clear that those decisions were taken on the basis of information that was badly flawed – for instance, on the number of nuclear warheads in Cuba, and on the degree to which decisions had been delegated to local commanders. Mr McNamara concluded, first, that the USA and USSR had come much closer than anyone then realized to a nuclear weapon exchange. Secondly, and more generally, he concluded: "The indefinite combination of nuclear weapons and human fallibility will lead to a nuclear exchange."

A Pugwash book of 1993 – *A Nuclear-Weapon-Free World: Desirable? Feasible?* – has its part in this history of ideas. It was read by Gareth Evans, Australian Minister of Foreign Affairs: it led him to persuade the Prime Minister, Paul Keating, to set up in 1995 the Canberra Commission, which had as its explicit mandate to: "... develop ideas and proposals for a concrete and realistic program to achieve a world totally free of nuclear weapons."

By the mid-1990s there was a whole battery of reports and statements arguing that the nuclear weapon powers should make an unequivocal commitment to a nuclear-weapon-free world. The arguments are not new: they have been kept alive by the peace organizations in various countries throughout the long period of nuclear weapon confrontation. The new element is the status and profession of many of the signatories to the reports – former generals and senior statesmen. Arguments have to be logical; but their effectiveness in changing policy is multiplied when they are presented by those who have, or have had, some status in a country's power structure.

There have been now three reports from a committee established at the Henry L. Stimson Center in Washington to guide a project "intended to encourage policy-makers, both in the United States and in other countries, to give serious consideration to the complete elimination of weapons of mass destruction from all countries as a long-term policy objective." The signatories include military men, nuclear weapon experts and ambassadors who were all prominent in directing nuclear weapon policy during the Cold War – General Andrew Goodpaster, General Charles Horner, General W Y Smith, Robert McNamara, Ambassador Paul Nitze, Ambassador Rozanne Ridgway.

The list of signatories to the Canberra Commission Report also includes names of men who have previously administered nuclear weapon policies: General Lee Butler, Field Marshal Lord Carver, Robert McNamara.

Two other documents should be added to this list. One, issued in December 1996, is a Statement on Nuclear Weapons by International Generals and Admirals, signed by 60 military professionals, including 17 from Russia and 19 from the USA. This states: "Long-term international policy must be based on the declared principle of continuous, complete and irrevocable elimination of nuclear weapons."

Then there is the advisory opinion of the International Court of Justice on the legal status of nuclear weapons, issued in July 1996. It had been widely assumed that the Court would refuse to rule on the matter. It did not refuse. This is its ruling:

> ... the threat or use of nuclear weapons will generally be contrary to the rules of international law applicable in armed conflict and in particular the principles and rules of humanitarian law. However, in view of the current state of international law, and the elements of fact at its disposal, the Court cannot conclude definitively whether the threat or use of nuclear weapons would be lawful or unlawful in the extreme circumstances of self-defence, in which the very survival of a state would be at stake.

The Court also unanimously stated that there existed: "an obligation to pursue in good faith and bring to a conclusion negotiations leading to nuclear disarmament in all its aspects under strict and effective international control." Under this ruling, any threat or use of nuclear weapons by one of the five nuclear weapon states against a "rogue state" would be illegal: a "rogue state," such as Iraq, could not put the very survival of the United States, Russia, China, France or the UK at stake. On nuclear disarmament, the ICJ ruling is stronger than the wording of Article VI of the NPT in two ways. First, there is no link to general and complete disarmament. Second, there is the requirement not just to negotiate in good faith, but to bring the negotiations to a conclusion.

The arguments presented in these various reports are powerful arguments, put forward by once-powerful men. If the sole function of nuclear weapons is to deter their use by another nuclear power, and if there are no other nuclear powers, then this function obviously lapses.

The ruling of the World Court implies that the use or threat of use against non-nuclear powers is illegal. It is also precluded by security assurances given to non-nuclear members of the Non-Proliferation Treaty and by the nuclear powers' accession to the protocols of nuclear-weapon-free zone treaties. The use, or threat of use, of nuclear weapons against non-nuclear weapon states is not acceptable. The conventional military capabilities of the major powers are fully adequate to deter "rogue states."

A structure in which a handful of states are permitted to own nuclear weapons and all the rest are forbidden to do so cannot last indefinitely. In the words of the Canberra Commission:

> Nuclear weapons are held by a handful of states which insist that these weapons provide unique security benefits, and yet reserve uniquely to themselves the right to own them. The situation is highly discriminatory and thus unstable; it cannot be sustained.

The combination of human fallibility and nuclear weapons would, in the long run, make their use inevitable.

These are the central arguments which emerge from the evolution of ideas about nuclear weapons, and which are presented in these reports. They amount to a powerful case.

A Nuclear-Weapon-Free World and the Objections

The immediate objective of those who want a nuclear-weapon-free world is a limited one – limited to the elimination of this particular weapon system. It is not to produce peace on earth; to eliminate disputes between states; to end all war.

It is not true that there would have to be some tremendous change in the nature of international relations to make the elimination of nuclear weapons possible. At Reykjavik in 1986 Presidents Reagan and Gorbachev came close to a joint acceptance of this objective. This was well before the demise of the Communist system in the Soviet Union, at a time when Reagan was still speaking of the Soviet Union as an "evil empire."

It is sometimes argued, for instance, that an NWFW would only be possible if all the present nuclear weapon powers were stable democracies. No doubt the standard democratic freedoms would help, for instance, with the effective use of societal verification. However, all democratic procedures do not necessarily work in favour of disarmament measures. In Russia, it is the new Parliamentary system, not the Presidency, that is delaying the ratification of START II. In the 1980s, had the Soviet Union been a democracy, it is not at all clear that Gorbachev would have been supported in the major concessions that he made to give an impetus to nuclear disarmament. There is no certain link between democracy and enthusiasm for disarmament or arms control.

Of course there are international political developments that would help the progress towards an NWFW, and others that would hinder it. For instance, the decision to expand NATO eastwards is probably the main factor delaying the Russian Duma's ratification of START II. The process works both ways. Progress in getting rid of nuclear weapons would have all kinds of beneficial by-products elsewhere on the international political scene. It would strengthen the non-proliferation regime in general; it would improve North-South relations. However, the general conclusion relevant here is this: in order to remove this particular category of weapons, there does not have to be some massive transformation in international political relations.

There are a number of descriptions of the steps along the road to zero. Most descriptions agree, for example, that there should be a process of de-alerting, and a move to an agreement on No First Use. However, there seems no good reason for the nuclear weapon powers to stretch the process out far into the next century.

In general, the Western nuclear weapon powers, in their statements about the objective of a nuclear-weapon-free world, have relegated the issue to a virtually unimaginably distant future by linking nuclear disarmament to general and complete disarmament. It waits for the lion and the lamb to lie down together. It is time for this link – between nuclear disarmament and general and complete disarmament – to be broken, and the ruling of the World Court goes some way to doing this. The elimination of nuclear weapons can be treated as a separate issue.

There should now be, as the Canberra Commission said, an unequivocal commitment by the nuclear weapon powers to the objective of zero nuclear weapons. It is more doubtful whether there should be a time-bound programme. A number of non-nuclear weapon states have suggested this; it is not hard to see why they have done so. For years after they signed and ratified the Non-Proliferation Treaty, the nuclear weapon powers continued frenetic competition in nuclear weapon developments, devising new weapon systems, extending ranges, improving accuracies. They took no notice of their obligation under Article VI of the NPT.

It is to a certain extent a similar situation now. The declared nuclear weapon policies of the major powers do include the possibility of some further reduction in numbers after START II. But there is no "declaration of intent" to move to zero. The argument of the non-nuclear weapon states is that, without a fixed timetable, the nuclear weapon powers will settle down to continue to own nuclear weapons in perpetuity.

The counter-argument to the demand for a fixed timetable is this. There may be some chance of getting the nuclear weapon powers to make some kind of unequivocal commitment to the zero objective; there is no chance of getting them to accept a time-bound framework. It is, therefore, a waste of effort to push the point at present. For specific steps along the way, once it is reasonably clear that there is a good chance of negotiating success, it may be sensible to suggest a completion date: it worked with the Comprehensive Test Ban Treaty. The idea of a timetable for the whole process from the present position to zero nuclear weapons is currently too ambitious.

What reasons are given for turning down the Canberra Commission proposal for an unequivocal commitment to a zero target? The proposal has been officially ignored. The probable reason is that any official reply would simply serve to draw attention to the issue. The governments of the nuclear weapon states do not want to revive public interest in nuclear weapon issues. The official line seems to be to lie low and say nothing, and hope that the ideas expressed in these various statements and reports will be buried in general apathy. So any criticism of the idea of a commitment to zero nuclear weapons is left to those outside the governments who still favour the indefinite retention of nuclear weapons.

The main theme of the criticism centres on verification. The argument is on these lines. If a state signs the Chemical or Biological Weapons Convention and then cheats, this does not provide it with any overwhelming military superiority. However, cheating on a Nuclear Weapons Convention could do exactly that. Further, it is not possible to provide a verification system which gives a total guarantee against such cheating.

The first objection, therefore, is the "bombs in the basement" objection – that a nuclear weapon power could hide a number of nuclear bombs in a basement; there is no way in which this could be detected. The second objection is the "Iraq example" objection – that a "rogue state" could secretly build up a nuclear weapon capability also without detection.

Sometimes the possibility of a terrorist bomb is added to this list. However, here the argument goes the other way. A nuclear weapon capability is of no use to counter a terrorist threat, since there would be no way of knowing what target should be attacked, and since even if it was known where the terrorists were hiding, nuclear weapons would be of no use in dealing with them. Further, the risk of terrorist theft, either of a weapon or of fissile material, is much greater while a large nuclear weapons industry still exists. In a world in which that industry had been dismantled, and in which there were much tighter safeguards over fissile material of all kinds, terrorist theft would be much more difficult. Terrorist threats are not an argument for keeping nuclear weapons; rather the contrary.

On the other two verification objections, there are a number of points to be made in rebuttal. A great deal can still be done to improve the techniques of technological verification: very little money has been spent on it, compared to the sums that have been devoted to the technological nuclear arms race. Some things should be done now. It is time for the nuclear weapon powers to provide full information and records: where exactly the nuclear warheads that now exist are located, together with a full account and records of past production of weapon-grade fissile material. Then there should be provision for international supervision of the processes of dismantling weapons. There will be much more confidence in verification procedures that begin when there are still thousands of nuclear warheads, rather than procedures that only begin right at the end of the dismantling process.

However, there will still be significant margins of error – in records of past production of fissile material, or possibly in records of the number of warheads destroyed in testing. If a nuclear weapon power were to decide, from the beginning of this process, that it intended to cheat and to conceal a certain number of warheads, or a certain amount of fissile material, it is quite possible that it could conceal the fact from an international inspecting body – if necessary by forged records.

There are a number of comments on this scenario. The verification of the final move to zero nuclear weapons would only come about after a long period in which the number of nuclear warheads had been coming down; in which, as a consequence, the whole idea of the actual use or threat of use of these weapons had become more and more unreal – they would have been marginalized as obsolete totems of an era long past; and in which, all being well, there would have been at least a decade of experience of international verification of the whole process of disarmament. In those circumstances, which are now difficult to imagine, the final verified move to zero might well carry much less risk than it seems to carry now.

Supposing that after years of reductions a nuclear weapon state did decide to cheat and conceal a cache of nuclear warheads, what would it hope to gain? The idea that it would use them without warning to blow up parts of the rest of the world is surely totally absurd. If it simply threatened to use them in the course of some dispute, then the other major powers would proceed rapidly to reconstitute their nuclear weapon capability. The cheating state would of course become a pariah state – an international outcast – in the international system. If the cheating state simply kept them, and never disclosed that it had them, what would be the point?

The second danger is that of the "rogue state" – a minor state, such as Iraq, that signs and ratifies a Nuclear Weapons Convention without any intention of observing its provisions, and that proceeds secretly to try to acquire a nuclear weapon capability. This would require substantial installations, and it must be assumed that the Nuclear Weapons Convention would include provisions for "anytime anywhere" inspections. In Iraq, before the Iraq-Kuwait war, there were no IAEA challenge inspections. There is an interesting contrast here with the inspections in Iran in the 1990s, when the IAEA was permitted by Iran to visit any sites that were considered suspect. For instance, in February 1992, the IAEA visited two Chinese-supplied nuclear research facilities in Isfahan, a small calutron supplied by China in Karaj, a training and recreation facility for the staff of the Atomic Energy Organization of Iran at Moallem Kalayeh, the site of a uranium exploration project at Saghand, the 1957 US-supplied 6-MW

Amirahad research reactor in Tehran, and an incapacitated uranium re-concentration facility at the University of Tehran. There have been other such inspections since then. If inspections on this scale were the norm, it would not be easy for a "rogue state" secretly to construct all the installations needed to establish a nuclear weapon capability.

An NWFW would be one in which all the declared nuclear weapon states had agreed to eliminate their nuclear weapons. They would, therefore, have a common interest in enforcing non-proliferation in the rest of the world. They would have, between them, overwhelming conventional superiority over any minor "rogue state." This conventional superiority would be fully adequate to impose total devastation on any minor state that actually used a nuclear weapon.

Perhaps the most important point of rebuttal concerns relative risk. The proponents of an NWFW do not claim that it would produce a world without risk. That is not attainable. The claim is rather to compare two worlds, and to ask in which of them the risks of a catastrophe are greater. One is the nuclear-weapon-free world, where the dangers are as described. The other is a world in which the nuclear weapon powers have retained substantial numbers of nuclear warheads with the apparent intention of keeping them in perpetuity, and where as a consequence a number of other states would eventually decide to follow their example, to withdraw from the Non-Proliferation Treaty, and to set out to acquire a nuclear weapon capability themselves. For, as the Canberra Commission argues, a two-tier system is simply not sustainable in the long run. The risk of the actual use of a nuclear weapon is greater in the second scenario.

There is one other element to be brought into the verification debate: societal verification, or citizen's reporting. This could significantly increase the chance that cheating would be discovered. The idea is simple – that citizens in general, and scientists in particular, should be encouraged to report any suspicions they might have that a Nuclear Weapons Convention was being violated.

There have been two objections to this idea. One is that it would not work in repressive dictatorships. The other is that nation states would not favour it, because the idea has too great a flavour of supra-national loyalty.

On the first of these objections, it is not easy now for any state to prevent communication across its borders, and the provisions for societal verification in any Convention should require that asylum should, if necessary, be granted to any person, in a state with a bad human rights record, who reports suspicions of Treaty violation.

On the second objection, in many states there is already increasing concern about the threat from a terrorist bomb. This might well be constructed by a group within the state itself. The main weapon against terrorist activity is information. Already in London there are posters asking citizens to report any suspicions of terrorist activity to the police. Governments would be concerned, not just with possible threats from other states, but with threats from possibly semi-lunatic groups within the state itself. Here citizen's reporting would be a valuable resource.

Further, so far as other states are concerned, the main preoccupation of the ex-nuclear weapon states is likely to be with the potential threat from small "rogue states." As a consequence, even if the ex-nuclear weapon states were doubtful about having citizen's reporting within their own borders, they might well consider it a price worth paying for the advantages of having citizen's reporting elsewhere in the world. Their priority would be to get advance information of possible treaty violations in those states that were for some reason considered to be hostile to the main industrial powers.

Violations of a Nuclear Weapons Convention would have to be made criminal offences under national law in each state. There is nothing new about that: this is also a requirement of the Chemical Weapons Convention, now in force. A Nuclear Weapons Convention should also include provision by which people could notify any suspicions directly to the International Verification Authority. States should also be required to give positive encouragement, particularly to scientific associations, to be on the watch for Convention violations. International associations of "Friends of the Convention" could be established, which could keep in touch with the verification authorities. Again, this is not new. International organizations concerned with chemical weapons, such as the Harvard Sussex Program, have had close contacts with the Preparatory Commission for setting up the Organization for the Prohibition of Chemical Weapons. They could be explicitly asked to watch out for violations.

Citizen's reporting of possible Treaty violations, and general critical scrutiny of the nuclear weapons industry by outside bodies, already exists – although it is true that up to now there has not been much official encouragement. In Russia a number of scientists have given accounts both of new chemical weapon developments and of alleged infringements of the Biological Weapons Convention. In the United States, there are a number of groups that will monitor the Stewardship and Maintenance Program for nuclear warheads, to check whether it is being used to design and develop new types of nuclear warhead.

Societal verification is not foolproof. However, it would serve to increase the chances that potential treaty violations were discovered in time; it would add to the inhibitions against cheating.

The main technical element of an NWFW verification process is a system that is needed now, to prevent nuclear theft: a rigorous system for the protection, accounting and control, not only of the dismantling of nuclear weapons, but also of all fissile material, both military and civil. The risk of theft, and its possible consequences, is just as great a danger now as it would be in an NWFW; indeed, it is probably greater. Precautions against this risk are not being given adequate priority. Action is needed on many fronts: improving security and accounting for nuclear materials; combating nuclear smuggling; increasing transparency in the management of weapon-usable nuclear material; halting or minimizing continued production of these materials; and carrying out disposition procedures to reduce the risk from excess fissile materials by making them far more difficult to use in nuclear weapons. Any fissile materials that could be used for making weapons – and that includes civil stocks of plutonium – should be guarded and accounted for as though they were nuclear weapons: the system should be brought up to the "stored weapon standard." These things need to be done whether there is a move to an NWFW or not. Making the needed improvements to nuclear security will cost several billion dollars over the next decade or more, a small fraction of the several hundred billion dollars the world spends annually in the name of "defence."

The arguments for a move to an NWFW, in preference to the alternative, are strong, and are much more widely accepted than they were ten years ago. A number of those who in the past have been in favour of defence policies based on nuclear weapons have now changed their minds. The next question is this: are we moving towards an NWFW or not?

Progress or Regress: Nuclear Weapon Policy and Deployment

US and Russian Policy

The nuclear weapon policy statements of the nuclear weapon powers seem as far away as ever from accepting the objective of zero nuclear weapons. The US nuclear policy statements still refer to the need for parity, and indeed still state as one objective the need to emerge in some sense victorious after a nuclear weapon exchange. Not much has been done to reduce the alert status of the nuclear weapon confrontation. The fact that the warheads are no longer targeted on Russia is not meaningful: they can be retargeted in minutes. This was a superficial move.

Indeed, in one respect nuclear policy seems to be going backwards. There are many more references now to the possible use of nuclear weapons against states that are parties to the Non-Proliferation Treaty as non-nuclear weapon states. (There are now only three significant states – India, Pakistan and Israel – that are not either signatories to the NPT or members of a nuclear-weapon-free zone.) There are strong suggestions that nuclear weapons might be used against any state that engaged in chemical or biological warfare, or indeed that built up a chemical or biological capability.

It is obvious that non-nuclear weapon states, parties to the NPT, are justified in requiring that they should be safe from a nuclear weapon attack, or threat, from any of the nuclear weapon states. The nuclear weapon states have indeed given security assurances: but they are not legally binding, and could be changed or withdrawn overnight. The nuclear weapon powers speak with forked tongues on this issue. These assurances have been given, and were explicitly repeated for the ex-Soviet states which have acceded to the NPT as non-nuclear weapon states. At the same time the nuclear weapon states want to leave an uncertainty; to imply that there are circumstances, mainly to do with chemical and biological warfare, that could invalidate the assurances that have been given.

The security assurances given to non-nuclear NPT states are not legally binding. However, assurances have also been given, by the signing of protocols, to the member states of three nuclear-weapon-free zones, in South America, the South Pacific and Africa – and these are legally binding.

The Libyan case provides an illustration of the schizophrenia on this issue. Libya is a party to the NPT, and a member of the African nuclear-weapon-free zone. Nonetheless, there was an open debate in the USA about the possible use of a bunker-busting nuclear warhead to destroy an alleged chemical warfare capability in Libya. It is true that it was subsequently denied that a nuclear warhead would be needed for this purpose; but the idea of the use of a nuclear warhead was rejected not on the grounds that it would be illegal, but on the grounds that a conventional weapon would be adequate.

At the time of the Cold War, the sole purpose of nuclear weapons was to confront the nuclear capability of the other side: it was a US:USSR, or NATO:Warsaw Pact confrontation. Today's doctrine, that they can be used against non-nuclear weapon states, is a new attempt to provide some justification for retaining them, now that the two-bloc confrontation seems obsolete. The new doctrine is not acceptable. It is clearly illegal in the eyes of the International Court of Justice. The security assurances that have been given are necessary props to the world non-proliferation regime. Given the immense conventional capabilities of the five nuclear weapon powers, which could destroy any of the "rogue states" with the use of conventional weapons alone, the threat of possible use of nuclear weapons against any non-nuclear state party to the NPT has no military justification either.

In Russia also there has been doctrinal regression from the period when President Gorbachev was advocating the elimination of nuclear weapons by the year 2000. This idea has disappeared from the Russian agenda. The doctrine of No-First-Use has been officially abandoned. Whereas in the United States those who want an NWFW are gaining ground, in Russia they are losing it.

There are a number of elements in this retreat. There is a general feeling that nuclear weapons are the only item left that can enable Russia to claim that it is still a great power, with the right to some kind of equal status with the USA.

There is also a more militarily specific reason – the inverse of the old NATO doctrine. NATO long claimed that its nuclear weapon deployments and its doctrine of flexible response (which was a euphemism for the possible first use of nuclear weapons) were necessary because of the Warsaw Pact's superiority in conventional forces. Now a number of Russian military experts are simply inverting this doctrine. If NATO brings in Poland, Hungary and the Czech Republic, it will have at least a 3:1 advantage in conventional forces over Russia. So Russia, they argue, needs nuclear weapons to deter a conventional attack. There are indeed specific demands for reintroducing land-based tactical nuclear weapons into the Russian force structure. These were removed by "reciprocal unilateral action," agreed between Bush and Gorbachev. No Treaty has been signed, and therefore there is no legal block to stop their reintroduction.

US and Russian Deployments

The USA actually increased the number of operational strategic nuclear weapons in the past two years, with the addition of the sixteenth and seventeenth Trident submarines. Its forward plans for improving some nuclear weapon capabilities stretch well into the next century: for instance, there is a $5 billion programme to improve the operational capability of the Minuteman III missiles, increasing their accuracy and updating them with Rapid Execution and Combat Targeting consoles; their operational life is to be extended to the year 2020. Russia has fewer upgrades in progress – one is a new variant of the SS-25 missile (called "Topol-M").

In the USA one of the results of the Comprehensive Test Ban is a Stewardship and Management Program scheduled to cost some $4 billion a year over the next ten years. The Department of Energy does not rule out using the enhanced capabilities to develop "new-design" nuclear weapons. Further, a number of zero-yield tests will be conducted underground, whereas they could be conducted safely, and transparently, in above-ground containment facilities of modest cost and design. These decisions are not likely to give much reassurance to Russia or China; they may well suspect that work on new types of nuclear weapons will be going on – particularly since the verification procedures of the CTBT are in limbo.

The impression has been given that, if START II comes into force, the total number of strategic nuclear warheads will come down to 3000 each in the USA and Russia. This is the total of deployed warheads. Both sides will keep a large stock of spare and "hedge" warheads – so that the total number of strategic nuclear warheads in the year 2007 is likely to be of the order of 10,000 on each side. The total megatonnage remaining then will still be equivalent to about a half a million Hiroshimas.

There is still a substantial research and development programme in the USA on ballistic missile defence. The label has been changed: it is now the Ballistic Missile Defense Program (BMDP), no longer the Strategic Defense Initiative (SDI) (on which some $40 billion had been spent with very little to show for it). The budget for the BMDP for the rest of the decade is around $3 billion a year, which nearly matches the level of funding provided by Congress during the first decade of SDI.

Congress has been pressing for programmes that go beyond the provisions of the Anti-Ballistic Missile Treaty, and the Administration has been trying to persuade the Russians to accept amendments to the Treaty. The Russians declined, and indicated that they are disturbed by some of the development work on theatre high-velocity defence systems. At Helsinki in March 1997 Presidents Clinton and Yeltsin both declared themselves committed to the ABM Treaty, and in September an agreement was signed imposing certain constraints on these high-velocity systems.

France, Britain and China

In their most recent statements on nuclear weapon policies, both France and Britain refer to their "sub-strategic" use. As in the United States, there is no indication of the way in which this could be reconciled with the security assurances both states have given.

By next year Britain's only nuclear weapon system will be the Vanguard submarines carrying the Trident missile. The "sub-strategic" nuclear warhead appears to be a missile that will carry a single warhead of some 100 kilotons – that is, the lethal power of some seven Hiroshimas. There is no indication of the sort of target on which a warhead of this size might be used.

The French Defence White paper, in much the same way, indicates that nuclear weapons can be used to demonstrate that France's vital interests are in some way threatened. The White Paper makes no reference at all to the security assurances that France has given: they seem to be regarded as irrelevant.

The forward plans for nuclear weapons, in both states, do not suggest any significant further reduction in the number of nuclear warheads at any time in the future. Both states plan further launch platforms. The fourth British Vanguard class submarine will not come into service before the year 2000. France is developing a new air-launched nuclear missile whose service entry is some ten years away.

China has a declared policy of No-First-Use. The nuclear weapon programme appears to be one of attempting to catch up with other nuclear weapon states in the sophistication of its nuclear weapon capability.

In sum, there are no signs, either in declared nuclear weapon policies or in actual deployments, that any of the nuclear weapon powers are seriously considering a move to zero. They seem to take the view that the indefinite extension of the Non-Proliferation Treaty has legitimized in perpetuity the existing division between nuclear weapon and non-nuclear weapon states.

Progress or Regress: Negotiations

The pattern of negotiations about nuclear weapons during the last two years suggests the same conclusion: that the nuclear weapon powers are still a long way from accepting the target of zero.

The main negotiations are, of course, still those between the USA and Russia. The USA has made some concessions. The date for completing the programme of START II reductions has been extended to the year 2007. The USA has reiterated its support for the ABM Treaty, and there is an outline agreement on the demarcation between Anti-Ballistic Missile systems and theatre missile systems – though that agreement still waits for an agreed text. Further, the USA has agreed that once START II is ratified by the Russian Duma, negotiations will begin straight away on START III, with a lower number of deployed strategic warheads on either side. However, all these further moves depend on the ratification of START II, and it remains to be seen whether the concessions will be enough to sway the vote in Russia: ratification is probably still held up more by the decisions about NATO expansion than by any specific complaints about START II provisions. If the Russian Duma fails to ratify START II, that may indeed be an irrational decision, since they could then end up with a greater degree of inferiority in nuclear weapon deployments. Parliaments have been known to make irrational decisions.

It is significant that there is no reference in the Helsinki communiqué to an eventual zero target. The prospect is still for thousands of nuclear warheads well into the next century. The unilateral reductions in US and Russian tactical nuclear weapons have been made under "soft" agreements, and the reductions could be reversed. No progress has been made in converting these agreements into legally binding treaties.

There has been no progress with the May 1995 Joint Statement on Transparency, covering nuclear stockpile data exchanges and reciprocal monitoring of fissile material storage sites.

There is no prospect that the Comprehensive Test Ban Treaty will enter into force this year or next, since this requires Indian ratification which will not happen. Consequently, the verification procedures will not come into force. Nothing more will happen until the states that have ratified meet to consider the situation in three years' time. The Test Ban should effectively constrain major nuclear weapon developments. If the threshold states observe it, then it should make it very difficult for them to acquire highly advanced nuclear warheads. The Ban will not prevent a good deal of "modernization" by the five declared nuclear weapon states.

The Conference on Disarmament in Geneva has now been enlarged to include 61 states. It cannot agree on its programme. The nuclear weapon powers want negotiations on a cut-off of the production of weapon-grade fissile material. The non-nuclear weapon states argue that this would be a cosmetic treaty, since all the nuclear weapon states have either stopped, or are about to stop, producing this material. It would serve to stop them from doing something which they do not want to do anyway. India, in particular, sees this proposal as one aimed at the near-nuclear weapon states. A large number of the non-nuclear weapon states want a working party to be set up on nuclear disarmament – not necessarily with a negotiating mandate.

There are the first signs that some Western non-nuclear weapon states are no longer willing to line up automatically with the USA, France and Britain on every nuclear weapon issue. Malaysia in 1996 put forward a resolution at the General Assembly which was in two parts: the first part simply required an endorsement of the International Court of Justice's ruling that the nuclear weapon powers had a legal obligation to bring about nuclear disarmament – a ruling that (as already described) went further than the wording of Article VI of the NPT. Nine European Union states voted in favour of this part of the resolution – Austria, Belgium, Denmark, Finland, Germany, Ireland, Italy, Luxembourg and Sweden. The German vote was particularly important. It indicates a certain restiveness among the non-nuclear states that are normally expected to align themselves with the USA. (The USA, France and Britain voted against this resolution.)

Among the non-nuclear weapon states, the non-proliferation regime is holding up well. The whole of the land masses of the Southern Hemisphere (with one or two minor exceptions) now form a nuclear-weapon-free zone: indeed NWFZs cover a good deal of territory north of the equator as well. There are suggestions that the three nuclear-weapon-free zones should come together to form one large Southern Hemisphere NWFZ. They might then work to make the seas of the Southern Hemisphere also nuclear-weapon-free – an idea that the nuclear weapon powers would no doubt jointly reject. However, it is difficult to see any reason why submarines carrying ballistic missiles should go south of the equator.

One other proposal for an NWFZ may move further – for a Central Asian zone: this is a joint proposal from Kazakhstan, the Kyrgyz Republic, Tajikistan, Turkmenistan, and Uzbekistan. However, there is not likely to be much progress for some time with the idea of a zone free of nuclear weapons, and indeed of other weapons of mass destruction, in the Middle East. There is a proposal for a NWFZ in Central and Eastern Europe; this proposal is also not likely to be successful, since Poland, Hungary and the Czech Republic have joining NATO as their main policy objective.

Conclusion

The arguments in favour of an NWFW are powerful arguments, and are now supported by once-powerful men. There are good reasoned replies to the main objection, on the difficulties of verification. There are, however, few signs that the nuclear weapon powers are much moved by the arguments. Nor are they much moved by pressure from non-nuclear weapon states. It is unfortunate that, although there are probably majorities in most countries in favour of a nuclear-weapon-free world, it is a matter that is no longer high up on the agenda of most people's concerns. The Canberra Commission concluded:

> There is no doubt that, if the peoples of the world were more fully aware of the inherent danger of nuclear weapons and the consequences of their use, they would reject them, and not permit their continued possession or acquisition on their behalf by their governments, even for an alleged need for self-defence.

For those who consider a move to zero nuclear weapons a matter of high priority, the main problem is to find ways of bringing pressure on the governments of the nuclear weapon powers.

PART ONE

A Nuclear-Weapon-Free World

1

The Anatomy of the Argument

Michael MccGwire

In recent years, there has been a sea-change in Western thinking about nuclear weapons. Until then, there was no real debate. Nuclear weapons were believed to be essential to the security of the West, and those who questioned that assumption were marginalized. Today, there is a significant body of influential opinion (including a sizeable number of retired Generals and Admirals), which outspokenly favours their elimination.

The circumstances of the Gulf War, the dissolution of the Warsaw Pact, and the disintegration of the Soviet Union combined to open up new avenues of thought, which led many in the US national security community to conclude that it would be very much in the interests of the United States if all nuclear weapons were "taken off the table of international affairs."[1] There remained the question of how that could be brought about, and the newly activated debate focused on the feasibility of a nuclear-weapon-free world (NWFW) and how to achieve that goal.

US thinking about this problem started from the benefits of eliminating nuclear weapons. Besides removing "all kinds of risks of catastrophic destruction," America would "be free to enjoy two extraordinary strategic advantages: first, as the least threatened of major states, and second, as the one state with modern conventional forces of unmatched quality."[2] It was these newly available advantages, coupled with the danger that nuclear proliferation would increase the threat of nuclear terrorism and could lead, on occasion, to US conventional superiority being neutralized, that made an NWFW seem desirable.

The elimination of nuclear weapons depends absolutely on the active commitment of the United States and it is essential that US interests should be served by such a policy. But when it comes to ways of achieving that goal, the US perspective tends to obscure the reasons why it is so important and to deflect attention from the urgency of the need for immediate action to initiate the process. I, therefore, start with a restatement of the problem that faces us.

Why an NWF World Is Necessary

We need to eliminate nuclear weapons because:

–   Nuclear weapons make nuclear war possible.
–   Of mankind's many enterprises, a major nuclear war has the unique capacity to destroy civilization as we know it and to jeopardize the survival of the human race.
–   Human fallibility means that a nuclear exchange is ultimately inevitable.

These facts, coupled with the current hiatus in international affairs, lead to the conclusion that governments should act *now* to initiate the elimination of nuclear weapons, a process that could take 20-30 years to complete.

The *aim* of such a policy would be: to reduce the probability of a major nuclear exchange to zero, while reducing the probability that nuclear weapons will be used by anyone in any way to as low a figure as possible.

This aim is specific, limited, and achievable.

The elimination of nuclear weapons is a "good" in its own right.

The aim of an NWFW policy is not, in itself, to eliminate war, to achieve comprehensive disarmament, to resolve regional conflicts, or to enhance global stability.

However, while not the aim of an NWFW policy, those objectives (to the extent they are achievable), and others of that kind would be furthered if the nuclear weapon states adopted "the firm and serious policy-goal" of an NWFW.[3] For example:

–   The number and variety of cooperative policy measures that would be involved in moving towards the goal of an NWFW would inevitably have a significant impact on national leaders and their electorates, and on the structure of the evolving international system.
–   The treaty-making process would help bridge the gap with the non-aligned nations and be a force for compromise and cooperation within the international community. By renouncing their nuclear capability, the most powerful nations would commit themselves to the greatest concessions. The transparency required to ensure control and verification of the NWFW regime would apply to all. And the universal goal of obviating a global catastrophe would generate a quite unusual coincidence of interests among participants.
–   Adopting the goal would defuse dissatisfaction with the Nuclear Non-Proliferation Treaty (NPT). Because halting proliferation would be essential to the process of achieving an NWFW, enforcement would become a matter of universal concern, rather than being seen by many non-nuclear weapon states as a dispute between haves and have nots.

– The goal would meet a key objection to the Comprehensive Test Ban Treaty (CTBT) and make it easier to police the Chemical and Biological Weapons Conventions.

These benefits flow *from* the goal of an NWFW and begin to take effect from the moment of its adoption. The logic is that of the "functionalist" approach to conflict prevention and international security, which has been demonstrated so powerfully in the genesis of the European Community. The EC grew out of the European Economic Community (founded in 1957 with just six nations), itself an extension of the European Coal and Steel Community (1950), which was the product of a policy decision to avoid further Franco-German conflict by intermeshing their heavy industry.

Although less tangible, the transformative effect of adopting a "firm and serious policy goal" was demonstrated by Mikhail Gorbachev's "new political thinking about international relations," which he publicized with increasing vigour throughout 1985. Within two years, the adoption by a superpower of that clearly articulated policy, reflecting as it did the principles underlying the UN Charter and the conclusions of the Palme Commission Report, had been largely instrumental in bringing about a relaxation of international tension from the heights it reached in the first half of the 1980s. This relaxation was achieved *without* noticeably softening Soviet policy towards America (that shift took place in Spring 1987); *before* the first concrete evidence of the change in Soviet military doctrine (the asymmetrical INF treaty signed in December 1987); and *despite* Gorbachev's "new political thinking" being dismissed in Washington and London as utopian propaganda.[4]

The Main Objection

It is increasingly accepted in the United States that nuclear weapons have no practical utility besides deterring their use by another state,[5] a function that would lapse in an NWFW. Today, the main objection to the logical corollary of that conclusion – eliminate nuclear weapons – is that to do so would create a new danger of "nuclear breakout," which would allow one state to hold the rest to ransom.[6]

The most persuasive rebuttal of that objection is comparative risk assessment. The subjects of comparison are the *likely outcomes over time* of alternative policies, neither of which is risk free. We tend to contrast the current post-cold-war hiatus with some future nuclear-weapon-free world, to the latter's disadvantage. The proper comparison is *between two unfolding processes* and not between two situations (one present, the other hypothetical) set years apart in time. The question to be answered is which policy is potentially the *least* dangerous and likely to bring the greatest benefits in the foreseeable future.

Risk is the product of the consequences of a calamity and the likelihood of its occurrence. In a nuclear world (such as we have known this half century), the worst case is a *full-scale nuclear exchange*. In an NWFW, the risk would be nuclear breakout, leading in the very worst case to the *limited use* of nuclear weapons.

Opinions will differ on how the probability of breakout from a tightly verified NWFW compares with that of accidental or inadvertent war in a high-salience nuclear world. But in terms of *risk*, we can be certain that if there were to be a significant difference between the probabilities,[7] the disparity will not be sufficient to balance the incomparable calamity of a nuclear exchange.

Meanwhile, cost-benefit analysis indicates that, in practice, there would be little (if any) political-military incentive to break out from an NWFW, the risk being correspondingly low.[8] The possible exception is the irrational rogue state, but while the probability may be somewhat higher, the calamity factor of such a breakout is by far the smallest (see Chapter 6).

To the gross disparity in risk once the NWFW threshold has been crossed must be added the steadily growing disparity, in the intervening period, in the relative risk of breakout from the NPT regime. As discussed elsewhere, current nuclear policies will face a steadily increasing probability of breakout.[9] Given the policy-goal of an NWFW, the risk will diminish over time, both for political reasons and as the heavy investment in verification bears fruit.

New Complications

As the debate has moved to the question of how best to achieve an NWFW, there has emerged a tendency to specify geopolitical conditions that would have to be met before we could adopt and implement the goal of eliminating nuclear weapons.

–   The weak version contends that the final stage of elimination requires the resolution of regional conflicts and the wide-ranging renunciation of the use of force.
–   The strong version claims that any move towards nuclear disarmament (and therefore ultimately to a nuclear-weapon-free world) can be made only as part of a wider move towards regional and global stability and security.

The strong version is essentially an argument for inaction. Given that we failed to achieve regional and global stability in the past, there is no reason to expect we will be able to meet the preconditions in the future, unless there is some external stimulus. The strong version can be seen as an attempt at political correctness by those who are not yet convinced of the *desirability* of an NWFW, let alone its feasibility.

The weak version of the argument is more worrisome because it is advanced by those who claim to believe that an NWFW *is* desirable.[10] The underlying rationale seems to embody three main strands, two of which may be largely subliminal.

One is the subconscious belief that nuclear weapons continue to have some use beyond simple deterrence of *nuclear* threats. Otherwise, why the need for regional and collective security regimes before reducing national nuclear arsenals to tens of weapons each?[11] The implication is that in the absence of such regimes, nuclear weapons are necessary to keep the peace. This is not, however, supported by the evidence of the last fifty years, including the 10-15 year period when the United States enjoyed an effective monopoly of the worldwide means of delivering such weapons. The irrelevance of nuclear weapons to the numerous conflicts since Hiroshima is notable, and they have provided no magic solution to the age-old problem of peace and security.

Nor do the other four "tasks" that were said to require the retention of nuclear weapons stand up to close analysis.[12] (1) The claim that nuclear weapons are needed to prevent major war once more becoming an option for settling serious disputes among advanced major powers can be dismissed as a case of *post hoc ergo propter hoc*.[13] (2) There are better ways of deterring or responding to attack by biological or chemical weapons;[14] and by relying on the overwhelming conventional capability enjoyed by the United States and its allies, we will gain the advantage of increasingly effective enforcement of the NPT and CWC. (3) The argument that nuclear weapons are needed to prevent breakout from an NWFW is both circular and ill-founded.[15] And (4), no example has been offered of how nuclear weapons "underpinned world order" in the past, or might do so in the future, particularly since extended nuclear deterrence has ceased to be credible, (particularly in Asia), outside very exceptional circumstances.[16] There remains the suggestion that nuclear weapons would be needed for the defence of Europe against a resurgent Russia. Given the time-frame, relative capabilities, and the state of the Russian political economy, this was implausible, even before NATO enlargement. It could, however, turn out to be a self-fulfilling prophecy.

The other subliminal strand seems to rate the "two extraordinary strategic advantages" that an NWFW would bring the United States as at least as important as eliminating the danger of a nuclear exchange.[17] While informed by the best kind of enlightened geopolitical thinking, this perspective tends to be agnostic about the beneficial effects of a decision by the nuclear states to commit themselves unequivocally to an NWFW, and continues to view the world in traditional geostrategic terms, with the United States as the global arbiter and peacemaker.

The third strand is fully committed to the elimination of nuclear weapons, but argues that "political realism" demands the specification of geopolitical preconditions.

All three strands are sustained by fallible expectations and false analogies. These must be addressed before we can turn to considering the third strand and the case for political realism.

Unsubstantiated Analogies

Regional Security. The contention that regional security is a prerequisite for adopting the goal of an NWFW is sustained by two interrelated ideas that are currently fashionable in the field of international relations. One is the optimistic belief that the kind of security that has been achieved in Northern America and Western Europe represents the leading edge of an evolutionary trend in world politics. The other is the claim that democratic states do not fight each other, the implication being that as democracy spreads, so will conflict recede.

Given the unique and radically different circumstances, historical, geographical, and political, that have led to the currently stable situations in Western Europe and Northern America, it is hard to see them as part of a trend. The idea of stabilizing the world, region by region, is an appealing one, but it reflects a Western view of the world, while ignoring the globalizing trends in international politics.

The claim that democracies do not fight each other depends on the period under review, what counts as war, and the precise definition of democracy. For example, Hitler came to power by constitutional means and probably had the support of a substantial majority of the German people until the Russian campaign. But even if the claim were true in the past, it still has to be shown that the consistent causal factor was the presence of democratic governments, rather than some external factor, such as being bound together in an anti-Soviet alliance, or a combination of factors. One suspects that the reason Greece and Turkey have not gone to war has more to do with the leverage exerted by Washington than the nature of the governments in Athens and Ankara.

Our experience this century tells us that democracies have not hesitated to resort to force when it served their purpose or when popular sentiment made it politically expedient to do so.[18] The democratic process benefits the domestic polity. It is not always a force for peace or progress in international politics. For example, would the Kremlin have been able to make the unilateral concessions that were needed to conclude the Treaties on Intermediate-range Nuclear Forces (INF) and Conventional Forces in Europe (CFE) if there had been a democratically elected government in Moscow in the 1980s? When one considers how strategic arms control became a political football in the United States, one suspects not. Would the Gorbachev leadership have been able to conceptualize the Soviet withdrawal from Eastern Europe and impose the change in military doctrine that created the essential preconditions? Again, one suspects not.

We come back to the point that the elimination of nuclear weapons is a good in its own right which would bring benefits in its wake, including an improvement in the climate of international relations. It may be true that, for industrially advanced nations, the world of military capabilities and geostrategy has been replaced by a world of economic strength and geofinance, in which national power derives from export industries and currency markets.[19] But there is nothing in past developments or current trends to suggest that we can afford to delay adopting the goal of a nuclear-weapon-free world in the expectation that the spread of Western-type democracies will bring peace to the world.

Strategic Arms Control. It is claimed that the various SALT and START agreements were only possible because of earlier improvements in the international security situation. The evidence argues otherwise. Negotiations on INF and START began in 1982-83, when the Reagan administration's confrontational policy was at its height and arms control negotiations were used as an instrument of that policy. Faced by the Warsaw Pact's superiority in conventional forces, Washington was not interested in negotiating away its advantage in strategic delivery systems.[20] The treaty was finally signed in 1991, but that was made possible by a reformulation of Soviet military doctrine in January 1987. This required the Soviet military to plan on the assumption that world war would be avoided by political means.[21]

As they no longer needed to cover the contingency of world war, the Soviets could accept a double-zero INF treaty in December 1987, despite the asymmetrical cuts involved. Similarly, the Soviets no longer needed to have conventional military superiority and an offensive posture in Europe, which allowed them to announce a 500,000 unilateral force cut in December 1988, breaking the MBFR stalemate and enabling the CFE treaty. And, since Eastern Europe was no longer needed as a defensive glacis or offensive springboard, political and economic factors could determine whether a Soviet military presence was advantageous, leading to withdrawal.

To underline the direction of causality, the reformulation of Soviet military doctrine followed a rambunctious year which saw a sharp deterioration in US-Soviet relations. It was the doctrinal shift that led to the subsequent relaxation of international tension and not vice versa.

Similarly, the SALT negotiations were made possible because the Soviets had replaced their long-standing objective of strategic superiority (which they shared with the United States) by the objective of parity at as low a level as possible; this flowed from a doctrinal shift at the end of 1966 regarding the likely nature of a world war. Détente was in part a byproduct of the SALT I negotiations. It had, however, been long dead when SALT II was finally signed in 1979, requiring major cuts in the planned deployment of Soviet fourth generation systems.[22]

Soviet military doctrine decreed that the benefits of curbing the strategic build-up outweighed the disruption of existing plans. It was that same objective of "parity at as low a level as possible" that provided the military rationale for the Soviets' proposal in January 1986 (and again at Reykjavik that October) of a programme to eliminate nuclear weapons by the end of the century.

In sum, while international circumstances may constrain policies, the choice of objectives can shape events and structure the circumstances.

It is true that agreement on dramatic reductions in nuclear weapons were only possible in the wake of the Soviet Union's (*de facto*) capitulation, but even then the initial US requirement was for an arsenal of 4500 warheads, which would be capable of destroying Russia as a functioning society several times over.[23] Similarly, a comprehensive test ban was only acceptable to America once Russia was in military disarray and after the USA had developed a satisfactory way of simulating nuclear testing by computer. But this says more about American domestic politics (which is, indeed, a crucial factor) than some general principle shaping the international system.

Political Realism

Political realism is the third and probably the most influential strand in the rationale underlying the weak version of the case for geopolitical preconditions; realism about the political problem of selling the elimination of nuclear weapons to the US electorate.

For some 40 years, the American people were told that nuclear deterrence kept the peace, that as long as enough money was invested in such weapons, deterrence couldn't fail, and that there was no danger of accidental or inadvertent nuclear war. War would only come about through a failure to deter aggression. Whatever the circumstances, it would be difficult to wean the US electorate from that version of the past.

But there are strong vested interests in its preservation, and redirecting US policy towards the goal of an NWFW will be to enter a political minefield. Throughout the Cold War, strategic weapons programmes and competing theories of deterrence were contentious issues in Presidential and mid-term elections, reflecting the electorate's separate concerns about the danger of war and America remaining Number One. It will require a bipartisan consensus if the electorate is now to be persuaded that the elimination of nuclear weapons is essential to the future wellbeing of the United States.

In the light of this political reality and the need to craft such a consensus, it is understandable that American advocates of elimination should make the process seem as evolutionary as possible. An NWFW would come about as the consequence (rather than the cause) of a fundamental change in the nature of international relations. Nuclear weapons would be progressively marginalized, and the process would be more one of atrophy than elimination.

The problem with this politically realistic scenario is that it ignores other realities that are outside American control. One is the international system.

The West has shown itself incapable of exploiting the opportunity for new political thinking about international affairs provided by the withdrawal of the Soviet Union from the Cold War and its subsequent disintegration. While the concept of "cooperative security" assumed a new prominence in Western discourse, cooperation as-between-equals was only on offer when vital interests were at stake, as in the redeployment and disposal of the former Soviet Union's nuclear arsenal. The most recent example of that incapacity was the decision (for parochial reasons) to incorporate former members of the Warsaw Pact into NATO, jeopardizing rather than enhancing future security in Europe.[24] Given the West's inept performance since the end of the Cold War and its seeming inability to adopt new ways of thinking, there is no obvious reason why the past pattern of world affairs should not continue in the future.

In fact, the conjunction of two historical trends increases the likelihood of confrontation or conflict in the years ahead. One is the end of the 500 year period that saw the peoples of Europe move out and effectively take over the world, a process that was not finally checked until the Second World War. Since then the Western flood has partly receded, but in many areas it left behind a deep resentment, (most notably in certain Muslim countries), a resentment that was renewed or reinforced by the experience of the last 30-40 years.

The other trend is the differential growth in world populations. Take Asia as stretching from the Indian sub-continent to the Pacific, and the West as comprising greater Europe and its colonial descendants around the world. Today, Asians outnumber Westerners by at least 2.5 times, but the West's economic and military power more than compensates for that disparity. Looking ahead 25-30 years, the disparity may be as much as 4-5 times, with no compensating advantages, and may well lead to a shift in hegemonic power away from the West. Historically, such shifts have been linked with international turbulence and war.[25] One need not subscribe to Samuel Huntingdon's "Clash of Civilizations" to conclude that 10-20 years from now, international relations are likely to be at least as conflictual as the Cold War years, maybe in ways that have yet to be foreseen.[26]

Another reality relates to nuclear weapons. For the time being, we have achieved what can be called a low-salience nuclear (LSN) world, in that US and ex-Soviet arsenals are being slowly dismantled and the idea of a nuclear exchange between Russia and America in the near future is no longer credible. But this came about because the Soviet Union withdrew from the Cold War and because Gorbachev's political and economic policies failed; it was not the outcome of some far-sighted Western policy. China, meanwhile, continues to add to its arsenals, and present Western policies appear unlikely to halt the proliferation of nuclear weapons.[27]

While war may no longer be considered an instrument of policy in great-power relations, arms races remain a feature of the international scene and, like a forest fire, will reignite with a change in wind, a change in the international climate. The present LSN world is a transient phenomenon related to the current hiatus in international affairs, and the last 50 years show that a high-salience nuclear (HSN) world is the norm, not the exception. This is because the nuclear arms race had a dynamic of its own, combining the crude logic of conventional advantage with the sophistries of deterrence theory. The requirement for an assured second strike combined with traditional targeting criteria justified an ever-increasing number of warheads[28] and diversity of delivery systems.[29]

In Sum

Attempts to specify or even postulate geopolitical preconditions for various phases of eliminating nuclear weapons are unnecessary and misleading. As the elimination process unfolds, national leaders will make their own judgments as to what is militarily prudent and what is politically practical, while predetermined specifications will favour the obstructionists. They are misleading because they posit constraints that are in fact amenable to change.

In political-military terms it will be easier to eliminate nuclear weapons than to eliminate regional conflicts, let alone achieve a world where mutual trust has reached a level where the main nuclear powers will be willing to hand over their weapons to a multilateral agency. There is no reason why, in the absence of some major new initiative, the conflictual pattern of world affairs should not continue in the future. A major attraction of a decision to eliminate nuclear weapons is that it would provide such an initiative. Because nuclear weapons are mainly in the possession of nations with great power status or pretensions, a voluntary decision by such states to join with other states in removing this threat to humanity would have far-reaching consequences and could start a virtuous spiral towards a more harmonious international system.

As for political realism, the minefield of American domestic politics must be weighed against the established pattern of international relations in general and arms racing in particular, plus the reality of a brief hiatus in that pattern of confrontation and conflict. Domestic politics have the unique advantage that they can be shaped by effective national leadership and public education.

The Nuclear States

The foregoing discussion has focused on the United States' circumstances, and for good reason. It was America that first built the fission and H-bombs; that based its national security policy on nuclear weapons; that developed and elaborated a complex theory of nuclear deterrence to underpin that policy. It was America that remained deeply ambivalent about the desirability of arms control rather than military superiority;[30] that had been poised to take the arms race into space. And it was influential members of the American national security community who, in the first half of the 1990s, began to argue that America's interests would be best served by the elimination of nuclear weapons.

The emergent opinion was particularly important because Russia (in the shape of the Soviet Union), had reached a similar conclusion in the mid-1980s, albeit for different reasons. The Soviets did not subscribe to Western theories of nuclear deterrence, nor did they believe that nuclear weapons prevented nuclear war;[31] rather, they recognized that nuclear weapons made nuclear war possible. And since their overriding concern was to avoid such a war,[32] the aim of eliminating nuclear weapons (an NWFW) was only logical. Hence the formal arms control proposal in January 1986 that all nuclear weapons should be eliminated within 15 years, a proposal that was elaborated at Reykjavik that October and had full military support.[33] Through 1992, Russia continued to advocate complete nuclear disarmament and in September 1994 at the United Nations, Boris Yeltsin advocated further cuts in strategic weapons, to provide for the possibility of an NWFW.

If Washington and Moscow agreed to adopt the goal of an NWFW, the other nuclear states would follow suit. China, given its conventional potential, has every reason to welcome an NWFW and is on record supporting the idea. This would remove the rationale for India's and hence Pakistan's capability; India has officially proposed an NWFW on several occasions. Israel recognizes its vulnerability to attack by primitive delivery systems, has shown that its territorial integrity can be ensured by conventional means, knows that the greatest danger now comes from internal forces that are impervious to nuclear threats, and is financially beholden to Washington. Britain and France would have no option but to go along.

Unfortunately, just as the window of opportunity has begun to open in Washington, it is closing in Moscow. Russia comprises some two-thirds of the former Soviet Union (FSU), but its population is now only one half that of the FSU and it has lost many of its defensible boundaries. Given China's growing population and the traditional enmity of Germany and Japan, Russia could legitimately claim a new need for "the great equalizer." Reflecting the reality of this concern, in 1993 the Russian military reversed the doctrine that had ruled in the 1970s and 1980s, renouncing no-first-use of nuclear weapons, bringing their policy into line with NATO.

At that date, Moscow was still committed to the goal of an NWFW, but in January 1994, President Clinton announced the expansion of NATO eastwards. With good reason, Moscow believes that this extension of NATO is a breach of the understandings reached in 1990-91.

If, despite these developments, Washington and Moscow were both to agree that it would be in their interests to eliminate nuclear weapons, it would be sensible to include China in the first tier of nuclear powers, rather than relegating it to the second tier with Britain and France. Unlike those two, China has always had a *demonstrable* requirement to deter nuclear attacks by the United States or the former Soviet Union and, although its arsenal is not comparable to America's or Russia's, China is still building up its forces and sees itself to be on a par in "great power" terms.

Such a categorization not only makes sense politically, but by concentrating on the three states in the first tier, we simplify the discussion about the complex process of progressively dismantling the arsenals and then moving to the final stage of elimination. If we can get the first tier right, the rest will fall (or can be pushed) into place.

These three states will share a situation of existential deterrence. However, if the political process of mutual disarmament and elimination is to be successful, we must be clear what is meant by that concept. In common parlance, to be deterred from doing something is to say that the potential costs are too high, be it the difficulty of a rock face, the price of certain goods, the level of military defences, or the penalty for breaking the law. However, in Western political-military parlance, the emphasis has shifted from the passive to the active mode, and the concept of deterrence has been personalized. While political scientists may talk of challenger and defender, themselves loaded terms, for Western policy-makers and public the image conjured up by "deterrence" is that of the magistrate and the law breaker, the latter only held in check by the threat of capital punishment.

It is in this Western sense that the concept of deterrence is wholly inappropriate to the process whereby the nuclear weapon states progressively divest themselves of their arsenals. If it is to succeed, the process will have to be a collaborative effort, based on a commonality of interests and concepts like collective and cooperative security. Verification, albeit rigorous, intrusive and uncompromising, will be mutual. And while the participants in this communal enterprise will assess their partners actions with tough-minded scepticism, none can claim the moral high ground and pretend to magisterial powers. A basic assumption will be that all parties to the process share the common goal of an NWFW. While there may be disagreements on how to get there, these will be resolved through negotiations involving the full range of political and economic trade offs and not by threats of punishment.

The project will surely fail if Western-style nuclear deterrence enters the picture, as it is inherently divisive.[34] We will, therefore, have to eschew using the concept to reassure domestic constituencies, who will need to be convinced that verification is truly effective, and re-educated to recognize that existing balances of advantage will not be changed by the phased reductions and to accept the reality of existential deterrence.

Nor is the Western concept of nuclear deterrence relevant to the final stage, when the USA, Russia and China eliminate their remaining weapons. The appropriate analogy is that of three gun-fighters, who have agreed to get rid of their weapons but are concerned to avoid getting shot in the process. Ideally, we would like there to be a well-armed, neutral sheriff to deter any attempt to cheat. But that is neither possible, nor necessary. In common parlance, all three states will be deterred from attacking the other two, because the possible benefits could not match the certain costs, let alone the probable ones.

The concept of an international "trustee" system or an integrated multilateral nuclear force at this final stage merely introduces another obstacle to progress. In the foreseeable future, none of those three nuclear powers are going to commit nuclear weapons into UN charge, and the last fifty years has shown that none of the Permanent Five is qualified (can be trusted) to act as a disinterested Trustee.

The Elimination Process

Even if the first tier of nuclear states adopted the goal of a nuclear-weapon-free world, the process of dismantling and eliminating the nuclear arsenals would be complex and lengthy, requiring the sustained political and financial commitment of the kind that drove the strategic arms race during the Cold War. It can be assumed that such a process would be mapped out in differing degrees of detail, starting with an overall conceptual plan blocking out the main phases of arms reductions, with each phase subsequently divided into stages and, ultimately, each stage broken down into successive and/or concurrent steps.

Underlying the disagreement on whether this process should be time-bound is a question of trust. This stems from the declared nuclear states' blatant disregard of their commitment under Article VI of the 1970 NPT to work for the elimination of nuclear weapons, and their refusal to be tied down on this point at the Review and Extension Conference in 1995 and the subsequent negotiations on a CTBT. The demand for a time-bound commitment is a natural response by those who see the NPT and CTBT as further enshrining the advantage of the declared nuclear states, while making no progress towards an NWFW.

In practice, the physical scale of the requirement, the complexity of the issues (political, military, legal, administrative, technological and scientific), the number of unknowns, and the cybernetic effects of the process, make it both impractical and counter-productive to establish a fully time-bound schedule for eliminating nuclear weapons, even if it were acceptable to all members of the top tier.

Nevertheless, the question of "good faith" must be addressed. An essential step would be for the main nuclear powers to make a caveat-free commitment to an NWFW, backed by a "treaty of intent" and a sustained public education programme on the urgency of that goal and its feasibility. Equally important, this political commitment would be reinforced by agreed (and inviolable) procedures for continually establishing new targets and deadlines and for signing interim protocols and agreements. These procedures would be designed to drive the process inexorably towards that ultimate objective to be achieved at some unspecified time in the future. However, while there would be no predetermined deadline for the final stage of elimination, a continuous series of successively agreed interim deadlines would be an essential feature of the process.

To Conclude

Among the growing body of influential advocates of eliminating nuclear weapons, the debate has moved on from the desirability of an NWFW to how to achieve that goal. There is, however, a very real danger that the process will get side-tracked by the distant details of how to get there, losing sight of *why* we are adopting the goal of an NWFW and *why* it is so urgent to initiate action in that direction.

To recap: we need to eliminate nuclear weapons because human fallibility makes a nuclear exchange ultimately inevitable; such an exchange will destroy civilization as we know it and jeopardize the survival of the human race. The urgency of initiating action stems from the fact that we are currently enjoying a hiatus in international affairs that makes it realistic in both domestic and international political terms to advocate adopting the goal of an NWFW. The hiatus is fortuitous, and the realities of the international system and the dynamics of arms racing argue that this window of opportunity will soon close.

Domestic political considerations require that advocates of a nuclear-weapon-free world be able to demonstrate that the elimination of nuclear weapons is feasible. This does not, however, require them to spell out every detail of how it is to be achieved, any more than a mountaineer attempting a new peak has to know exactly what route he will take before launching his assault. Eliminating nuclear weapons will involve a *controlled process*; initiating action to achieve that goal does not require a leap in the dark. During the lengthy process of elimination, the viability of the concept will be under continual review in the light of new knowledge and revised projections, and political leaders will be making informed judgments before agreeing on incremental steps.

Advocates of an NWFW must also be able to demonstrate that the elimination of nuclear weapons is not merely desirable, it is *essential*; it is that their very existence threatens the survival of the human race. In consequence, the risks of present inaction are of a different order to the risks inherent in an NWFW.

To persuade electorates of these facts requires a major reeducation programme to make them aware of how close we came to accidental or inadvertent war in the 1960-85 period and how these dangers will increase exponentially in the multi-polar world that lies ahead. They will also need to be disabused of the idea that "nuclear weapons kept the peace" and made to realize that the great achievement of the last 50 years was to have *avoided* war, despite the corrosive effective of nuclear deterrence on all aspects of East-West relations.[35]

The fact that eliminating nuclear weapons would allow America "to enjoy two extraordinary strategic advantages" is important in terms of persuading the US electorate. And that, of course, is the key to the whole process. But this must not be allowed to obscure the primary reason for elimination, the fact that nuclear weapons make nuclear war possible, a reason that applies to all nations in the world.

Of all the realities we face, the one over which we have least control is the inexorable closing of the window of opportunity provided by the ending of the Cold War. Hence the urgency. We need to stop agonizing over the elimination *process* and seize this fleeting opportunity to adopt the *goal* of an NWFW. To argue about the international circumstances needed to allow the process to proceed is to waste precious time. It will be up to future leaders to decide whether the world situation will allow progress, and we are not in a position to prejudge their decisions.

Today, our focus should be on the complexities of the elimination process and the as yet untapped potential for verification, which is still low on its learning curve. If the process of eliminating nuclear weapons is to succeed, we may need to invest as many resources in the science and technology of control and verification as we were prepared to invest in the Strategic Defence Initiative. That was also intended to enhance US security, but while an NWFW will eradicate nuclear arms racing, the SDI would have fuelled the existing race and extended it into Space.

We are left with the problems of persuading the US electorate of the urgent need for action. It may not be too difficult to convince them that in a multi-polar world there will be an inherent danger of accidental or inadvertent nuclear war. It will, however, be much harder to challenge the verities of nuclear deterrence theory and the Cold War depiction of the Soviet threat. But this may be essential if we are to resolve the new problem of Russia. How otherwise can we persuade Moscow that, contrary to everything the West proclaimed during the Cold War, nuclear weapons are not essential when faced by potential enemies who enjoy overwhelming conventional superiority, as well as geostrategic advantage.

Notes

1. McG. Bundy, W.J. Crowe Jr, S.D. Drell, *Reducing Nuclear Danger: The Road Away from the Brink*, New York: Council on Foreign Relations Press, 1993, p. 5. For an account of the US debate see S.A. Cambone and P.J. Garrity, "The Future of US Nuclear Policy," *Survival*, Winter 1994-95, 36:4, IISS: London, pp. 74-77.

2. Bundy, Crowe & Drell, *Reducing Nuclear Danger*, p. 5. Bundy was Special Assistant to the President for National Security Affairs, 1961-66; Admiral Crowe was Chairman of the Joint Chiefs of Staff 1985-89, and subsequently US Ambassador to London; and Sidney Drell, a nuclear physicist, is a long-time advisor to the US government.

3. In his article "Is there a Future for Nuclear Weapons?," Michael Quinlan asked whether there were adequate reasons for *not* adopting the "firm and serious policy goal" of a non-nuclear world (*International Affairs*, 69:3, 1993, pp. 485-596). He ruled that the onus of proof rested upon those inclined to answer "yes." The qualifiers "firm and serious" were needed to distinguish such a policy goal from Western pronouncements prior to 1991, which claimed that such was the ultimate goal but insisted on the immediate need for additional nuclear weapons. Sir Michael Quinlan, by then retired, had been the senior permanent official in the British Ministry of Defence, and his article was intended to provide an affirmative answer to the first question.

4. See M. MccGwire, *Perestroika and Soviet National Security*, Washington D.C.: Brookings Institution, 1991, pp. 179-86, 204-39, 253-57.

5. See *An Evolving US Nuclear Posture*, The Second Report of the Steering Committee, Project on Eliminating Weapons of Mass Destruction (Chair: A.J. Goodpaster), The Henry L. Stimson Center, Report No.19, December 1995, p. vi.

6. This objection usually ignores the scientific, technological and administrative advances in verification theory and practice that would be the natural corollary of adopting the goal of an NWFW.

7. The difference has yet to be demonstrated. Assertions about the likelihood of breakout often fail to allow for improvements in verification techniques and procedures.

8. M. MccGwire, "The Elimination of Nuclear Weapons" in *Old Issues and New Strategies: Proceedings of the Fifth Annual Conference on Arms Control and Verification*, ed. J. Brown, Amsterdam: UV University Press, 1995; A. Mack, "Nuclear Breakout: Risks and Possible Responses," *Background Papers for the Canberra Commission on the Elimination of Nuclear Weapons*, Australian Government, August 1996.

9. See M. MccGwire, "The Possibility of a Non-Nuclear World," *Brassey's Defence Year Book*, 1995, pp. 345-48.

10. For example, *An Evolving US Nuclear Posture*, pp. 9, 25.

11. *An Evolving US Nuclear Posture*, pp. vii, 31.

12. Quinlan's argument for retaining nuclear weapons relied on the perceived need to discharge five political-military tasks. I dissected these in MccGwire, "Is there a future for nuclear weapons?" *International Affairs*, 70:2, 1994, pp. 211-228.

13. MccGwire, "Is there a Future for Nuclear Weapons?," pp. 215-219.

14. *An Evolving US Nuclear Posture*, p. 16.

15. *An Evolving US Nuclear Posture*, p. 25. MccGwire, "The Possibility of a Non-Nuclear World," pp. 359-60.

16. On this point see MccGwire, "Is there a Future for Nuclear Weapons?," p. 219, particularly the extended footnote.

17. I would stress that *An Evolving US Nuclear Posture*, which is closely argued, carefully balanced, and finely nuanced, provides no explicit evidence of this perspective. However, Robert McNamara, who has long insisted that "the indefinite combination of nuclear weapons and human fallibility will lead to a nuclear exchange," found it necessary to dissent from the Steering Committee's conclusions concerning a range of preconditions. *Ibid*, notes 6, 7, 20, 24, 26, 28.

18. During the Cold War it was the West that most frequently resorted to military force as an instrument of foreign policy outside its National Security Zone, and committed the largest resources to this role. Western intervention was often coercive, whereas Soviet intervention (outside its NSZ) was always supportive. Moreover, Soviet intervention was always protective of the client (e.g. air defence), whereas US supportive intervention usually included a strong punitive element, such as strikes on the client's enemy (e.g. bombing Haiphong or shelling Druze villages). MccGwire, *Military Objectives in Soviet Foreign Policy*, Washington D.C.: Brookings Institution, 1987, pp. 220-224. These differences reflected political calculations and world views, rather than moral attitudes, but they belie the impression that the authoritarian Soviet Union was especially prone to the use of coercive force. Inside their respective NSZs, the two sides reacted equally strongly to perceived threats, although the very different geostrategic circumstances allowed the use of a much wider array of instruments to secure US interests.

19. M. Walker, *The Cold War*, London: Fourth Estate, 1993, pp. 336-8, 348.

20. Secretary of State Alexander Haig noted that the Soviets were eager to enter into arms control talks on almost any basis. Haig, *Caveat: Realism, Reagan and Foreign Policy*, Macmillan, 1984, p. 228. He also described the US START proposals as a "non-negotiable package" and a "two-faced proposal." R. Gutman, *Newsday*, 12 August 1984. See also Haig, *Caveat*, p. 223. Richard Burt, Haig's principal arms control deputy, described the purpose of the concurrent INF negotiations to be "the maximum political advantage. It is not arms control we are engaged in its alliance management." S. Talbot, "Behind Closed Doors," *Time*, 5 December 1983, p. 19. For Haig's comments on the US INF proposals, see *Caveat*, p. 229.

21. MccGwire, *Perestroika and Soviet National Security*, pp. 312-318.

22. MccGwire, *Perestroika and Soviet National Security*, pp. 55, 63-66.

23. This was the number originally proposed by the United States at START II; the Russians proposed 2500. The final agreement (1/93) set a ceiling of 3500 by the year 2003, a figure that accorded with the 3000-4000 warheads recommended in a study published by the US National Academy of Sciences in 1991.

24. M. Mandelbaum. *The Dawn of Peace in Europe*, New York: Council on Foreign Relations, 1966. M. MccGwire, *NATO Expansion and European Security*, Oxford: Brasseys, 1997, London Defence Studies No. 37.

25. The only peaceful transfer was from Britain to the USA, which took place during WWII, at which time their relations were governed by a formal alliance, constructed to defeat other challengers. Note, however, that in the 1920s and early 1930s, US naval war plans for the Pacific region assumed that Britain would be the enemy.

26. S.P. Huntingdon, "The Clash of Civilizations?," *Foreign Affairs* 72:3, 1993, pp. 22-49. More pertinent, Brad Roberts draws attention to the recent emergence of a new tier of states technically capable of producing high-leverage weapons: "1995 and the End of the Post-Cold War Era," *The Washington Quarterly* 18:1, Winter 1995, pp. 5-25.

27. MccGwire, "The Possibility of A Non-Nuclear World," pp. 345-48.

28. Even as the superpowers were actively negotiating the successive treaties on strategic arms "limitations" and "reductions," the number of warheads on each side rose from under 2000 to over 11,000. Between 1970 and 1975 (the height of the SALT negotiations), the number of US strategic warheads rose from about 1900 to 6850, while the Soviet inventory rose from about 1700 to 2700. During the START negotiations (1982-90), US numbers went from about 11,000 to 13,000, while the Soviets went from about 8800 to just under 11,000.

29. Nor was this a quirk of communist intransigence, as it was the USA that consistently led the strategic arms race. In 1959, when the Soviets still lacked an effective means of delivering nuclear weapons on North America, the US Strategic Air Command had 1750 bombers and was beginning to deploy ICBMs. Ten years later, when the Soviets adopted the 1970s strategy (and the goal of strategic parity), their ICBM force still lagged behind the US force in numbers, accuracy, reliability, and response time. The USA was the first to diversify into multiple independently-targeted reentry vehicles (MIRV), followed by strategic cruise missiles (SLCM, ALCM), and in 1983 embarked on the Strategic Defense Initiative (SDI), which would take the arms race into space. MccGwire, *Perestroika and Soviet National Security*, pp. 45-79, 186-204.

30. See the Council on Foreign Relations book by M Krepon, *Strategic Stalemate: Nuclear Weapons and Arms Control in American Politics*, St Martin's Press, 1984, particularly pp. 1-2, 108-20. For a comparison of US and Soviet arms control objectives and negotiating behaviour, see MccGwire, *Perestroika and Soviet National Security*, pp. 45-79, 186-204.

31. MccGwire, *Perestroika and Soviet National Security*, pp. 416-417. The Soviets did, of course, recognize the reality of Mutual Assured Destruction, which was a feature of the prevailing state of existential deterrence.

32. See MccGwire, *Military Objectives in Soviet Foreign Policy*, pp. 36-40 and Fig 3-1.

33. The policy was articulated in 1984 and was pursued with particular vigour by Mikhail Gorbachev after taking office. See MccGwire, *Perestroika and Soviet National Security*, pp. 186-204, 375-77. In December 1989, the Soviet military recognized that to accommodate Western doctrine it would have to accept limited deterrence as a way

station. But note the subsequent *Pravda* interviews with the Minister of Defence, Army General D T Yazov, 23 February 1990, in which he talks of "the accelerating slide towards global catastrophe" and asserts that "the elimination of weapons of mass destruction [is] an indispensable condition for survival." p. 377. Through 1992, Russia continued to advocate complete nuclear disarmament.

34. I discuss the damaging effects of "Nuclear Deterrence" in a paper with that title for the Canberra Commission, to be found in the volume of Background Papers, August 1996, pp. 229-40. For an early version of this argument see MccGwire, "Deterrence - The Problem, not the Solution," *International Affairs*, 62:1, Winter 1985-86.

35. For an important empirical analysis of this issue see R.N. Lewbow and J. G Stein, *We All Lost the Cold War,* Princeton University Press, 1994.

2

The Phased Elimination of
Nuclear Weapons

Cathleen Fisher

Since the fall of the Berlin Wall, the debate about the long-term nuclear future has been transformed. Measures of arms control and disarmament, which only a few years ago could not have been discussed seriously in governing circles, have been implemented. The United States and Russia are reducing their nuclear arsenals; a number of countries have moved away from programmes to acquire or retain nuclear weapon capabilities. After decades of failed efforts, a Comprehensive Test Ban Treaty (CTBT) has been concluded. These steps represent real progress towards reducing the role of nuclear weapons in interstate relations.

Support is growing, moreover, for more far-reaching changes. A number of retired military and civilian leaders and respected strategic analysts are challenging long-standing beliefs about the political and military utility of nuclear weapons; many are giving serious consideration to the goal of nuclear disarmament. In 1991, for example, the Committee on International Security and Arms Control of the US National Academy of Sciences said that nuclear weapons "should serve no purpose beyond the deterrence of, and possible response to, nuclear attack by others." Although the Committee did not at that time endorse a "zero" objective, it recommended further reductions in the USA and Russian strategic nuclear arsenals to 1000 to 2000 nuclear warheads each.[1] In 1993, three prominent US strategists urged reductions to a level of 1000 to 1500 warheads for the US and Russia, noting that this was by no means the "lowest level obtainable by the early twenty-first century."[2] In August 1993, General Andrew J. Goodpaster, a former Supreme Allied Commander in Europe, proposed step-by-step reductions that would end in the complete elimination of all nuclear weapons.[3] Two years later, a committee of retired senior military commanders, former US defence officials, and civilian security experts convened by the Henry L. Stimson Center outlined a four-phase process to eliminate all nuclear weapons.[4] The report of the Canberra Commission on the Elimination of Nuclear Weapons recommended that nuclear disarmament be pursued through "a series of phased verified reductions that allow states to satisfy themselves, at each stage of the process, that further movement toward elimination can be made safely and securely."[5]

These and other studies of the phased elimination of nuclear weapons share important themes. First, they emphasize the importance of a "realistic approach" and the need to think in terms of pragmatic, concrete steps. Second, they underscore both the necessity and opportunity to re-think long-standing assumptions about nuclear costs and risks, and about the feasibility and desirability of eliminating nuclear weapons. Third, although a rich menu of steps towards elimination is offered, deadlines for achieving the ultimate objective – a nuclear-weapon-free world – are rejected as unrealistic because progress towards disarmament is viewed as hinging on certain domestic, regional, and international circumstances that would facilitate – *although not precondition* – movement towards that objective. Recent studies of phased elimination, in short, attempt to tackle "the vexed problem of transition,"[6] and to explore the politics of process as well as the technical measures that would have to be undertaken to eliminate nuclear weapons.

This chapter reviews current thinking about the step-by-step elimination of nuclear weapons.[7] It begins by describing the rationales for elimination typically presented, then surveys the menu of actions that could accompany each phase in the disarmament process. It then considers two common critiques of phased approaches to elimination: first, the absence of deadlines and, second, the notion that progress will depend on the achievement of certain "preconditions." It concludes with some general observations on issues for further study, and on the next steps towards elimination.

The Case for Phased Elimination

Recent studies of phased nuclear disarmament appear to be rooted in several common concerns and conclusions: this section summarizes the arguments presented. First, that the current international environment offers a unique, but probably fleeting, opportunity to significantly reduce or eliminate the risks that nuclear weapons pose. Second, the utility of nuclear weapons has diminished in the post-Cold War period, while the risks associated with continued reliance on nuclear deterrence may be growing. In particular, the current "two-tier" non-proliferation regime is unsustainable unless the nuclear weapon states demonstrate greater diligence in pursuing nuclear disarmament.

Unfortunately, despite the dramatic changes in the global strategic environment, thinking about nuclear weapons remains mired in the assumptions and beliefs of the past. Although the Cold War antagonisms that led to the stockpiling of tens of thousands of nuclear weapons have abated, as the Canberra Commission observes, "assertions of their [nuclear weapons'] utility continue."[8] What is needed is a fundamental reappraisal of the traditional assumptions that have guided nuclear policy for over four decades.

The political and military benefits provided by nuclear weapons are diminishing.[9] Nuclear weapons are not usable on the battlefield, and their use against non-nuclear weapon states is unthinkable. Other emerging security threats cannot be effectively addressed with the threat of mass destruction. Preferable alternatives exist to reliance on nuclear weapons both to deter and to respond to the use of chemical or biological weapons. The only role for nuclear weapons is to deter the use of other nuclear weapons. Therefore, if all states were to eliminate their nuclear weapons, these weapons would no longer be needed.

While it is recognized that achievement of a nuclear-weapon-free world is likely to take many years or even decades, if it can be achieved at all, the goal appears more feasible than in the past. For example, recent arms control agreements have introduced highly intrusive verification regimes that only a few years ago would have been inconceivable. The experience gained through these arrangements could provide a foundation on which to build an effective verification regime to monitor compliance with a global ban. Other trends, such as the slow spread of democracy, and commercial and financial ties across national borders, suggest the possibility of a world in which concepts of sovereignty and security might be fundamentally transformed. In such a world, although sovereign states would continue to exist, the threat of mass destruction would be inconceivable.

The opportunity to move progressively towards a world of reduced nuclear risks could be short-lived, however. The non-nuclear weapon states will not be willing to tolerate indefinitely the basic *political* inequity embodied in a regime that sanctions the possession of nuclear weapons for five states, yet forbids all others from acquiring them. Although the incentive to acquire nuclear weapons may be more closely related to states' particular security concerns, or to national objectives that have little to do with the specific policies of the United States, Russia, China, France, and Britain, the continued possession of nuclear weapons by these five states is an advertisement of their utility and therefore, albeit indirectly, a "constant stimulus to other states to acquire them."[10] "By continuing to maintain ... large nuclear arsenals," the CSIS Nuclear Strategy Study notes, "Washington and Moscow send a strong signal about the persisting value of nuclear weapons, a signal that cannot be lost on leaders in the developing world."[11] The Canberra Commission states: "This situation is highly discriminatory and thus unstable: it cannot be sustained."[12]

Concern about the rising risks of proliferation, indeed, would appear to be a central motivating factor in recent studies of the phased elimination of nuclear weapons. In the post-Cold War world non-proliferation efforts must be radically altered. Unless the nuclear weapon states do something to fulfill their commitment to nuclear disarmament, a commitment reaffirmed at the time of the NPT's extension in April 1995, support for the non-proliferation regime could erode. The result could be a general weakening of the international norm against the acquisition of nuclear weapons. "To deal effectively with proliferation," the Canberra Commission concludes, "means also tackling head on the problems of nuclear disarmament and the elimination of nuclear weapons at the earliest possible time."[13] "Without a more radical approach to non-proliferation," the Stimson Center report cautions, "the challenges posed to the non-proliferation regime can only mount over time."[14]

The Phases of Elimination

In general, creative thinking about the steps that a process of phased elimination might entail has advanced further than systematic investigation of the domestic, regional, and international conditions that would make these actions more feasible. Like proposals for the time-bound elimination of nuclear weapons, gradualist programmes for disarmament contain a rich menu of incremental steps and measures; most describe a similar progression of actions. Bilateral (US-Russian) agreements and actions are to lead to multilateral constraints among the five declared nuclear weapon states, with some provision made to include the three "threshold" nuclear weapon states – India, Pakistan, and Israel – either at this stage or at a later point in the process. In some studies, subsequent progress towards the complete elimination of nuclear weapons would be achieved after an interim period of "neutralization" or "de-nationalization," during which the remaining nuclear weapons would either be held by states "in trust" or pooled in an international nuclear deterrent force. During this period, the relative risks and benefits associated with moving towards complete elimination would be assessed; if elimination were then viewed as a preferable nuclear "end state," even these residual nuclear forces would be destroyed.

Throughout the process of phased elimination, flexibility would be essential. For example, virtually all of the studies surveyed identify an additional round of bilateral reductions as the next step in the elimination process, but some leave open the possibility that such reductions might be pursued outside of formal negotiated accords through a series of reciprocated unilateral actions.[15] The Canberra Commission report indeed implies the greatest degree of flexibility with regard to process, presenting "notional objectives" and declining to describe in any detail the phases that might lead to the achievement of those objectives.

Although there is general agreement that the principal responsibility for initiating the elimination process must belong to the five declared nuclear weapon states, the cooperation of all nations is viewed as essential if a nuclear-weapon-free world is to be achieved. "At the very least," the Stimson Center report argues, "China, France, and Britain have the responsibility not to undertake any actions that might weaken the non-proliferation regime, such as increasing their nuclear arsenals or producing more fissile material for weapons."[16] Similarly, the Canberra Commission says, it is essential that "states with a presumed nuclear weapons potential take early action and enter into international legal constraints as they will have to resolve their ambiguous nuclear status before the nuclear weapon states will finally move to zero nuclear weapons."[17] All states are called upon to strengthen the non-proliferation regime and to create effective regional and global cooperative security mechanisms.

The elimination process must be pursued in a step-by-step fashion because any other approach would be unrealistic. States will only be willing to take steps towards nuclear disarmament if convinced that political conditions permit them to do so without harm to their security interests. Disarmament, therefore, must be an evolutionary process that moves in tandem with gradual changes in international, regional and, perhaps, domestic politics. The creation of an environment conducive to disarmament and concrete steps towards elimination can be mutually reinforcing, however. Just as favourable developments in the broader political environment can accelerate progress towards elimination, successes in reducing nuclear dangers, in turn, can contribute to creating the conditions under which subsequent steps become possible. For example, new arms control initiatives by the major nuclear powers, the Atlantic Council notes, "can themselves make an important contribution to improved and improving relations among nations."[18] The Canberra Commission strikes a similar note: "Successful nuclear weapon negotiations will benefit other security related negotiations and progress in regional and other political and security related negotiations will enhance the prospect of building a nuclear weapon free world."[19]

The most important characteristics of specific phases in the elimination process are summarized below. A more detailed comparison of the specific measures proposed by selected strategies for phased elimination can be found in the Appendix.

Initial Phase: Bilateral Reductions and Operational Changes

The step-by-step elimination of nuclear weapons would begin with further bilateral reductions, as well as changes in the operational status of the weapons remaining in the US and Russian arsenals. Preparatory steps for multilateral arms reductions would begin during this phase as well.

Initial steps towards elimination could be undertaken in the current environment. Regardless of the outcome of democratic and economic reforms in Russia, both countries' strategic needs could be met at lower force levels. Views vary on just how low the United States and Russia could go without fundamental changes in the principles that guide nuclear policy or in the structure of their nuclear forces. Several groups have recommended bilateral reductions during this first phase to a level of 1500 to 2000 warheads each; one study proposes a two-step process of bilateral reductions to even lower levels, with the first step bringing US and Russian arsenals down to a level of 1000 warheads each, and a subsequent agreement further shrinking forces to between 500 and 1000 warheads.[20] Various provisions are made for tactical nuclear weapons, with some studies advocating a complete ban on non-strategic nuclear weapons and the immediate deactivation of all such weapons.

During this initial phase, operational arms control measures would take on added importance. The United States and Russia are called upon to reduce significantly the alert status of their remaining nuclear forces, or to adopt a "zero-alert" posture. Both states could move immediately to separate warheads from delivery vehicles on the systems slated for destruction. Some proposals advocate changes in the operational practices that are no longer compatible with improving US-Russian political relations, such as restrictions on the daily operations of SLBMs to areas near each country's respective coastline, and the installation of an early-warning system on the missile fields of the other state. Other measures to build mutual confidence would include comprehensive data exchanges and a dialogue on the safety and security of nuclear weapons. There are differing views on the importance of a no-first-use treaty or pledge during this first phase. The CSIS Nuclear Weapons Study Group, for example, suggests that this phase might include the completion of a treaty that would ban the first-use of nuclear weapons and impose sanctions if the prohibition were violated. The Canberra Commission similarly calls on the nuclear weapon states to undertake a reciprocal no-first-use pledge and proposes a non-use undertaking in relation to non-nuclear weapon states as well.

The first steps towards solving the problems of verifying and safeguarding a ban on nuclear weapons would have to be taken at an early point in the elimination process. There would have to be an accurate global system of accounting for nuclear weapons and materials. Serious study of possible verification regimes and of response mechanisms would also begin during this period.

Parallel policies designed to further de-legitimize weapons of mass destruction as instruments of policy and to address the security concerns of all states would help to facilitate progress towards subsequent phases. Important components would include confidence-building measures (CBMs); the expansion of regional nuclear-weapon-free zones; the strengthening of non-proliferation regimes for nuclear, chemical, and biological weapons; a ban on nuclear testing; and a ban on the production of fissile materials for military purposes. Most studies also point to an increasingly important role for regional and international institutions and organizations, in particular, the United Nations. Diplomacy and trade could also play a reinforcing role in this process of building a more cooperative security order.

The Transition to a Multilateral Arms Control Regime

The process of bilateral cooperation, including the regime of nuclear transparency and confidence-building measures, would be extended to the three smaller nuclear weapon states. During this phase, the five declared nuclear weapon states would reduce their arsenals to hundreds of weapons each.

Some provision also would have to be made for the threshold nuclear weapon states during this phase, if not earlier. Just how these three states might be integrated into existing regimes is less clear, however. Current proposals range from pledges by the three threshold states to "freeze" their weapons at comparable levels, to formal inclusion in the existing non-proliferation regime and "roll-back" of these countries' nuclear programmes.

There are differing views regarding the political conditions that would facilitate advancement to this stage. Some argue that the only role of nuclear weapons – to deter other nuclear threats – could be met at much lower levels in the current strategic environment. In this view, there is no compelling strategic rationale preventing all five declared nuclear weapon states from moving immediately to a "minimum deterrent" posture. Others admit that the principal rationale for higher force levels is political, but argue that the transition to a multilateral arms control regime, realistically, will require the development of generally amicable relations among all of the major powers. A strong non-proliferation regime is also seen as essential, since the governments of the nuclear weapon states will be reluctant to agree to reductions to this level without a high degree of confidence in the ability of the international community to detect and respond to new proliferators.

Towards Elimination

Studies of the step-by-step elimination of nuclear weapons offer alternative visions of the nuclear "end state."

– Neutralization. Those who remain most sceptical of the feasibility of a nuclear-weapon-free world foresee a prolonged interim phase during which nuclear weapons would be politically and militarily "neutralized." Under one proposal, all remaining nuclear weapons would be separated from their delivery systems and both warheads and delivery systems placed under multilateral control on the territory of the owner states.[21] Advocates of "neutralization" argue that such an interim nuclear "end state" would provide time for states to build confidence in a global system of cooperative security. If the political conditions for complete elimination could be created, then this phase of "neutralization" might lead either to the transfer of all remaining stocks of warheads and weapons-grade fissile material to an international body, such as the United Nations, or, alternatively, to their complete destruction.

– De-nationalization. Other proposals suggest that the final path to zero may include a phase in which all remaining nuclear weapons are "de-nationalized." One proposed alternative would be to create trustee arrangements, under which the remaining nuclear weapon states agree to hold small numbers of nuclear weapons in "trust" for the international community and to bear all costs and risks associated with retaining these small arsenals. The only role for nuclear weapons would be to provide extended deterrence for all states. Residual nuclear forces would be subject to international safeguards so as to reduce the opportunities for collusion among the national "trustees." An alternative arrangement would involve the creation of an integrated multilateral force, subject to international control and multilateral decision making.[22] During this period of "de-nationalization," states would assess the relative risks and benefits of elimination. A key question is whether it would be easier to maintain stability and mutual confidence at a very low level of internationally controlled weapons, as some have suggested, or whether the complete elimination of nuclear weapons, in the end, would prove more stable and sustainable. More study is needed to determine the desirability and viability of such schemes.[23]

– Elimination. If effective verification and safeguards could be designed, the final step would be the complete elimination of all nuclear weapons.

An Early Commitment to the Goal of Elimination

To create and sustain momentum towards disarmament, some groups recommend that the governments of the nuclear weapon states re-commit themselves seriously at the outset of the process to the goal of eliminating all nuclear weapons. As signatories to the NPT, the United States, Russia, China, France, and Britain are already pledged to pursue "negotiations in good faith on effective measures relating to the cessation of the nuclear arms race at an early date and to nuclear disarmament," a commitment that was reaffirmed at the 1995 NPT Review and Extension Conference.[24] As the Stimson Center report notes, however, "most observers correctly view this as a rhetorical goal; active governmental efforts to identify and solve the problems that would have to be overcome to achieve the elimination of all nuclear weapons have been noticeably absent."[25] An unequivocal commitment to the elimination of all nuclear weapons is necessary, the Canberra Commission argues, to "propel the process [of elimination] in the most direct and imaginative way."[26]

"Preconditions" and Deadlines

Critics of phased nuclear disarmament commonly take issue with two characteristics of "step-by-step" proposals for disarmament: (1) the assumption that progress will depend on the achievement of certain "preconditions"; and (2) the lack of a timetable for achieving disarmament.

"Preconditions"

Many reject the assertion that progress towards elimination will depend on the achievement of certain political conditions. "The only true barrier" to a nuclear-weapon-free world, some argue, is "lack of political will, especially on the part of the nuclear weapons states."[27] In this view, if the nuclear weapon states could be convinced to embrace elimination, then it would be achievable. Emphasis on the "preconditions" for disarmament could become an excuse for delaying steps towards nuclear disarmament indefinitely, and inaction may entail high security risks. Linking progress towards disarmament to broader political changes could block progress towards ends that might be achievable in the present international political context.

In fact, proposals for the phased elimination of nuclear weapons do not suggest that progress towards disarmament should be linked formally to the creation of specific political conditions.[28] With the exception of references to the creation of effective verification and non-proliferation regimes, the word "precondition" does not appear to be used in the sense of "necessary" or "essential" conditions. Rather, the "preconditions" for progressive disarmament are depicted as ameliorating developments that would help to persuade states to take concrete steps towards a nuclear-weapon-free world. In the broadest sense, the "preconditions" for disarmament are those features of the broader strategic environment that would move governments to view progressive denuclearization as preferable to a continuation of the status quo. Without concurrent progress towards building "an environment conducive to nuclear disarmament and non-proliferation,"[29] governments are likely to remain reluctant to pursue nuclear disarmament diligently.

Identifying the conditions or circumstances under which states might be willing to disarm is, of course, a highly speculative exercise. One must envisage both a dynamic strategic environment and a dynamic elimination process, as well as posit causal linkages between changes in the strategic context and the evolution of the elimination process. While noting that it is impossible to describe specifically an environment "conducive" to disarmament, several types of changes in the strategic environment feature prominently in gradualist strategies for disarmament, including:

– increasing cooperation between the major powers;

-   progress towards addressing the security concerns of all states, and particularly those in regions of tension; and
-   greater transparency.

Virtually all gradualist studies identify two conditions as absolutely necessary to achieve a nuclear-weapon-free world. First, the willingness of states to move towards elimination depends on steady progress towards controlling proliferation – a task that becomes even more important as very low levels of nuclear weapons are approached. A breakdown of the non-proliferation regime, or the emergence of a new nuclear weapon state, would endanger the elimination process. A second essential precondition is the creation of an effective verification regime and of a system of response capabilities against cheating or breakout; states must have high-levels of confidence in the collective power of the international community to detect violations and to respond – economically, politically, and even militarily – to such violations. Both of these conditions imply enhanced international cooperation.

There is less consensus on the degree of domestic change that would be required to create a cooperative international security environment and thus to achieve a nuclear-weapon-free world. Some suggest, for example, that the success of future US-Russian reductions may well hinge on the consolidation of democratic reforms in Russia, and that, ultimately, a world free of nuclear weapons would require the slow spread of democracy or at least the transformation of authoritarian regimes so that governments would submit to intrusive inspections and other verification measures necessary to monitor a ban on nuclear weapons. Without such a transformation, mistrust and the fear of cheating or breakout would likely diminish the willingness of other states to agree to further disarmament measures.

There appears to be a consensus that nuclear disarmament *does not* require the creation of world government and the end to an international system characterized principally by sovereign states. The Stimson Center report observes: "The continuation of an international system founded on state sovereignty does not imply a perpetual state of nuclear deterrence. Other outcomes would preserve the state system in recognizable form, yet offer effective alternatives to the threat of mass violence."[30] Two contributors to the SIPRI study *Security Without Nuclear Weapons?* argue similarly:

> The achievement of nuclear weapon abolition requires a political transformation in relations between states, but not one as revolutionary as is required by the world government school of thought. It would involve something comparable to Western Europe's transition from a state of war to a security community taking place in all the other major areas of regional conflict."[31]

The critical component of such a political transformation is a fundamental shift in perceptions of the political or military value of nuclear weapons: "Nuclear weapons would ... have to be seen as having no part to play in assuring any state's national sovereignty and independence."[32] Governments would have to "see so little value in the threat of mass destruction that nuclear weapons and nuclear deterrence would wither away."[33]

This is not to underestimate the degree of change that would be required to achieve a nuclear-weapon-free world, however:

> A world ready to eliminate nuclear weapons would be very different from today's world.[34]

> The objective [of elimination] will only be achieved – if it can be achieved at all – after far-reaching changes occur in the principles that guide state policies and actions.[35]

> It [complete disarmament] may one day be seen as appropriate to the circumstances of international politics. For that to occur, the transformation of the world system would have to be more profound than that envisioned as a context for non-operational or international nuclear forces.[36]

> The abolition of nuclear weapons will require a major transformation in international relations.[37]

The prospects for a transformation of global politics are not as utopian as once assumed. A number of studies observe that certain developments and changes suggest a "considerable potentiality for improved security within a condition of anarchy."[37] The increasing obsolescence of war, at least among the major states of the world, multiplying transnational links, and increasing economic interdependence create the possibility of a truly international society of states bound by common norms of behaviour. There is broad consensus, however, that much can – and indeed must – be done in the current political environment to reduce nuclear dangers and to build trust in an eventual elimination regime.

Deadlines

A secondary concern relates to the absence of any deadlines for achieving the steps outlined in phased strategies for nuclear disarmament.

Proponents of a time bound framework for disarmament call for the achievement of a nuclear-weapon-free world within a specific period of time. For example, the "Programme of Action for the Elimination of Nuclear Weapons" put forward by the Group of 21 in the Conference on Disarmament assigns specific deadlines for the achievement of particular interim measures, and calls for completion of global nuclear disarmament by 2020.[38]   Such proposals reflect deep suspicions that the nuclear weapon states have no intention of fulfilling their NPT commitment and that, therefore, they must be forced to undertake steps towards elimination through legally binding international obligations that identify clearly the time at which sanctions for failure to honour such obligations are introduced.

In contrast, most gradualist studies reject a target date for achievement of a nuclear-weapon-free world as unrealistic. The Atlantic Council report, for example, observes, "Any attempt to suggest specific time-lines for warhead reduction to the levels examined ... would at this time be almost impossibly speculative."[39]   "A long time-scale is ... unavoidable," the SIPRI study cautions.[40]   Three American experts likewise observe that a "nuclear-weapon-free world – desirable as it is as an ultimate objective – is at best a distant prospect." [41] The Stimson Center report suggests that a nuclear-free world "could be achieved in one or two generations," but makes no specific projections as to the number of years required to reach this "end-state."[42] While noting the importance of "agreed targets and guidelines which would drive the process inexorably towards the ultimate objective of final elimination, at the earliest possible time," the Canberra Commission, too, elected not to set out a precise timetable.[43]

Although studies of phased disarmament seldom explain the rationale for rejecting a timetable for elimination, the lack of deadlines follows logically from the importance that such studies place on the political context in either advancing or retarding progress towards elimination.   Most gradualist proposals, either explicitly or implicitly, assume that the complete elimination of nuclear weapons will be achieved only when governments and publics come to see that nuclear weapons are of little value in protecting the lives, territories, and interests of states, yet impose significant costs and risks.   Such a fundamental shift in perceptions of the utility of nuclear weapons is likely to depend, in turn, on domestic, regional, and international changes that gradually diminish the insecurities of states and transform our understanding both of national security and sovereignty.

The pace and nature of such changes cannot be predicted. A deadline for achieving the ultimate objective is, therefore, unrealistic and apolitical. If states already had come to identify positively with each other to the extent that the security of one was viewed as the responsibility of all, and national interests were viewed as identical to international interests, then calls for disarmament in ten or twenty years might not be inconceivable. Such a re-conceptualization of "national security" – though desirable – is as yet far from complete, however. Although the dangers of the nuclear age, like the threat of global ecological problems, are generating increasing demands for "world security," in the main, we continue to "think and act only in terms of the security of states."[44] A true society of nations of course remains a possibility, and in some regions states have already made advances towards commonly shared rules and institutions for managing their mutual relations. At present, however, a global security community remains an aspiration only, and states are likely to abjure actions that they see as harmful to their *national* security, even if they would be of benefit to humanity. Nuclear disarmament may be of "universal relevance," but the weapons, or their components, remain in the hands of sovereign states.

The issue of deadlines, however, need not be viewed as an "either-or" proposition. Although deadlines for the completion of particular phases or for the elimination process as a whole may be unrealistic, interim deadlines for specific measures can be helpful under certain circumstances. When key states are in fundamental accord that a particular step must be taken, and the shape of a possible agreement is in sight, then a deadline for the completion of that step can be useful, as the negotiations for a Comprehensive Test Ban Treaty demonstrate. In order for such interim deadlines to be useful, however, they must be realistic.[45] As one expert on negotiations cautions: "A deadline that does not leave enough time for negotiation will either not be respected or will produce only a symbolic agreement."[46]

The Way Forward

Strategies for the phased elimination of nuclear weapons and proposals for time-bound disarmament in fact share many common elements. First and foremost, both embrace the goal of elimination. Second, both approaches propose many of the same steps along the path to elimination. Both approaches, either explicitly or implicitly, suggest that these "building blocks" are likely to be achieved only in a series of phases.

The principal difference lies in the assumptions that are made about the conditions under which elimination is most likely to be achieved. Gradualist approaches proceed from the assumption that international politics will determine whether and how quickly a nuclear-weapon-free world can be achieved. While acknowledging that action is urgently needed, proponents of a step-by-step approach to elimination believe that "there is no alternative to a prolonged transition. The road to abolition will require many small steps, not one big jump."[47] A grand design for disarmament, complete with deadlines, makes little sense, since we cannot at this point even identify the conditions that would persuade governments to consent to nuclear disarmament. The only alternative therefore is to "identify sets of goals and attend to the major issues at hand."[48] In practice, this means:

> mitigating the effects of the new instabilities occurring as the cold war recedes, and taking every advantage of the new opportunities to place security

on a sounder footing. If, each year, the nuclear risks can be lowered a little
more than the previous year, the threat will eventually be eliminated.[48]

Recent studies of phased elimination have made an important contribution
to the debate about the long-term nuclear future. In challenging long-standing
beliefs about the utility of nuclear weapons, these studies are forcing political
and military leaders to re-examine traditional beliefs and assumptions about the
value – and costs – of nuclear reliance. By emphasizing concrete, pragmatic
actions, they are helping to reframe the debate about the feasibility of
elimination. And by considering seriously the once "heretical" goal of nuclear
disarmament, they are helping to legitimize discussion of the elimination option.

Additional exploration of the timing and modalities of subsequent steps
towards disarmament is needed. This is particularly true of the verification and
safeguards challenges that the transition to zero, and the maintenance of an
elimination regime over time, would involve. Could a ban on nuclear weapons
be effectively verified? How would the international community safeguard itself
against potential cheaters? What would be the cost of creating and maintaining
effective verification and safeguards regimes, both nationally and
internationally? What would be the role of defensive systems in such a
safeguards regime? How are the capabilities of the threshold nuclear weapon
states to be treated – and at what point in the elimination process? When is it
appropriate to begin multilateral arms control negotiations among the five
declared nuclear weapon states? What role can and should international
organizations, such as the United Nations and the International Atomic Energy
Agency, or regional organizations, play in the elimination process, and in the
final regime? What should be the relationship between a nuclear weapons
elimination regime and the conventions banning chemical and biological
weapons?

There is also a great need to think more systematically about the conditions
that could facilitate progress. It is not enough to simply blame the nuclear
weapon states for a failure of political will. One must ask why the governments
of the nuclear weapon states cling to traditional beliefs about the political and
military value of nuclear weapons, and, secondly, what kinds of political,
economic, or social changes might encourage a shift in thinking. Much
progress has been made in fleshing out the menu of technical steps that might
be undertaken. Much more thinking needs to be done about the conditions that
would help to make these steps more feasible. Achievement of these conditions
should not be linked formally to specific steps in the elimination process, but
a better understanding of the influence of various domestic, regional and
international environments on the security calculations of states could be useful
in thinking about strategies for moving towards a nuclear-weapon-free world.

As all proponents of elimination argue, efforts should be intensified to
persuade the five declared nuclear weapon states to commit themselves to the

objective of elimination. A commitment at the highest political level, backed by concrete actions, is necessary, both to overcome domestic resistance to far-reaching changes in nuclear policy and to "ensure that resources and personnel are devoted to finding solutions to the problems associated with moving to zero, and to crafting appropriate transition strategies."[49] A clear view of the long-term goal would also help to provide direction and coherence to a long-term programme for nuclear elimination. Finally, such a commitment would send a powerful signal to the non-nuclear nations of the world and to potential proliferators that the five declared nuclear powers are prepared to make good on their international obligations under the global non-proliferation regime.

Notes

1. *The Future of the U.S.-Soviet Nuclear Relationship*, Washington D.C.: National Academy Press, 1991, p.3. In a subsequent report, the Committee concluded that "the potential benefits of a global prohibition of nuclear weapons are so attractive relative to the attendant costs" that further study of the conditions that would make prohibition feasible and desirable is warranted. See *The Future of U.S. Nuclear Weapons Policy*, Washington D.C.: National Academy Press, 1997, p. 10.

2. McG. Bundy, W.J. Crowe, Jr., and S.D. Drell, *Reducing Nuclear Danger: The Road Away From the Brink,* New York: Council on Foreign Relations, 1993.

3. A.J. Goodpaster, *Further Reins on Nuclear Arms: Next Steps for the Major Nuclear Powers*, Consultation Paper Series, Washington D.C.: The Atlantic Council, August 1993.

4. *An Evolving US Nuclear Posture: Second Report of the Steering Committee, Project on Eliminating Weapons of Mass Destruction*, Washington D.C.: The Henry L. Stimson Center, December 1995.

5. *Report of the Canberra Commission on the Elimination of Nuclear Weapons*, Canberra: Department of Foreign Affairs and Trade, 1996, p. 10.

6. K. Booth and N.J. Wheeler, "Beyond Nuclearism," in *Security Without Nuclear Weapons? Different Perspectives on Non-Nuclear Security*, ed. R. Cowen Karp, Oxford: Oxford University Press, 1992, p. 36.

7. Although many different sources were consulted for this paper, the narrative focuses principally on four detailed studies on the phased elimination of nuclear weapons. All four studies eschew firm deadlines for the completion of particular phases, although some posit target time lines for completion of the process. The proposals include: *Toward a Nuclear Peace: The Future of Nuclear Weapons in U.S. Foreign and Defense Policy*, Report of the CSIS Nuclear Strategy Working Group, Washington D.C.: Center for Strategic and International Studies, June 1993; Goodpaster, *Further Reins on Nuclear Arms: Next Steps for the Major Nuclear Powers; An Evolving US Nuclear Posture: Second Report of the Steering Committee, Project on Eliminating Weapons of Mass Destruction;* and the *Report of the Canberra Commission on the Elimination of Nuclear Weapons.* The paper also draws on the insights of two earlier volumes exploring in depth the various components of a nuclear-weapon-free world: *Security Without*

Nuclear Weapons? and *A Nuclear-Weapon Free World: Desirable? Feasible?*, ed. J. Rotblat, J. Steinberger and B. Udgaonkar, Boulder, Colorado: Westview Press, 1993.

8. *Report of the Canberra Commission*, p. 7.

9. See, for example, *An Evolving US Nuclear Posture*, p. 7; *A Nuclear-Weapon-Free World*, pp. 41, 54, pp. 56-62; and *Report of the Canberra Commission*, p. 24.

10. *Report of the Canberra Commission*, p. 7.

11. CSIS, *Toward a Nuclear Peace*, p. 12. See also C. Kaysen, R.S. McNamara, and G.W. Rathjens, "Nuclear Weapons After the Cold War," in *A Nuclear-Weapon-Free World: Desirable? Feasible?*, p. 49.

12. *Report of the Canberra Commission*, p. 7.

13. *Ibid.*, p. 27. See also *An Evolving US Nuclear Posture*, p. 39.

14. *An Evolving US Nuclear Posture*, p. 39.

15. Kaysen, McNamara, and Rathjens, "Nuclear Weapons After the Cold War," for example, suggest that movement to a minimum deterrent level might more easily be achieved through a series of unilateral actions, rather than "by the tedious and interminable-seeming process of negotiation on which we have relied so far" (p. 47). The Stimson Center study, *An Evolving US Nuclear Posture*, similarly, suggests that cuts below START II levels could be achieved outside of a negotiated accord, as long as reductions proceeded in parallel and in a transparent and verifiable manner (p. 19).

16. *An Evolving US Nuclear Posture*, p. 20.

17. See *Report of the Canberra Commission*, p. 65. The Atlantic Council report recommends that, during the second phase of elimination (multilateral reductions to 100-200 warheads each), an exception be made for the three threshold nuclear states – Israel, Pakistan, and India – in the no-first-use rule that the five declared nuclear weapon states would adopt. See *Further Reins*, p. 13.

18. *Further Reins*, p. 1.

19. *Report of the Canberra Commission*, p. 51.

20. Both the Atlantic Council and the Steering Committee of the Stimson Center's Project on Eliminating Weapons of Mass Destruction propose reductions to a level of 1500-2000. The CSIS report calls for two-phase reductions.

21. For one proposal for how nuclear weapons might be "neutralized," see J. Dean, "The Final Stage of Arms Control," PRAC Paper no. 10, Center for International and Security Studies at Maryland, College Park, MD, August 1994, p. 21.

22. On the idea of an international nuclear force, see R. Speed, *The International Control of Nuclear Weapons*, Center for International Security and Arms Control, Stanford University, June 1994; R.L. Garwin, "Nuclear Weapons for the United Nations?," in *A Nuclear-Weapon-Free-World: Desirable? Feasible?*, pp. 169-180; and V.I. Goldanskii and S. Rodionov "An International Nuclear Security Force," in *A Nuclear-Weapon-Free World: Desirable? Feasible?*, pp. 181-190. But see also a different view by Francesco Calogero, "An Asymptotic Approach to a NWFW," *A Nuclear-Weapon-Free World: Desirable? Feasible?* pp. 191-200.

23. See P.M. Lewis "Verification of Nuclear Weapons Elimination," in *Security Without Nuclear Weapons*, pp. 128-150; and P.M. Lewis, *Verification Matters: Laying the Foundations: Verifying the Transition to Low Levels of Nuclear Weapons*, Preliminary Report, London: VERTIC, April 1997.

24. Treaty on the Non-Proliferation of Nuclear Weapons, *Arms Control and Disarmaments Agreements: Texts and Histories of Negotiations*, Washington D.C: United States Arms Control and Disarmament Agency, 1982 ed., p. 93; 1995 Review and Extension Conference of the Parties to the Treaty on the Non-Proliferation of Nuclear Weapons, New York, 17 April-12 May 1995, NPT/CONF 1995/L.5, 9 May 1995.

25. *An Evolving US Nuclear Posture*, p. 3.

26. *Report of the Canberra Commission*, p. 7.

27. "Non-Governmental Organization Abolition Caucus Statement," at the NPT Review and Extension Conference, New York, April 25, 1995.

28. The Canberra Commission is most specific on this point: "Progress towards a nuclear weapons free world should not be made contingent upon other changes in the international security environment" (p. 51).

29. *Report of the Canberra Commission*, p. 67.

30. *An Evolving US Nuclear Posture*, p. 35.

31. Booth and Wheeler, in *Security Without Nuclear Weapons?*, p. 40.

32. *Report of the Canberra Commission*, p. 67.

33. *An Evolving US Nuclear Posture*, p. 35.

34. *Report of the Canberra Commission*, p. 67.

35. *An Evolving US Nuclear Posture*, p. 37.

36. CSIS, *Toward a Nuclear Peace*, p. 78.

37. Booth and Wheeler, in *Security Without Nuclear Weapons?*, p. 39.

38. Group of 21, "Programme of Action for the Elimination of Nuclear Weapons," August 1996.

39. *Further Reins*, p. 23.

40. Booth and Wheeler, in *Security Without Nuclear Weapons?*, p. 40.

41. Kaysen, McNamara, and Rathjens, in *A Nuclear-Weapon-Free World: Desirable? Feasible?*, p. 42.

42. *An Evolving US Nuclear Posture*, p. 39.

43. *Report of the Canberra Commission*, p. 71.

44. R.B.J. Walker, "Security, Sovereignty, and the Challenge of World Politics," *Alternatives* XV, 1990:3.

45. When the negotiating parties have already arrived at a general formula for agreement, negotiations analyst William Zartman observes, "deadlines tend to facilitate agreement, lower expectations, call bluffs, and produce final proposals...." See I. W. Zartman and M.R. Berman, *The Practical Negotiator,* New Haven: Yale University Press, 1982, p. 195, 147.

46. *Ibid.*, p. 193.

47. Booth and Wheeler, in *Security Without Nuclear Weapons?*, p. 40.

48. *Ibid.*, p. 42.

49. *An Evolving US Nuclear Posture*, p. 38.

Appendix

Comparison of Select Proposals for Phased
Elimination of Nuclear Weapons*

CSIS Nuclear Strategy Study Group, *A Nuclear Peace: The Future of Nuclear Weapons in U.S. Foreign and Defense Policy* **(June 1993)**
Envisages a two phase process for changing US nuclear strategy, with various possible end-states, from maintenance of "nonoperational" national nuclear forces, to an international nuclear force to replace national forces to complete disarmament.

PHASE	ACTIONS	FEATURES OF STRATEGIC ENVIRONMENT
I	US and Russia: • Reduce first to 1000 warheads each, then to 500–1000, and consider ban on tactical nuclear weapons. • Reduce operational tempo – move almost all ICBMs to non-alert status, install early-warning system on missile fields of other state, restrict daily operations of SSBNs. US: • Take lead in establishing global treaties and agreements providing specific sanctions for nuclear use. • Begin discussions with other declared NWSs on non-operational nuclear forces. • With NATO, consider total ban on tactical nuclear weapons, and NFU pledge for regional conflicts. UK, France, PRC agree to restrict arsenals to 200 operational strategic warheads.	No change in major assumptions regarding nuclear strategy and roles of nuclear weapons: • Anarchic international system, in which nuclear weapons may help to keep peace. • US nuclear policy based on MAD. • Extended deterrent role for nuclear weapons. • Bilateral nuclear balance. Russian government willing to cooperate in arms control. Treaty banning first-use of nuclear weapons and establishing "clear and credible political, economic, and military sanctions (short of direct intervention) for use of nuclear weapons".

---

* For each proposal, the phases listed here are as described by that particular proposal, and thus the phases will not be parallel between the different proposals; likewise, some proposals do not define clearly distinct phases. Blank cells in the table reflect the lack of material on the corresponding topic in the proposal. Some proposals are vague as to which items are considered actions and which are elements of the strategic environment; thus, action-oriented items appear under the latter heading in some cases. In some proposals, deadlines are assigned to the completion of specific phases; others reject timelines.

CSIS Nuclear Strategy Study Group, *continued*		
PHASE	ACTIONS	FEATURES OF STRATEGIC ENVIRONMENT
II	Move to "end-state". Alternative end-states include: • Non-operational nuclear forces. • International nuclear force. • Complete and total disarmament.	End to anarchic international system; "considerable progress" toward rule of law in international affairs. Leaders of major states no longer view nuclear weapons as necessary to deter war, enjoy friendly relations, and have faith in conflict resolution system. May require: • Movement toward representative democracy in major states. • Development of international organizations able to mediate disputes, prevent and control conflict. • Web of economic, military, political treaties and commitments. • Dispute resolution and crisis management mechanisms. • Robust security guarantees. • Stiff penalties/sanctions for resort to war.

General Andrew J. Goodpaster, Atlantic Council, *Further Reins on Nuclear Arms* (August 1993)
Proposes three phases: bilateral, multilateral, and "zero level," and explores the corresponding pre-conditions for complete disarmament

PHASE	ACTIONS	FEATURES OF STRATEGIC ENVIRONMENT
I	US and Russia reduce to 1500–2000 total warheads each. Five declared NWSs adopt NFU policies. Threshold nuclear states: • Resolve nuclear issues between Israel and Pakistan. • Create NWF-zone in South Asia. Reinforcing measures: • Efforts to build & maintain highly capable detection mechanisms. • Assess adequacy of interim level of 200 for all NWSs. • Mideast peace efforts, and Israeli commitment to 200 warhead level. • Agreement on positive security assurances. • Discussions of response mechanisms for violations. • Discussions of cut-off of fissile material production for military purposes. • Discussions of CTB. • Study of desirability/feasibility of global ban on intermediate and long-range land-based ICBMs.	START ratification. Denuclearization agreements between Russia & Ukraine. Russian progress toward democratization, internal stability, non-confrontational foreign policy.

GOODPASTER, ATLANTIC COUNCIL, *CONTINUED*		
PHASE	ACTIONS	FEATURES OF STRATEGIC ENVIRONMENT
II	Five declared NWSs reduce stockpiles to 100–200 warheads each.	• Cooperative security environment among industrialized democracies, including Japan and Germany. • Continued Russian progress toward democratization, internal stability. • Adoption of NFU by 5 declared nuclear powers. • Strengthened non-proliferation regime. • Agreement to reassess and halt reductions if "rogue" is detected to have built or be near to building nuclear weapons. Agreement by Israel, India, Pakistan to a level not exceeding 200, and commitment that nuclear weapons are "defensive last resort". Acceptance of START verification procedures.
III	Abolish and eliminate all nuclear weapons.	• High-confidence in procedural safeguards and response capabilities against proliferation, breakout, clandestine cheating. • Additional NWF zones. • Monitored ban on production of weapons-grade nuclear materials. • Ban on nuclear testing. • Elimination of land-based ballistic missiles. • Tactical ballistic missile defense as safeguard against breakout/cheating. • Rigorously enforced nonproliferation regime.

The Henry L. Stimson Center, *An Evolving US Nuclear Posture: Second Report of the Steering Committee, Project on Eliminating Weapons of Mass Destruction* **(December 1995)**
Recommends an "evolutionary" approach to disarmament.

PHASE	ACTIONS	FEATURES OF STRATEGIC ENVIRONMENT
I	NWSs commit seriously to objective of eliminating all nuclear weapons. **US and Russia:** • Implement START II. • Reduce arsenals to roughly 2000 warheads each. • Engage UK, France, & China in policy negotiations on non-proliferation, nuclear safety & security, long-term arms control. • Gradually extend bilateral exchanges on nuclear safety, security, & accountability. • Reduce readiness levels. • Increase cooperation on nuclear safety and security. **US:** • Limit nuclear roles to deterrence of other nuclear threats only. • Support actions reducing prestige attached to NW possession (UNSC reform). • Support negotiation of ban on producing fissile material for military purposes. • Begin official studies to find solutions to key challenges: (1) Verification of elimination. (2) Safeguards against breakout. (3) Implications of phased elimination on relations with allies. (4) Implications of phased elimination on conventional military forces. (5) Potential role of defensive systems in safeguarding a ban on nuclear weapons. UK, France, China and threshold nuclear states should not undertake actions to undermine non-proliferation regime. Reinforcing policies: • Build strong cooperative relationship with Russia • Promote cooperation with China & Asia • Progress toward eliminating nuclear and chemical weapons.	US and Russia able to cooperate to reduce nuclear dangers.

The Henry L. Stimson Center, *continued*		
PHASE	ACTIONS	FEATURES OF STRATEGIC ENVIRONMENT
II	Declared NWSs: • Reduce arsenals to hundreds of weapons each. • Remove most, if not all, nuclear weapons from active alert status. • Extend bilateral regime of nuclear transparency measures to UK, France, China. • Explore possible cooperative deployment of defensive systems. • Begin to address capabilities of threshold nuclear states. Reinforcing policies: • Measures to address security concerns of states in volatile regions and of threshold nuclear states. • Commit to build or strengthen regional and international organizations and institutions. • Strengthen global non-proliferation regimes for nuclear, chemical, and biological weapons.	• Stable and cooperative relations among declared NWSs so that nuclear deterrence no longer plays central role in their mutual relations. • Russia finds role in Europe that others would accept without concern for security. • China participates in multilateral cooperation in Asia. • Effective and robust non-proliferation regimes for nuclear, chemical, and biological weapons. • Significant progress toward resolution of conflicts in Europe and Asia to minimize risks of new security threats. • Value of nuclear weapons as symbols of global status greatly diminished.

The Henry L. Stimson Center, *continued*		
PHASE	ACTIONS	FEATURES OF STRATEGIC ENVIRONMENT
III	"De-nationalization" of nuclear weapons. NWSs reduce arsenals to tens of weapons, then: • Create international "trustee" system; *OR* • Create integrated multilateral nuclear force through pooling of remaining NWSs' arsenals. Reinforcing policies: • Strengthen ability of regional organizations and states to anticipate, resolve, and respond to threats to national and international security.	Movement toward new guiding principles for national security policy, including: • Functioning and reliable regional and global collective security regimes. • High levels of transparency, with access to accurate information on NW & fissile material stockpiles of remaining NWSs. • Intrusive verification regime. • Effective system of incentives and penalties to ensure compliance with constraints on military force and WMD acquisition. • Nuclear weapons' only role to provide reassurance that international community could respond to unexpected threat. States remain sovereign.
IV	Eliminate nuclear weapons. Preserve reconstitution capability under international safeguards.	State system with effective security alternatives to threat of mass violence. May require spread of democracy. National and international verification regimes capable of detecting violations of nuclear weapons' ban in a timely manner. Safeguards against risks of non-nuclear world, including: • Mechanisms to impose economic, political, and military penalties on violator attempting to extract short-term gain.

Canberra Commission, *Report of the Canberra Commission on the Elimination of Nuclear Weapons* **(August 1996)** Proposes immediate negotiation by the NWSs of a commitment to eliminate nuclear weapons and begin work on practical steps leading toward elimination. Thoroughly examines arguments for and against elimination.		

PHASE	ACTIONS	FEATURES OF STRATEGIC ENVIRONMENT
Immediate	5 NWSs: • Commit unequivocally "to proceed at all deliberate speed to a world without nuclear weapons". • Take nuclear forces off alert. • Remove warheads from delivery vehicles. • End deployment of tactical nuclear weapons. • Initiate negotiations to further reduce US/Russian arsenals; begin bringing UK, France, & China into disarmament process. • Agreement among NWSs of reciprocal NFU; & non-use undertaking in relation to NNWSs.	• All states must cooperate to develop and support an "environment favourable" to elimination. • Progress should not be contingent upon other changes; progress toward elimination will benefit progress in other political/security negotiations and vice versa. Horizontal proliferation under control: • Incorporation of states outside NPT regime an "essential" step in elimination process. • Identification & solution of security needs of all parties in situations of regional tension. Effective verification arrangements, with high level of confidence in early detection of cheaters; confidence that violations will be addressed.
Reinforcing Steps	• Action to prevent further horizontal proliferation. • Develop verification regime. • Cease production of fissile materials for military purposes.	

Canberra Commission, *continued*		
PHASE	ACTIONS	FEATURES OF STRATEGIC ENVIRONMENT
Steps Concurrent with Entire Process	Actions to build an environment conducive to nuclear disarmament & non-proliferation: • Constraints on strategic nuclear ballistic missiles. • Nuclear Weapon Free Zones. • Constraints on nuclear trade and export controls. • Elimination of other WMD.	
Final Steps	• Bring other NWSs into the process: UK, France, and China join nuclear reductions when US/Russian arsenals "sufficiently reduced." • States with "presumed" NW potential enter into international legal constraints. • New legal arrangements (nuclear weapon convention or separate but mutually reinforcing instruments)	

Pugwash, *A Nuclear-Weapon-Free-World: Desirable? Feasible?* **(1993)** Examines whether the goal of zero nuclear weapons is desirable and feasible. Various scenarios for achieving disarmament are described by different authors; the following represents the main points made in the book's Executive Summary.		
PHASE	ACTIONS	FEATURES OF STRATEGIC ENVIRONMENT
I	• Steady reduction of nuclear forces, aiming at zero. • Universal adoption of a doctrine of No First Use. • Formalized agreement to stop the development of new delivery platforms or new warheads. • Strengthened NPT and IAEA safeguards regime. • More nuclear-weapon-free zones. • Increased confidence and cooperation among the existing nuclear-weapon powers.	
II	Negotiation of an NWFW treaty, making it illegal to possess or use nuclear weapons. There would be no right of withdrawal from the treaty. The treaty would have provisions for enforcement and verification, including: • Verified, physically-secured, dismantlement of all nuclear weapons, and disposal of nuclear materials. • Comprehensive safeguards regime, covering: all civil nuclear activities; research institutions; sites previously involved in nuclear weapons work, *etc.* • Verification that no nuclear-weapon state has hidden nuclear weapons or weapon-usable material. • Verification that there are no clandestine nuclear weapons production facilities. • Legal arrangements for societal verification.	• The idea of a war between any of the major industrial nations is greatly diminished. There are still disagreements and tensions between states, but the idea of trying to settle them by military force appears absurd. • Security Council prepared to take action, with conventional forces, to prevent development of nuclear weapons by any state.

Gorbachev Foundation (Moscow/USA) and Rajiv Gandhi Foundation, *Global Security Programme* **(October 1994)**
Proposes a comprehensive programme calling for nuclear and conventional disarmament; new security and peace-keeping arrangements; new mechanisms for conflict prevention & resolution. Nuclear disarmament programme should be tied to a time-bound framework.

PHASE	ACTIONS	FEATURES OF STRATEGIC ENVIRONMENT
I	US and Russia make START reductions irreversible: • Full data exchange & bilateral or multilateral monitoring of nuclear warhead stocks and fissile material for weapons. • Global agreement to ban production of fissile material for military purposes. • Further drastic reductions of deployed weapons. • Obligatory dismantling of reduced nuclear warheads and storage of fissile material under multilateral supervision. • Obligatory destruction of missiles reduced by agreement. • For deployed systems, separation of warheads from delivery systems and storage under international monitoring.	
II	US and Russia: • Undertake post-START reductions to roughly 1,000 warheads each. • Bring in UK, France, and China for series of further reductions. • Bilateral measures agreed in phase I extended to other declared NWSs.	
III	5 NWSs: • Reduce arsenals to level of 100 warheads each. • Separate remaining warheads from delivery systems. • Place warheads and delivery systems under multilateral control on owner state's territory. Threshold states would have option of giving up fissile materials or placing in monitored storage on own territory.	Strengthening of IAEA and its verification capabilities Adequate safeguards over nuclear capabilities of all UN member states UNSC mechanisms to punish violators of ban on nuclear weapons
Final	• Reductions to scores of nuclear weapons. • Elimination of nuclear weapons.	An international security system of real effectiveness

INESAP, *Beyond the NPT: A Nuclear-Weapon-Free World* **(April 1995)** Steps would be part of a Nuclear Weapons Convention; order does not imply chronological preference.		
PHASE	ACTIONS	FEATURES OF STRATEGIC ENVIRONMENT
I	• Reduction in nuclear arsenals and deployment. • Nuclear test moratorium and CTBT. • Closure, dismantling of NW production facilities. • NFU Treaty. • Treaty to ban use and threat of use of nuclear weapons. • Global moratorium on further production/development of nuclear weapons. • Test ban for ballistic missiles. • Production cut-off of weapon-grade fissile material; improved safeguards/monitoring system on all nuclear facilities. • Ban on tritium production. • Full implementation of CWC and verification system for BWC. • UN register of conventional arms and UN reports on military expenditures.	
II	• Additional deep reductions in 5 declared NWSs' arsenals. • Constraints on NW deployments to territorial bounds. • NWFZs in Africa, SE Asia, other regions. • Removal of nuclear warheads from strategic/tactical missiles into national storage under international inspections. • International inventory of fissile material.	
III	• "Transformation" of NWSs into NNWSs. • Dismantling of remaining global nuclear arsenal under international inspection. • International control of all fissile material. • Ban on national uranium enrichment and spent fuel reprocessing facilities. • Global nuclear weapons convention.	

Group of 21: *Programme of Action for the Elimination of Nuclear Weapons* **(August 1996)**
Proposes a step-by-step programme for the elimination of nuclear weapons within a specified timeframe.

PHASE	ACTIONS	FEATURES OF STRATEGIC ENVIRONMENT
Phase I: 1996–2000	Reduce the nuclear threat by negotiating immediately: • Treaty to eliminate nuclear weapons. • Prohibition on use/threat of use of NWs. • Legally binding instrument providing the NNWSs with negative security assurances. • Cut-off treaty. End qualitative improvements to nuclear weapons by agreeing on: • Ending nuclear testing, closing test sites. • Prohibition of nuclear weapon R&D, & other measures to upgrade NWs. Declarations of all NW stocks and NW usable materials. Full implementation of existing NWFZs and creation of new zones. Other measures of nuclear disarmament (taken verbatim from the "Programme"), including: • Stand down nuclear-weapon systems from a state of operational readiness. • Preservation of the ABM Treaty. • Moratorium and prohibition on testing of outer space weapons systems. • Ratification and implementation of the START II Treaty. • Commencement and conclusion of negotiations on further reductions of nuclear arsenals (START III). • Placement under IAEA safeguards of nuclear fissile material transferred from military to peaceful uses by the NWSs. • Further negotiations for nuclear disarmament by all NWSs, including the cessation of production of nuclear warheads. • Recommendations to the General Assembly to declare the decade 2000-2010 as the "Decade for nuclear disarmament".	

Group of 21, *continued*		
PHASE	ACTIONS	FEATURES OF STRATEGIC ENVIRONMENT
Phase II: 2000–2010	Measures to reduce the nuclear arsenals and to promote confidence between States (taken verbatim from the "Programme"): • Entry into force of the treaty to eliminate nuclear weapons and establishment of a single integrated multilateral comprehensive verification system to ensure compliance, including measures such as: • Separation of nuclear warheads from their delivery vehicles. • Placement of nuclear warheads in secure storage under international supervision leading to the removal of special nuclear materials from warheads. • Transfer of nuclear materials, including fissile materials and delivery vehicles, to peaceful purposes. • Preparation under international auspices of an inventory of nuclear arsenals, including fissile materials, nuclear warheads and their delivery vehicles. • Progressive and balanced reduction of missiles intended for carrying nuclear warheads. • Recommendation to the General Assembly to declare the decade 2010-2020 as the "Decade for the total elimination of nuclear weapons".	
Phase III: 2010–2020	Consolidation of a NWFW (verbatim): • Adoption of principles and mechanisms for a global cooperative security system. • Full implementation of the treaty to eliminate all nuclear weapons and of its verification regime through the completion of further measures such as: • Conversion of all facilities devoted to the production of nuclear weapons to peaceful purposes. • Application of safeguards on nuclear facilities on a universal basis. • Elimination of all nuclear weapons.	

3

Verifying Nuclear Disarmament

Steve Fetter

Commentators differ on whether nuclear disarmament would be desirable, but many argue that disarmament is impractical because it could not be verified. Three reasons are offered for such pessimism. First, nuclear weapons are small and difficult to detect, and one could not be sure that a few weapons had not been hidden away. Second, nuclear weapons are so destructive that a mere handful would confer enormous military and political advantages over non-nuclear adversaries. Third, nuclear know-how cannot be eliminated, and any nation that had dismantled its nuclear weapons would be capable of quickly assembling a new arsenal from scratch or using civilian nuclear materials. Because of the difficulty of verifying that other states had eliminated all their weapons, and of providing adequate warning if they rearmed, it is argued that states would not agree to disarm in the first place.

While a degree of scepticism is healthy, the recent elimination of nuclear weapon programmes in South Africa and Iraq gives some hope that disarmament could be verified adequately, particularly in the sort of international environment in which disarmament was under serious consideration. This paper examines the techniques that could be used to verify that nuclear arsenals had been dismantled and to provide timely warning of any attempt to build nuclear weapons. Although no verification regime could provide absolute assurance that former nuclear weapon states had not hidden a small number of nuclear weapons, verification could be good enough to reduce remaining uncertainties to a level that might be tolerable in a more transparent and trusting international environment. And although the possibility of breakout will be ever-present in modern industrial society, verification could provide the reassurance that would be necessary to dissipate residual fears of cheating. Verification will never be so effective that it can substitute for good relations between nations, but it can play an essential role in consolidating the trust that is necessary to support the process of reducing nuclear arsenals, perhaps all the way down to zero.

Standards for Verification

For an agreement to be verifiable, parties must be able to detect militarily significant violations in time to respond and deny the other side the benefit of the violation.   What would constitute adequate verification of a nuclear disarmament agreement? How confident must we be that all nuclear explosives had been dismantled? How sure must we be that an attempt to build a small nuclear arsenal would be detected? How much warning must we have of such an attempt? How many illegal nuclear weapons would constitute a "militarily significant" violation?

Unfortunately, it is impossible to answer these questions in general terms. The demands that we would place on the verification regime would depend on the nature of the world order in which disarmament is considered.   Nuclear disarmament could be pursued under conditions of unprecedented world peace and tranquillity, or under widespread and intense fear of nuclear weapons triggered by chaos in Russia, accidental or unauthorized use of nuclear weapons, war in Korea, the Middle East, or South Asia, or blackmail by rogue states or terrorist groups that somehow obtain nuclear weapons. Our standards for disarmament and verification are likely to be considerably lower if disarmament is motivated by a general recognition of the irrelevance of nuclear weapons to maintaining peace and security, rather than by a belief that their continued existence is maleficent and destabilizing.

The standard of verification also will depend on the safeguards that are established in connection with the disarmament agreement to protect against the possibility of violations. Safeguards might include defences against nuclear weapons delivered by aircraft, missiles, or covert means; security guarantees that pledge states to aid victims of nuclear attack or to punish nuclear aggressors; international nuclear or conventional forces of sufficient strength to deter or punish the use of nuclear weapons; or preparations to rebuild national nuclear forces. Some analysts promote the deterrent effect of nations being ready to "go nuclear" in response to a violation of the disarmament agreement; in this view, disarmament might mean not having assembled weapons, but maintaining the capacity to assemble them in a matter of weeks.[1]   Others recommend a ban on nuclear activities of all kinds – civilian as well as military – to build the biggest possible firebreak to rearmament.[2]

It is possible to imagine an international environment in which the standard of verification might be relatively low. If the collective political will and military ability to punish violators is strong, or if states believed that any advantage that could be obtained by violating the agreement would be short-lived, then incentives to defect from the regime would be small. Unfortunately, it is easier to imagine situations which would call for a much higher standard: the existence of technically capable aggressive states; the lack of a strong cooperative security regime that incorporates all the major powers; or technical breakthroughs or political breakdowns that made it easier for states or subnational groups to acquire weapons clandestinely.

The political and technical circumstances in which nuclear disarmament would be considered seriously by the nuclear weapon states cannot be predicted with any accuracy. Thus, we cannot say whether one weapon or one hundred weapons would be a significant violation, or whether one day or one year would represent timely warning of such a violation. What we can do is investigate the range of possible verification techniques, intelligence capabilities, and inspection privileges and infer from this what sort of verification standard might be achievable. Having determined what standard of verification is *possible*, we can discuss the sort of international political environment and types of safeguards that would be necessary to make this standard *adequate* for disarmament.

Dismantling Nuclear Arsenals

The first job of the verification regime would be to certify that the nuclear arsenals of all nations had been eliminated. For verification purposes, nuclear arsenals can be considered to have three types of components: delivery vehicles and their launchers, nuclear warheads, and fissile materials. Each of these components has an associated complex of production and support facilities that also must come under control. The goal of verification is to ensure that these items, materials, and facilities have been dismantled, destroyed, or converted to peaceful or non-nuclear military uses under appropriate international monitoring.

The verification process would begin with a declaration by each state possessing nuclear weapons of the location and characteristics of the weapons and related facilities, followed by a series of "baseline" inspections to verify the accuracy of the declaration. Once an agreed inventory was established, each item would be dismantled or converted to peaceful use according to specified procedures under international monitoring. Continuing inspections would verify that facilities had not been recommissioned or diverted to military use. During the reduction process, and for a very long time thereafter, surprise or "challenge" inspections would be conducted to search for evidence of hidden weapons or undeclared facilities.

The following sections describe how the process of declarations and inspections would be applied to delivery vehicles, warheads, and fissile materials. This is followed by an analysis of the only example of voluntary and verified nuclear disarmament – the case of South Africa. I then draw general conclusions about the degree of confidence that states would be likely to have that nuclear arsenals had been eliminated.

Delivery Vehicles

To date, nuclear arms control has focused on restricting the number of delivery vehicles – particularly ballistic missiles and long-range aircraft. The reasons for this are simple: delivery vehicles and their launchers are easy to count using spy satellites; they are the most expensive components of a nuclear arsenal; and they are the primary determinants of strategic capability. Delivery vehicles thus have been the chief currency of nuclear capability, and their elimination would be a natural focus of disarmament efforts.

Recent US-Russian arms control agreements provide a useful model for verifying the elimination of nuclear delivery vehicles on a multilateral basis. The Intermediate Nuclear Forces (INF) and START treaties are particularly instructive in three respects. First, these treaties established comprehensive and on-going exchanges of data on the number, location, and characteristics of all long-range US and Soviet (now Russian) nuclear delivery vehicles, as well as facilities for their production, testing, storage, maintenance, repair, and training. The accuracy of these data is confirmed by initial and continuing inspections of the declared facilities. Second, these treaties established procedures by which delivery vehicles and launchers can be verifiably eliminated or converted to a non-nuclear mission. The elimination or conversion is verified by a combination of national technical means and on-site inspections, depending on the type of delivery vehicle. Third, the treaties provide for "suspect-site" inspections to verify that equipment or activity limited by the treaty is not present at other, undeclared facilities.

In most respects, the INF and START treaties provide a complete set of tools to verify the elimination or conversion of nuclear delivery vehicles and associated launchers and facilities. To make use of these tools in a disarmament agreement, it would be necessary to apply them in a more comprehensive manner. For example, the START treaties specify procedures for verifiably eliminating only certain types of delivery vehicles and launchers: silos for intercontinental ballistic missiles (ICBMs), "heavy" ICBMs, mobile ICBMs and launchers, launch tubes for submarine-launched ballistic missiles (SLBMs), and heavy bombers. The START treaties do not require the elimination of SLBMs, non-heavy silo-based ICBMs, and air-launched cruise missiles (ALCMs), however. Moreover, aside from the INF Treaty's requirement that all ground-launched ballistic and cruise missiles with ranges between 500 and 5500 kilometres be eliminated, there is no requirement to eliminate other non-strategic delivery systems, such as tactical aircraft and sea-launched cruise missiles (SLCMs).

A disarmament agreement should require the elimination of all nuclear delivery vehicles. In some cases, the conversion to non-nuclear missions or peaceful applications might be permitted under strict guidelines and verification. For example, START allows the conversion of nuclear bombers to conventional roles, provided that the converted bombers are based separately from nuclear bombers and at least 100 kilometres from nuclear weapon storage sites, that they are modified so that they cannot carry nuclear armaments, and that they have observable differences from nuclear bombers of the same type. A similar approach could be used to convert other types of nuclear delivery vehicles, such as tactical aircraft, ALCMs, and SLCMs, to conventional roles. Small numbers of ballistic missiles might be converted for use as space launch vehicles, subject to realistic projections of future demand and on-going monitoring. But because aircraft and missiles could be converted back into nuclear delivery vehicles, ultimately verification would depend on ensuring that the nuclear warheads for these systems had been eliminated.

Nuclear Weapons

US-Russian efforts to control nuclear arsenals have largely ignored their most fearsome components – the nuclear explosives themselves. This is due to the inherent difficulties in verifying limits on nuclear warheads. National intelligence is incapable of accurately counting an adversary's warheads; US estimates of the number of Russian warheads have an uncertainty measured in the thousands.[3] Cooperative means of verification have been resisted because they might reveal sensitive information about the design of nuclear weapons or the status of nuclear forces.

This attitude has begun to change recently. In September 1994, Presidents Clinton and Yeltsin agreed to exchange data on their countries' nuclear arsenals, and instructed their experts to meet to discuss what information could be provided to the other side. Such an agreement has not yet been reached, and the parties are likely to begin with a modest exchange of information. Preparations for nuclear disarmament, however, would require a comprehensive declaration, including:

– the location, type, status, and serial number of all nuclear explosive devices;
– the location, status, and description of facilities at which nuclear explosives had been designed, tested, assembled, stored, deployed, repaired, and dismantled; and
– the location, status, and description of facilities that produced key nuclear weapon components, such as high-explosive assemblies and neutron generators; and of facilities that fabricated special warhead materials, such as plutonium and highly-enriched uranium (HEU).

This information would allow parties to verify the current status of nuclear stockpiles and production complexes, as a basis for verifying the dismantling of warheads and the decommissioning of related facilities. To provide confidence that this information was complete, it also would be helpful to have complete information about the history of the stockpiles, including:

– the history of each nuclear explosive device, including the dates of assembly, movement between various declared facilities, and its dismantling, destruction in an explosive test, or accidental loss; and
– the operating records of the warhead-related facilities listed above.

Data on the history of stockpiles and the operation of warhead-related facilities cannot be verified directly, but could be checked for internal consistency and for consistency with archived intelligence data.   If, for example, US satellites had detected the movement of nuclear warheads from a particular facility on a certain date, this could be checked against the records that had been provided.   The fact that countries would not know what information might be available to other parties would act as an incentive to provide complete and accurate records.

As with declarations on delivery vehicles, the current status of nuclear warhead stockpiles would be verified by inspections of declared facilities, combined with challenge inspections to verify the absence of warheads at other locations.   During inspections of declared facilities, for example, inspectors could count the number of warheads in a particular storage bunker and compare this to the number listed in the data exchange.

Unlike verification of missiles or silos, however, warhead verification raises the question of how inspectors could be sure that objects declared to be warheads were authentic. Without such assurances, parties might fear that fake warheads had been substituted for real ones, with the real warheads hidden to avoid dismantling.   Simple radiation detectors could confirm the presence of fissile materials, but not necessarily the authenticity of a nuclear device.

One possibility would be to use a combination of radiation and other signatures to "fingerprint" types of nuclear warheads.   Either the country being inspected or the inspecting party could select a nuclear warhead of a particular type for fingerprinting.   Detectors could then measure the rate at which gamma-rays and neutrons were emitted from the device at several locations; size, weight, and heat output also could be measured.   A signature with such detail would be extremely difficult to counterfeit, but it might raise concerns that sensitive design information was being revealed.   To deal with such concerns, the data could be encoded in such a way that the inspection instrument would give only a "yes" or "no" answer when inspecting a particular device.   Such a system has, in fact, been developed by the United States.

During inspections, it also would be necessary to assure that other, undeclared objects do not contain warheads.   If the object was not too large, gamma-ray and neutron detectors could confirm the absence of fissile materials. Large objects could contain enough shielding to prevent such detection in a reasonable amount of time, however, in which case the inspected party should be required to use other methods to demonstrate that no warheads were contained within.

Verification of the declaration would be enhanced and simplified if all declared nuclear warheads were equipped with a unique identification number or "tag" that was specified in the declaration. First, tags would simplify verification because the discovery of an untagged warhead would be *prima facie* evidence of a violation. Second, tags would facilitate the use of random sampling, thereby decreasing monitoring effort, cost, and intrusiveness.[4] Third, tags would allow particular warheads to be tracked as they moved among facilities. If combined with perimeter-portal monitoring, tags would allow the declaration to be updated continuously, and would foreclose the possibility that untagged warheads could make use of declared facilities. A nation intending to cheat would be forced to develop a parallel, clandestine system to store, maintain, repair, or deploy illegal warheads – thus increasing the cost of cheating and the risk of exposure.

Perimeter-portal systems are conceptually simple. A monitored perimeter – for example, an existing fence equipped with intrusion sensors – would be installed around facilities where nuclear warheads were kept. The perimeter would contain a portal equipped to detect the passage of a warhead into or out of the facility. Thus, nuclear warheads could not enter or be removed from the facility without detection. One could begin perimeter-portal monitoring with a single storage facility for warheads slated for dismantling. The next logical step would be to install such systems at other storage facilities, dismantling facilities, and finally at facilities where warheads are deployed.

The monitoring of assembly and dismantling facilities deserves special attention. Unlike the elimination or conversion of delivery vehicles and launchers, the dismantling of nuclear warheads cannot be verified directly without revealing sensitive design information. The most straightforward solution would be to install perimeter-portal systems at dismantling facilities, and to monitor the flow of nuclear warheads into the facilities and the flow of plutonium pits out.[5] A particular nuclear warhead would be counted as dismantled when the corresponding pit had been placed in monitored storage. If desired, pits could be fingerprinted and associated with particular warhead types. At specified intervals, all the warheads within the facility could be dismantled and interior inspections allowed to verify that a stockpile of warheads or warhead materials had not been accumulated within the dismantling facility.

A possible complication is that warhead remanufacturing and maintenance activities may take place even at very low levels of nuclear weapons, often in the same facility as dismantling activities. To illustrate how this might be handled, assume that the facility had a single portal through which all materials must enter or exit. Entering the portal would be warheads for dismantling;

warheads for maintenance or remanufacture; and new warhead components (pits, tritium bottles, high-explosive assemblies, *etc.*) for stockpile maintenance activities. Leaving the facility would be reconditioned warheads and old components from dismantled and reconditioned warheads. Inspections at the portal would ensure that objects declared to be warheads or pits of a particular type were authentic, and that no warheads or pits entered or left the facility without being detected and accounted for. There would then be a balance between warheads entering the facility for dismantling and pits of the corresponding type leaving the facility; and between warheads of a particular type (and associated warhead components) entering and leaving the facility for stockpile maintenance activities. Because this balance might not be exact during dismantling or maintenance campaigns, the facility's inventory would have to be taken at agreed intervals.

Regarding warhead components, various levels of accounting, control, and recycling could be permitted:

–   Plutonium pits and other fissile components should receive the same degree of control and accounting as warheads, and should be stored and ultimately converted for disposal or for peaceful use under international safeguards. So long as nuclear stockpiles were permitted, pits from remanufactured warheads could be recycled for use as new pits.
–   So long as nuclear stockpiles were permitted, tritium from dismantled and remanufactured warheads could be recovered and recycled; thereafter tritium would be used only for peaceful purposes under international safeguards.
–   Other important warhead components, such as high-explosive implosion assemblies, neutron generators, and fusing and firing systems, should be destroyed or, while stockpiles are yet permitted, recycled for use in remanufactured warheads.

In all of these procedures, nuclear weapon states would have to balance the desire for effective verification with the need to protect sensitive nuclear weapon design information. Initially, this balance might be served best by having the United States and Russia inspect each other. As the number of nuclear weapons drops, the other three nuclear weapon states could be invited to join the process on a more-or-less equal basis. At some point, verification would be the responsibility of the IAEA or some other international agency, perhaps using nationals from the nuclear weapon states for more sensitive tasks.

It is important to begin verifying warhead declarations as far in advance of a disarmament agreement as possible. As the number of nuclear weapons falls into the hundreds, states would be more likely to have confidence in a declaration whose accuracy had been verified for years and for tens of thousands of nuclear warheads, than one whose verification had begun recently and only after thousands of warheads had been dismantled. Failure to verify the dismantling and consolidation of the huge US and Russian nuclear stockpiles could undermine confidence in declarations made later about much smaller numbers of weapons. There is little pressure for warhead-verification measures today because stockpiles are so large as to make existing uncertainties unimportant. But unless the nuclear powers begin now to describe and verify their warhead stockpiles, when the need for verification is not pressing, they will have failed to lay a foundation that is strong enough to bear the weight of a disarmament regime.

Fissile Materials

Fissile materials – highly-enriched uranium and plutonium – are the essential ingredients of all nuclear weapons. Control and accounting for these materials, therefore, must be a fundamental element of any comprehensive disarmament regime, just as it is the basis for the current non-proliferation regime.

As with delivery vehicles and warheads, the first step would be a declaration of existing stockpiles of all fissile materials. In this case, parties would declare:

–   the mass, chemical and isotopic composition, status, and location of all fissile materials;
–   a description of all facilities that had been used to produce these materials;
–   the production records and a material balance for each facility;
–   an account of materials otherwise acquired (*e.g.*, from other countries); and
–   an account of all fissile materials removed from the inventory (*e.g.*, consumed in weapon tests or nuclear reactors, dispersed in accidents, lost to waste or radioactive decay, or transferred to other countries).

There are two major differences between this declaration and those previously described. First, record keeping is far better and more accurate for missiles and warheads than for fissile materials. Second, missiles and warheads are subject to simple item accounting; fissile materials are not. Material accounting is susceptible to errors of measurement and estimation. Although the mass of a finished piece of plutonium or uranium metal can be measured with high accuracy, the amount of material that remains in inaccessible locations within a facility, or that is lost to waste streams, often is not measured accurately.

It is likely that the nuclear weapon states know, with very little uncertainty, how much plutonium and HEU are in their fabricated weapon components, fresh fuel rods, and various storage forms. More problematic is the plutonium and HEU in spent fuel; in metal scraps; in powders lining pipes, glove boxes, and ventilation ducts; and in various liquid solutions and wastes. A recent accounting of US plutonium stockpiles revealed that, of the 111.4 tonnes of plutonium produced or otherwise acquired by the United States, nearly 3.4 tonnes is estimated to have been lost to waste.[6] Such estimates, however, are subject to large uncertainties, as is illustrated by the fact that the total amount of plutonium actually in wastes is estimated at 3.9 tonnes.

Estimates of national inventories may contain uncertainties of a few per cent. For example, the estimate of the total amount of plutonium produced or otherwise acquired by the United States is 2.8 tonnes higher than the measured amount of plutonium in current stockpiles (99.5 tonnes) plus the estimated amount removed from the inventory in tests, wastes, reactors, decay, accidents, and transfers (9.1 tonnes).[6] This 2.8 tonnes is the sum of inventory differences at a dozen facilities over fifty years. There is no evidence that any of this plutonium was lost or stolen. Most, if not all, of the inventory difference is the result of errors in measurement and record-keeping, overestimates of the amount produced in reactors, and underestimates of the amount in wastes. In the latter case, a significant fraction of the "missing" plutonium may be recovered as facilities are decommissioned and decontaminated.

Inventory differences are likely to be even larger for US production of HEU, because the United States did not measure how much HEU went into waste streams and did not keep precise records of the enrichment of various product streams. In addition, Russian and Chinese production records probably are considerably less dependable than those of the United States. Although concerted efforts could be made to minimize inventory differences, it seems unlikely that they could be reduced below several per cent of the total inventory.

The large uncertainties in fissile-material inventories could prove to be the largest obstacle to verifying nuclear disarmament. As Table 1 indicates, the amount of fissile material reserved for military use in the nuclear weapon states is huge. An uncertainty of five per cent in the US or Russian stockpiles corresponds to enough material to build about 5000 nuclear explosives; in the case of the United Kingdom, France, or China, about 100 nuclear explosives; in the case of Israel or India, about five explosives. To this challenge we also must add the difficulty of accounting for hundreds of tonnes of civilian fissile materials in these states that have not been safeguarded by the IAEA, but which could be used for weapons.[7]

It would be fairly straightforward, if time-consuming, to verify the accuracy of some categories of information provided in a fissile-material data exchange. For example, inspectors could verify that selected storage canisters contained material of the amount and isotopic composition specified in the declaration. In some cases, such as scraps and wastes, verification will be complicated by physical barriers, safety considerations, and measurement uncertainties. Other information, such as the amount and composition of fissile materials in a particular type of warhead, would be likely to remain unverified. Of course, as disarmament proceeds, weapons will be dismantled and the pits and other components they contain will be converted to forms appropriate for disposal or peaceful use under international safeguards, as will materials recovered during the clean-up and decommissioning of production and fabrication facilities.

Table 1. Estimated amount of military fissile material in the nuclear weapon and threshold states, and the corresponding number of nuclear explosives that could be built with this material.

Country	Plutonium (tonnes)	HEU (tonnes)	number of explosives*
Russia	130	1050	120,000
United States	100	645	80,000
United Kingdom	12	8	4,000
France	5	25	3,000
China	4	20	3,000
Israel	0.5	---	100
India	0.3	---	80
Pakistan	---	0.2	20
Total (rounded)	250	1750	210,000

Source: D. Albright, F. Berkout, and W. Walker, *Plutonium and Highly Enriched Uranium 1996: World Inventories, Capabilities, and Policies*, Oxford: Oxford University Press, 1997.

*Assumes 4 kg of plutonium or 12 kg of uranium-235 for each fission explosive.

At the final stage of nuclear disarmament, more precise measurements could be made and compared with the initial declaration.

One problem is that this final stage of disarmament might come long after the delivery vehicles and warheads had been dismantled. The United States, for example, does not have a facility to process plutonium pits. A decision to build such a facility probably will await a final decision on the ultimate disposition of the plutonium. The clean-up of production and fabrication facilities also may take decades to complete. A full accounting of fissile-material stockpiles is therefore likely to lag considerably behind the rest of the disarmament process.

But even if one could measure precisely the amount of material in the various forms enumerated in the declaration, there would remain the difficult problem of ensuring that there were no undeclared stocks of material. This would be accomplished primarily by confirming declarations about the total amount of material that had been produced, but, as noted above, it is unlikely that it will be possible to confirm such declarations with an uncertainty of less than five or ten per cent.

Verifying declarations of HEU production would begin with a material balance for each enrichment facility. Recorded receipts of uranium hexafluoride would be compared with shipments of enriched product and discharges of depleted uranium. In addition to the total amount of uranium, a mass balance would be done for uranium-235, based on recorded isotopic assays of enriched and depleted material. The overall design and enrichment capacity of each plant would be verified through on-site inspections. Records of the total amount of separative work performed by the plant would be compared with its design capacity, the amounts and enrichment levels of product and tails, and, in the case of gaseous diffusion plants, records of electricity consumption. As an added check, the total amount of uranium mined or imported could be compared with the amount used as feed for enrichment plants, taking into account other demand for uranium. The production of low-enriched uranium (LEU) also could be compared with records of fuel fabrication and reactor fuel loadings. Even if records were complete and accurate, however, uncertainties of at least several per cent could be expected in estimates of the amount of HEU produced.

Verifying plutonium production would involve examining records of the fabrication of uranium fuel and target rods for plutonium-production reactors; the design of the fuel and the reactors, typical fuel loadings in the core, and dates of fuel loading and discharge; monthly production of thermal energy; shipments of spent fuel; the design and chemical flowsheet of the reprocessing plants; monthly production of plutonium product; and the volume, isotopic concentrations, and disposition of the various waste streams. If the records were complete and accurate, this information would allow plutonium production to be estimated with an uncertainty of perhaps five per cent.

The value of this method of verifying production declarations would depend almost entirely upon the accuracy, completeness, and authenticity of the records that were provided. One could check that operating records were consistent with declarations, and that the records were internally consistent, but this should not be confused with independently verifying their accuracy. Records can be falsified, and even authentic records may be inaccurate or incomplete. For example, the rigid quota system imposed on Soviet facilities may have led operators to manipulate official production records.

Therefore, it would be helpful to have access to physical evidence that could be used to verify the accuracy of the records. Production facilities are possible sources of such physical evidence.[8] In plutonium-production reactors, for example, the ratio of isotopes in permanent components of the reactor (*e.g.*, the graphite moderator, steel fuel supports, or reactor vessel) can provide an estimate of the total thermal energy, and therefore the total amount of plutonium, produced during the reactor's lifetime. Although estimates derived in this way would have an uncertainty margin of five or ten per cent, they would be largely independent of record-keeping by the host country, and, therefore, would provide an independent check on the declaration. In the case of uranium enrichment facilities, isotopic ratios in depleted uranium stored on site could confirm records of product and tails assays over a particular time period. Even these types of measurements are not foolproof, however: production reactors might be dismantled before measurements could be made, and depleted uranium could be hidden or used for other purposes (*e.g.*, ballast, bullets, or blending stock).

South Africa: A Case Study in Disarmament

South Africa is the only country known to have crossed the nuclear threshold in both directions. Having built six Hiroshima-type nuclear bombs during the 1980s, South Africa decided in the early 1990s to dismantle its weapons and join the nuclear Non-Proliferation Treaty (NPT) as a non-nuclear weapon state. South Africa's experience in convincing the international community that it had disarmed is, therefore, particularly instructive about the promise and problems of verifying disarmament.

Beginning in July 1990, South Africa disarmed in secret. Within a year, the nuclear bombs had been dismantled, documents destroyed, production and assembly facilities decommissioned, and HEU weapon components cast into standard shapes for storage and international inspection.[9] Only in March 1993 did President de Klerk announce that South Africa had built, and had dismantled, six nuclear bombs. The IAEA was given a full history of the nuclear weapon programme, and was granted permission to conduct inspections at any relevant location and to interview former managers and workers about the programme. A special team of inspectors verified that six bombs-worth of HEU had been placed under safeguards, that other components had been rendered unusable for weapons, and that weapon-related activities had ceased at various facilities.

IAEA inspectors easily verified that the *declared* weapons and facilities had been dismantled and decommissioned, and that the *declared* stocks of HEU had been placed in safeguarded storage. Verifying that South Africa did not have any *undeclared* weapons or stocks of HEU was considerably more difficult, however. This is, of course, the central problem in verifying nuclear disarmament.

In this case, the major obstacle was verifying the accuracy and completeness of South Africa's declaration of the amount of HEU it possessed. South Africa claimed that the Valindaba enrichment plant had produced considerably less HEU than its design capacity would have allowed, primarily, the South Africans stated, because accidents caused plant shutdowns, and because the plant was also used to produce LEU for reactor fuel.

In the end, the IAEA concluded that "the amounts of HEU which could have been produced by the pilot enrichment plant are consistent with the amounts declared."[10] This conclusion was based largely on an analysis of the original operating records of the plant which were provided to the Agency, and which the IAEA judged to be authentic. Estimates of the amount of enriched uranium produced by the plant based on these records and the plant's specifications matched the South African declaration within an acceptable margin of uncertainty.[11] A materials balance of the plant, however, revealed much greater uncertainties because plant operators kept poor records of the enrichment of the depleted-uranium tails. Although an assay of the 370 tonnes of tails, which are stored on-site in some 600 cylinders, would have reduced greatly the uncertainty in the material balance, the IAEA decided that the increased confidence provided by such measurements would not justify their considerable expense.[12]

The lessons of the South African experience for verifying nuclear disarmament are both positive and negative. On the positive side, the experience suggests that when a government makes a full and complete disclosure of past nuclear activities; offers international inspectors unfettered access to all relevant facilities, records, materials, and personnel; and cooperates fully with the investigation to resolve any discrepancies that may arise, the international community can gain considerable confidence in a government's claim that it had disarmed. This conclusion should, however, be tempered by the unique situation of South Africa.

Unlike other nuclear-armed countries, South Africa did not fear attack from adversaries armed with nuclear weapons or superior conventional forces. Indeed, the South African government's greatest concern focused on an internal risk: maintaining control over nuclear weapons in the turmoil that might accompany the movement towards majority rule. That the South African government had little incentive to cheat on its pledge of nuclear disarmament was undoubtedly a major factor in building confidence in that pledge. The standard of verification required by the international community might be considerably greater for countries that are viewed as having powerful incentives to cheat, or in cases in which adversaries would have strong reasons to fear the possibility of cheating (see Chapter 6). This underscores the importance of viewing verification in its political context, and the need for other mechanisms to reduce incentives to cheat.

On the negative side, the South African experience shows the difficulty of verifying declarations of even small inventories of fissile material. As noted by IAEA Director General Hans Blix, "There is inherent difficulty in verifying the completeness of an original inventory in a country in which a substantial nuclear programme has been going on for a long time."[13] Although South Africa's nuclear programme may have been substantial and sustained by IAEA standards, it was tiny and transient compared to those of the nuclear weapon states. Like South Africa, we can expect that the nuclear weapon states have not kept good records of certain parameters that, while valuable for verification, were not relevant for the production of materials and weapons. If the IAEA had difficulty in verifying the production of a few hundred kilograms of HEU in South Africa, how will it cope with stockpiles a thousand times larger? What if original records are not available or cannot be authenticated? What if production facilities have been dismantled or if plant managers are unavailable for interviews? These are difficult questions that will have to be addressed if disarmament is to be considered seriously.

How Confident Could We Be of Disarmament?

In the end, then, we come back to the fundamental question: "How confident could we be that states had disarmed?"

We could be confident that the nuclear weapon states had eliminated the ICBMs and SLBMs that now dominate their strategic nuclear forces. Although a hidden stockpile of mobile missiles might escape detection, it soon would lose its military utility without the regular test, maintenance, and exercise activities which would, if carried out, greatly increase the risk of exposure. Of more concern would be long-range aircraft and cruise missiles. Even if we could verify that all nuclear-armed aircraft had been destroyed, conventional variants would exist and could be converted to deliver nuclear warheads with little or no warning. Of course, even civilian aircraft or ships could be used to deliver nuclear warheads. Verifying nuclear disarmament, therefore, must rely on verifying that no hidden stockpiles of nuclear explosives exist.

We could be confident that a declared number of nuclear warheads had been dismantled if dismantling facilities and fabricated weapon components were subject to verification during the reduction process. Unfortunately, the process of dismantling excess warheads is already well underway in the United States and Russia without the benefit of any verification or transparency measures. As long as the pits remain intact, it may yet be possible to gain a high degree of confidence that the corresponding warheads were dismantled. If, however, the pits are recast or reused, it will be impossible to verify independently the number or type of weapons that have been dismantled. In that case, one would have to rely primarily on records and assurances provided by the inspected party.

A statement that *all* warheads had been dismantled would be even more difficult to verify, resting largely on the perceived accuracy and authenticity of records provided by the inspected party and the testimony of relevant officials, supplemented by an imperfect accounting of the stocks and production of fissile materials. Regarding the latter, the inspection agency at best could conclude that there was no evidence that materials had been hidden, that the declarations of amounts of material produced and stockpiled were consistent with available records and physical evidence, and that any discrepancies were within the uncertainties inherent in the estimating procedure. Unfortunately, these uncertainties will be very large – at least several per cent of the total amount of material produced. A declaration that is verified to the best of our abilities would not prove, therefore, that weapon states had not hidden significant amounts of fissile materials – perhaps enough to make hundreds of warheads – from international inspectors.

From a purely technical point of view, it would not be difficult to hide the existence of a few dozen (or perhaps even a few hundred) nuclear devices – or enough material to build dozens or hundreds of bombs – from inspectors. A nation could falsify records to show that the hidden warheads or materials had never been produced. Alternatively, a country could claim that hidden warheads had been destroyed in accidents or nuclear tests, or that hidden materials had been lost in wastes.[14]

The infrastructure required to support and maintain a small, secret arsenal need not attract attention or require significant amounts of money. The warheads themselves are small; several bombs or cruise-missile warheads could be transported in a common delivery truck and stored in any warehouse. Only a small cadre of trained personnel would be required to examine the warheads from time to time for signs of deterioration. Some weapons would require a fresh supply of tritium to give their design yield, but the required tritium could be diverted from civilian stocks only if and when the weapons were needed. A hidden stockpile of fissile materials would, by itself, be easier to hide than a stock of warheads. The strategic value of such stocks would depend, however, on a country's ability to produce weapons quickly using these materials, and maintaining or creating a capability to do so would be far more difficult to hide.

It is unlikely that hidden warheads or stocks of fissile materials would be discovered unless someone aware of their existence leaked information about their location. Because of the inherent weakness of technical means of verification in detecting small violations, some analysts stress the importance of "whistle-blowing" or "societal verification," a subject which is taken up in detail in Chapter 4.

In short, one could never be certain that a country that had built a substantial nuclear arsenal had disarmed completely. It is unlikely that an international inspectorate would be able to prove beyond a reasonable doubt that the United States or Russia had not sequestered a dozen or so "bombs in the basement" (or enough plutonium to build a dozen bombs), short of administering truth serum or polygraph tests to the nation's political and military leaders. But this conclusion, while important, is intuitively obvious. The more important question is whether the theoretical possibility of cheating makes disarmament impossible in practice.

No treaty is perfectly verifiable. Fortunately, perfection is not the appropriate standard. A verification regime can reduce the likelihood of cheating and the magnitude of cheating that could go undetected, but it cannot make undetected cheating impossible. Ultimately, states must judge whether the benefits of nuclear disarmament outweigh the risks of possible cheating. The risks of cheating depend less on the characteristics of the verification regime than on the probability that states that disarm might become hostile, on the perceived value of small numbers of nuclear weapons in securing the goals of such hostile states, and on the precautions states had taken to protect against the possibility of cheating.

Detecting Rearmament

Besides verifying that all nuclear weapons had been dismantled and that all fissile materials had been placed under international safeguards, the verification regime would have to be able to provide timely warning of any attempt to build new nuclear weapons or to reconstruct dismantled nuclear arsenals. In contrast with verifying disarmament, the international community already has considerable experience with verifying that countries are not building nuclear weapons, at least with respect to the non-nuclear weapon states that are parties to the NPT. Much of this experience would be directly applicable to monitoring a comprehensive nuclear disarmament regime, although the standards for verification would have to be higher than they are at present, for two reasons. First, the former nuclear weapon states have considerable experience in producing nuclear weapons, and presumably would find it much easier to circumvent current safeguards without detection than states that had never produced nuclear weapons. Second, the nuclear weapon states are likely to require that barriers to the acquisition of nuclear weapons be increased as one condition for agreeing to dismantle their own arsenals.

Under the NPT, non-nuclear weapon states promise "not to manufacture or otherwise acquire nuclear weapons or other nuclear explosive devices." The Treaty acknowledges the right of these states, in forgoing nuclear weapons, to enjoy the peaceful uses of nuclear energy. To prevent the "diversion of nuclear energy from peaceful uses to nuclear weapons," the non-nuclear weapon states agree to accept IAEA safeguards on all their nuclear activities. In addition, all parties agree not to transfer nuclear materials or equipment to any other state unless those materials or equipment are subject to IAEA safeguards.

IAEA safeguards are designed to detect diversions of significant quantities of nuclear material with high confidence, and to provide warning of such diversions in a timely manner.[15] The safeguards are based on audits of each country's records of nuclear-material inventories and changes in those inventories at each facility, and on the collection of data to verify the accuracy of those records. IAEA inspectors count items such as fuel rods, estimate amounts of nuclear material, affix seals to indicate whether items have been moved or tampered with, and install video cameras and radiation detectors to monitor the movement of nuclear materials. Inspectors also verify the design of facilities to understand their capacity and the flow of nuclear materials within them, and to evaluate the operator's measurement systems. The frequency of inspections depends on the quantity and quality of nuclear material present. Facilities containing spent reactor fuel, for example, are inspected less frequently than those with separated HEU or plutonium, but more frequently than facilities containing only natural or low-enriched uranium.

Improving IAEA Safeguards

Revelations in the wake of the Persian Gulf War that Iraq had pursued an extensive nuclear weapon programme while a member of the NPT, focused international attention on the shortcomings of IAEA safeguards. Among these are the weak authority of the Agency to conduct inspections on short notice and at undeclared facilities, the inability to concentrate inspection effort on states of proliferation concern, the focus on nuclear materials to the exclusion of other weapon-development activities, the right of states to refuse certain inspectors or inspectors from certain states, and a shortage of funding to achieve inspection goals.[16]

At a minimum, these defects would have to be corrected before IAEA safeguards could be used as a basis for monitoring a comprehensive disarmament agreement. The single most important factor in the failure of safeguards in Iraq was the inability to detect undeclared facilities. IAEA inspections are designed to detect the diversion of significant amounts of material from declared facilities, and they have been highly effective in accomplishing this goal. It is precisely for this reason that countries have been, and would continue to be, more likely to cheat by constructing clandestine nuclear facilities.

If discovered, the mere existence of an undeclared nuclear facility would be *prima facie* evidence of a violation sufficient to prompt the international community to take action. The challenge is to detect undeclared facilities in the first place. With a reasonably high probability, the verification system must provide clear and convincing evidence of an undeclared facility, if one exists. Just as important, it must provide adequate reassurance when no such facilities exist.

At least four major changes in the current safeguards regime are required to deal with the possibility of undeclared facilities. First, high-quality intelligence information, particularly high-resolution imagery and signals intelligence that might reveal the construction and operation of clandestine nuclear facilities, must be incorporated in the verification process. Today, this information is available only through national intelligence. The quality of commercial imagery will continue to improve in the coming decades, but it is unlikely that any commercial service will approach the overall intelligence capabilities of the United States. Before the Persian Gulf War, governments did not share information about the Iraqi nuclear programme, if they had any, with the IAEA. The United States and other countries subsequently have been more forthcoming, and US satellite photographs were vital in mobilizing international support for IAEA efforts to uncover undeclared nuclear activities in Iraq and North Korea.

Such informal mechanisms are unlikely to be adequate under a general disarmament agreement, however. As long as the best intelligence information is in the hands of a few countries, observers will expect that these countries will use the information for their own purposes. The fact that intelligence assets are concentrated in the hands of the current nuclear weapon states may be particularly troubling. Although some might hope that these countries would keep an eye on each other, others might fear that they would collude to keep secrets from an international inspectorate. If, on the other hand, high-quality intelligence information became more widely available, it would be more likely that countries that wished to cheat would learn how to hide their nuclear activities.

Second, extensive environmental monitoring would improve substantially the ability to detect undeclared facilities, by detecting the distinctive radioactive or chemical substances emitted during their operation.[17] Environmental sampling would be especially effective in detecting plutonium separation, since large amounts of radioactive gases are released into the environment when the spent fuel is dissolved. These gases can be trapped with considerable difficulty and expense, but releases cannot be eliminated entirely. Uranium enrichment is much harder to detect because emissions are low and uranium exists in nature. High concentrations or unusual chemical forms of uranium in the air or water, however, could indicate the presence of undeclared uranium mining, purification, or conversion operations.

The operation of most existing nuclear facilities can be detected rather easily because of their large size, and because precautions usually have not been taken to disguise their emissions. Nuclear reactors, for example, typically are built above ground on the shores of a large body of water, and are easily recognized by their distinctive appearance and the discharge of large quantities of heat. Releases of radioactive gases from existing reprocessing plants can be detected thousands of kilometres downwind, and particles of enriched uranium from commercial enrichment plants can be detected at distances of tens of kilometres. Nuclear facilities sized to produce only a few bombs-worth of material each year, however, would be more difficult to detect, especially if precautions were taken to disguise the facility and to minimize emissions. In those cases, detection would rely primarily on the possibility of accidents and societal verification.

Third, the chance of detecting clandestine nuclear facilities could be increased by expanding the scope of safeguards to include uranium mining and milling operations. Currently, safeguards begin when uranium is converted into a chemical form suitable for fuel fabrication or uranium enrichment; inventories of refined natural uranium ("yellowcake") are neither reported nor safeguarded. A clandestine effort to produce plutonium or HEU would require substantial quantities of uranium – 5 to 10 tonnes of yellowcake per significant quantity.[18] A programme to produce enough material for five weapons per year would require 25 to 50 tonnes of yellowcake per year, which is about 1 to 2 per cent of the amount currently mined by the United States, Russia, China, and France. Extending safeguards to yellowcake would make it difficult to divert uranium from safeguarded mines and mills to clandestine fuel-fabrication or uranium-enrichment facilities, and it would make undeclared mining and milling vulnerable to detection.

Fourth, the IAEA's authority to inspect undeclared sites on short notice could be improved dramatically. Current safeguards agreements include provisions for "special" inspections at undeclared sites, but these inspections must be carried out in consultation with the state. In practice, the IAEA must notify the state in advance, provide reasonable justification for the inspection, and obtain the state's permission. The requirement for notification and consultation severely weakens the IAEA's ability to deter or detect the construction and operation of clandestine facilities.

Special inspections can be compared to the "challenge" inspections provided for in the Chemical Weapons Convention (CWC). Any CWC party can request a challenge inspection of any location or facility within the territory of any other party. The state being challenged has no legal right to refuse the inspection; under the terms of the Convention, it must provide prompt access to the site in question.[19] Access to the site can be "managed" by the challenged party, however, to protect proprietary or national-security information; papers can be removed, equipment shrouded, or access can be restricted to randomly selected rooms. This level of access should be more than sufficient to verify compliance with a nuclear disarmament agreement, since ultra-sensitive sampling techniques could detect the distinctive isotopic or chemical signatures of nuclear facilities even if attempts had been made to clean facilities, trap emissions, or move equipment.

The preceding discussion has focused on the possibility of detecting undeclared facilities for the production of plutonium or HEU. Some have criticized the IAEA's exclusive focus on safeguarding nuclear materials, reasoning that the NPT's prohibition on the "manufacture" of nuclear explosives applies to the entire research, development, and production process.[20]

Although monitoring authorities certainly should be alert for other signs of weapon development, they should not put much hope in the possibility of detecting the research, development, and manufacture of nuclear weapons, simply because these activities are so easily hidden from spy satellites and on-site inspectors. The United States, with its massive intelligence-gathering apparatus, was unable to identify specific sites of such activities in Iraq, South Africa, or North Korea, but it had much more success in identifying fissile-material production. Weapon-development activities probably would be revealed only through sloppiness or leaks of information. High-explosive assemblies might be tested in distinctive facilities, for example, or a disaffected employee might reveal the location of key facilities. Such discoveries would be serendipitous, however, and it is difficult to outline a systematic programme for ferreting out such information, aside from general intelligence collection (but see Chapter 4).

One possibility would be to expand the scope of safeguards to materials other than plutonium and HEU that are uniquely useful in nuclear weapons, such as tritium and enriched lithium. In the absence of nuclear weapons, tritium and enriched lithium would be used mostly in nuclear fusion and other scientific research, and therefore might be subjected to safeguards without too much trouble. Other important materials (*e.g.*, beryllium and high explosives) and subcomponents (*e.g.*, neutron generators and high-speed switches) are used in such a wide variety of industrial applications that safeguards of the type now applied to nuclear materials would be impractical and ineffective. Export controls are applied to such items by the Nuclear Suppliers Group, but these controls have been circumvented many times in the past, and this mechanism has inherent weaknesses that limit its reliability.

Although the existing verification regime appears to have been highly successful in deterring the diversion of significant amounts of materials from safeguarded facilities, it is important to improve the effectiveness and efficiency of safeguards as the number and size of nuclear facilities grow. Of particular concern are facilities that handle large quantities of weapon-usable material in bulk form: reprocessing, enrichment, and mixed-oxide fuel-fabrication facilities. As the size of these facilities grows and as older facilities in the nuclear weapon states are placed under safeguards, measurement errors could grow so large that detecting significant diversions of material might be problematic with current techniques. In addition, the current standard for "significant quantity" would have to be revised downwards as the current nuclear weapon states came under safeguards, since these countries know how to build nuclear weapons with far less than the 8 kilograms of plutonium or 25 kilograms of HEU that the IAEA judges necessary for a state to make its first nuclear explosive.[21] The standard for "timely detection" also would need to be revised from one month to perhaps one week or less, since the nuclear weapon states presumably could convert diverted material into a fabricated weapon component in a matter of days.

Meeting even the current safeguards standards at large reprocessing plants would strain the limits of safeguards technology, and it may not be possible to meet the more stringent standards suggested here with a reasonable level of monitoring effort. Meeting current standards would require moving to near-real-time accountancy, in which sensors accurately and automatically measure and track the movements of nuclear material within the plant. Facility operators also would have to impose fewer restrictions on the access of inspectors to the plant and demonstrate less concern about the release of proprietary information. Unless inspectors know as much about a plant and its operation as the facility operators themselves, it probably will be impossible to obtain an adequate level of assurance of non-diversion.

Beyond the NPT

The preceding discussion of safeguards has taken place within the constraints of the NPT and the IAEA charter. The NPT does not provide an adequate basis for complete disarmament, however. It is likely that a disarmament agreement would replace the NPT and other existing nuclear arms control treaties. This new agreement would present an opportunity to completely revamp the safeguards regime to include not only the incremental measures noted above, but more far-reaching measures that could alter fundamentally the nature of the nuclear industry and the authority of the IAEA or its successor agency.

A central issue is how nuclear power and other peaceful nuclear activities should be structured and managed in a disarmed world. The first nuclear disarmament proposal, the Baruch Plan, envisioned the creation of an "International Atomic Development Authority" that would manage or own all "potentially dangerous" nuclear activities, inspect and license all other nuclear activities, and be at the forefront of all nuclear research and development. The Authority would control all mining, refining, and distribution of uranium, as well as all facilities capable of producing fissile materials.[22]

An agency with the scope and authority envisioned by the Baruch Plan would be impractical today. When the Baruch Plan was presented by the United States to the United Nations in 1946, nuclear power was a distant dream; today more than 430 nuclear reactors in over 30 countries account for nearly 20 per cent of global electricity production. Also, at the time of the Baruch Plan, scientists believed that nuclear fuels could be "denatured" or made unusable for weapons. We now know that *all* nuclear fuel cycles must involve fuels (fresh or spent) that contain weapon-usable materials that can be obtained through a relatively straightforward chemical separation process. Still, it is wise to ask whether aspects of the nuclear fuel cycle that are especially worrisome should be limited or brought under international control as part of a disarmament agreement.

The most severe shortcoming of the current regime is that non-nuclear weapon states are permitted to own and operate facilities capable of producing plutonium and HEU in forms that are directly usable in nuclear weapons, and can produce, stockpile, and use these materials so long as they are subject to safeguards. For example, states can enrich uranium, separate plutonium from spent reactor fuel, use plutonium and HEU reactor fuels, and stockpile fresh HEU and separated plutonium. Some of these activities are hard to safeguard, and all of them pose the risk of rapid breakout from the disarmament regime.

Some analysts believe that the risks associated with civilian uses of HEU and plutonium are so great that commerce in these materials should be discouraged or even outlawed. The United States has been the leading proponent of this view, having decided in the late 1970s to discourage the civilian use of HEU and plutonium world-wide. As a result, the United States adopted the "once-through" fuel cycle, in which plutonium-bearing spent fuel is treated as waste, and launched a programme to develop LEU fuels for HEU-fueled reactors. The United States reaffirmed its opposition to the use of plutonium fuels in 1993, although it promised not to interfere with the plans of allies with comprehensive non-proliferation commitments and established civilian reprocessing or plutonium facilities.

Few countries share the US view of the dangers of the civilian use of plutonium. Indeed, this policy has been a major point of contention between the United States and three of its closest allies, France, Japan, and the United Kingdom, which have major programmes for the separation and use of plutonium. These programmes were developed in the 1970s, when demand for nuclear power was projected to grow rapidly and uranium was thought to be relatively scarce. Increased supply and decreased demand has pushed uranium prices to record lows, however, making plutonium uneconomical as a reactor fuel for the foreseeable future. Belgium and Germany have abandoned their domestic reprocessing programmes, but several countries, including Russia and India, cling to ambitious plans to expand the use of plutonium fuels in spite of the now obvious economic disadvantages of doing so.

In the long term, plutonium use is tied to the future of nuclear power and uranium extraction. If nuclear power does not expand much beyond the current level, then the price of uranium should remain low and we might avoid building a new generation of reprocessing facilities twenty or thirty years from now. If, on the other hand, the demand for nuclear power grows, then the price of uranium will increase. This might make the use of plutonium fuels economically attractive, triggering a huge expansion in the separation, handling, and transport of plutonium.[23]

If the civilian use of plutonium continued over the longer term, additional technical and institutional barriers could be introduced to increase the probability of detecting diversions, as well as to raise the amount of warning time available. Fissile materials could be placed in forms that would not be directly usable for weapons, or reprocessing and fuel-fabrication processes could be altered so that plutonium would not be present in weapon-usable forms. Schemes that have been suggested include mixing or precipitating uranium with plutonium and adding neutron emitters. These would be significant barriers for subnational groups, but not for most nations that host nuclear industries. Adding highly radioactive materials to the fuel, moreover, would add significantly to the costs and hazards of fabricating and handling reactor fuel.

The risks of diversion of weapon-usable materials also could be reduced by internationalizing certain parts of the nuclear fuel cycle. As noted above, traditional IAEA-type safeguards may be unable to detect the diversion of significant quantities of weapon-usable materials in a timely manner from large facilities that handle these materials in bulk form, such as reprocessing, enrichment, and fuel-fabrication plants. If such activities were managed directly by the IAEA or, as envisioned in the Baruch Plan, an "International Atomic Development Authority," it would be easier to deter or detect diversions by states. Similar arrangements could be extended to the storage and use of fresh plutonium and HEU fuels. National reactors might be permitted to burn only LEU fuels, with the spent fuel turned over to international reprocessing or storage centres; reactors burning plutonium or HEU fuels would be managed by an international authority.

Some analysts believe that the continued use of nuclear energy is incompatible with the goal of a disarmed world. As noted above, all fuel cycles involve weapon-usable materials; therefore, the use of nuclear energy carries with it the ever-present danger that the host nation would decide to use these materials to build nuclear weapons. The existence of a civilian nuclear industry also maintains technical expertise that could be applied to a weapon programme, and provides a background of legal activity against which it would be more difficult to detect an illegal programme. Internationalizing certain aspects of the fuel cycle could help deter and detect decisions to go nuclear, but could not prevent civilian nuclear facilities and materials from being redirected to weapons uses. In this view, Article IV of the NPT, in which non-nuclear weapon states are guaranteed the right to "research, production and use of nuclear energy" and "the fullest possible exchange of equipment, materials and scientific and technological information for the peaceful uses of nuclear energy," is fundamentally flawed.

This view is unlikely to become widespread, at least while nuclear power is an important energy source. Global energy use continues to grow, and many countries do not have abundant energy resources. The prospect of climate change has redoubled efforts to replace fossil fuels, and nuclear power is one of the few non-fossil energy sources that can meet a large fraction of global energy demand. It would be difficult to convince policy makers that nuclear energy is incompatible with disarmament; if forced to choose between them, some might value the benefits of nuclear energy more than those of disarmament. There are, moreover, important precedents in the Biological Weapons Convention and the Chemical Weapons Convention, which, in banning biological and chemical weapons, did not infringe on the right of states to use biological and chemical agents for peaceful purposes.

The knowledge of how to build nuclear weapons cannot be eliminated. Even the complete elimination of peaceful nuclear activities would not eliminate the possibility of breakout from a disarmament agreement. The time required for a country to build nuclear weapons would, however, depend largely on the type of civilian nuclear facilities and materials that would be available for use in a weapon programme. Based on the experience of Iraq and North Korea, it would take five or more years for a developing country with little or no existing nuclear infrastructure to produce fissile materials and fabricate a workable bomb. Industrialized countries with reprocessing or enrichment facilities or stocks of fissile material, on the other hand, might require as little as a few months to make a nuclear bomb. Even if an industrialized country had no nuclear facilities or chose not to use them for a weapon programme, a weapon could be produced in one to two years in a national emergency, assuming access to a modest stock of uranium.

These breakout times set a standard for "timely warning" under a disarmament agreement – the time period in which the international community must be ready to respond to indications of cheating or breakout. As noted above, a response could include economic sanctions designed to cripple an offender's economy, military action designed to destroy the nuclear programme or remove the government responsible for initiating it, the readying of conventional forces (or, if they exist, international nuclear forces) to deter or respond to the use of nuclear weapons, or the rebuilding of national nuclear arsenals for the same purpose.

The possibility of rapid breakout could have both positive and negative effects on the prospects for disarmament and the operation of a verification system. On the one hand, the industrialized countries might not worry excessively about the possibility of cheating, because they would be confident in their ability to assemble a nuclear arsenal quickly in an emergency. For this reason, these countries might not be viewed as having strong incentives to violate the agreement clandestinely, and the international community might be satisfied with the reassurance provided by the verification system that such countries were not cheating. On the other hand, the speed with which breakout could occur might put pressure on the verification system to detect cheating at the earliest possible moment. Dangerous instabilities might result, in which countries, fearing that some other country was cheating and preparing to break out of the agreement, would respond hastily and disproportionately to evidence of cheating – evidence that ultimately might prove to be erroneous.

A disarmament regime would have to be structured to avoid such instabilities by allowing the inspection agency time to investigate fully any evidence of cheating without triggering a premature response.

Conclusions

This paper has outlined the technological possibilities for verifying compliance with a nuclear disarmament treaty. Many of these possibilities do not depend on dramatic improvements in world politics, and could be implemented soon. In particular, it is important for the nuclear weapon states to declare in detail their stockpiles of nuclear devices and fissile materials and to allow these declarations to be verified. Unless the nuclear weapon states begin this process today, when stockpiles are huge and shrouded in secrecy, they will fail to lay the necessary foundation for nuclear disarmament, because today's uncertainties will be magnified greatly as we move from tens of thousands to hundreds of warheads and ultimately to zero.

In the final analysis, however, no conceivable verification regime could provide absolute assurance that former nuclear weapon states had not hidden a dozen or even a hundred "bombs in the basement" (or enough plutonium or HEU to build such a stockpile), no matter how cooperative and transparent the parties had agreed to be. In other words, even the most intrusive inspection regime could not detect a small stockpile of carefully hidden bombs or plutonium with high confidence. And although improved and expanded IAEA safeguards, together with internationalization of certain aspects of the civilian nuclear fuel cycle, would give states reasonably high confidence that parties were not clandestinely producing fissile materials for nuclear weapons, any state with a substantial nuclear industry would be technically capable of producing or diverting fissile materials and building nuclear weapons in less than a year, and perhaps in as little as a few months.

We, therefore, are driven to the conclusion that nuclear disarmament would be verifiable only in a world in which such scenarios were generally regarded as highly unlikely or unimportant. For example, if relations between all the nuclear powers were as congenial as are today's relations between the United States, the United Kingdom, and France, then we would not worry about the possibility of "bombs in the basement" or rapid breakout. If, moreover, the decision-making processes of these and other key governments were as transparent as those of the US government, then states might judge that the probability of hiding bombs or plutonium from inspectors for many years was negligible. Achieving and maintaining such good relations and transparency probably would require having stable democratic governments in place in Russia and China, which would itself increase the prospects for self-enforcement of international obligations.

It may seem as if verification thus has been reduced to a trivial task: in order for disarmament to be possible, states would have to possess a degree of mutual trust and transparency that would make verification (and disarmament itself) a mere formality. This formulation is too simplistic, however, because the disarmament process is iterative. Parties agree to reductions on the assumption of shared goals; the verification of these reductions builds confidence between the parties in that assumption, making increased transparency and deeper reductions possible. The START negotiations made dramatic progress only after relations between the United States and the Soviet Union improved, but START would not have been signed or ratified without the extensive verification provisions it contained. The successful implementation of the INF Treaty a few years earlier also was important in creating the environment that made improved relations and the START treaties possible. Indeed, dramatically improved relations between Russia, China, and the other nuclear weapon states may be possible only in an environment in which they are engaged in a process of mutual and progressive restraints on their nuclear arsenals, since those arsenals are potent symbols of continuing mistrust.

The cheating and breakout scenarios outlined above also would become unlikely or unimportant if adequate precautions had been taken to deal with these possibilities. If, for example, the nuclear weapon states and other great powers had pledged to defend each other against aggressors, or to act together to punish nations that violated the nuclear disarmament agreement, then this would decrease the benefits and increase the costs of cheating substantially (assuming, of course, that such pledges were, and were widely believed to be, genuine). Alternatively, an international nuclear force might be retained to deter or punish cheaters. Somewhat paradoxically, however, the implementation of such safeguards would require a degree of trust and cooperation that would be possible only if cheating by the cooperating states was considered highly unlikely.

One type of safeguard that might not require such dramatic improvements in international relations would be to allow nuclear weapon states to maintain a capability to build nuclear weapons. States could, for example, be allowed to maintain a small stockpile of plutonium pits and other bomb components in separate storage areas, under international monitoring. An attempt by any state to retrieve these components would trigger alarms in other countries, leading them to assemble and disperse their nuclear components. The knowledge that any attempt to cheat or break out of the disarmament agreement would produce an instant and offsetting response by other states would deter cheating in the first place, because cheating could produce no lasting advantage. Maintaining the capacity to rebuild nuclear weapons also would remove the incentive for states to keep a few "bombs in the basement" as a hedge against the possibility that other states might do the same. It would be necessary to protect the bomb-building capacity of each state against pre-emptive attack by other states, of course, through a combination of multiple sites, deep burial, or provisions for rapid dispersal.

There are two potential problems with this type of safeguard arrangement, however. First, allowing states to maintain the capability to build nuclear weapons on short notice would make it easier for a state to cheat while at the same time making it more difficult to detect cheating. States would argue, for example, that they would need nuclear weapon design laboratories, testing facilities, and facilities to produce tritium and fabricate weapon components. These activities would be of great value for a clandestine programme, and would create a background of legal activity against which it would be more difficult to detect illegal activities. Second, having states poised to resume manufacture and deployment could create dangerous instabilities in which states might rush to rearm during a crisis. The possibility of rearming could lead states to disperse their weapon components to protect them from attack, worsening the crisis. If "rules of the road" could be developed to prevent such instabilities, then this sort of arrangement might be a useful way station on the path to a more complete elimination of nuclear weapon capabilities.

In summary, it would be wrong to believe that nuclear disarmament would be adequately verifiable only when we had learned how to detect with high confidence every hidden bomb or every kilogram of hidden plutonium, and when we had figured out how to prevent or detect any diversion of nuclear materials from peaceful uses. Available verification techniques, if implemented vigorously in a spirit of cooperation, could verify the absence of large-scale cheating, but they could not rule out the possibility of "bombs in the basement" or rapid breakout. Nuclear disarmament will be possible not when small-scale cheating or breakout is impossible, but rather when nations become convinced that such cheating no longer seems very likely or very important. In the meantime, verification of the reductions process will play an essential role in moving us towards a world with the degree of trust and transparency necessary to make this possible.

This chapter is a shorter version of a report written for the Henry L. Stimson Center's Project on Eliminating Weapons of Mass Destruction.

Notes

1. See J.Schell, *The Abolition,* New York: Avon, 1984, and M.J. Mazarr, "Virtual Nuclear Arsenals," *Survival*, 37:3 (Autumn 1995), pp. 7–26.

2. T.B. Taylor, "A Ban on Nuclear Technologies," *Technology Review*, 98:6 (August/September 1995), p. 76.

3. In 1992, the CIA estimated that Russia had 30,000 nuclear weapons, "plus or minus 5000." (See "Testimony of Lawrence Gershwin before the House Defense Appropriations Subcommittee," 6 May 1992.) Subsequent statements by Russian Minister of Atomic Energy Victor Mikhailov that the Russian stockpile peaked at 45,000 warheads cast doubt on the CIA estimate, and emphasized further the difficulty of estimating warhead stockpiles with national intelligence alone.

4. Without sampling, inspectors would have to count every warhead at a site, and possibly verify the authenticity of each warhead. Sampling could reduce greatly the number of warheads that would be examined. For example, a detailed inspection of only 28 randomly selected warheads would provide 95 per cent confidence that at least 90 per cent of these warheads were authentic (or that the actual number of warheads did not exceed the declared number by more than 10 per cent). Even a 1 per cent violation would have a 25 per cent chance of detection.

5. Such a scheme is described in T.B. Taylor and L.P. Feoktistov, "Verified Elimination of Nuclear Warheads and Disposition of Contained Nuclear Materials," in *Verification: Monitoring Disarmament*, ed. F. Calogero, M.L. Goldberger, and S.P. Kapitza, eds, Boulder, Co.: Westview Press, 1991, pp. 45–66. See also T. Taylor, "Technological Problems of Verification," in *A Nuclear-Weapon-Free World: Desirable? Feasible?*, ed J. Rotblat, J. Steinberger and B. Udgaonkar, Boulder, Co.: Westview Press, 1993.

6. "Plutonium: The First 50 Years," Washington D.C.: US Department of Energy, February 1996.

7. By 2000, the nuclear weapon and threshold states will have produced about 900 tonnes of plutonium in civil reactors. Of this, about 185 tonnes will be separated; the remainder will be contained in spent fuel. Although most of this material will be available to the IAEA under the voluntary safeguards agreements between the nuclear weapon states and the IAEA, very little will actually be under IAEA safeguards. See D. Albright, F. Berkhout and W. Walker, *Plutonium and Highly Enriched Uranium 1996: World Inventories, Capabilities, and Policies*, Oxford: Oxford University Press, 1997, pp. 142-3, 184-91.

8. S. Fetter, "Nuclear Archaeology: Verifying Declarations of Fissile-material Production," *Science and Global Security*, 3:3-4 (1992).

9. D. Albright, "South Africa's Secret Nuclear Weapons," *International Security Information Service Report*, May 1994.

10. Quoted in Albright, "South Africa's Secret Nuclear Weapons."

11. The acceptable margin was one significant quantity, or 25 kilograms of HEU. See Albright, "South Africa's Secret Nuclear Weapons," and Office of Technology Assessment, *Nuclear Safeguards and the International Atomic Energy Agency*, OTA-ISS-615, Washington D.C.: U.S. Government Printing Office, June 1995, p. 85.

12. See T.B. Cochran, "Highly Enriched Uranium Production for South African Nuclear Weapons," *Science and Global Security*, 4:2 (1994), pp. 161–178; and D. Howlett and J. Simpson, "Nuclearisation and Denuclearisation in South Africa," *Survival*, 35:3 (Autumn 1993), pp. 154–173.

13. Quoted in Howlett and Simpson, "Nuclearisation and Denuclearisation in South Africa."

14. The United States and Russia have lost a small number of nuclear weapons in submarine sinkings, airplane crashes, and other accidents, and it would be difficult or impossible to verify independently the number of weapons lost. In addition, many nuclear weapons were used, but probably not destroyed, in nuclear-weapon-effects tests.

15. The IAEA defines "high confidence" as a 90-per cent probability of detecting the diversion of a significant quantity of nuclear material. A "significant quantity" is defined as 8 kilograms of plutonium or 25 kilograms of uranium-235 in the form of HEU, which represents the amount thought to be needed for a state to make its first nuclear explosive, taking into account processing losses. "Timely warning" is based on the time it would take for a state to convert the diverted material into a finished weapon component; for unirradiated plutonium or HEU, the IAEA goal is to detect diversions within one month; for irradiated plutonium or HEU (*e.g.*, spent fuel), three months; for natural or low-enriched uranium, one year. See OTA, *Nuclear Safeguards*, pp. 45, 57.

16. This section draws heavily on chapter 3 of OTA, *Nuclear Safeguards*.

17. Office of Technology Assessment, *Environmental Monitoring for Nuclear Safeguards*, OTA-BP-ISS-168, Washington D.C.: U.S. Government Printing Office, 1995.

18. Producing 1 kg of weapon-grade HEU (90 per cent U-235) requires 180 to 420 kg of natural uranium feed (assuming a tails assay of 0.2 to 0.5 per cent U-235), or 5 to 12 tonnes of yellowcake per 25-kg significant quantity. Producing 1 kg of weapon-grade plutonium (6-per cent Pu-240) requires about 1000 kg of natural uranium (assuming a burnup of 1.2 GWd/te(U) and 0.9 kg(Pu)/GWd for a reactor fueled with natural uranium and moderated with graphite or heavy water), or about 10 tonnes of yellowcake per 8-kg significant quantity.

19. Requests can be rejected by the CWC Executive Council, however, if they are deemed frivolous, abusive, or beyond the scope of the Treaty.

20. L.S. Spector, "Repentant Nuclear Proliferators," *Foreign Policy*, 88 (Fall 1992), pp. 30–31.

21. The amount of material in nuclear weapons is secret, but the U.S. Department of Energy recently stated that "Hypothetically, a mass of 4 kilograms of plutonium...is sufficient for one nuclear explosive device." (Classification Bulletin WNP-86, 8 February 1994; quoted in OTA, *Nuclear Safeguards*, p. 67.) Nuclear explosives can be built with even less; press reports of the destruction of a Russian nuclear device buried at the Semipalatinsk test site in Kazakhstan stated that the device contained about 1 kilogram of plutonium and would have yielded 1 kiloton.

22. US Department of State, *Documents on Disarmament, 1945–1956*, Washington D.C.: US Government Printing Office, 1960, pp. 10–15.

23. Alternatively, it might be cheaper to extract uranium from sea water. Although present at low concentrations, the amount of uranium contained in sea water is huge, and economical extraction would make plutonium use unnecessary.

4

Societal Verification

Frank Blackaby

Introduction

Societal verification (SV) is a straightforward idea. The suggestion is that citizens in general, and scientists in particular, should assist the authorities in enforcing the law – in this case the law (which does not of course yet exist) that prohibits the production or possession of nuclear weapons.

There is a general principle here. It is widely accepted that citizens have a duty to help the authorities to enforce the law. Indeed, a great deal of national law enforcement depends on "information received." (That is why it would be necessary to embody the provisions of any treaty or convention into the national law of each signatory state.)

There are some particular points about SV as an aid to the verification process of a Nuclear Weapons Convention. First, an NWC would need all the verification it can get. The requirements are much tougher than they are, for example, for a Chemical or Biological Weapons Convention. This is because, if a State infringes a CWC or a BWC, it is not considered that it would obtain an overwhelming military advantage – certainly not as against the major powers. For an NWC, this is one of the main reasons that some believe the idea is not feasible: that a state which secretly acquired a nuclear weapon capability in an NWFW would be able to blackmail virtually any other state with the threat of war. The validity of this objection is discussed elsewhere in this book (Chapter 6). However, whether valid or not, it is generally agreed that the verification requirements of an NWC would be much stricter than those for a CWC or BWC. Any measure which makes any improvement to the verification process at virtually no cost should be accepted.

The secret construction of a nuclear weapon capability is not something that can be done by one or two people in a garage. Even if stolen fissile material were used, it would require relatively large installations, and a number of skilled physical scientists and engineers. It is difficult to believe that this could be done without some people outside the group concerned having suspicions. The more people who would be on the look-out for violations, the better. Good verification is labour-intensive. An SV system would not simply permit people to notify suspicions. It would positively encourage them to do so. If there were a system in which people in general, and scientists in particular, were urged to report suspicions; if there were a formal and well-publicized process, with a safe information channel through which suspicions could be notified; then verification capacity could be multiplied manyfold.

A treaty-based system of worldwide SV, added to the technical processes of verification, would add to the difficulties of a treaty-breaking attempt. There would always be the risk of a whistle-blower. It is not suggested that this would provide total security. The requirement for moving to an NWFW is not total security, but a lower risk of catastrophe than the alternatives.

Objections and Rebuttals

There are four common objections to the idea of SV. First, it would require citizens to act as citizens of the world, rather than as citizens of any particular nation, and not many people are willing to do that. Secondly, it is an idea that would work where it is least needed – in liberal democracies, and would not work where it is most needed – in authoritarian "rogue sta s." Third, politicians and civil servants dislike the idea of any kind of "power to the people;" the idea of SV is not one that is likely to appeal to treaty negotiators. A fourth objection is that there would be a great many hoax or bizarre complaints.

National Loyalty

It is suggested, then, that people would be asked to do something that ten years ago would have been regarded as high treason. Unfortunately, the idea of world citizenship seems still to hold little attraction, and there is not much evidence of a worldwide decline in nationalistic feelings – rather the contrary.

However, the basic premise of this objection – that some kind of world loyalty would be needed – is open to question. An NWFW would be one in which all the major nuclear weapon states had decided that an NWFW was in their interest: that would be a necessary condition for an NWFW to come about. It would be logical in such a world that the ex-nuclear weapon powers – and indeed other signatories of an NWC – would want as rigorous a verification system as possible. The issue of "world loyalty versus national loyalty" would not then arise. Further, they might well see one of the main threats to be terrorist acquisition of nuclear weapons; these could be terrorist groups within the country. A number of states – including the USA, Japan and Britain – have learned that not all terrorist threats come from beyond state borders. In detecting possible terrorist activity on home territory, citizens reporting could help – and indeed is already encouraged.

So there should not be a conflict between world loyalty and national loyalty – except in those few states that signed the Convention but which intended to violate its provisions if they could do so without discovery: that point is dealt with in the next section.

Although world loyalty and national loyalty should not, therefore, in general be in conflict, nonetheless the concept of world loyalty is germane to this issue. It is those for whom the concept of world citizenship has some meaning who are most likely to support the SV idea and who would be willing to help to make it work. Physical scientists will perhaps be more ready than others to take a planetary view of issues such as that of nuclear weapons: national borders are after all irrelevant to their academic disciplines. It may seem particularly absurd to them that the human race should continue to keep self-destructive capabilities of this appalling scale. Indeed, most people find nuclear weapons singularly repulsive. In a world officially declared nuclear-weapon-free, there would be a large number of people who would be prepared to do something to keep it so.

"Rogue States"

To be fully effective, citizen's reporting requires that the government should not act to prevent it. However, even in "rogue states," if there were a full international verification system with asylum provisions, there could be a significant risk to the regime that one or two citizens might be prepared to report their suspicions. Throughout history there have been individuals prepared to take great personal risks for causes they believe in.

The number of likely "rogue states" is limited. There are only seven states in the world that have not signed the Non-Proliferation Treaty, and four of them are parts of nuclear-weapon-free zones. The vast majority of the states that have signed the Treaty as non-nuclear weapon powers have done so with every intention of observing the Treaty's provisions. So far as societal verification of the Nuclear Weapons Convention is concerned, a "rogue state" would be one that has signed the Convention, which nonetheless plans and prepares secretly to develop a nuclear weapon capability, and which denies freedom of expression to its citizens. The standard list of states likely to fall into that category numbers four – Iran, Iraq, Libya and North Korea.

There is no realistic prospect of a Nuclear Weapons Convention coming into force – at the most optimistic estimate – for at least a decade: two decades is more probable. By then the nature of the regimes in some or all of those four states might well have changed. Fortunately, dictators are mortal. Even if the regimes have not changed, it is possible – through perhaps not probable – that they might be less anxious to try to acquire a nuclear weapon capability in a world where the nuclear weapon states were getting rid of these weapons. Libya, for example, considers itself threatened by US nuclear weapons; there has been open discussion in the USA about the use of a nuclear warhead on an alleged chemical weapon facility in Libya. If the US nuclear weapon threat were removed, then Libya might be less concerned to try to acquire nuclear weapons itself.

It is not easy now for any state to control completely communication with the world outside – to monitor all communications through the Internet, by fax machines and by telephone. If governments can be persuaded to take SV seriously, then they should put into the Nuclear Weapons Convention a requirement that states should not put any impediments in the way of citizen's communication with the International Verification Authority. Further, they can add that if such impediments are believed to exist, then the Verification Authority should be empowered to provide for asylum to be granted to any citizen of the impeding state who reports suspicions.

Because it may be difficult to introduce SV into a handful of significant states, that is not a sufficient reason for refusing to introduce it into the large majority of states where there would be no difficulty. Further, even in that handful of states, a powerful international SV system would increase the probability of discovering treaty infractions.

Official Attitudes to Societal Verification

In matters of arms control and disarmament, governments have so far not shown much interest in the possibilities of SV. For example, it might have been considered an obvious adjunct to the Comprehensive Test Ban Treaty. A nuclear weapon test could hardly be conducted without a large number of people knowing about it. A provision, therefore, that encouraged the report of any suspicion of infraction to the Verification Authority might have seemed a fairly obvious idea to propose. It was not proposed. It would improve confidence in the CTBT if there were unrestricted civil access to the US test site in Nevada, to the Russian test site in Novaya Zemlya, and to the Chinese test site at Lop Nor.

Governments in general are not very happy about the idea of unauthorized civilians poking around in military matters. There is a link here to a broader issue – the tension between the old idea that military secrecy must be preserved, and the new idea that transparency improves security. There has certainly been some shift from secrecy to transparency. For instance, in Europe now, the participating states in the OSCE are required to provide to all other members photographs of all their major weapon systems. However, the preference for military secrecy is still strong: behaviour that is kept secret cannot be criticized.

Governments, therefore, will have to be persuaded that SV could strengthen an international verification regime considerably, and that, therefore, they should encourage it on their own territory as well. The links with anti-terrorist activity is of help here. The most potent weapon against terrorist activity is information. In Britain, threatened by terrorist activity from the Irish Republican Army, this is now widely recognized. There is an extensive spread of posters throughout London asking anyone with information about terrorism to ring a Metropolitan Police telephone number.

This is also relevant to the final, minor objection to societal verification: that there would be hoax calls. Probably there would be some – there are hoax calls on all the emergency services. This does not render them impotent. Hoax calls would be no more than a minor irritation.

The following sections of this chapter comment, first, on the history of the idea of citizen's reporting; second, on the fact that many of the elements of this idea are already here. The final section describes what a more systematic structure for societal verification might look like.

History

The idea of SV to support the verification of disarmament dates back to the period when general and complete disarmament was still on the agenda. Once it became clear that there was not going to be any significant disarmament, and the concept of disarmament was replaced by that of arms control, the idea lapsed. It had no place in arms control treaties that simply limited numbers – citizens cannot go around counting missiles or tanks. SV has been brought back into discussion mainly because there are now "abolition conventions" – the CWC and BWC to abolish chemical and biological weapons, with the eventual possibility of an NWC, to abolish nuclear weapons.

Most of the literature on citizen's reporting therefore dates back some forty years. In the immediate post-war period the thinking about a new world order was more radical than it is today. There was a strong world government movement which for a short period had wide support – for instance, in the United States some 21 state legislatures voted in favour of strengthening the role of the United Nations in the direction of world government. This coincided with the period when the idea of general and complete disarmament was taken seriously.

The idea that a disarmament regime should be strengthened by citizen's reporting fitted in well with the world government approach. One of the advocates wrote:

> Verification by the methods of citizen reporting has many advantages besides
> potential efficiency in detecting violations. It would tend to foster world-
> mindedness, decentralized democratic control, abhorrence of war crimes, and
> civic responsibility.[1]

The point was made already in the early literature that physical scientists
in particular, and those involved in handling materials or processes that could
secretly be turned to weapon uses, should be encouraged to watch for
violations.

Johan Galtung examined the conditions that would have to be satisfied if
ordinary people were to report violations to an international body:

> The general populace should be explicitly told by its own governments to
> function as an inspecting body: access must be provided to report channels,
> possibly in the form of a citizen's hot line; citizens must be protected from
> retribution from their own government.[2]

To help to get over the problem of the transition from treason to duty, Karl
Deutsch suggested the use of national legitimacy symbols of various kinds to
support the idea of citizen's reporting. There should be royal endorsement of
the idea; it should be included in the codes of the Boy Scout movement, and so
on. Systems of authoritative communications should be used to remind citizens
of their duty to cooperate with inspectors and if necessary to do some inspection
on their own.[3]

Grenville Clark and Louis Sohn proposed a revision of the UN Charter to
include a UN Inspection Service, responsible for disarmament verification.
Two sections of the relevant Article deal with citizen's reporting:

> Any person having any information concerning any violation of this Annex or
> of any law or regulation enacted thereunder shall immediately report all such
> information to the United Nations Inspection Service. The General Assembly
> shall enact regulations governing the granting of rewards to persons supplying
> the Inspection Service with such information, and the provisions of asylum to
> them and their families.

> No person shall penalize directly or indirectly any person or public or private
> organization supplying information to the United Nations with respect to any
> violation of this Annex.

Clark and Sohn also called for the provisions of any arms control treaty to be
incorporated into national law. There should be

> ... a provision in the original arms control agreement requiring all
> participating governments to pass laws making it a crime, punishable by

domestic law, to violate the provisions of the arms control agreement or to keep secret from the agency for international control any information of such a violation. Moreover, these provisions of the law of the land should be publicized by each government and failure to support them by such publicity (or by other ways) should be declared to be a major violation of the control treaty.[4]

As the Cold War began and intensified, these various ideas withered and died. Any ideas connected with world government were condemned as bourgeois cosmopolitanism in the Soviet Union, and as pro-Communist in the USA. Disarmament was replaced by arms control, and citizen's reporting disappeared from the arms controller's lexicon. It is only now, with disarmament and indeed weapons abolition on the agenda, that it has been found to be relevant once more.[5]

Existing Elements of Societal Verification and Whistle-Blowing[6]

A number of the elements of SV already exist – particularly concerning the two "abolition treaties," the CWC and the BWC. There have already been citizen's reports of Treaty infractions. This is not, of course, a fully-fledged SV system: there is no international verification regime for the BWC, and one is only just being established for the CWC. The allegations have come to public attention through the press, sometimes with help from non-governmental organizations (NGOs).

In the nuclear weapon field, although the Comprehensive Test Ban Treaty has no provision for SV, certainly in the USA there will be concerned citizens, working through NGOs, who will try to do some monitoring. In particular, they will watch as best they can the Stockpile Stewardship and Management Program; they will want to make sure that it is not used for the development of new types of nuclear warhead. Already, the Natural Resources Defense Council has published a critique, using the declassified portions of the Department of Energy's (DOE) publications.[7] This critique argues that some of the ongoing and planned activities of the DOE's programme conflict with US policy statements, that the US "is not seeking to find technological alternatives to build new weapon types, absent testing." In Russia, in the nuclear weapon field, the main whistle-blowing activity has not concerned any of the nuclear weapon arms control treaties, but rather the radioactive contamination risks from the submarine dismantlement programme.

Another main requirement of an SV system is that scientists and scientific associations should concern themselves with possible treaty violations. This is already the case. For example, the international scientific community of microbiologists has had a long-standing concern with biological warfare. At the

General Assembly of the International Association of Microbiological Societies in Mexico City in August 1970, a resolution was passed in total condemnation of microbiological methods of warfare (Appendix). Since this was before the BWC existed, the resolution could not call for the scientists to report any violations of this principle. However, it did call for states to agree to proposals that went beyond the Geneva Protocol (which banned use, but not development or production). This resolution was one of the precursors of the BWC.

In the field of biological weapons, the relations between scientists and those concerned with the Convention have been close and cooperative. This was clear at the Third Review Conference of the BWC in September 1991. In its final declaration the Review Conference appealed to the scientific community

> to continue to support only activities that have justification under the ... Convention for prophylactic, protective or other peaceful purposes, and refrain from activities which are in breach of obligations deriving from provisions of the Convention.

Since the Convention has as yet no verification procedures, it could not have asked scientists to report violations. However, if a verification structure of some kind is established, then it would be appropriate to push the language of the Third Review Conference a little further, and invite scientists to cooperate closely with the inspection and reporting procedures.

Article IV of the BWC does invite states party to the Treaty to incorporate the relevant prohibitions into their national legislation:

> Each State Party to this Convention shall, in accordance with its constitutional procedures, take any necessary measures to prohibit and prevent the development, production, stockpiling, acquisition or retention of the agents, toxins, weapons, equipment and means of delivery specified in Article I of the Convention, within the territory of such State, under its jurisdiction or under its control anywhere.

So far, not many states have enacted national legislation. If this is done, then it is open to any citizen to report any violation of that legislation to the national authorities.

The threat with which SV is concerned is not just from other states: it is also from terrorist activity which may well be within the state. That is why national legislation is needed. When the Japanese authorities were faced with a sarin attack on their underground system, they found that they had no national legislation making the production of sarin illegal, and had to proceed to pass a law to this effect.

The US Director of the Arms Control and Disarmament Agency has given a precise example of the effective combination of national legislation and SV:

Even though they are aimed mainly against countries, these treaties – and especially their implementing legislation – can have important anti-terrorist effects. In 1995, for example, a member of a hate group in Ohio fraudulently ordered the bubonic plague bacillus by mail from a specialized supplier in Rockville (Maryland). The order was filled. But the supplier also notified law enforcement officials, who in turn searched the would-be terrorist's home, and stymied whatever foul plans he was brewing. This happened in part because of a law – the Biological Weapons Anti-Terrorist Act – that is required to be on the books because of the Biological Weapons Convention.[8]

The CWC, now in force, explicitly requires national legislation. Article VII reads:

Each State Party shall, in accordance with its constitutional processes, adopt the necessary measures to implement its obligations under this Convention. In particular, it shall: (a) Prohibit natural and legal persons anywhere on its territory ... from undertaking any activity prohibited to a State Party under this Convention, including enacting penal legislation with respect to such activity ...

The Article requires States to specify whether its penal legislation will cover only activities prohibited by the CWC or also other actions that undermine the CWC but which are not explicitly prohibited by it (for example, impeding the verification process).

Further we do already have, in both biological and chemical weapons, examples of citizen's reporting leading to on-site inspection. In September 1992 a report was published by two Russian scientists in Moscow News about the development of a new toxic agent at a chemical technology research institute in Moscow. The *Baltimore Sun* published an expanded version of the article, based on an interview with one of the scientists. Extensive details were given – the new agent was named Novichok-8 (Russian for "newcomer"); the first industrial batch was manufactured at the Khimprom plant in Volgograd; field tests were conducted at a chemical test site on the Ustyurt plateau near Nukus in Uzbekistan. Both scientists were officially accused of revealing state secrets, and one – Vil Mirzayanov – was arrested and charged with unauthorized disclosure of information. However, he was released following protests from the international scientific community, and in June 1994 was awarded 30 million roubles in compensation by a Russian court for having been unjustly arrested. However, he has not received the money.

There has also been whistle-blowing in Russia on biological weapons. Dr S. Leskov, writing in *Isvestia* in June 1993, gave a long account of BW activity in the then Soviet Union after the BW Convention had been signed:

In the middle of the 1970s, a strictly secret Research and Technology

> Committee was formed under the Central Administration of the Microbiology Industry ... Production tasks were given to a large industrial complex, "Biopreparat" – eighteen R&D Institutes with 25,000 staff, were included in the programme. The Institute in Kor'sovo near Novosibirsk worked on the lethal virus of haemorrhagic fever and on Venezuelan (equine) encephalitis ...

The article continued with further information of this kind.

More information on continuing work on biological weapons was given by a certain A.A. Makhly in a television interview on a Moscow television channel. This gave details of work being done at the Virological Centre of the Microbiological Research Institute at Sagorsk (now Sergiyev-Posad), on spotted fever and other agents. Substantial information was also given by Vladimir Pasechnik, who defected to Britain in 1993. He had previously been Director of the Leningrad (now St Petersburg) Institute for Ultrapure Biological Preparations at the Biopreparat complex.

It was later officially admitted in Russia that the USSR had continued research, testing and production of biological weapons after ratifying the BWC. However, it was claimed in 1993 that all such programmes had been closed down, and foreign observers were invited to inspect a number of research institutions named by the scientists or journalists who had reported previous violations of the BWC. Thus foreign official observers did inspect the Institute of Ultrapure Biological Preparations; a facility at Berdsk, bear Novosibirsk; and a facility at Pokrove, near Moscow.

Unfortunately this short outbreak of whistle-blowing in Russia may have been just a flash in the pan. There are signs that the authorities are returning to doctrines of military secrecy. For example, a retired Russian naval captain, Alexander Nikitin, has been working in the St Petersburg office of a Norwegian environmental group, the Bellona Foundation. The Foundation has published material on the environmental threat from 88 nuclear submarines due for decommissioning; the Foundation fears that they may sink before they are dealt with. The Foundation also says that radioactive waste from 90 reactor cores is stored in unsafe conditions; that full overhauls of active submarines have been suspended on cost grounds; and that fleet commanders admit that crews are inadequately trained to maintain and operate the reactors. Mr Nikitin is accused of giving away state secrets, although the Foundation claims that the source documents were in the public domain.

A Structure for Societal Verification

The creation of a more systematic SV structure for disarmament treaties, therefore, would not be a leap into the dark. Most of the elements already exist in embryonic form.

To avoid accusations of disloyalty to the state, the relevant provisions of any disarmament treaty should be embodied into national law. This is not new: it is already required in both the BWC and the CWC. There would, therefore, be no problem in including a provision to this effect in an NWC.

The review conferences of the BWC have already recognized the importance of scientific cooperation – with explicit appeals to microbiologists to observe the provisions of the Convention. It would only be a short further step, once some verification provisions for the Convention have been established, to invite scientists to report suspicions.

Although the BWC has as yet no verification authority, and although the CWC Verification Authority is only just in the process of being established, there have already been examples of scientists – through the press – bringing out into the open alleged infringements – or potential infringements – of both treaties. As a consequence, inspections by foreign nationals have taken place. In the USA there is the Ohio example of the way in which the relevant national law on BW was used to prevent terrorist activity. These various examples are on a small scale, of course: but they serve to establish the principle. SV would not be a leap into the dark; it would be an extension and formalization of things that have already been happening.

What is missing is any strong government enthusiasm for the idea. This may change during the next decade or so, helped by fear of terrorist activity, which may be from within the state itself. The standard state-to-state verification procedures would not be of much help in detecting activities such as those of the Aum Shinrikyo (Supreme Truth) cult in Japan. An active programme of encouraging information could be much more useful.

What might be needed to provide more pro-active encouragement of SV? In a Nuclear Weapons Convention, it might be sufficient to have a general Article instructing the verification authorities on this matter. This Article should say that the authorities should provide facilities for the reporting of suspected infringements; it should also ensure that the public knew that this was an important duty, and also knew the way in which reporting should be done. It should specify that it would be an infraction of the Convention for a State to put any impediments in the way of the reporting process. It would probably be a good idea to arrange that any reports go both to the national and to the international verification authority at the same time, to ensure that they are not unaccountably delayed. The Article should also instruct the international authority to arrange for the provision of asylum where necessary – for example, for those living in states with a bad human rights record who reported infractions. Finally, the Article should propose close cooperation with scientific bodies and with the relevant non-governmental organizations. International "Friends of the Convention" associations could be set up, which would keep in close contact with the verifying authorities, and which would act as auxiliary watchdogs.

Summary

A Nuclear Weapons Convention would need all the verification it can get. Societal Verification, or citizen's reporting, could help. It would increase the chances of detecting infractions of the Convention. The cost/benefit ratio of an SV structure is good. The costs would be low. It is hard to think of significant detrimental consequences.

Now that it is difficult for states to stop communication across borders, ways could be found to make SV effective, in a limited way, even in states with a bad human rights record.

The elements of an SV structure already exist. The other two "abolition conventions," the BWC and CWC, have a requirement that the main provisions should be incorporated into national law, which is one of the main prerequisites. That principle is already established. There have already been examples of whistle-blowing in Russia that have led to international inspections. There are also already international groups of scientists and others, not employed by governments, who are concerned to help in any way they can to make the BWC and CWC effective.

A Nuclear Weapons Convention should include an article that instructs the national and international verification authorities to provide facilities for the reporting of infringements of the Convention. These authorities should explain to the public the importance of detecting infringements, and should ensure that the public knows how to go about notifying suspicions. Further, the international verification authority should be instructed to make provisions for granting asylum where necessary – to whistle-blowers in states with bad human rights records. The verification authorities should encourage the formation of "Friends of the Convention" associations, formed from international scientific bodies and from concerned NGOs, which would act as auxiliary watchdogs.

Notes

1.   H. Newcombe, "Citizen Reporting as a Method of Arms Control Verification," *Proceedings of the Fortieth Pugwash Conference on Science and World Affairs: Towards a Secure World in the Twenty-First Century,* Pugwash: London, 1991, pp. 321-331.

2.   J. Galtung, "Popular Inspection of Disarmament Processes," *Cooperation and Conflict,* 2:3/4, 1967, pp. 121-138.

3.   K W Deutsch, "The Commitment of National Legitimacy Symbols as a Verification Technique," *Journal of Conflict Resolution,* September 1963, pp. 360-369.

4.   G. Clark and L.B. Sohn, *World Peace Through World Law* (2nd edition), Harvard University Press: Cambridge, 1960, p. 267.

5. J. Rotblat, "Societal Verification," in J. Rotblat, J. Steinberger and B. Udgaonkar eds., *A Nuclear-Weapon-Free World: Desirable? Feasible?*, Boulder, Co.: Westview Press, 1993, pp. 103-118.

6. The material for this section is drawn from successive SIPRI Yearbooks, and in particular from the following chapters, which gives detailed references: T. Stock, "Chemical and Biological Weapons: Developments and Proliferation," (Chapter 7), *SIPRI Yearbook 1983;* T. Stock and A. De Geer, "Chemical Weapon Developments," (Chapter 9) and E. Geissler, "Biological Weapons and Arms Control Developments," (Chapter 18), *SIPRI Yearbook 1984;* S.J. Lundin, T. Stock and E. Geissler, "Chemical and Biological Warfare and Arms Control Developments," (Chapter 6), *SIPRI Yearbook 1992;* T. Stock and A. De Geer, "Chemical and Biological Weapons: Developments and Destruction," Chapter 10, *SIPRI Yearbook 1995.*

7. *End Run: The U.S. Government's Plan for Designing Nuclear Weapons and Simulating Nuclear Explosions under the Comprehensive Test Ban Treaty,* Natural Resources Defense Council, August 1997.

8. J. Holum, "ACDA Director Remarks on Arms Control Agenda," *Disarmament Diplomacy*, January 1997, pp. 40-42.

Appendix

6.F. **Resolution adopted by a General Assembly of the International Association of Microbiological Societies, August 1970**

The microbiologists taking part in the conference on biological warfare at the 10th International Congress for Microbiology in Mexico, 1-14 August, 1970, have studied and discussed in detail much material including:

1. Report of the UN Secretary-General (1969), *Chemical and Bacteriological (Biological) Weapons and the Effects of their Possible Use.*
2. Report of a WHO Group of Consultants (1970), *Health Aspects of Chemical and Biological Weapons.*
3. Stockholm International Peace Research Institute (SIPRI) (1970), *The Problem of Chemical and Biological Warfare*, Provisional Edition, Parts I, III and IV.

Therefore they are cognizant of the great potential dangers of human, animal, and plant infections to the welfare of mankind;

Know what grave consequences could result from the use of harmful microorganisms (bacteria, fungi and viruses) or their products as instruments of warfare;

Declare that microbiological methods of warfare should not be employed, even in retaliation;

Believe also that no country should produce, sell or acquire microbial agents in quantity, except for peaceful purposes or to improve the health and wellbeing of Mankind;

Convinced also that

1. the search for truth in science is enhanced by non-secret research, and that secret research tends to increase mistrust and international tension;
2. the results of scientific investigation should be published and widely disseminated; and
3. the free movement of scientists from one laboratory or one country to another is an important aspect of science;

Realizing that the pursuit of these aims is shared by the vast majority of Mankind as indicated by:

a. the fact that a majority of UN member states have already signed and ratified The Protocol for the Prohibition of the Use in War of Asphyxiating, Poisonous or Other Gases, and Bacteriological Methods of Warfare (Geneva, 17 June, 1925);
b. the scope of the United Nations General Assembly Resolutions 2162 (XXI) of 5 December, 1966, and 2454 (XXIII) of 20 December, 1968, which called for strict observance by all states of the principles and objectives of the Geneva Protocol;
c. the trend among nations to go beyond the provision of the Geneva Protocol, for instance by unilateral renunciation of use under any circumstances of biological weapons and of any further research and development of such weapons;

    d.   the fact that several nations have by treaty renounced the use of weapons of mass destruction;

    e.   the resolution passed by many professional societies and congresses;

Affirm, support and welcome further positive activities of the same kind, and particularly *We urge that*:

    a.   all countries that have not signed or ratified the Geneva Protocol should do so, and

    b.   all installations (laboratories, academies, institutes, *etc.*) where established microbiological programmes have been carried out expressly for offensive or defensive biological warfare purposes be converted to peaceful uses, if possible with international participation, and that no new installations should be commissioned.

    c.   all stockpiles of biological weapons should be destroyed as soon as possible.

We believe that existing installations for military microbiology could usefully be converted to any of the following uses:

    applied environmental microbiology; biogeochemical transformations; conservation of soils; crop productivity and biological nitrogen fixation; production of proteins and other food substances; production of enzymes and hormones; purification and recycling of sewage for drinking water; rapid diagnosis of infectious diseases; improved means of mass-vaccination; problems of viral carcinogenesis; problems of molecular biology; microbiological pest control, *etc.*

Although microbiology is our field of competence, we feel that similar principles could usefully be applied as well to chemical, atomic and other means of mass destruction.

We recommend the use of arbitration in the solution of problems connected with matters related to this resolution.

5

Reducing the Threat of Nuclear Theft

John P. Holdren and Matthew Bunn

A comprehensive approach to reducing the risk of nuclear theft will require action on many fronts: improving security and accounting for nuclear materials; combating nuclear smuggling; increasing transparency in the management of weapon-usable nuclear materials; halting or minimizing continued production of these materials; and carrying out disposition procedures to reduce the risks from excess fissile materials by making them far more difficult to use in weapons. Although such an approach entails the need for action in all the nuclear weapon states and, to some extent, elsewhere as well, the biggest burdens fall naturally on the United States and on the former Soviet Union – where by far the largest inventories of nuclear materials are to be found.

We therefore focus primarily, in this paper, on the particular problems of reducing the threat of nuclear theft in the United States and the former Soviet Union, including cooperative approaches linking the capabilities and interests on both sides. In doing so, we draw extensively on three recent studies in which we have both been heavily involved: the National Academy of Sciences (NAS) study of plutonium management and disposition; the President's Committee of Advisors on Science and Technology study of cooperative programmes between the United States and the former Soviet Union on nuclear materials, protection, control, and accounting (MPC&A); and the Independent US-Russian Scientific Commission on the Disposition of Excess Weapon Plutonium.[1]

We begin by surveying the five classes of measures enumerated in our opening sentence, before turning to an additional category unique to the former Soviet Union – the need to improve the economic conditions of the people responsible for managing nuclear weapons and materials, including, particularly, the diversification and strengthening of the economic base of the nuclear cities.

Improved Security and Accounting

The first priority is to ensure that all nuclear weapons and weapon-usable materials are secure and accounted for – that is, to establish effective materials, protection, control and accounting. This involves: facility-level security and accounting systems for both weapon-usable materials and nuclear weapons themselves; new, secure storage facilities; consolidation of weapons and materials at a smaller number of locations; high security for transport of weapons and materials (often the most vulnerable point in their life-cycles); effective national-level systems of accounting, control, and regulation; and, ultimately, more stringent international standards.

Nuclear Materials: Facility-Level

Excluding sites for the storage of intact nuclear weapons, there are about 100 separately fenced areas in the former Soviet Union (FSU) – at about 50 separate sites – handling kilogramme-quantities of weapon-usable nuclear materials (separated plutonium and highly-enriched uranium (HEU)), and perhaps a couple of dozen such sites in the United States. Approximately a dozen of the former – all research or training reactors using HEU – are outside Russia (including facilities in Kazakhstan, Ukraine, Belarus, Latvia, Georgia, and Uzbekistan).

Direct expenditures for safeguards and security programmes in the US Department of Energy (DOE) complex have been estimated at some $800 million per year, including protection for materials, sites, information, and personnel, as well as the entire classification and security clearance programme; expenditures directly related to security and accounting for weapon-usable nuclear material probably account for well over $200 million of this total. The owners of private facilities handling weapon-usable material (such as research reactors using HEU, or the facility that fabricates HEU naval fuel) pay separately for protection of the material at their facilities. It is widely held that the resulting MPC&A measures in place at the relevant US sites are adequate or close to adequate. Although this conclusion deserves scrutiny – and might not withstand scrutiny in every instance – the task of repairing any major deficiencies in MPC&A at the relevant US sites is undoubtedly a much easier one than the task of improving the MPC&A at the sites in the former Soviet Union to approximately the current US standard.

Comparable figures for spending in Russia and the other former Soviet states are not available. The Department of Energy estimated in 1995 that modernizing the MPC&A systems at the separately fenced areas in the FSU might cost roughly $5 million each, on average. Currently, US and former Soviet experts are engaged in at least some level of MPC&A cooperation at well over 40 of the roughly 50 sites in the former Soviet Union where such materials exist. If the Department of Energy estimate turns out to be correct, the one-time cost of continuing this cooperative programme until MPC&A has been modernized at all of the locations in the FSU handling weapon-usable material would be roughly $500 million (excluding the operating costs once modernization is completed). This is, of course, a highly approximate estimate – between $300 million and $1.5 billion might be a better way to put it – and there are a number of important caveats.

First, this cost will not be borne by any one country: while the states of the FSU themselves bear the ultimate responsibility for protecting the materials on their territory and must bear a significant part of the cost, their capacity to pay is limited, and it is in the self-interest of the United States and other members of the international community to assist financially.

On the other hand, it is likely that the figure of $5 million per facility will turn out to be an underestimate. A number of these sites include many individual buildings and facilities where MPC&A should be modernized, each of which may involve substantial costs. Nor does the $5 million figure represent, in general, the cost of upgrading to a level of security and accounting comparable to that currently required for nuclear-weapons-complex facilities in the United States. Approaching US standards would cost more. It would also take longer and require a larger cultural shift by nuclear workers. For the near term, it makes more sense to modernize MPC&A rapidly at a large number of sites than to upgrade only a few sites to the highest possible standards.

Modernization of MPC&A in the FSU could not be accomplished over-night, even if budgets far larger than those available today became available. Given the limited number of individuals in the former Soviet Union expert in state-of-the-art safeguards technologies – and the limited infrastructure for organizing and applying such skills – the absorptive capacity for cooperation in this area is limited. Nor is modernization of MPC&A technologies a full or complete answer: a new "safeguards culture" is needed as well. If equipment is not used or maintained, if guards wave trusted workers through without having them pass through inspection systems, if scientists and technicians refuse to accept the inconveniences associated with more stringent safeguards, if managers refuse to put up with increases in costs of production, then no amount of technology will adequately reduce the risk of theft. To help build the needed safeguards culture, a continued focus on genuine participation and engagement by users at these sites is critical. This will not be accomplished quickly.

These disclaimers notwithstanding, cooperative MPC&A programmes remain limited by the budgets available. With a redoubled focus on expanding the cadre of trained experts in the former Soviet states available to work on implementation of improved MPC&A, budgets substantially higher than the $137 million proposed for the US contribution to this cooperative effort in fiscal year 1998 could be spent effectively and would allow faster progress towards reducing the risk of nuclear theft.

Because not everything can be accomplished at once, the MPC&A panel of the President's Committee of Advisers on Science and Technology (PCAST) emphasized the importance of preparing a prioritized MPC&A action plan identifying specific near-term, mid-term, and long-term goals and objectives, and the resources needed to accomplish them. The PCAST panel recommended that the near-term objectives should include: modernizing security and accounting for weapon-usable materials at the largest civilian facilities in open cities in Russia, and at all the former Soviet facilities outside Russia where weapon-usable materials are stored; working with Russia to establish a programme to identify additional high-priority steps to be taken; helping to establish a Russian programme to take accurate inventories of the nuclear material at all the various nuclear sites; establishing a cooperative programme to modernize security and accounting for naval and icebreaker fuel; cooperating with Russia to initiate mass production of state-of-the-art MPC&A equipment; and cooperating with the former Soviet states to establish effective training programmes and regulatory structures in this area.

As part of the effort to accomplish these near-term goals, the PCAST report identified several specific near-term actions that should be undertaken:

–   *Training and equipping Russian MPC&A assessment and improvement teams.*   Such teams could provide a rapid and consistent assessment of comparative upgrade needs at Russian sites – information that could provide a foundation both for Russia's unilateral modernization programmes and for the ongoing cooperative efforts. The cost of such training and equipment might be around $10 million.

–   *Training and equipping Russian inventory teams.*   There is a pressing need to carry out measured, physical inventories of the weapon-usable nuclear materials at each site (EURATOM has also targeted measured, physical inventory as a high priority.) Unlike the vulnerability assessments just described, such inventories are a labour-intensive, time-consuming process requiring a significant amount of equipment – particularly where nuclear materials are handled in bulk forms rather than countable items, and where they are in difficult-to-measure forms, such as when they are mixed with other scrap and waste. The cost of initial training and equipment for a few inventory teams might be a few tens of millions of dollars, but the total cost of taking measured inventories at all the relevant sites will be large enough to be among the factors which suggest that $500 million is likely to be an underestimate of the total MPC&A modernization cost.

–   *A fast-paced programme to improve security for highly-enriched naval and icebreaker fuel.*   Preliminary discussions of cooperation in this area are underway, but more remains to be done. The cost of this part of the programme could be in the range of $100 million or more, particularly if it is determined that new buildings or vaults are needed, rather than merely upgrades to existing facilities.

- *Training additional US and former Soviet personnel to participate in these cooperative programmes, and assigning additional qualified personnel to manage and implement these programmes at the Department of Energy.* As a rough estimate, the cost of paying and training these additional participants might amount to some $30 million per year.

- *Establishing a "quick response" team with the expertise and resources needed to respond rapidly and effectively to opportunities such as Project Sapphire.* Project Sapphire was the programme in which the Kazakh and US governments cooperated to airlift over 600 kilogrammes of insecure HEU from Kazakhstan to the United States in November 1994.[2] The personnel already participating in the cooperative programmes would have the expertise to be designated as members of such a quick-response team, but additional training and flexible funding sources would be needed to provide the capability for rapid response. At the same time, the United States should cooperate with Russia in activities comparable to those of the US Nuclear Emergencies Search Team (NEST). If the same personnel were used, this would probably cost a few million dollars per year, in addition to providing a funding source that could be drawn on when a specific mission arose.

- *Establishing a small cadre of full-time US personnel in Moscow to help manage and oversee these programmes, and maintain constant contact with Russian participants.* We estimate the cost of this effort at approximately $1 million per year.

These programmes can only succeed if they are based on genuine cooperation and mutual trust and respect. Maximum success requires maximum flexibility – meaning that Congress should resist the temptation to impose burdensome restrictions on how business can be conducted, such as "buy American" requirements and specified audit and examination procedures. Many of the sites involved are highly sensitive, and there are locations at which American auditors are not likely to be allowed broad access, but where it is nevertheless deeply in the US interest to cooperate with Russia in modernizing MPC&A and reducing proliferation risks. The PCAST panel concluded that the flexible procedures being used in the lab-to-lab programme, for example, were effective in ensuring that the taxpayers' funds were being appropriately spent.

Storage Facilities

An important supplement to efforts to upgrade MPC&A at existing facilities where weapon-usable materials are located is the Nunn-Lugar programme to build, at Chelyabinsk-65 (now renamed Ozersk, and also sometimes known as Mayak, the name of the principal production association at the site), a new safe and secure storage facility for plutonium and HEU from dismantled weapons. The new facility would offer greatly improved security and accounting, and the United States would be offered transparency measures in return for its assistance.

Despite the many delays that have plagued this programme, the establishment of a modern facility with a highly effective MPC&A system and some degree of US oversight is important, and this programme should continue – assuming that MINATOM demonstrates a good-faith commitment to investing its own resources in the project as well. Total costs for the first facility (including both US and Russian inputs) are estimated at $300-$500 million. No definite decision has yet been taken as to whether to build a second $300-$500 million facility at Tomsk.

Nuclear Weapons: Facility-Level

Nuclear weapons in the former Soviet Union appear to be held under comparatively high standards of security and accounting. Nevertheless, given the grave consequences that could result if a nuclear weapon were actually stolen, it is important to continue pursuing the recently expanded dialogue between the US Department of Defense and the Russian Ministry of Defence regarding upgrades to security for nuclear weapons.

According to unclassified CIA testimony, Russia has already reduced the number of sites where nuclear weapons are stored from over 600 in 1989 to roughly 100, comparable to the number of sites with non-weaponized weapon-usable material.[3] This figure does not include actual deployment sites, such as missile silos.

The Department of Defense is cooperating with Russia to upgrade equipment for securing and accounting for stored nuclear weapons (as well as weapons in transport, described below). The initial emphasis was on improved accounting and tracking equipment, such as computerized warhead-accounting systems. Today, work is underway on improving physical protection systems at individual sites as well. Active nuclear weapo. storage sites are particularly sensitive, so flexible procedures are being worked out to ensure that US-provided material is used appropriately, without unduly compromising sensitive information – perhaps without even requiring US visits to the individual warhead sites. Since these sites already have substantial physical protection systems in place, and the programme does not face the complex material accounting issues that arise at sites that carry out bulk processing of nuclear materials, the programme is expected to be significantly less expensive than the MPC&A programme. Just as in the case of nuclear materials, nuclear weapons are Russia's responsibility, and it will ultimately have to bear the lion's share of the cost of protecting them.

Consolidation

As noted above, Russia has already accomplished a drastic reduction in the number of sites where nuclear weapons are stored. The PCAST report recommended that the United States begin discussing with the former Soviet states, and Russia in particular, the need for a similar consolidation in the number of sites with weapon-usable nuclear materials. This includes reducing the number of areas where such materials are handled at individual facilities, and reducing the total number of facilities where such materials are located. Such consolidation could greatly reduce the costs of ensuring adequate safeguards.

With the end of the Cold War, a contraction of the Russian nuclear complex is inevitable and consolidation of nuclear materials should be a key part of that contraction – as it has been in the United States. The US Department of Energy should prepare a detailed briefing for the Russian side on the US experience, including the very large reductions in safeguards and security costs that have been achieved at some sites through consolidating materials, and the reduction in the number of research reactors using HEU (which has resulted in part from the high cost of meeting MPC&A regulations for such strategic materials). Both in work at individual sites and in discussions of the overall programme, the United States should actively encourage Russia to undertake consolidation.

In particular, there is a wide range of small civilian research facilities using HEU in Russia, many of which no longer have a strong rationale for continuing to use weapon-usable material. Because these facilities have always been regarded as civilian, standards of security traditionally have been low. Iraq's recent admission that after its invasion of Kuwait it planned to undertake a "crash" atomic bomb programme using HEU from its research reactors highlights the serious risks such facilities can pose. Soviet-designed research reactors using HEU fuel exist not only in many countries of the former Soviet Union, but in Libya and North Korea as well.

Given the crisis of funding for scier   in the FSU, many of these facilities are likely to be having trouble fundii .. ... research, and some may no longer be able to afford research related to HEU. These institutes might be quite happy if someone were to offer to purchase their remaining HEU supplies, rather than having to protect them in place. Such an approach would be simpler and less politically sensitive if carried out on a commercial basis by private companies rather than by the US government; the private companies could blend the material to low-enriched uranium (LEU) for sale on the commercial market. In this case, there would be no substantial cost to the US government.

For those institutes that will continue to do nuclear research with the reactors now running on HEU, it is important to offer opportunities to continue research while converting to proliferation-resistant low-enriched uranium. The United States initiated such a reactor-conversion programme, known as the Reduced Enrichment for Research and Test Reactors (RERTR) programme, in 1978, and it has been quite successful in converting reactors in the United States and all over the world to the use of proliferation-resistant fuels. A small programme to develop similar fuels for Soviet-designed research reactors is now underway. This programme should be expanded from fuel development to actual conversion of reactors – including not only those in the former Soviet Union, but even more urgently, those in nations such as North Korea and Libya – to low-enriched fuels. A few tens of millions of dollars over several years would probably be sufficient for this purpose.

Transport

During transport, nuclear weapons and weapon-usable nuclear materials are particularly vulnerable to theft by armed groups. Ensuring effective security during transportation should therefore be a high priority. The US Department of Defense is already providing warhead-transportation equipment that the Russian Ministry of Defence has indicated has made a major difference in improving security of Russian warhead transport. A substantial cooperative programme to improve transport security for weapon-usable nuclear materials is underway as well.

National-Level Systems

Efforts at individual sites should be co-ordinated so that they fit together and contribute to the goal of creating national systems providing a generally consistent level of MPC&A for all weapon-usable materials. Improving national-level tracking and accounting systems for nuclear materials, as well as regulatory functions, must be a fundamental priority of any comprehensive programme. While regulations are often taken to have less urgency than securing materials on the ground, only a sound set of regulations requiring effective MPC&A, backed up by enforcement, will provide facility managers with the incentives necessary to lead them to invest in, operate, and maintain MPC&A systems.

In most of the states of the former Soviet Union, where nuclear regulatory agencies exist at all, they are new and are suffering the growing pains of fledgling organizations with large mandates and small staffs. In Russia's case, the relative authority of the principal nuclear ministries (MINATOM and MOD) and the civilian nuclear oversight agency (GAN) is still evolving; both these ministries are far larger and more powerful than GAN, and unenthusiastic about independent regulation. President Yeltsin, after initially giving GAN authority to regulate safety and security of all nuclear activities, both military and civilian, recently signed a decree removing GAN's authority to regulate MOD activities. Ultimately, these ministries themselves must have effective internal regulatory programmes, in addition to independent regulation.

The US Nuclear Regulatory Commission (NRC) and DOE have established promising programmes of regulatory support, including work with GAN in Russia. Several areas of cooperation are underway:

–   development of effective regulations and standards;
–   equipment and training for inspectors and regulators;
–   establishment of national computerized material accounting systems;
–   in Russia, MPC&A at non-MINATOM, non-MOD sites (where GAN is serving as the point of contact for facilities controlled by a wide array of different agencies and groups).

Development of a strong regulatory system in this area will take years; funding from the international community, in the range of a few tens of millions of dollars over the period, will be needed.

Tougher International Standards

The need to modernize MPC&A systems is a global issue, not limited to the states of the FSU. Materials in many countries are not protected to standards that meet today's threats. For these reasons, the NAS report on management and disposition of excess weapons plutonium recommended that new international arrangements should be pursued to improve safeguards and physical security over all forms of plutonium and HEU worldwide.[4]

The most difficult technical obstacle to producing nuclear weapons is gaining access to the necessary fissile materials – plutonium or HEU. With such materials in hand, many countries, and even some subnational groups, could produce nuclear weapons. The NAS report, therefore, recommended that, to the extent possible, weapon-usable materials, whether military or civilian, should be guarded and accounted for as though they were nuclear weapons – a goal the NAS report called the "stored weapons standard" – and that international standards should be updated to meet this goal.

Current international standards fall far short of this objective. Although an attempt to set international standards for nuclear materials security was made in the 1980 Convention on the Physical Protection of Nuclear Material, that convention was drafted at a time when today's threats – from nuclear smuggling to the use of weapons of mass destruction by terrorist groups – did not yet exist. US approaches have changed radically since then, resulting in more than a doubling of annual spending on safeguards and security. The Convention is vague in its requirements, applies primarily to international transport of materials, and has no provisions for verification or enforcement. Similarly, although the IAEA has published more detailed guidelines for physical protection of nuclear materials, these are purely advisory. Neither the IAEA nor any other organization monitors or compiles accurate, up-to-date information on physical security procedures worldwide. Moreover, no comparable convention setting standards for material control and accounting exists.

International standards should be updated to reflect the "stored weapons standard," and provisions should be made to allow an international body (probably the IAEA) to organize site visits to make recommendations for improvements (as has been done successfully, for example, with nuclear safety). There is a growing international consensus on the need for such steps, reflected in similar recommendations – including specifically endorsement of the stored weapons standard – made in 1995 by an international panel organized by the American Nuclear Society, which included high-level representatives from the United States, Russia, France, Britain, Germany, and Japan.[5]

A major international effort to improve security and accounting for weapon-usable nuclear materials worldwide would be costly, probably adding tens of millions of dollars a year to the costs currently paid for such activities. This cost, however, should be considered an essential part of the cost of operating a facility that uses weapon-usable materials – just as the costs of pollution prevention and mitigation should be paid by the polluters – and would represent a small additional burden on the global nuclear power industry.

Stopping Nuclear Smuggling

The most critical part of the effort to reduce the threat of nuclear theft and nuclear smuggling is ensuring that nuclear weapons and weapon-usable nuclear materials are not removed from the sites where they are intended to be. Once such materials are stolen, the difficulty of finding and recovering them before they can be used in weapons rises dramatically. Nevertheless, if MPC&A systems fail and material is stolen, anti-smuggling efforts form an important second line of defence. Some modest efforts to train and equip police, investigators, customs officials, and border guards in the relevant states, to share analyses of seized material, and to co-ordinate nuclear smuggling intelligence are underway, but these efforts have been halting and piecemeal. Further efforts along these lines are needed. This is a global problem requiring intensive international cooperation.

To date, the principal successes in finding and seizing stolen weapons-usable nuclear materials have been the result of informers and sting operations – which is to say, they have resulted from the efforts of police, intelligence, and "special services." Some nuclear materials have been seized by border guards and customs agents, but these have been relatively inconsequential in comparison. The lesson is the importance of information, of knowing where to look.

Therefore, increased police and intelligence cooperation across borders – as is already occurring – must be a top priority, and energetic efforts should be made to work out ways in which information can be shared without unduly compromising law-enforcement and intelligence sensitivities (such as protection of sources). In particular, information about the sources of smuggled materials (likely to be more available to Russian agencies than to those in other countries) should be linked, to the extent possible, to information on buyers and transit routes (likely to be more available to European countries). For example, the FBI's office in Moscow should include a cadre of experts on nuclear smuggling, who could cooperate with Russian counterparts. The monetary cost would potentially run to a few million dollars per year.

At the same time, there is room for a substantial increase in the amount of training and equipment provided to police, border guards, and customs agencies in a variety of states, including particularly the FSU, and likely transit states in central Asia and Europe. Already, for example, the FBI is opening an international training centre in Eastern Europe to help states cope with threats from organized crime (including nuclear smuggling), and the United States is organizing international conferences to discuss how to handle the forensic analysis of nuclear smuggling cases. The following are a few examples of additional items a comprehensive approach would include:

–   *Analysis centres.* A small number of certified analysis centres should be established at several key points in Eurasia, where seized materials could be sent. These centres should be equipped to provide sufficiently detailed analyses to make it possible to trace the origin of a particular batch of material. This would not require establishing an international database of nuclear material fingerprints (an immense job, and an approach that the nuclear weapon states, among others, are not likely to agree to).

–   *Nuclear smuggling law enforcement units.* Each key country should have at least a small unit of law enforcement officers capable of investigating nuclear smuggling cases. These officers would have the training and equipment to distinguish between, for example, intensely radioactive caesium and weapon-usable plutonium, or between relatively innocuous low-enriched uranium and weapon-usable highly-enriched uranium. Key states could be helped to establish, train, and equip such units relatively rapidly, for a cost in the range of a few millions to a few tens of millions of dollars.

–   *Training and equipping border patrols and customs.* The immense volume of traffic that crosses international borders every day, and the vast and sparsely-populated length of the borders between some of the key countries, makes the task of interdicting nuclear materials as they cross international borders extremely difficult – as evidenced by the massive flows of drugs and other contraband that governments have so far been unable to stop. Nevertheless, US nuclear detection equipment and training provided to border patrols and customs officers in some countries has already paid off in seizures of radioactive materials. Ultimately, border guards and customs agencies in each of the key potential source states and transit states should have sufficient equipment and trained personnel to monitor at the least the main border crossings and international exit/entry points. In some cases, this might mean little more than ensuring that border units had a Geiger counter; in other cases, substantially more sophisticated equipment might be used, such as systems that can detect both nuclear materials and metal containers that might be used to conceal their radiation. New technologies for drive-through portal monitoring might be applied to some key bridges and border crossing points. As one obvious example, there could be a significant deterrent benefit in a programme to scan selected luggage at airports, such as Moscow, for nuclear materials. Because of the very large job that customs agencies and border guards must do, involving many sites, thousands of individuals, thousands of miles of border, spreading such equipment and training broadly could be expensive – potentially mounting into hundreds of millions of dollars over time.

It will not be possible to accomplish everything that might be done at once. Hence, the intelligence community should examine where the greatest weaknesses and the highest leverage points for improving the response to nuclear smuggling lie.

Weapon Dismantlement and Monitoring

Past arms control agreements have concentrated primarily on limiting the numbers of missiles and launchers. Now the objective is to bring about irreversible nuclear arms reductions and also to reduce the risk of nuclear theft. Consequently, the next generation of agreements must focus on controlling nuclear weapons themselves and the fissile materials needed to make them. The NAS report on the management and disposition of excess plutonium recommended that the United States should work to reach agreement with Russia on a broad, reciprocal regime that would include:

–   declarations of stockpiles of nuclear weapons and all fissile materials;

- cooperative measures to clarify and confirm those declarations (including physical access to production facilities and production records);
- an agreed, monitored halt to the production of fissile materials for weapons; and
- agreed, monitored stockpile reductions.

The regime would initially be bilateral and later international. It would monitor warhead dismantlement (using a perimeter-portal monitoring system in addition to monitoring the build-up of weapon components in storage); it would also monitor the commitment of excess fissile materials to non-weapon use or disposal; and there would be some form of monitoring of whatever warhead assembly continues. Such a regime would build confidence in the knowledge each side had of the size and management of the other side's nuclear stockpiles and the progress of nuclear arms reductions, and the information exchanged and site visits conducted would provide critical additional information to support cooperative MPC&A efforts.

The more such information that can be exchanged, the greater the potential synergistic benefit for MPC&A cooperation. Reciprocal visits to a wide range of plutonium and HEU storage and production sites (as envisaged in the NAS report and in a US proposal tabled in December 1994), could be of great benefit for MPC&A. (There is no substitute, in judging what MPC&A improvements are needed, for actual visits to the relevant sites.) It was for reasons such as these that the Senate required the Administration to begin pursuing such a weapons and fissile materials regime in the Biden Condition to its ratification of the START I treaty.

Such a broad regime could be approached step-by-step, with each step adding to security while posing little risk. The regime the NAS recommended would involve measures applying to each phase of the life cycle of military fissile materials: production and separation of the materials; fabrication of fissile material weapon components; assembly, deployment, retirement, and disassembly of nuclear weapons; and storage and eventual disposition of fissile materials. While such a regime could never be rigorously verified, in the sense of absolutely confirming that a few dozen nuclear weapons or a few tonnes of fissile material had not been hidden away somewhere, these measures would be mutually reinforcing, building confidence that the information exchanged was accurate and that the goals of the regime were being met. With a sufficiently inclusive approach, it would be difficult to falsify the broad range of information exchanged in a consistent way, so as to hide a stockpile large enough to be strategically significant.

The United States and Russia have been discussing measures to meet the objective of "transparency and irreversibility" of nuclear arms reductions, including many of the elements of such a broad regime. A number of key elements are agreed at the level of broad Presidential statements, including the reciprocal data exchange on nuclear weapons and fissile material stockpiles, and mutual inspections of the stored fissile materials resulting from weapon dismantlements, but implementation is so far lacking.

Removing large quantities of fissile material from the stockpiles available for weapons is a key element of such a regime. This can be accomplished, as President Clinton is doing, through political or legal commitments never again to use designated materials in weapons, confirmed by bilateral or international monitoring. (To date, however, the United States has declared only a small amount of the material from actual dismantlements excess to its military needs, keeping most of it for military reserves. The NAS study recommended, by contrast, that a very large fraction of this material be declared excess.)

The NAS study recommended that excess fissile materials committed to non-weapon use or disposal by the United States and Russia should be placed under international safeguards (possibly combined with bilateral monitoring). In the interest of speed, monitoring of storage could initially be a bilateral US-Russian effort, but the IAEA should soon be brought into the process. In the case of plutonium stored as "pits," the NAS report concluded that adequate safeguards could be provided without compromising sensitive weapon-design information by declassifying the mass of plutonium in the pits, and allowing IAEA monitors to assay the sealed containers holding the pits without observing the components' dimensions. Preparing a site for IAEA safeguards requires that a reasonable material control and accounting system be in place, so there is a potential synergy with MPC&A efforts here, as well.

The NAS report recommended further that this regime be internationalized, so that all states would ultimately declare their holdings of fissile material, and all the declared weapon states would declare their holdings of nuclear weapons.

The cost of data exchanges and limited numbers of reciprocal visits to fissile material production and handling sites would be relatively modest. Perimeter-portal monitoring of dismantlement facilities would be somewhat more costly, possibly amounting to a few tens of millions of dollars per year. (A variety of technologies for automated monitoring might reduce substantially the number of inspector-days, and therefore the costs, required to confirm dismantlement figures effectively.)

In addition, the United States should consider how to provide incentives (financial and otherwise) for participation by key Russian parties in such a transparency programme, and how to build it step-by-step. For example, taking a cue from the lab-to-lab MPC&A programme, US laboratories are working with their Russian counterparts to develop and demonstrate technologies and approaches for such transparency on a reciprocal basis – potentially creating a motivated cadre of Russian experts and advocates in this area, as in MPC&A.

In addition, financial assistance could be provided for the actual dismantlement of nuclear weapons. If the United States were to offer a reciprocal regime for verification of warhead dismantlement, for example, while simultaneously offering financial assistance to help pay for the costs of warhead dismantlement itself, once verification of that dismantlement was in place – as envisaged in the original Nunn-Lugar legislation, but never implemented – this could provide a significant incentive for Russian officials to do the hard work necessary to overcome decades of Communist secrecy and implement a transparency regime. Russian officials have estimated that it costs roughly $15,000 to dismantle each warhead; if the United States financed half this cost, and the Russians continued to dismantle roughly 2000 warheads per year, the cost would be $15 million per year. If financial assistance allowed Russia to accelerate dismantlement, the resulting increase in cost would be a small price to pay for the large resulting benefit to US security.

Safeguards on excess fissile material also involve significant costs (potentially as high as a few tens of millions per year, counting the costs of hosting inspections, if both the United States and Russia place all their excess material under safeguards). Costs are particularly high when material is in difficult-to-monitor forms, such as scrap and waste. More broadly, to carry out its expanded, post-Gulf War missions, along with the new missions of monitoring excess nuclear material and a global fissile material production cut-off, the IAEA's safeguards budget will have to be substantially increased. Other steps should be taken as well to strengthen the IAEA's ability to carry out its responsibilities.

Limiting Accumulation

If the world has too much weapon-usable material, it should stop making more. Any comprehensive plan to reduce the risks of theft of these materials would obviously be helped if the world stockpiles of weapon-usable nuclear material were to stop growing. Already, in addition to the hundreds of tonnes of excess fissile material building up as a result of nuclear arms reductions, there are over 150 tonnes of separated, weapon-usable civilian plutonium in storage around the world – a figure that increases by many tonnes every year, as reprocessing of additional plutonium continues to outpace its use as reactor fuel.

Unfortunately, even the first step in the effort to limit accumulation of these materials – initiated in a US-Russian agreement signed in 1994 to end production of plutonium for weapons – has not yet been completed. After extensive debate about how to avoid the problems that would be created by simply shutting down three Russian reactors that produce not only weapon plutonium but also heat and electric power for the surrounding regions, it was finally agreed that the cores of these reactors will be converted to operate with fuels that do not produce weapon plutonium and do not require near-term reprocessing. This will cost tens of millions of dollars, rather than the hundreds of millions, or billions, of dollars required for entirely new plants. The reactors are now expected to be converted by the year 2000.

The second step in this path is a worldwide fissile cut-off convention, banning production of plutonium or HEU for nuclear explosives or outside of international safeguards. Such an agreement would be a considerable non-proliferation achievement – and would mean placing enrichment and reprocessing plants worldwide, including those in the former Soviet Union, under international safeguards, inevitably requiring a major improvement in MPC&A at some of these facilities. The costs of monitoring such an agreement might increase the IAEA's annual safeguards budget by $40-$90 million; the costs of initially preparing older reprocessing plants for safeguards would also be significant.

It is also important to limit the build-up of civilian separated plutonium around the world. Reprocessing operations in France, Britain, Russia and Japan continue to proceed far faster than the use of the resulting plutonium as fuel, with no end in sight to the resulting build up of separated plutonium. Utilities are contracting for reprocessing not because they need the plutonium for their planned programmes, but because they need to get their spent fuel out of their cooling ponds. For example, despite having no commercial scale plutonium fuel fabrication capability – and therefore no near-term need for civilian plutonium – Russia continues to reprocess at the Mayak plant, adding another tonne or more annually to the roughly 30 tonnes of plutonium in storage there, and is considering construction of a massive new reprocessing plant at Krasnoyarsk-26. MINATOM would like to be able to change Russian law to permit it to offer reprocessing contracts to foreign utilities under which Russia would keep the waste and plutonium separated during reprocessing, meaning that utilities could send their spent fuel to Russia and never have to worry about it again. This could result in a major increase in global reprocessing. For the moment, however, prospects for financing this plant and for such a change in the atomic law in Russia appear slim.

Disposition

The end of the Cold War and the dismantlement of tens of thousands of nuclear weapons is leaving the United States and Russia with a daunting legacy: hundreds of tonnes of HEU and plutonium that are no longer needed for military purposes and must be securely managed and ultimately transformed into forms that would be more difficult to use for nuclear weapons. As the NAS report warned, the existence of these huge stocks of excess material "constitutes a clear and present danger to national and international security." This is a critical security challenge of the post-Cold War period. In addition to its direct security implications, disposition will involve significant sums of money – billions of dollars of potential profit in the case of HEU, and hundreds of millions or billions of dollars in required subsidy in the case of plutonium.

A substantial period of storage of this material – lasting, for some portion of the material, for decades – will be required for all plausible disposition options. For that period, as noted earlier, it is essential to ensure that this material is stored safely and securely, and with adequate transparency (both bilateral and international) to confirm commitments that it will never be returned to weapons.

Although intermediate storage is an inevitable interim step, it should not be extended longer than necessary. It would be bad for the cause of non-proliferation and arms reduction to maintain these vast stocks of excess material in a readily weapon-usable form over the long term. Whether storage is secure against the risks of breakout and theft depends entirely on the durability of the political arrangements under which storage is conducted. Indeed, one of the key criteria by which disposition options should be judged is the speed with which they can be accomplished, and thus how rapidly they could curtail these risks of storage.

The NAS report recommended that the United States and Russia pursue long-term disposition options that:

–   minimize the time during which this material is stored in forms readily usable for nuclear weapons;
–   preserve material safeguards and security during the disposition process, seeking to maintain the same high standards of security and accounting applied to stored nuclear weapons (the "stored weapons standard" described above);
–   result in a form from which the plutonium would be as difficult to recover for weapon use as the larger and growing quantity of plutonium in spent fuel – the "spent fuel standard;" for uranium, an analogous standard, not addressed in the NAS report, is that disposition should result in a form from which the uranium would be as difficult to recover for weapon use as ordinary commercial low-enriched uranium; and
–   meet high standards of protection for public and worker health and the environment.

For HEU, it is technically straightforward to achieve these goals. Highly-enriched uranium can be blended with other forms of uranium to produce proliferation-resistant LEU, which is a valuable commercial fuel. The United States has agreed to purchase 500 tonnes of excess Russian HEU, blended to LEU, over 20 years; if current prices persist, the value of the deal over that period will be roughly $12 billion. The United States is planning to undertake a similar blending process for most of its own stockpile of excess HEU (currently declared to amount to approximately 175 tonnes of material).

While disposition of HEU is technically straightforward, the details of arranging this material's entry into the commercial market have proved to be complex. After considerable initial difficulties, LEU blended from Russian HEU is now being delivered and money transferred. The soon-to-be-privatized US Enrichment Corporation and the firm representing Russia's Ministry of Atomic Energy have recently signed a new contract setting the prices and quantities to be shipped for five years, which is expected to keep the agreement moving along at least for that period of time. After a series of difficult negotiations, transparency measures to ensure that the LEU the United States is purchasing comes from HEU, which in turn comes from weapon stockpiles, and to ensure that the United States uses this material only for peaceful purposes, have been agreed and are being implemented.

There are strong security arguments for increasing the size and pace of the HEU deal. Currently, the deal is for 500 tonnes of material to be purchased over 20 years. Russia has indicated informally that it has substantially more than 500 tonnes of excess HEU, and has sent out feelers concerning possible additional sales in the USA or other countries. Additional purchases would help to reduce the stockpiles of weapon-usable material in Russia, create an additional incentive for weapon dismantlement, and provide much-needed hard-currency – all at zero or modest net cost to the US taxpayer. Arrangements might be reached, moreover, under which the profits from additional purchases might be used to fund high priority nuclear security objectives, such as upgrading MPC&A or undertaking plutonium disposition (see below). Speeding up the deal would reduce the time during which this material remained in weapon-usable form. Even if the commercial market cannot absorb the material now, or sufficient facilities for blending the material more rapidly to a commercial-quality product cannot be made available, it would be highly desirable to blend the material to an intermediate level below 20 per cent enrichment, so that it was no longer usable in weapons.

Plutonium raises more difficult issues. As nearly all isotopes of plutonium are weapon-usable, plutonium cannot, like HEU, be blended to a proliferation-resistant form. Moreover, given the current worldwide supply of cheap uranium, the use of even "free" plutonium as fuel in reactors is currently uneconomic, so that essentially all plutonium disposition options will require subsidies of hundreds of millions or billions of dollars.[6]

The NAS study concluded that the two most promising options for plutonium disposition are:

–   fabrication into mixed-oxide fuel for use as fuel in existing or modified nuclear reactors; or
–   vitrification (combining the material with molten glass) in combination with high-level radioactive waste.

Both of these options would result in forms that met the spent fuel standard. The technical panel on reactor-related options that supported the NAS study recommended that both of these options should be pursued in parallel, to ensure that at least one of them would succeed. The panel concluded that each of the most promising options would have a net discounted present cost of between $500 million and $2 billion, for 50 tonnes of excess US plutonium. Costs in Russia are difficult to predict, (particularly as a disposition campaign would not be likely to begin for several years, by which time economic conditions are sure to be markedly different), but are not likely to be dramatically less. It appears very likely that if disposition of Russian plutonium is to be accomplished in the relatively near term, the United States and other members of the international community will have to help to finance it, as an investment in global security.

Following up the NAS study, the DOE undertook a major programme of analyses and experiments to study the advantages and disadvantages of the various options for disposing of excess US weapon plutonium. This effort generated three major reports – a Technical Summary Report, a Programmatic Environmental Impact Statement, and a Nonproliferation and Arms Control Impact Assessment – which were completed in mid- to late-1996 and arrived at conclusions similar to those reached by the NAS reports: that the two most attractive options for disposition of excess weapon plutonium beyond interim storage are MOX, for once-through use in a limited number of currently operating power reactors, and immobilization, by mixing with high-level radioactive wastes in glass logs.

Many of the basic conclusions of the NAS study have been endorsed by other nations as well. At the April 1996 Moscow Nuclear Safety and Security Summit, Presidents Clinton and Yeltsin, along with the other leaders of the Group of Seven industrialized nations, agreed that disposition of excess fissile material should be accomplished as quickly as practicable; endorsed the "spent fuel standard;" agreed that use as MOX or vitrification were the two best available approaches for meeting this standard; and agreed that disposition should be carried out with stringent security and accounting measures and international safeguards applied as early in the process as practicable. Further, the assembled leaders endorsed international cooperation to carry out necessary demonstrations and pilot projects, and called for an international experts meeting, held in Paris in October 1996, to lay out next steps in international cooperation.

Russia's planned programme of research and analysis on plutonium disposition beyond interim storage includes, analysis and tests of weapon-plutonium/MOX use in existing VVER-1000 light-water reactors and the existing BN-600 fast-neutron reactor; plans to construct larger BN-800 fast-neutron reactors (for which, however, sufficient funding is not yet available); and studies of high-temperature gas reactor systems. In addition, Russia has joint studies underway with France and Germany on MOX use in light-water and fast-neutron reactors, and these three countries have jointly proposed the construction of a pilot-scale MOX fabrication plant in Russia, capable of processing 1.5 tonnes of plutonium per year. Russia also has a joint study with Canada on the use of Russian weapon plutonium in CANDU reactors, and a joint study with the US firm General Atomics on the use of high-temperature gas reactors. A joint US-Russian government-to-government cooperative study analysing the technical characteristics of a wide variety of reactor, immobilization, and geologic-disposal options was completed and published in September 1996, and has been followed by joint analyses and tests of specific technologies, including a plan, still in its early stages, for a pilot plant for conversion of plutonium metal to oxide.

In mid-1996 the governments of Russia and the United States agreed to form an Independent US-Russian Scientific Commission on the Disposition of Excess Weapon Plutonium to make recommendations to Presidents Clinton and Yeltsin, through the Gore-Chernomyrdin Commission, on appropriate next steps. In an Interim Report completed in September 1996,[7] this Bilateral Commission recommended that the two most promising disposition options – the MOX/current-reactors option and the immobilization-with-wastes option – should both be developed to the point of large-scale operation in both countries. The Commission argued that this "dual track" approach provided the best opportunities for stimulating full cooperation between the two countries, the best possibilities for international financing, and, as a result of these features, and of not putting all the eggs in one basket, the best prospects for making plutonium disposition operational in both countries without excessive delay.

This two-track approach, which as noted above had also been recommended in the report of the Reactor Options Panel of the NAS study, stimulated some adverse comment from a number of US non-governmental organizations, who claimed that US use of the MOX option – putting weapon plutonium in civilian reactors – would violate US non-proliferation policy and would encourage proliferation-prone civilian recycle of plutonium in commercial reactors around the world. Proponents of the two-track approach replied that US non-proliferation policy opposes separating plutonium from spent nuclear fuel by reprocessing (whereafter the plutonium could be used in bombs) but does not and should not oppose putting already separated plutonium into fuel (where, after irradiation in a reactor, it cannot be used in bombs unless the fuel is reprocessed). Proponents also argued that limited once-through MOX use for weapon plutonium disposition would be unlikely to stimulate the commercial recycling of plutonium, especially since the latter remains uneconomic in comparison with once-through use of low-enriched uranium fuel. In mid-January 1997, the Clinton Administration announced in a formal Record of Decision that it would proceed with the dual-track approach. It is to be hoped that a similar decision by the Russian government will be forthcoming.

Both countries have some, but not all, of the facilities they would need to undertake plutonium disposition. For the reactor option, existing light-water reactors (LWRs) could, possibly with some modification, handle plutonium fuel in either one-third or 100 per cent of their reactor cores. A number of LWRs in Europe are already running with one-third MOX cores, though neither Russia nor the United States has substantial experience with MOX use in its commercial reactors. The NAS study concluded that building new reactors for plutonium disposition (such as the breeder reactors favoured by many MINATOM officials) is unnecessary, and would involve higher costs and longer delays. A single large LWR operating with uranium-plutonium mixed-oxide fuel containing 6-7 per cent plutonium by weight in 100 per cent of its core could use 50 tonnes of plutonium during its 30-year operational life. Unlike previous Soviet designs, the VVER-1000 LWRs are safe enough to continue to operate for decades to come, and with appropriate attention to modifications that may be necessary, use of plutonium fuel should not reduce their safety. Thus, if Russia decides that 100 tonnes of its weapon plutonium is no longer needed for weapon purposes, and if it proves to be possible to modify the VVER-1000s to use MOX in 100 per cent of their reactor cores, a single site such as Balakovo, where there are four VVER-1000 reactors, could handle the job. If the existing reactors can only use MOX in one-third of their reactor cores, additional modern VVER-1000 plants are operating in Ukraine – already fuelled by Russia, on contract – which could provide the necessary reactor capacity if associated political, transport and security issues could be satisfactorily resolved.

Neither Russia nor the United States, however, has an operational commercial-scale facility for fabricating MOX fuel or a facility for converting metallic plutonium weapon components to oxide. Providing such a facility is the long pole in the tent – in both time and cost – for beginning a large-scale plutonium disposition campaign using the reactor option. The NAS panel on reactor-related options concluded that in the United States, an existing unfinished MOX facility at Hanford could be made ready by 2001, with a capacity that could allow the last of 50 tonnes of excess plutonium to be loaded into reactors by 2026. The panel concluded that timing in Russia was not likely to be faster. More recent DOE studies have posited a slower, though still aggressive, schedule, on which a domestic US MOX plant would begin production in 2007.

Another option for dealing with the MOX fabrication problem would be to ship the plutonium to Western Europe for fabrication in existing and planned MOX plants there. These MOX facilities, however, have been designed to provide sufficient capacity to handle the plutonium being produced by commercial reprocessing in Europe. As a result, using these plants for weapon plutonium would require either delaying the fabrication of a similarly large stockpile of civilian plutonium, building additional fabrication capacity, or delaying or canceling some planned reprocessing. Nevertheless, this option is worth considering, particularly in the case of Russian plutonium, which would not have to travel far to get to these facilities: at fabrication plants in Western Europe, excellent MPC&A, international safeguards, and political and economic stability would be assured.

Similarly, both the United States and Russia have some but not all of the facilities that would be needed to mix plutonium with glass and high-level wastes. In the United States, a major effort to vitrify high-level wastes from past reprocessing is about to begin at Savannah River, and is planned at Hanford. Plutonium could be added to such waste glasses, but this would require either substantial modifications of existing facilities or the construction of new ones. The NAS panel estimated that vitrification of plutonium could not begin on a substantial scale in the USA until 2005, but could then be completed in less than a decade thereafter. Recent DOE studies similarly estimate a start time of 2006, and roughly a decade of operation. Russia is already vitrifying high-level wastes at Chelyabinsk, using a type of glass somewhat less suited for plutonium disposition. If it decided to do so, Russia could probably undertake vitrification of its plutonium on a similar schedule.

It is critical that disposition of excess HEU and plutonium should be carried out under stringent standards of security and accounting, and international monitoring. Disposition will inevitably involve substantial bulk handling of plutonium and HEU – which, if stringent procedures are not in place, could increase rather than decrease the risk of theft. Even a single documented case of theft of weapon-usable material from the disposition programme – a programme designed to reduce proliferation risks – could have a devastating political impact on the entire fissile material cooperation effort, in addition to the serious security risks that any such theft would pose. In the case of the HEU deal, it is critically important that both the sites where the HEU weapon components will be converted to HEU oxide, and the sites where the material will be blended to HEU, be provided with effective MPC&A systems. The United States and Russia should agree now that whatever disposition options are chosen, a stringent standard of safety, security, and international accountability will be maintained.

The US-Russian Independent Commission, in its interim report, recommended not only that both countries pursue a two-track approach to plutonium disposition, but that the two countries agree on a range of non-proliferation and monitoring provisions as well. In particular, the Commission recommended that the United States and Russia begin negotiations with the aim of ensuring that their warhead dismantlement and materials-disposition programmes proceed in parallel, ultimately reducing to equivalent remaining levels of plutonium and HEU in their two military stockpiles.

Once the excess weapon plutonium has been transformed into forms that are no easier to use in nuclear weapons than plutonium in spent fuel, the weapon plutonium disposition campaign itself can be considered complete. The urgent security problem posed by large stockpiles of excess weapon plutonium will then have been reduced to a part of the broader, longer-term problem of management of spent fuel and other nuclear wastes. The forms resulting from plutonium disposition will be suitable for secure storage for decades, while approaches for their final fate are being prepared. Nevertheless, in the long run, whatever plutonium remains in spent fuel or in immobilized waste forms will need to find final resting places with appropriate levels of protection against intruders, of isolation from the biosphere, and of monitoring to verify that the protection and isolation are being maintained.

This last stage of the management process might involve direct disposal of spent fuel and immobilized waste forms in geologic repositories, or it might involve additional treatment (with or without reprocessing, in advanced reactors or accelerator-driven subcritical reactors, or otherwise) to fission more of the plutonium or to increase the durability of its packaging, before it is emplaced in its final resting place. In this last stage, the residuals from the utilization or other disposition of military plutonium will represent only a small fraction of a larger quantity of similar residuals from civilian nuclear energy activities and from the management of other military radioactive wastes. Extensive studies of the options for ultimate disposal of these similar waste forms are underway in Russia, the USA, and elsewhere; and, while the addition of the residuals from disposition of military plutonium adds a few complications to these studies, there is much less urgency about making the final decisions than there is about the three prior stages of nuclear explosive materials management.

Of course, the ultimate disposition of separated civilian plutonium is also an issue. This plutonium, amounting to over 150 tonnes today, is not much more difficult to use in nuclear explosives than is separated military plutonium and so requires a comparable degree of protection. The United States and Russia should cooperate with each other and with other countries to ensure that stockpiles of separated civilian plutonium and HEU worldwide are publicly declared to enhance transparency, placed under international safeguards, and handled with stringent standards of MPC&A as appropriate to the threat of theft or diversion of this weapon-usable material. How to minimize the total quantities of this material in storage prior to its irradiation in reactor fuel – or its immobilization with pre-existing radioactive wastes – is a matter for further study and discussion.

In the long run, the security risks from spent fuel will increase as the fission-product radioactivity decays and as the technical sophistication needed to separate out the plutonium becomes more widespread. It may then be appropriate to protect spent fuel (including the spent fuel from reactor disposition of military plutonium) to a greater degree than has been thought necessary up until now, to accelerate the process of placing it in geologic repositories, or to burn up more of the contained plutonium using advanced reactors or accelerator-driven systems.

If nuclear energy is to make a large contribution to world electricity generation over the long run, it will be necessary either to tap the vast but dilute uranium resources in seawater or to recycle large quantities of bomb-usable plutonium "bred" from uranium-238 (or, equivalently, bomb-usable uranium-233 "bred" from thorium). Recycling plutonium or uranium-233 on such a large scale without creating significant security risks is likely to require MPC&A measures at least as challenging as those being contemplated currently for military plutonium, or to require the use of proliferation-resistant advanced reactor and fuel cycle technologies that are not yet fully developed.

Reform and Diversification of Nuclear Cities

All of the measures described above are essential parts of reducing the risk that nuclear weapons and weapon-usable material fall into the wrong hands. None of these efforts will be successful in the long run, however, absent a still broader agenda of reform, including improving the economic conditions of those responsible for nuclear weapons and materials. Desperate people are ingenious in overcoming obstacles; whatever technologies are deployed, significant proliferation risks will continue to exist if the personnel who must guard and manage nuclear weapons and fissile materials are underemployed, ill-paid, embedded in a culture of growing crime and corruption, and confronted with an uncertain future offering no assurance that they will be able to provide the necessities of life for themselves and their families. These issues can only be addressed as part of a broad effort devoted to economic renewal in the FSU and the establishment of a strengthened legal system able to cope with crime and corruption.

A critical step in that broader effort will be developing new businesses to diversify the economic base of the nuclear cities in the FSU. Economic collapse in these cities would pose a serious threat to the security of the United States, given the large quantities of nuclear weapons and nuclear materials stored there. Moreover, as long as these cities have no new mission, they will continue to lobby energetically for the continuation of their past missions – production of nuclear weapons and weapon-usable materials. The 1994 episode in which a sit-down strike by unpaid workers at Krasnoyarsk-26 ultimately provoked President Yeltsin to come to the site to promise a new nuclear reactor and completion of a gigantic new plutonium reprocessing facility, is a case in point. Thus, diversifying the economic base of these cities will be a fundamental part of achieving US security objectives over the long term.

This will not be easy. These cities were created for one purpose and one purpose only: the production of nuclear weapons and their essential ingredients. By design, they are remote and isolated, limiting the opportunities for trade. They remain "closed cities," meaning that no one can enter or leave without special permission. In general, they have seen less of the benefits of reform than virtually any other part of Russia. They are, in the words of one US defence conversion expert, economic "basket cases." Thus, efforts to develop new businesses in these cities are certain to be difficult, and are likely to require substantial subsidies.

Some programmes designed to foster such diversification are already underway. The International Science and Technology Centre (ISTC) in Moscow, the similar centre in Kiev, and a variety of lab-to-lab programmes, are already employing thousands of former Soviet weapons scientists in useful civilian work. (Thousands more, however, are still focusing their efforts on weapons of mass destruction, or remain underemployed.) Existing defence conversion programmes have begun contributing to the shift of some facilities from commercial to civilian production. While the programme that is planned to play the principal role in US defence conversion efforts in the future, the government-industry partnership known as the Defense Enterprise Fund (DEF), is targeted specifically to conversion of facilities involved in weapons of mass destruction, it is also targeted to enterprises likely to be profitable after getting a kick-start from outside funding. As a result, few, if any, of the initial 82 enterprises to be funded are in the closed cities. The Industrial Partnering Programme (IPP), which finances (with both government and industry funds) partnerships linking US industry with technologies developed in US and Russian laboratories is promising but has not yet led to the creation of self-sustaining commercial enterprises.

These efforts simply do not match the huge scale of the task. A substantial international effort is needed to identify new projects that could diversify the economic base of these cities. In some cases, nuclear cities are already diversifying, and have considerable potential for developing profitable new enterprises. In other cases, however, major cultural change and substantial subsidies will be required if these cities are to have any economic future independent of production of nuclear weapons.

A useful first step might be to organize business development conferences in each of the major nuclear cities, bringing together local interests with ideas for new businesses, Russian and foreign investors, and international banks and financial institutions. Such conferences could work to identify new enterprises that could be developed strictly through private investment, as well as outlining the scale of the subsidy that might be required for other enterprises to ultimately become self-sustaining. The emphasis should be on partnership with private industry, in order to target funds toward projects that business identifies as having a substantial chance of being a success. Ultimately, the international community may have to provide loans and grants of hundreds of millions or billions of dollars to provide a reliable economic future for these cities. This should be viewed as an investment in security, not simply a subsidy to another nation's economy. (This could be compared, for example, with the substantial sums in energy improvements in Ukraine which the G-7 appear to be prepared to provide, to enable the shut-down of the Chernobyl reactor.)

Synergies

The plan outlined above would involve a wide array of major programmes, each with its own complexities and issues, stretching for years into the future. In implementing any such a programme, it will be essential to prioritize the key objectives, co-ordinate the efforts closely, and seize opportunities for synergies between different parts of the programme.

All of the parts of this programme can and should contribute to each other. Technologies and institutional relationships developed in the course of upgrading MPC&A will also contribute to building transparency. Data exchanges and reciprocal visits carried out under the transparency programme will provide vital information for the effort to upgrade MPC&A. Storage and disposition of excess plutonium and HEU will inevitably be integrally linked. New businesses for the nuclear cities will inevitably include efforts in all these areas, including fissile material disposition, production of MPC&A equipment, and the like.

In particular, the large sums of money involved in the HEU purchase can provide substantial leverage for accomplishing other nuclear security objectives. Looked at in isolation, raising the billion dollars or more that might be required to finance plutonium disposition in Russia might seem extremely difficult. But, as one example, the United States could agree to purchase another 100 tonnes of HEU – a 20 per cent addition to the 500-tonne deal already underway – linked to a Russian commitment to spend the resulting income on financing disposition of 50-100 tonnes of plutonium. If considered together, disposition of the plutonium and HEU from dismantled weapons is likely to make a profit overall. Alternatively, such an additional purchase might be linked to a Russian commitment to finance specific steps to upgrade MPC&A.

Conclusions

The control of plutonium and HEU – the essential ingredients of nuclear weapons – is one of the most serious and urgent security challenges facing the world in the coming decade. Nothing could be more central to world security than ensuring that nuclear weapons and the materials needed to make them do not fall into the hands of rogue states or terrorist groups.

Meeting this challenge will require a comprehensive programme of action on many fronts. To succeed, this programme will require more energetic leadership and substantially more money – from the United States, from Russia, and from other countries – than it has had to date. The programmes outlined above will cost several billion dollars over the next decade or more. Although substantial, particularly in the current atmosphere of budget constraints, these sums are tiny by comparison to the several hundred billion dollars the world now spends annually in the name of "defence."

Notes

1.   Committee on International Security and Arms Control (CISAC), National Academy of Sciences, *Management and Disposition of Excess Weapons Plutonium*, National Academy Press, 1994; Panel on Reactor-Related Options for the Management and Disposition of Excess Weapons Plutonium, CISAC, *Management and Disposition of Excess Weapons Plutonium: Reactor-Related Options*, National Academy Press, 1995; President's Committee of Advisors on Science and Technology (PCAST), *Cooperative US/Former Soviet Union Programs on Nuclear Materials Protection, Control, and Accounting* (Secret), Office of Science and Technology Policy, Executive Office of the President, March 1995 (summarized in unclassified testimony by J. Holdren before the Subcommittee on Europe, Senate Foreign Relations Committee, and the Permanent Subcommittee on Investigations, Senate Committee on Governmental Affairs, U.S. Congress, 23 August 1995); and Independent Bilateral Scientific Commission on Plutonium Disposition, *Interim Report*, President's Committee of Advisors on Science and Technology, the White House, and Russian Academy of Sciences, 16 September 1996. The current article draws heavily on a November 1995 paper entitled "Reducing the Threat of Nuclear Theft in the Former Soviet Union: Outline of a Comprehensive Plan" commissioned from J. Holdren by Senator Richard Lugar and published in abbreviated form in the September 1996 issue of *Arms Control Today.*
    We are also indebted to the publications on this subject by Frank von Hippel and his colleagues at the Federation of American Scientists and the Center for Energy and Environmental Studies at Princeton University; by Thomas Cochran, Chris Paine, and their colleagues at the Natural Resources Defense Council; by William Potter and his colleagues at the Monterrey Institute of International Relations; by Arjun Makhijani and his colleagues at the Institute for Energy and Environmental Research; and the book Avoiding Nuclear Anarchy (Cambridge, MA: MIT Press, 1996) by Graham Allison and his colleagues at Harvard's Center for Science and International Affairs.
    2. For a detailed account of Project Sapphire, see W.C. Potter, "Project Sapphire: US-Kazakhstani Cooperation for Nonproliferation," in J.M. Shields and W.C. Potter eds., *Dismantling the Cold War: US and NIS Perspectives on the Nunn-Lugar Cooperative Threat Reduction Program*, Cambridge, MA: MIT Press, 1997.
    3. Testimony of Gordon Oehler, Director, Nonproliferation Center, Central Intelligence Agency, Senate Armed Services Committee, January 31, 1995, Senate Hearing. 104-35, p. 4.
    4. Committee on International Security and Arms Control, National Academy of Sciences *Management and Disposition of Excess Weapons Plutonium*, National Academy Press, January 1994.
    5. American Nuclear Society, *Protection and Management of Plutonium*, Special Panel Report, La Grange Park, Il.: American Nuclear Society, August 1995.

6. Panel on Reactor-Related Options, Committee on International Security and Arms Control,National Academy of Sciences, *Management and Disposition of Excess Weapons Plutonium: Reactor-Related Options*, National Academy Press, July 1995.

7. John P. Holdren (U.S. Co-Chair), Evgeniy P. Velikhov (Russian Co-Chair), John F. Ahearne, Richard L. Garwin, Wolfgang K. H. Panofsky, John Taylor, Alexei Makarov, Fedor Mitenkov, Nikolai Ponomarev-Stepnoi, Fedor Reshetnikov, Dmitri Tsourikov, and Matthew Bunn (Independent Bilateral Scientific Commission on Plutonium Disposition), *Interim Report*, President's Committee of Advisors on Science and Technology, the White House, and Russian Academy of Sciences, 16 September 1996.

6

Breakout from a Nuclear Weapons Convention

Tom Milne and Joseph Rotblat

Introduction

Although the argument that nuclear disarmament is desirable in principle is gradually being won, many of those who are persuaded that it is desirable still doubt that it is feasible. They have two main reservations. First, a nuclear weapon state might circumvent the verification system and hide some bombs "in the basement." Second, a state might secretly build up a nuclear arsenal *after* the Nuclear Weapons Convention (NWC) has entered into force.

No-one denies that there are potential dangers: verification is not foolproof, the nuclear genie is out of the bottle. But these are not arguments against nuclear disarmament. If they were, then they would argue against *all* disarmament. The same points apply to chemical weapons, for example, yet we have the Chemical Weapons Convention (CWC).

The CWC was agreed because the nations that have signed it believe that it will make the world safer from chemical warfare than it would be if the Convention did not exist. To argue that nuclear disarmament is feasible one needs only to show that an NWC would likewise provide more security than the alternative, namely, widespread reliance on nuclear deterrence.

But the enormous destructive power of nuclear weapons does make them a special case. An NWC will have to move beyond the CWC in two fundamental respects. First, adherence to an NWC must be universal. Second, there must be a high degree of openness in all scientific research. We elaborate on these two pre-requisites below. In other ways, an NWC could be modelled on the CWC, according to which states undertake never to "develop, produce, otherwise acquire, stockpile, or retain chemical weapons ... use chemical weapons ... assist, encourage or induce, in any way, anyone to engage in any activity prohibited by the CWC."

The discussion of breakout in this chapter is based on the assumption that such a convention banning nuclear weapons – with a verification regime to detect violations and with provision for punishing violators – has been agreed and come into force.

Pre-requisites for a Nuclear Weapons Convention

It is most unlikely that the nuclear weapon states will sign an NWC if even one nation refuses to do so, thereby implying that it might retain nuclear weapons or acquire them in the future. The Convention will have to be adhered to by all nations without a right of withdrawal. When a clear majority of nations, including all the nuclear weapon states, have agreed on the terms of the Convention, it will be made binding on all states. At present there is no mechanism to compel a nation to become a party to an international treaty against its wishes. But, given the political will, the legal and practical means to impose an absolute ban on a class of weapon would be found.

With 187 nations already members of the NPT, universal adherence to an NWC should not be too difficult to achieve, once the nuclear weapon states have signed up. The three significant states outside the NPT – India, Pakistan and Israel – could be brought in. India has always favoured an NWFW and is unlikely to oppose an NWC. Pakistan links its policy to India's. Israel, subject as it is to US pressure, could not stand alone outside an NWC. In any case, Israel is seeking a zone free of weapons of mass destruction in the Middle East.

The second pre-requisite, openness, is based on the same logic. An agreement to ban nuclear weapons will never be reached if any country is allowed to run an establishment in which secret research is carried out. This, in effect, would be equivalent to permitting the retention of nuclear weapons.

Openness will mean that the nuclear establishments, such as Los Alamos and Livermore in the USA, Chelyabinsk and Arzamas in Russia, Mianyang in China, Aldermaston in the UK, and the planned Mégajoules laser facility in France, will have to close down or convert completely to peaceful research carried out in the open. Here too difficulties will arise about research that is genuinely peaceful but is carried out in secret to protect commercial rights or a potential Nobel Prize-winning idea.

Incentives for Breakout

With these pre-requisites met, and a convention banning nuclear weapons in force, we begin by asking what incentives a state might have to break out. We also ask the related question, what would happen if breakout were to occur?

As we have said, there are two main ways in which an NWC could be violated: (i) one or more of the current nuclear weapon states could secretly retain a number of weapons, or a quantity of fissile material; (ii) a state could build up a clandestine nuclear arsenal after the NWC has entered into force. (Strictly speaking, only the latter should be called "breakout," but clearly both must be considered when discussing security in an NWFW.) The first is probably more important because it is easier to hide away a small number of weapons from a large arsenal than it is to build up an arsenal from scratch in secret.

(i) *Illegal Retention of Nuclear Weapons by a Nuclear Weapon State – the "Bomb in the Basement"*

A state might hide away a number of nuclear weapons from its arsenal, or a quantity of fissile material for weapons, for one of three purposes: (a) offensive – to use nuclear weapons to conquer the world or a specific region; (b) defensive – to use nuclear weapons if attacked; (c) as a hedge against another state violating the Convention.

(a) The retention of nuclear weapons by one of the nuclear weapon states for offensive purposes appears to us to be inconceivable. Let us consider what such a scenario would involve. An inner governing circle, together with a number of scientists and technicians, would maintain a secret nuclear arsenal in the face of an unequivocal, legal commitment to nuclear disarmament made by the government, both to its own people and to the rest of the world. At some point in time, out of the blue, the Head of State would announce that the government's stated policy had been a sham, a deliberate ploy to acquire a monopoly on nuclear weapons in order to conquer other countries. Frankly, if the world is such that a Machiavellian plot of this sort is in any way plausible, we will not get close to eliminating nuclear weapons in the first place.

Fortunately the world is not like this. Those who take seriously the "offensive" motivation for cheating on an NWC ignore the fundamental changes that have occurred in the world since the end of World War II, and in particular since the end of the Cold War. The division between Communism and anti-Communism that dominated the world is gone. Classical colonization has come to an end. Democratic regimes are on the increase. National sovereignty is being given up as international treaties acquire near universal acceptance. The globe is shrinking thanks to the fantastic progress in communications and transportation. We are all becoming more and more interdependent. The notion of any nation trying to conquer the world, or even any region within it, is outdated.

To be more specific, let us look at the five nuclear states that will have signed the Convention. Which of them could be considered an expansionist power, desiring territorial expansion, and needing nuclear weapons for this purpose? The United States has no territorial ambitions. The idea that France or the UK might try to recreate their imperial past is ludicrous. China has always adhered to the doctrine that its nuclear weapons are solely to deter the USA and Russia. As for Russia, it will for years be concerned with its internal problems. The idea that it would try to recreate dominance over Eastern Europe by means of nuclear weapons, after having agreed to nuclear disarmament, is not realistic. Similar arguments apply to the threshold nuclear weapon states.

(b) The second incentive, to keep nuclear weapons to use *in extremis* in conventional war, ceases to be valid once the Convention banning nuclear weapons comes into force. A global no-first-use policy will precede the Convention, *i.e.* the Convention will have as its basis the conviction that nuclear weapons are not needed to counter conventional forces. Before nuclear weapons are eliminated the powerful countries in the world will have agreed explicitly that nuclear weapons are needed only to deter the use of other nuclear weapons – not for any other purpose.

(c) The most plausible, but still very unlikely, incentive for cheating is the third: as a hedge against cheating by another nuclear state for one of the above purposes. We see it as the most plausible because it would be understandable if a state was not one hundred per cent confident that all other states were adhering fully to the terms of the Convention.

We say, however, that it is unlikely to be an incentive for illegally retaining nuclear weapons because each of the nuclear weapon states, if thinking logically, is bound to arrive at the conclusion that its potential opponents have no incentive to cheat, except as an insurance against others doing this, and if so, that there is no need for any of them to take this course. The small temptation for a state to hedge against cheating by another is far outweighed by the high probability that, in an open world, it will be caught cheating by the Convention's verification system, and face the ensuing opprobrium and punishment.

(ii) Build up of a Clandestine Nuclear Arsenal – Breakout

Even if the NWS have strictly adhered to the Convention, and eliminated all their nuclear weapons, there is still the possibility that one of them, or another state, might at some future date decide to build up a nuclear arsenal in secret. In our opinion this too carries a very low probability.

In discussing the possible reasons for breakout some time in the future, we have to bear in mind the changed attitude to nuclear weapons that will form in the course of nuclear disarmament. There is likely to be a widespread process of re-education in parallel with the disarmament process in order to secure popular support for the elimination of nuclear weapons. There will be clear statements from governments that the risks from nuclear weapons outweigh the benefits, that nuclear weapons pose an intolerable danger, along the lines of the statement made by the Canberra Commission. Nuclear weapons will become marginalized in the public eye. They will be declared illegal, and their use in any circumstances deemed a crime against humanity. Already the prospect of using nuclear weapons is, for most people, quite unimaginable. This change in thinking on nuclear weapons will have advanced further by the time that nuclear weapons are finally eliminated. All this will greatly reduce the incentives for breakout.

In the light of this change of attitudes, the arguments that we advanced for thinking that it is unlikely that a nuclear weapon state would hide nuclear weapons during the disarmament process apply with greater force to breakout by one of these states after the Nuclear Weapons Convention is in place. They also apply to other governments that base their security policies on rational lines. Countries, such as Israel, that feel threatened by neighbours will seek security in alliances with powerful countries, and enforceable international treaties, rather than relying on an illegal nuclear arsenal.

The above arguments may not apply, however, to a "rogue" state, characterized by an irrational leader, or by the adoption of an irrational doctrine. The history of this century has shown that fanatics may come to power, that irrational leaders hankering after world domination may emerge.

The most serious situation would be if a rogue regime were to come to power in one of the world's most powerful countries, a former nuclear weapon state, for example. But changes of this kind do not occur without warning. There would be time for other major powers to adjust their policies, warn the new regime of the consequences of a breach of the Convention, and, if necessary, to take pre-emptive action, including, possibly, reacquiring nuclear weapons.

If the rogue state was a minor power, then it would know that it would incur the wrath of the world, and be defeated in a conventional military operation. Currently, international military actions tend to depend on the region of the world affected, and on the parochial interests of a few powerful countries. There has been no systematic planning for dealing with aberrant nuclear threats. In a nuclear-weapon-free world, the possibility of breakout will have been carefully thought through, and plans for responding to breakout worked out. The major powers will have an overwhelming preponderance of conventional forces and there will be a common interest among these countries in preserving the Nuclear Weapons Convention, ensuring that concerted action will be taken against a rogue aggressor.

Prevention of Breakout

The central element of a Nuclear Weapons Convention will be a verification system designed to detect any violation of the Convention early enough for preemptive action to be taken, and in this way to deter attempts to break out in the first place.

As Steve Fetter argues in this book (Chapter 3), we do not have the technology that could give us a hundred per cent assurance that a nuclear weapon state has not hidden away a number of bombs or an amount of fissile material. Neither are we able to quantify the risk in terms of numbers of nuclear weapons that a state could hide or produce in secret without being detected. The risks vary from country to country. They also depend on the existing verification technology, technical advances that may be made (those that would make verification easier and those that would make it more difficult), and the supporting societal verification processes. Fetter discusses, in broad terms, the upper bounds of what might be successfully concealed.

At the same time, a cheating state could not be certain that it would avoid detection. Even if it believed that it could avoid detection by technical means, there would always be the possibility that accidents, serendipity, or plain bad luck might take a hand. All this would make the offending state less confident, and the uncertainty this created would have a deterring effect.

The technological means for detecting a secret nuclear weapons programme are much better than those for detecting the "bomb in the basement." There are powerful techniques for detecting secret nuclear reactors, reprocessing plants, and enrichment facilities. Besides this, more people would be involved in a programme to build weapons than would be needed to maintain a hidden arsenal, further increasing the probability that the programme would be discovered early enough to take action. Once again, perfect verification is not possible, but it should be possible to ensure that there is a strong probability of detecting any secret programme, and near certainty of detecting a programme on a significant scale.

Supplementing the technological verification regime would be arrangements to encourage verification by the society at large (see Chapter 4). The basis of societal verification is that in the Convention banning nuclear weapons there will be a clause requiring every country to enact national legislation that makes it the right and the duty of its citizens to notify an international authority about any activity that contravenes the Convention. Even in a dictatorial regime, citizen's reporting cannot be completely controlled by the authorities; indeed, reporting will become easier as electronic communications develop. Established systems of citizen's reporting, supplemented by organized monitoring by the scientific community, and legal protection for whistle-blowing, will further deter a nation contemplating breaking out from a nuclear-weapon-free regime.

Operating in parallel, these two systems of verification, technological and societal, should go a long way towards deterring breakout, or, failing that, detecting breakout in its early stages.

Comparable Risks Over Time

Let us summarize the argument. A NWFW will be maintained by a Nuclear Weapons Convention of which every nation is a member. The NWC will be vigorously verified in a climate of openness. There will be a general preparedness among the world's powerful nations to preserve the NWC with conventional forces. Nuclear weapons will, in general, be thought of as dangerous relics of a past age. Even in such a world, it remains possible that one or more states would try to break out, but there is no good reason to expect this. Conversely, there are many reasons to think that a state would be deterred from breakout by the prospect of early discovery, and by the inevitable hostile reaction of the rest of the world should it succeed.

This is not to suggest that breakout carries only trivial risks, but it does bring into question whether these risks justify abandoning the goal of nuclear disarmament. To answer this question we need to consider the *comparable* risks that would face the world if nations retain their nuclear weapons. As stressed at the beginning of this chapter, and throughout this book, the core of the case for nuclear disarmament is the quest for a world more secure than at present, not for a world that is completely safe. The following are a few examples of relative risk considerations.

–   It is argued that if small numbers of nuclear weapons were to be reacquired by one or more states, the situation would become unstable, with races to rebuild nuclear arsenals and increasing pressures for pre-emptive use of nuclear weapons. There could indeed be a new arms race, but it does not follow that all the moral restraints on the use of nuclear weapons would evaporate; that all the arguments that had persuaded nations to disarm in the first place would go out of the window; and that counsel for calm and restraint would not be heard in the period when the weapons were being produced. No justification is given for thinking that such a total reversal of reasoning would take place. If, in the extreme case, a few nuclear weapons were used following breakout, this would be a catastrophe, but one from which the world would recover. On the other hand, if there is no NWC and nuclear weapons remain in national arsenals, there is a real danger of large scale nuclear war that could annihilate the human species.

–   The chance of nuclear weapons passing into "irrational" hands will be greater if nuclear weapons are retained by a number of countries than if global disarmament is pursued. If a nuclear capability is acquired by a leader who does not care if he loses a city to a nuclear strike, or is totally fanatical and consequently undeterrable, then the nuclear weapon states will be no better equipped to deal with such a madman if they retain their nuclear arsenals than they would be in an NWFW. A national leader so reckless as to take on the world with nuclear weapons, after a Nuclear

Weapons Convention is in place, fits this description. If we are worried about so-called irrational dictators acquiring bombs, then the case for nuclear disarmament is very strong.

- Nuclear terrorism is less likely in a nuclear-weapon-free world than it is today. If nuclear terrorism is held to be a realistic threat, then this is another argument in favour of disarmament. As in the case of an irrational state leader, the nuclear weapon states have no means to respond to, or deter, nuclear terrorism today. In fact, in a nuclear-weapon-free world it would probably be easier to trace the source of the fissile material used, and perhaps identify a government that had assisted the group with money or resources, than it would be today.

- At a philosophical level, if nuclear disarmament is rejected because of the possibility of breakout, it would signal that human society has still not found a way to deal with undesirable outcomes of advances in science and technology. It is not just nuclear weapons that threaten the human species – other technical means of mass destruction will come along in the future. If we are to survive, then we have to find ways to regulate societal behaviour, starting by outlawing nuclear weapons.

It is wrong-headed to contrast the danger of breakout from an NWC with what seems *today* to be a low risk of major nuclear conflict, a point made by Michael MccGwire (Chapter 1). The proper comparison is with the nuclear dangers that might develop over the coming decades if nuclear weapons are retained. The proponents of nuclear weapons do not give any reason to suppose that new nuclear tensions will not develop, that there will not be nuclear proliferation. Instead, they emphasize that the future is uncertain and unpredictable.

Getting to Zero: Breakout in the Final Stages of Disarmament

While the main concern in this chapter is breakout in a world in which nuclear weapons have been banned, the problem of breakout during the process of disarmament, before getting to zero, is also of great importance. There is a widely held concern that the disarmament process would be unstable when the numbers of nuclear weapons were reduced to hundreds or tens – more unstable than when disarmament is complete.

We do not see why this should be so. A state would not be likely to embark on a crash programme to produce new nuclear weapons in the late stages of a disarmament process, or reveal that it had concealed a number of warheads, for the same reasons that it would not be likely to break out after a nuclear-weapon-free world had been established. In both cases, a state would have reached a careful judgement that global nuclear disarmament was in its best interests. It would not readily reverse this weighty decision. The general change in attitudes to nuclear weapons, in the minds of both decision-makers and the general public, would have begun to set in.

Since the verification regime may not be fully operational throughout the disarmament process, it is possible that, at some stage, one party may have a temporary preponderance of nuclear weapons. It is hard to see what a state could hope to gain from such an "advantage." It could not possibly achieve a first strike capability. States would make provisions to station their remaining nuclear weapons invulnerably in the case of a rise in international tensions. The idea that any of the nuclear weapon states would attempt a disarming first strike against another is far fetched in any case. The more basic point is that nuclear disarmament will not take place in a climate of fear and hostility.

An idea that has been put forward – to try to reduce the chance of disarmament breaking down in its final stages – is that the residual nuclear weapons, though physically remaining in the control of national military authorities, would formally be put at the service of the United Nations. This can be envisaged as a half-way house towards an international nuclear force. It has been further suggested by a number of people, including some who have had direct experience of managing nuclear weapons, that serious consideration should be given to providing the United Nations with an autonomous nuclear force in order to deter breakout. The United Nations force is usually conceived of as a temporary construction – designed as an insurance against cheating in the early years of an NWFW – that would be disbanded as soon as all nations were confident that their opponents had destroyed their nuclear weapons as they had stated that they had done.

There are many reasons to doubt the credibility and desirability of a UN force. It is difficult to imagine the UN authorizing the use of a weapon that would cause death and disease among innocent people, including inhabitants of countries not involved in the conflict. These doubts aside, decisive arguments against such a force have been made. Foremost is the argument that if the nuclear weapon states decide that they do not need nuclear weapons then there is no case for a UN nuclear force either. The converse is equally true: if a case can be made for the UN having nuclear weapons, then the same case can be made for nuclear weapons remaining in national hands. To take the example of the most powerful country today, it is far easier to imagine that the USA would embrace the idea of an NWFW than it is to imagine that it would rely on the United Nations to guarantee its protection against a continuing nuclear danger.

To make a case for transferring nuclear weapons to UN control would involve contradicting all the arguments made in this chapter. It would imply that breakout is a realistic danger, that it presents a grave threat, and that a non-nuclear response to breakout would be inadequate. For these reasons, a UN nuclear force would hinder nuclear disarmament, not advance its cause.

Conclusion

Although breakout is a potential danger, this danger can be exaggerated. There are formidable political constraints, arising from rational thinking on world affairs, working to deter any state from this action. The incentives for breakout are less weighty than is often imagined, and the probability of early detection of attempts to cheat is quite high. A state that defied the world by producing nuclear weapons in an NWFW would have little to gain and everything to lose from this action. It should be obvious to a minor government considering breakout that any advantage that it might gain would be short-lived, and that its long-term survival chances, with the whole world ganged up against it, would be almost non-existent. It seems inconceivable that a state would not rehearse these arguments before deciding to break out from an NWC and therefore decide against going along such a suicidal path. Equally, it should be obvious to a powerful country, or alliance of countries, contemplating breakout that this would only have the effect of returning the world to a Cold War situation. For these reasons alone, the breakout problem is not likely to arise in an NWFW. The risks that breakout would present, if it did occur, are far lower than the comparable risks that nations will face if they continue to rely on nuclear deterrence. Our conclusion is that the threat of breakout does not provide a reason for abandoning the goal of a nuclear-weapon-free world.

PART TWO

The Road to Zero: Progress and Regress

7

Progress in Nuclear Weapons Reductions

Thomas B. Cochran, Robert S. Norris
and Christopher E. Paine

The Disarmament "Obligation" of the Nuclear Weapon Powers

Since March 1970, the nuclear weapon parties to the Treaty on the Non-Proliferation of Nuclear Weapons (NPT) have been subject to the nuclear disarmament obligation contained in Article VI, which requires that "effective measures related to cessation of the arms race" – such as the Comprehensive Test Ban Treaty (CTBT) and a "cut-off" of fissile material production for weapons – be pursued in good faith "at an early date." Good faith negotiations, not necessarily at an early date, are also required on "effective measures related to nuclear disarmament," which the NPT Preamble further describes as "effective measures *in the direction of* nuclear disarmament," leading to "the elimination from national arsenals of nuclear weapons and their means of delivery *pursuant to* a treaty on general and complete disarmament under strict and effective international control" (emphasis added).

Despite the failure of the nuclear weapon powers to achieve the cessation of the arms race at an early date, this race had indeed abated considerably by the time of the NPT's 25 year Review and Extension Conference in May 1995, with several arms reduction and arms race cessation measures already in place or pending. The Conference agreed to extend the NPT indefinitely; it also endorsed a "programme of action" to achieve the "full realization and effective implementation of Article VI," including "the determined pursuit by the nuclear weapon-states of systematic and progressive efforts to reduce nuclear weapons globally, with the ultimate goals of eliminating those weapons, and by all States of general and complete disarmament under strict and effective international control."

A recent advisory opinion of the World Court finds that "there exists an obligation to pursue in good faith and to bring to a conclusion negotiations leading to nuclear disarmament in all its aspects under strict and effective international control." This ruling differs from the wording of Article VI of the NPT; there is no link between this obligation on nuclear weapons and a wider move to general and complete disarmament. The obligation stands without conditions or caveats attached.

In this chapter we assess the progress made by the nuclear weapon states (NWS) towards the ultimate goal of a nuclear-weapon-free world (NWFW) in the following areas:

–   US and Russian strategic arms reductions;
–   reduction in the overall size of the nuclear weapon stockpiles;
–   data exchange, transparency and nuclear stockpile verification measures.

Strategic Arms Reductions

START I and II

START I entered into force on 5 December 1994, and by the end of 2001, the treaty requires each side to have reduced its strategic nuclear forces to 1600 deployed delivery vehicles having 6000 "accountable" warheads, of which 4900 can be ballistic missile warheads.

Presidents Bush and Yeltsin concluded a framework agreement for START II on 17 June 1992, negotiated a further seven months and signed START II on 3 January 1993. Beginning 1 January 2003, the Treaty limits the warheads on each side's intercontinental strategic forces to 3500 "accountable warheads," of which no more than 1750 may be deployed on MIRVed Submarine-Launched Ballistic Missiles (SLBMs), and the balance on single-warhead ballistic missiles and/or bombers.[1] "Heavy" intercontinental ballistic missiles (ICBMs) and MIRVed ICBMs are banned. "Reserve" stocks of strategic nuclear warheads, and nuclear weapons deliverable by shorter range systems, such as sea-launched cruise missiles and tactical aircraft, are not covered by the agreement.

On 26 January 1996 the US Senate approved a resolution consenting to ratification of START II by a vote of 87 to 4. However, the Russian State Duma has not done so, and a substantial body of opinion in Russia views the treaty as giving the United States a nuclear advantage. The Treaty is also regarded as too costly to implement on the agreed timetable because it requires the early retirement of Russian ICBMs before the end of their useful service life, and the production and deployment of an additional 500 single warhead ICBMs just to reach the 3000 warhead level by 2003. To maintain parity with the USA, additional resources would have to be dedicated for missile submarine and SLBM modernization, silo conversion, and improved C^3I systems.

Moreover, since 1995 the proposal to expand NATO eastward to include such nations as Poland, Hungary, and the Czech Republic has provided Russian hard-liners with an argument for not ratifying START II and for retaining large stocks of non-strategic nuclear weapons to offset a conventional imbalance, a logic reminiscent of NATO's during the Cold War. The Russian military leadership sees nuclear weapons as pre-eminent in deterring both conventional and nuclear war.

START III Negotiations

In the negotiations wh¹ ¯ resulted in the Joint Statement by Presidents Yeltsin and Clinton after their meeting in Helsinki in March 1997, the USA has recognized some of the Russian difficulties with START II. (The Joint Statement is given in Appendix A.) The deadline for the elimination of strategic nuclear delivery vehicles under that Treaty is extended to the end of 2007. It was also agreed that one basic component of a START III agreement would be to establish, by end-2007, lower aggregates of 2000-2500 nuclear warheads for each side. Further, the statement on START III components includes a reference to measures to prevent a rapid increase in the number of warheads. There is also the outline agreement limiting the capability of higher-altitude theatre missile defence systems. However, the requirement for the ratification of START II before START III negotiations begin still stands. The Duma may well wait to see the outcome of the NATO-Russian negotiations which are linked to NATO's proposed eastward expansion.

Implementation of START I. Implementation of START I by the five parties to the Treaty – the United States, Russia, Ukraine, Kazakhstan, and Belarus – is moving forward. The Treaty has been implemented in an orderly fashion since entering into force in December 1994. In fact, the USA had already reduced its operational strategic forces to START I levels before the Treaty entered into force, while continuing several modernization programmes. Modernization of Russian strategic forces proceeds at a very modest pace.

START I requires exchanges of data, at periodic intervals, about the status of strategic forces of the five parties. Since entry into force of the Treaty on 5 December 1994 there have been four updated memoranda of understanding (MOU) about the strategic forces. They have occurred at six month intervals – mid- and end-1995, and mid- and end-1996. After 90 days have elapsed they are made public.

United States Strategic Arms Reductions. There have been increases in the number of operational strategic nuclear weapons since 1994 due to the addition of the sixteenth and seventeenth Trident submarines. At the end of 1996 there were roughly 7000 strategic nuclear warheads deployed with US operational forces (Table 1). The number could rise in 1997 when the eighteenth and final submarine joins the force.

ICBMs. In 1995 the Air Force made the decision to consolidate the 500 Minuteman III ICBMs at three bases, from the current four. On 4 October 1995 the first of the Minuteman IIIs to be phased out at Grand Forks AFB, North Dakota began its transfer to Malmstrom AFB, Montana. The transfer will proceed at the rate of about one missile per week over three years. The schedule is to complete the emplacement at Malmstrom by April 1998. Then there will be 200 Minuteman IIIs at Malmstrom, and 150 each at Minot AFB, North Dakota and F.E. Warren AFB, Wyoming.

During 1995 work was completed in removing Minuteman IIs from their silos at three bases. Work then proceeded to blow up the silos in accordance with START. On 13 September 1996 the 149th silo was blown up at Ellsworth AFB, South Dakota, completing the programme well ahead of schedule. It is proposed that the 150th silo (Delta Nine) at Ellsworth AFB should become a museum, along with its launch control facility (Delta One), eleven miles away. Eventually the 150 Minuteman III silos at Grand Forks will be blown up after the transfer is completed.

At the time of writing, 300 missiles have the higher yield W78 warhead and 200 have the W62 warhead. To comply with the ban on MIRVs under START II, each of the 500 Minuteman III missiles will have the number of warheads reduced from three to one, if the Treaty enters into force (Table 2). It has been decided to replace the higher-yield W78s and older, lower-yield W62s with single W78s removed from the 50 Peacekeeper (MX) missiles. The W87 warhead has the preferred safety features, including insensitive high explosive (IHE), fire resistant pit (FRP), and enhanced nuclear detonation safety (ENDS), whereas the W78 only has ENDS.

A $5.2 billion programme is underway to extend the operational life of the Minuteman IIIs to the year 2020 and improve their capability. There are three major parts to the programme. First, launch control centres have been updated with Rapid Execution and Combat Targeting (REACT) consoles. The REACT programme was completed by the end of 1996. Second, improvements to the missile's guidance system will be implemented between 1998 and 2002. These measures eventually will increase the accuracy of the Minuteman III to near that of the current MX – a circular error probable of 100 metres. The third part involves "repouring" the first and second stages, incorporating the latest solid propellant and bonding technologies. The third stage will either be refurbished or rebuilt.

SSBNs and SLBMs. One new Ohio-class submarine, the USS *Maine* (SSBN-741), the sixteenth of the class, joined the fleet on 29 July 1995. The USS *Wyoming* (SSBN-742) joined the fleet on 13 July 1996 and the USS *Louisiana* (SSBN-743) will be delivered in 1997, completing the nuclear powered ballistic missile submarine (SSBN) fleet.

This is in keeping with the conclusions of the 1994 Nuclear Posture Review (NPR), which decided to complete construction of 18 Ohio-class submarines, and to retire four older SSBNs of the same class based in the Pacific at Bangor, Washington. Which four of the eight is under review. The current plan is to retain the four submarines until close to the 2003 target date for full implementation of the START II force reductions. If START II is implemented sooner, then the retirement dates could be advanced.

Another decision in the NPR was to purchase additional Trident II D-5 SLBMs for the four Bangor-based submarines that will remain. The increased Trident II programme now calls for purchase of 462 missiles at a cost of $27.7 billion, or $60 million per missile. This is an increase of 45 missiles and $2.2 billion in costs from previous levels. The Bangor base will have to be adapted to support the Trident II. The backfitting of the four SSBNs will take place from FY 2000 to FY 2005. Eventually, two or three submarines will be shifted from Kings Bay, Georgia to Bangor to balance the fourteen submarine fleet. To comply with START II, SLBMs will be "downloaded" from eight to five warheads each.

A third decision in the NPR was to have more SSBNs patrolling on "modified-alert" status than "alert" status. Modified alert apparently means that a lower percentage of SSBNs at sea routinely patrol within range of potential targets and maintain continuous communications with command authorities. This is a very minor adjustment. Two-thirds of the SSBNs are still at sea at any given time; patrol rates equal to those at the height of the Cold War remain unaltered, as does the practice of each SSBN having two crews. Reducing the patrol rate and going to one crew would constitute major changes. The Congressional Budget Office estimated that switching to single crews could save $300 million per year, or a total of $4.5 billion by the end of year 2010.

Like the ICBM force SLBM targeting and retargeting is being improved. The SLBM Strategic Retargeting System (SRS) operational requirement document was approved in 1995. When, and if, the SRS achieves an operational capability, ballistic missile submarines will have the ability to rapidly target and retarget Trident IIs to any spot on the globe.

Bombers. The first B-2 bomber was delivered to the 509th Bombardment Wing at Whiteman AFB, Missouri on 17 December 1993. The wing will have two squadrons, the 393rd and the 715th, each with eight planes. The first squadron, the 393rd, is scheduled to become operational in FY 1997. During 1994 four B-2s were delivered, another three in 1995, six in 1996, and one is planned for delivery in 1997. The 20th and last operational B-2 is scheduled to be delivered on 31 January 1998. In a change of plans all of the six (instead of five) aircraft now in the test programme will be modified to achieve an operational capability. The planes will be delivered in 1998, 1999, and 2000.

The B-2 remains controversial. The General Accounting Office concluded in an August 1995 report that, "After 14 years of development and evolving mission requirements, including six years of flight testing, the Air Force has yet to demonstrate that the B-2 design will meet some of its most important mission requirements." A congressionally mandated study, done by a Pentagon think tank and provided to Congress on 3 May 1995, concluded that the planned force of 20 B-2s is sufficient to meet future contingencies, a finding in concert with the Air Force and Defense Department positions.[2]

According to an Air Force estimate the programme acquisition costs for 20 operational aircraft, expressed in then-year dollars totals $44.389 billion, or $2.2 billion each. By comparison an average Boeing 747 costs about $155 million, and the new Boeing 777 costs about $130 million. By using other categories, such as "flyaway cost" or "procurement cost," which leave out significant expenses, such as $25 billion in development costs, unit costs for the B-2 can be made to seem half of what they really are.

Under START II the B-1B bombers will no longer be counted as nuclear weapon carriers. This transition to a conventional role is already occurring, though START II has not entered into force. By the end of 1997 the B-1 will be out of the SIOP mission altogether and oriented to conventional missions. However, under the "bomber hedge" option of the NPR, sufficient nuclear weapons will be retained in a reserve status to reconvert the B-1Bs to a nuclear role.

In 1994 the NPR determined that 66 B-52Hs would be retained, but the Department of Defense (DOD) later decided to keep 71, with 12 serving as trainers and another 15 put on attrition reserve/depot maintenance status. The Air Force estimates the B52Hs will be structurally sound until about 2030.

Russian Strategic Arms Reductions. With implementation of START I and the break-up of the Soviet Union, operational strategic nuclear forces have decreased markedly – over 325 ballistic missiles have been withdrawn from active service and over 3400 strategic warheads that were deployed in Ukraine, Kazakhstan, and Belarus have been transferred to Russia. From Kazakhstan all warheads were removed by April 1995; from Ukraine all strategic warheads – some 1900 – were removed between March 1994 and 1 June 1996, and all non-strategic warheads – some 2500 – were removed by May 1992; and from Belarus all warheads were removed by the end of 1996. The array of Russian nuclear forces at the end of 1996 is shown in Table 3.

Under START I counting rules, as of 1 January 1996, there were 1497 operational strategic launchers and 6681 warheads in Russia. In reality, some of the systems are not operational, and the bombers are capable of carrying more warheads than are attributed to them under START counting rules. By our estimates Russia's operational strategic force as of 1 January 1996, consisted of about 1253 launchers carrying about 6,685 warheads.

In Table 4, we have projected how Russian operational strategic forces might look in 2003, the previously agreed date for full implementation of START II reductions. We have projected four scenarios, two that assume START II will not be ratified by the Russian State Duma, and two that assume that it will be ratified. With respect to each of these two assumptions we project force levels based on two budget scenarios: (a) a "High Budget," which assumes sufficient funds will be made available to provide for extending the service life of some existing systems; and (b) a "Low Budget" that assumes a more rapid retirement of older systems. An interesting result of our projections is that, if START II is ratified, the permitted START II force level of some 3000-3500 strategic warheads is not reached under either of these two budget scenarios. This situation should provide incentives for the Russian security establishment to seek a nuclear balance with the USA at a lower, and more economically sustainable, level of forces, and for the United States to cuts its own costs by further reductions in the size and operating tempo of its nuclear forces. The Helsinki Joint Statement suggests that this point has now been recognized by both sides.

ICBMs. At full deployment there were 308 SS-18s in the Soviet Union, 104 in Kazakhstan and 204 in Russia. By the end of 1996 all SS-18s in Kazakhstan, and 24 in Russia are assumed to be non-operational, leaving 180 operational SS-18s in Russia as of 1 January 1997. Six silos at Dombarosvki and 12 at Uzhur have been blown up. Under START I Russia is permitted to retain 154 SS-18s. If START II is fully implemented, all SS-18 missiles must be destroyed, but Russia may convert up to 90 SS-18 silos for deployment of single-warhead, non-heavy, SS-25 type ICBMs.

As of the end of 1996 there were approximately 160 deployed SS-19s in Russia. If START II is not ratified, we assume about 120 SS-19 will be retained with six warheads each. Under the START II limits, Russia could retain up to 105 SS-19 missiles "downloaded" to a single warhead. Some in Russia would like to increase this number. As part of an agreement with Ukraine announced in November 1995, 32 SS-19s will be returned to Russia. After transfer they will be used as spares and for parts to support the SS-19 force that will remain deployed in Russia, with the purpose of extending the service life of the weapon system. The other SS-19s, once deployed in Ukraine, are being withdrawn and put in storage.

Of the original 56 silo-based SS-24 M2s, 46 were in Ukraine at Pervomaysk, and 10 are in Russia at Tatishchevo. Only the 10 in Russia are considered operational. In addition, there are 36 rail-based SS-24 M1s – 12 each at Bershet, Kostroma and Krasnoyarsk in Russia. If START II is ratified, these missiles must be converted to single warhead missiles or retired altogether.

SS-25s are deployed only in Russia. SS-25 deployment in Belarus peaked in December 1991 at 81 missiles at Lida and Mozyr. By the end of 1996 all had been removed.

The SS-25 is deployed in regiments of nine launchers, as was the SS-20. The SS-25 shares a nearly identical first-stage with the SS-20. Several of the bases (*e.g.*, Kansk and Novosibirsk) were used for the SS-20. The missile can be fired from field deployment sites or through the sliding-roof garage it occupies at its base. The SS-25 has a throwweight of 1000 kg, slightly smaller than the US Minuteman III at 1150 kg.

The SS-25, which is assembled at Votkinsk in Russia, is the only strategic weapon system still under production and will likely be the mainstay of the ICBM force if and when START II is implemented. On 20 December 1994 the Russians first flight-tested a variant of the SS-25 (called "Topol-M"). Flight tests continued during 1995 and 1996. The Topol-M, unlike earlier models, is being produced entirely in Russia, under the direction of designer Boris Lagutin. Previously various components were made in Ukraine and other republics. The Topol-M was scheduled to be operational at the end of 1996, but that schedule has now apparently slipped. It is planned for silo-basing but could also supplement or replace the mobile force.

SSBNs and SLBMs. More than one-half of the SSBN fleet have been withdrawn from operational service since 1990. Table 3 assumes that all the Yankee Is, Delta Is, Delta IIs, and one Delta III have been withdrawn, leaving 26 SSBNs of three classes (13 Delta III, 7 Delta IV and 6 Typhoon). These SSBNs are based on the Kola Peninsula and on the Kamchatka Peninsula.

The first Typhoon submarine, which entered the Severodvinsk shipyard in 1991 for overhaul, is still there. Five others await overhaul and missile conversion, giving rise to rumours that the entire class may be retired in the next five to ten years. One of the Typhoons is used for training, after an accident in 1992. No SSBNs or SLBMs are presently in production. The slow process of upgrading the six Typhoon-class submarines with a new missile (the so-called SS-N-26 to replace the SS-N-20) continues. A second new SLBM, for the Delta V, a new class of SSBN that might replace the Typhoon and Delta IV, is also under development.

Strategic Bombers. For the strategic bomber force (*Dalnyaya Aviatsiya-*DA) and tactical aircraft – always lesser priorities in Soviet/Russian armed forces – maintenance and modernization have been cut drastically and in some cases deferred completely. This is, in part, the result of a shrinking budget, but the fighting in Chechnya consumed a large share of the Russian Federation Air Force's (RFAF) operating funds, leaving units without fuel, spare parts, or adequate bases.

The 19 Blackjacks at Priluki air base in Ukraine are poorly maintained and basically non-operational, as are the 25 Bear H bombers at Uzin air base. An agreement, announced on 24 November 1995, calls for Ukraine to eventually return all the Blackjack and Bear bombers, and more than 300 cruise missiles, to Russia. The precise timing of the transfer and the amount of money to be paid were not made public. Bear H and Blackjack production has been terminated. It is likely that most of the planes will be used for spare parts to support the bombers in Russia, with only a very few, if any at all, returning to service.

Bear H bombers are configured in two ways, those that carry 16 ALCMs and those that carry 6 ALCMs. According to the 1 June 1996 START I MOU the bombers are deployed as follows: Bear H16 – 19 at Mozdok, 16 at Ukrainka, and 21 at Uzin (Ukraine). Bear H6 – 2 at Mozdok, 26 at Ukrainka, and 4 at Uzin (Ukraine). In addition to the 19 Blackjacks at Priluki there are six at Engels AFB near Saratov in Russia.

Reduction in the Overall Size of Nuclear Weapon Stockpiles

There is a wide disparity in what has been publicly revealed about the history of the nuclear warhead stockpiles of the various weapon states. More is known about the history of the US nuclear warhead stockpile than that of Russia or those of other weapons states, due in part to the Openness Initiative of the US Department of Energy (DOE). But even in the case of the United States, the DOD continues to insist that the inventory of currently stockpiled warheads remains classified.

The estimated, year-by-year, total stockpile and megatonnage of US nuclear forces is given in Table 5. Table 6 gives the number of warheads, strategic and non-strategic, for the Soviet Union and (later) Russia.

The US Nuclear Weapon Stockpile

The US nuclear weapons stockpile peaked in 1967 at about 32,000 warheads (Figure 1). The estimated inventory of US nuclear warheads, as of the end of FY 1990 (30 September 1990) – a year before the breakup of the Soviet Union – was about 21,000 warheads. At the end of 1996 there were about 8500 warheads in DOD's operational (deployed) stockpile and another 2600 spare and reserve warheads[3] (Table 1). The total DOD stockpile is estimated to be about 11,000 warheads. In addition, there are an estimated 2800 retired warheads in Air Force, Navy and DOE depots that are in a queue, awaiting their turn on the Pantex disassembly line. In Table 1 in the reserve category, we have included 192 warheads for the 24 Trident II SLBMs that will be on the eighteenth and final Trident submarine, which was expected to enter the force in July 1997. Even now, the mindless momentum of the arms race continues, as the US operational stockpile has actually *increased* over the past two years with the Navy's addition of a sixteenth and seventeenth Trident submarine, and a further increase in the summer of 1997 with the addition of the eighteenth.

The dismantlement goal for FY 1995 was 2000 warheads, but only 1393 were dismantled in that year, and an estimated 1166 were dismantled in FY 1996. At the end of FY 1996 (30 September 1996) there was still a backlog of about 2800 retired nuclear warheads awaiting dismantlement. Under current

DOE plans, and assuming no further significant reductions in the stockpile, this backlog should be eliminated by the end of FY 1999. Currently, there are no further planned reductions in the stockpile beyond those warheads that will be removed for evaluation disassembly and disposal. Between FY 1997-2003, the DOE estimates that the number of warheads that will undergo evaluation disassembly and disposal will reduce from 73 to 42 annually, averaging 51 warheads annually over this seven year period.[4] Some of these will be replaced by new warheads manufactured at the Los Alamos National Laboratory. An average of 58 warheads annually are projected to undergo evaluation disassembly and reassembly during the same seven year period.

While the public perception is that the US and Russian nuclear weapon stockpiles will be reduced to about 3500 warheads by 2003 under START II, the truth is that the Clinton Administration is planning a stockpile some three times this amount – approximately 11,000 warheads (Table 2). In addition to the 3500 operational strategic warheads in the US arsenal in 2003, the Pentagon plans to retain another 950 warheads for non-strategic forces, and presumably additional spares which we estimate will equal about 10 per cent of the active inventory. The strategic reserve, originally created for use after a nuclear war with Russia, now is conceived as a force allowing the USA to resist potential coercion by such nations as China, North Korea, and Iran which might attempt to take advantage of the United States following a nuclear war. The reserve force could also be directed towards these or other countries irrespective of the Russian context, should the national command authorities so decide.

In addition, another 2500 warheads are destined for what the DOD calls the "hedge." When fully implemented in 2003, the hedge will be a contingency stockpile made up of warheads removed from active strategic forces pursuant to START II, but not dismantled. The purpose of retaining them intact is so that they can be "uploaded" on existing strategic delivery systems, thereby "reconstituting" US strategic forces to something close to the START I force levels.

Finally, the Pentagon plans to retain about 3400 warheads in "inactive reserve." These warheads will be retained without maintaining the tritium inventory, and presumably without servicing other limited life components, such as batteries. DOD has said that if START II is not ratified by Russia, it intends to retain these warheads in an active status, thus increasing the tritium requirements about 25 per cent – equivalent to five years of tritium decay.

At the end of FY 1996 there were about 9200 pits in storage at Pantex. By the end of FY 1999 there will be about 12,000 pits in storage at Pantex; and Pantex has been approved for future storage of up to 20,000 pits.

Some 5000 of the 12,000 plutonium intact pits recovered in the warhead disassembly process will be retained as a "strategic reserve." This pit reserve is estimated at about 15 tonnes (t) of plutonium, or roughly half the 32t that will remain in intact weapons, for a total of 47t to be retained for weapons use, out of a total stockpile of 85t of weapon-grade plutonium. The US government has declared that the balance of 38t of WGPu - almost half of it not in pit form - is surplus to military needs and may be permanently withdrawn from the US weapons stockpile.

On highly-enriched (> 20 per cent U-235) uranium (HEU) from weapons, the US DOE has announced that it produced 994t for all purposes by the end of 1992. Current estimates assume that the USA had about 500t of "orally" (Oak Ridge Alloy - 93.5 per cent U-235), and about 230t between 20 per cent and 90 per cent enriched, in weapons or assigned for weapons use. The US government has declared 14t of HEU excess to its military requirements; only about one half of this figure was ever in weapons or produced for weapons use. It follows that the USA is continuing to reserve around 530 tonnes of HEU for potential military use, including an estimated 330t for weapons and about 200t of oralloy for the Navy, sufficient for a 100 + year reserve.

The Russian Nuclear Weapon Stockpile [5]

The size of the Russian nuclear weapon stockpile - past, present, and future - is still cloaked in secrecy. Our best estimate, presented in Figure 2, is highly uncertain and is based on the following conflicting information. According to Ministry of Atomic Energy (MINATOM) Minister Viktor Mikhailov, the Soviet nuclear weapons stockpile grew rather steadily until it peaked in 1986 at 45,000 warheads;[6] and then declined more than 20 per cent to about 35,000 warheads by May 1993.[7] An official CIA estimate given in May 1992 placed the stockpile of the former Soviet Union at 30,000 nuclear weapons with an uncertainty of plus or minus 5000.[8] The upper limit of the CIA estimate is consistent with the MINATOM figures.

According to Russian sources, Russia had 21,700 air defence and tactical warheads in service in 1991. President Mikhail Gorbachev in October 1991 pledged to dismantle all atomic land mines by 1998, all nuclear artillery shells by 2000, half of the surface-to-air missile warheads by 1996, half the tactical naval warheads by 1995 (with the other half stored ashore), and half of the bombs for the non-strategic air force by 1996. According to a Russian official, as of mid-1996 this schedule was still being followed. Thus, the 1991 Gorbachev initiative called for the elimination of about 14,200 of these warheads. Accounting for the 3,000 warheads already withdrawn as a result of the 1988 INF Treaty, brings the total withdrawn to about 17,200.

According to MINATOM the stockpile was projected to decline to 40-50 per cent of its mid-1992 level as a result of arms control initiatives agreed to up to early-1992.[9] Assuming the mid-1992 stockpile was 35,000 warheads, this implies a planned reduction of 14,000 to 17,500 warheads, which is consistent with the estimated reduction of 17,200 warheads. The CIA, on the other hand, stated in May 1992 that:

... the Russians have something on the order of 9000 to 16,000 nuclear weapons slated for dismantling. They have not given us an official figure for how many weapons are slated for dismantling as a result of the Gorbachev-Yeltsin initiative. This is our estimate. We have a highly uncertain estimate of the size of their tactical nuclear weapon inventory. Their initiative included something on the order of 1200 strategic [air defense] weapons; 5000 to 12,000 tactical nuclear weapons, and our estimate of 2700 weapons remaining from the INF treaty.[10]

The CIA's upper limit of 16,000 warheads slated for dismantlement in 1992 is reasonably consistent with our estimate of 17,200 warheads derived from MINATOM and other Russian data.

We assume that 20,350 strategic air defence and tactical warheads will be retired from the operational stockpile by 2003-2004, because most of the remaining fractions of weapons in the stockpile under the Gorbachev initiative will become obsolete. Adding approximately 3000 INF warheads already retired and 1900 strategic warheads from Ukraine, gives some 25,250 warheads that were potentially available for disassembly beginning in 1991. These can all be disassembled by about 2004, assuming an average disassembly rate of 2000 warheads per year. By our estimates this would leave Russia with a stockpile of about 11,000 warheads, at which point it would be comparable in size to the US stockpile.

On 17 June 1992, Presidents Bush and Yeltsin announced that the US and Russian strategic arsenals would each be reduced to 3000-3500 strategic warheads no later than 1 January 2003. This agreement was codified as START II. Depending on many decisions about the future composition of Russian forces, the Russian operational, or active, stockpile in the 2003-2004 period could be anywhere from 1800 to 4300 warheads (Table 4). Since, at the projected retirement rate of 2000 warheads per year, it is estimated that the number of intact Russian warheads will be about 11,000 warheads in 2004, it is likely that Russia also will retain a reserve of several thousand intact warheads; and if START II is ratified, Russia surely will follow the US lead and retain a "hedge" category of warheads to enable rapid uploading of SS-19 and SS-24 ICBMs. Our projection of likely candidates for the "hedge" and reserve warhead categories is presented in Table 4.

While we have assumed a disassembly rate of about 2000 warheads per year, information about the pace and scope of Russian warhead dismantlement is very sketchy. In the United States the public is provided with a detailed accounting of the number and kinds of warheads that have been dismantled, but in Russia, secrecy about such matters is still the rule. Dismantlement work is performed at Sverdlovsk-45 at Nizhnaya Tura, Zlatoust-36 at Yuruzan, and the Avanguard facility at Arzamas-16. The combined dismantlement rate at these three facilities, according to statements made by Mikhailov in 1992, was about

1500 to 2000 per year, or slightly higher than the average rate of dismantlement at Pantex in the United States during the past few years.

In sum, we believe the Russian nuclear stockpile, including retired but still intact warheads awaiting dismantlement, is about 25,000 warheads, and that warheads are being dismantled at a rate of about 2000 per year. Should Russia continue at this dismantlement rate, the stockpile would reach about 11,000 warheads in about 2004 – comparable in size to the currently planned US stockpile level for the same period.

We estimate that Russian reactor production of WGPu since 1948 amounts to some 150-170t, of which 115-130t was actually fabricated into weapon components, with the balance in production scrap, solutions, residues and losses to nuclear waste and the environment. An additional 30t of separated reactor grade plutonium is stored at Chelyabinsk-65. This estimate for Russian WGPu in pits is roughly double the 66t of WGPu contained in US weapon pits, and Russia's total separated plutonium inventory of close to 200t is roughly double that of the US. Given the agreement between the two sides that US and Russian plutonium disposition programmes should proceed in parallel with the goal of reducing to equal levels of military plutonium, Russia will be required to dispose of its plutonium at a rate three times that of the USA to reach equal levels by a given date.

While the total production of Soviet/Russian HEU has never been officially disclosed, it is believed to be on the order of 1200t. Under a 1994 contract for US purchase of HEU derived from Russian weapons, Russia agreed to sell the US up to 500t of HEU equivalent (in the form of LEU) at a rate of 10t per year for the first five years, and 30t per year for the next 15 years. Thus far, the US Enrichment Corporation, executive agent for the US side of the deal, has taken delivery of 6t of HEU equivalent in 1995, and 12t in 1996.

While we are projecting that the process of nuclear weapons disarmament will continue in Russia over the next eight years, the disarmament process could be halted or reversed as a consequence of political changes within Russia, or changes in Western policies toward Russia. In an article written in 1996, Mikhailov and two senior colleagues from the Arzamas-16 weapons laboratory raised the prospect of a radical reworking of Russia's nuclear arsenal to adapt to the changed circumstances of NATO's expansion eastward and the precipitous decline in Russia's capabilities to mount a credible conventional defence. According to Mikhailov *et al.*:[11]

> If Russia sees its interests ignored or NATO expansion proves spearheaded against Russia, it will have to take economic and military measures that should be prepared well in advance.
>
> ... Nuclear arms modernization can be carried out within the framework of the Comprehensive Test Ban Treaty, though this would require maximum mobilization of the Russian Atomic Energy Ministry capacities.

In the military-political field, Russia should not rush to ratify START-II cuts in its strategic offensive arms, except for systems which have already exhausted their potential – until the political picture has taken shape.

... We should be aware that for all the pledges and declarations made by the West, in the near future Russia cannot afford to carry out nuclear disarmament, otherwise it may find itself defenceless after a possible turnaround in the West's policies.

Russia could make one move to change the perception of nuclear arms as arms of mass destruction, and the next step – to diminish the nuclear threat. These moves are: modernization of all adopted nuclear arms, creation of an additional yield level not exceeding several hundred tons of TNT equivalent. This lower yield level should be the routine state of nuclear warheads. If there were no such means, a nation may prove unable to retaliate for a strike from any point of the globe, its deterrence potential being illusory. If there arises a threat of a full-scale nuclear attack on Russia, its nuclear warheads must be upgraded to a higher yield level. Technically, this is feasible, and the Ministry of Atomic Energy is capable of solving this problem without additional nuclear tests and great expenses. Russia could make these moves even unilaterally.

United Kingdom: Reductions and Trends

Over the past six years British armed forces have given up all but two of their nuclear roles. By 1998 there will be only one British nuclear weapon system, the submarine-launched ballistic missile.

British reductions came in the aftermath of the dissolution of the Soviet Union. Following the Bush-Gorbachev initiatives of 27 September and 5 October 1991, British Secretary of State for Defence Tom King said that, "we will no longer routinely carry nuclear weapons on our ships." On 15 June 1992 the Defence Minister announced that all nuclear weapons – the WE177C – had been removed from surface ships and aircraft, that this nuclear mission would be eliminated and that the "weapons previously earmarked for this role will be destroyed." The C version of the WE177 bomb was assigned to selected Royal Navy Sea Harrier FRS.1 aircraft and ASW helicopters. The arsenal was thought to number about 25. It existed in both a free-fall and depth-bomb modification and had an estimated yield of approximately 10 kilotons (kt).

The Royal Air Force (RAF) has been progressively decreasing its stockpile of nuclear bombs over the past few years, and the number of aircraft squadrons with nuclear missions. Currently the RAF operates eight squadrons of dual-capable, strike/attack Tornado GR.1/1A. Each squadron has 12 aircraft. These include four squadrons at RAF Bruggen, Germany (Nos. 9, 14, 17, 31). The three strike/attack Tornado squadrons at RAF Laarbruch, Germany were disbanded between September 1991 and May 1992, and the base will be closed in 1999. Two squadrons previously at RAF Marham were redeployed to RAF

Lossiemouth in 1994. They replaced the Buccaneer S2B in the maritime strike role. Tornado reconnaissance squadrons 2 and 13 are at RAF Marham. It i likely that less than a full complement of bombs is assigned to the Tornadoes that have maritime strike and reconnaissance roles.

The total number of WE177 nuclear gravity bombs produced was estimated to have been about 200, of which 175 were versions A and B. The 1992 White Paper stated that, "As part of the cut in NATO's stockpile we will also reduce the number of British free-fall nuclear bombs by more than half." A number of British nuclear bombs were returned to the UK from bases in Germany. The 1993 Defence White Paper stated that the WE177, "is currently expected to remain in service until well into the next century," but the government announced in March 1994 that this meant until the year 2007. On 4 April 1995 the government announced that the remaining WE177s would now be withdrawn from service by the end of 1998; this was later advanced to the end of March 1998. On 1 May 1996 Defence Secretary Michael Portillo announced that RAF Bruggen would close in 2002. The Tornadoes (four years after becoming non-nuclear) will be reassigned to bases in the UK.

Britain also ended its involvement in operating several tactical nuclear weapon systems. The US nuclear weapons for certified British systems have been removed from Europe and returned to the United States, specifically for the 11 Nimrod ASW aircraft based at RAF St Magwan, Cornwall, UK, the single Army regiment with 12 Lance launchers and the 4 Army artillery regiments with 120 M109 howitzers in Germany. Squadron No. 42, the Nimrod maritime patrol squadron, disbanded in October 1992. The 50 Missile Regiment (Lance) and the 56 Special Weapons Battery Royal Artillery were disbanded in 1993.

Britain built and deployed four *Resolution*-class SSBNs, commonly called Polaris submarines after the missiles they carry. The first boat (HMS *Resolution*) went on patrol in mid-June 1968, the fourth (HMS *Revenge*) in September 1970. *Revenge* was retired on 25 May 1992. *Resolution* was retired in 1994 and *Renown* and *Repulse* were retired in 1996.

Construction, training, testing, and sea trials continue with the Vanguard-class SSBN system. Each Vanguard-class SSBN carries sixteen US produced Trident II D-5 SLBMs. The first submarine of the class, the HMS *Vanguard*, went on its first patrol in December 1994. The second submarine, *Victorious* entered service in December 1995. The third submarine, *Vigilant* was launched in October 1995 and will enter service in the summer or fall of 1998. The fourth and final boat of the class, *Vengeance* is under construction. Its estimated launch date is 1998 with service entry in late 2000 or early 2001. The current estimated procurement cost of the programme is $18.8 billion.

We estimate that the British stockpile as of the end of 1996 to be approximately 260 warheads of two types. The British stockpile peaked in the mid-1970s at some 350 warheads. We estimate that it will increase slightly to about 275 warheads of only one type at the turn of the century.

France: Reductions and Trends

On 22 and 23 February 1996 President Jacques Chirac announced several dramatic reforms for French armed forces for the period 1997 to 2002. The most significant will be the introduction of a professional armed force and the phasing out of conscription over a six year period, ending in 2001. The size of the armed forces will decrease from almost 400,000 to 260,500.

The decisions in the nuclear area were a combination of the withdrawal of several obsolete systems with a commitment to modernize those that remain. Already many of the programmes announced in the early 1980s to increase the size of the French stockpile had been cancelled, modified, or scaled back for budgetary and geopolitical reasons. More recently, in May 1992 it was announced that the number of new *Triomphant*-class SSBNs would be reduced from six to four. There was some speculation that President Chirac might not purchase the fourth boat, but he reaffirmed that he would and also stated that a new ballistic missile, the M51, would replace the M45 in the 2010-2015 time period.

The lead SSBN, *Le Triomphant*, was rolled out from its construction shed in Cherbourg on 13 July 1993. It entered service in September 1996, armed with the M45 SLBM and new TN 75 warheads. The second SSBN, *Le Téméraire*, is under construction, and will not be ready until 1999. The schedule for the third, *Le Vigilant* has slipped and it will not be ready until 2001. The service date for the fourth SSBN is approximately 2005. We estimate that eventually there will be 288 warheads for the fleet of four new *Triomphant*-class SSBNs, because enough missiles and warheads will be purchased for only three boats. This loading is the case today with five submarines in the fleet – only four sets of M4 SLBMs were procured.

After considering numerous plans to replace the silo-based S3D IRBM during President Mitterrand's tenure, President Chirac announced in February that the missile would be retired and there would be no replacement. On 16 September, all 18 missiles on the Plateau d'Albion were deactivated.

The number of Mirage 2000N aircraft committed to nuclear missions was scaled back in 1989 from 75 aircraft in five squadrons to 45 aircraft in three squadrons. On 11 September 1991, President Mitterrand announced that as of 1 September the AN 52 gravity bomb, once carried by Mirage IIIEs, Jaguar As and Super Etendards, had been withdrawn from service. From that point on France no longer had a nuclear gravity bomb. The Air-Sol-Moyenne-Portée (ASMP) supersonic missile was deployed in 1988 and today there are 45 ASMPs with two Mirage 2000N squadrons at Luxeuil and one at Istres. The number of nuclear-armed Super Etendard aircraft scheduled to carry the ASMP was also reduced due to budgetary constraints, from about 50-55 to 24 planes with 20 ASMPs allocated to them.

The Pluton short range ballistic missile was retired by the end of 1993. The longer range Hadès was to have replaced it. The original programme called for 60 launchers and 120 missiles (and warheads). The programme was reduced several times, eventually to 15 launchers and 30 missiles. The first regiment was activated at Suippes, in eastern France, on 1 September 1991. Further introduction was impossible given geopolitical events and the Hadès was shelved. The missiles and warheads were stored intact allowing them to be reintroduced if need be. In a significant action President Chirac announced that the Hadès system would be dismantled and the regiment reassigned to other duties.

In July 1996, after thirty-two years of service, the Mirage IVP relinquished its nuclear role and was retired. Five Mirage IVPs will be retained for reconnaissance missions at Istres. The other planes will be put into storage at Chateaudun.

The three squadrons of Mirage 2000N have now assumed the "strategic" role, in addition to their "pre-strategic" one. A fourth Mirage 2000N squadron at Nancy – now conventional – is scheduled to be replaced with Mirage 2000Ds. Those aircraft may be modified to carry the ASMP and distributed to the three 2000N squadrons at Luxeuil and Istres, along with the Mirage IVP's ASMP missiles. President Chirac also said that a longer-range ASMP (500 km vs. 300 km, sometimes called the "ASMP plus") will be developed for service entry in about a decade.

The Rafale is planned to be the multi-purpose Navy and Air Force fighter/bomber for the next century. Its roles include conventional ground attack, air defence, air superiority and nuclear delivery of the ASMP and/or ASMP+. The carrier-based Navy version will be introduced first with the air force Rafale D attaining a nuclear strike role in approximately 2005.

We estimate that the French stockpile as of the end of 1996 is approximately 450 warheads of three types. The historical peak of 538 was reached in 1991-92. We estimate that the future stockpile of 2005 will decrease slightly to around 400 of two types.

China: Trends

The Chinese have been very effective in keeping secret the details about the size and composition of their nuclear stockpile. Thus there remains uncertainty about the size of the nuclear bomber force, the number of ballistic missiles deployed, and whether or not there are "tactical" nuclear weapons. We estimate that the Chinese stockpile, as of the end of 1996, was approximately 400 warheads in two basic categories: some 250 "strategic" weapons structured in a "triad" of land-based missiles, bombers, and submarine-launched ballistic missiles; and about 150 "tactical" weapons – low yield bombs for tactical bombardment, artillery shells, atomic demolition munitions, and possibly short range missiles.

The mainstay of Chinese nuclear forces is the ballistic missile, which varies in range from 1700 to 13,000 kilometres, with only a handful capable of the longest ranges. More advanced systems have long been under development with emphasis on improved accuracy and guidance, increased range, mobile launch platforms, solid fuel technology, and multiple warheads. It is logical to assume that the last series of nuclear tests was aimed at providing warheads with improved yield-to-weight ratios for the next generation of ballistic missiles. The yield estimates of the 11 nuclear tests since 1990 suggests that one warhead may be in the 100 to 200 kt range and a larger one in the 600 to 700 kt range.

One feature of all Chinese weapon system programmes is that it takes a long time for the missile, submarine or bomber to enter service. From initial research through development and testing to deployment can take a decade or two, by which time it is largely obsolete. It is important to keep China's military modernization in perspective. Is its purpose a routine upgrade or, as some would have it, evidence of aggressive designs in the region? As a close observer of China, David Shambaugh, has recently written, "It is important ... not to confuse ambition with capability." "The PLA's current weapons inventory remains 10 to 20 years or more behind the state of the art in almost all categories, although some gaps are being closed."[12] While the size of China's military budget is difficult to calculate, many Western experts believe it is in the $28 to $36 billion range, seven to nine times smaller than the US military budget.

The bomber force is antiquated, as it is based on Chinese-produced versions of 1950s-vintage Soviet aircraft. The Hong-5, a redesign of the Soviet Il-28 Beagle, has been retired from air force service. The main bomber is the Hong-6, based on the Tu-16 Badger, which entered service with Soviet forces in 1955. Under a licensing agreement the Chinese began producing the H-6 in the 1960s. It was used to drop live weapons in two nuclear tests in 1965 and 1967.

For more than a decade China has been developing a new supersonic fighter-bomber, the Hong-7 (or FB-7) at the Xian Aircraft Company. According to a 1995 RAND study on China's Air Force, the FB-7 is for the Chinese navy and does not have air force participation.[13] The FB-7 will not be ready for deployment until the late 1990s and then will only be produced in very small numbers – not more than 20. It will not have a nuclear mission.

A quicker route for China to modernize its bomber force would be to adapt aircraft for a nuclear role that it has already purchased from abroad, or may purchase in the future. In the former category are 26 Soviet/Russian Su-27 Flankers that were delivered in 1992 at a cost of $1 billion. They are currently with the 3rd Air Division at Wuhu airfield, 250 kilometres west of Shanghai. Under a new agreement Russia intends to sell production rights to China to assemble and produce Su-27s in China. The Su-27 does have an air-to-ground capability though there is no evidence that the PLAAF is modifying it for a nuclear role. Many reports of purchases or licensed manufacturing of other types of Russian aircraft (for example, MiG-31, Tu-22M, and Su-25) remain unsubstantiated.

With only one operational SSBN to date China has had a difficult time with developing and deploying this leg of its Triad. Technical difficulties with solid fuel for the missiles and nuclear reactors have slowed the programme. The Julang-1 SLBM was China's first solid fueled ballistic missile. A second generation SLBM is also under development. It seems unlikely that a future fleet will number more than four to six submarines.

Information on Chinese tactical nuclear weapons is limited and contradictory, and there is no confirmation from official sources of their existence. China's initial interest in such weapons may have been spurred by worsening relations with the Soviet Union in the 1960s and 1970s. Several low yield nuclear tests in the late 1970s, and a large military exercise in June 1982 simulating the use of tactical nuclear weapons by both sides, suggests that they have been developed.

Data Exchange, Transparency and Verification Measures

On 10 May 1995 Presidents Clinton and Yeltsin issued a "Joint Statement on the Transparency and Irreversibility of the Process of Reducing Nuclear Weapons" (reproduced in Appendix B). This Joint Statement represents the fullest and most recent description of the intentions of the two countries with regard to warhead dismantlement and transparency. Among the key provisions of this joint statement, the USA and Russia agreed to establish:

- an exchange on a regular basis of detailed information on aggregate stockpiles of nuclear warheads, on stocks of fissile materials and on their safety and security;
- a cooperative arrangement for reciprocal monitoring at storage facilities of fissile materials removed from nuclear warheads and declared to be excess to national security requirements to help confirm the irreversibility of the process of reducing nuclear weapons, recognizing that progress in this area is linked to progress in implementing the joint US-Russian programme for the fissile material storage facility at Mayak; and
- other cooperative measures, as necessary to enhance confidence in the reciprocal declarations on fissile material stockpiles.

With respect to transparency, the agreement also states that:

> The United States of America and the Russian Federation will also examine
> and seek to define further measures to increase the transparency and
> irreversibility of the process of reducing nuclear weapons, including
> intergovernmental arrangements to extend cooperation to further phases of the
> process of eliminating nuclear weapons declared excess to national security
> requirements as a result of nuclear arms reductions.
>
> The United States of America and the Russian Federation will seek to
> conclude in the shortest possible time an agreement for cooperation between
> their governments enabling the exchange of information as necessary to
> implement the arrangements called for above, by providing for the protection
> of that information. No information will be exchanged until the respective
> arrangements enter into force.

Unfortunately, there has been no progress between the United States and
Russia on implementation of the agreed upon data exchange, or any warhead
dismantlement and fissile material storage transparency and verification
measures, since October 1995, when without explanation Russia cut off bilateral
talks directed toward concluding an Agreement for Cooperation, the legal
instrument that would permit the data exchange and transparency measures to
go forward. Russian hard-liners among President Yeltsin's inner circle were
apparently responsible for this turn of events.

Russia's refusal to move forward with an Agreement for Cooperation has
brought to a halt virtually all reciprocal transparency initiatives related to
nuclear warhead dismantlement and warhead component storage, including (a)
a US proposal for mutual inspections of warhead storage and dismantlement
sites to verify the rate at which nuclear warheads are being dismantled, the
number that await dismantlement, and the number that have been dismantled
already, and (b) the demonstration of techniques for verifying the presence of
pits and other nuclear weapon components in sealed storage containers.

Even if these political issues are resolved, the US DOD and the Russian
Ministries of Defence and Atomic Energy are likely to keep most, if not all, of
the data classified and available only to the two governments, even though most
of the data could be publicly released without harm to either side's national
security. Moreover, the US proposal was weakened considerably by the
exclusion of operational nuclear warheads and tritium inventories from the
proposed categories of data to be exchanged.

At their Helsinki meeting in March 1997, the two Presidents agreed that
START III negotiations should include "measures relating to the transparency
of strategic nuclear warhead inventories and the destruction of strategic nuclear
warheads," and would also consider "issues related to transparency in nuclear
materials." However, these negotiations are waiting for the Russian Duma's
ratification of START II.

The two countries could have implemented the data exchange and extensive transparency with regard to warhead dismantlement had the United States availed itself of a window of opportunity and moved on these issues in 1991 and 1992 instead of waiting until 1994.

Summary and Conclusions

While the public and media perception is that US and Russian nuclear weapon stockpiles under START II will be reduced to no more than 3500 warheads each by 2003, the truth is that both nations are planning stockpiles that are three times this amount, on the order of 10,000-11,000 warheads.

The various forward plans of the five nuclear weapon states still indicate that they intend to retain nuclear weapons into the indefinite future. The Joint Statement of March 1997 on nuclear weapon policy, by Presidents Clinton and Yeltsin, does not have any reference to an eventual objective of eliminating them altogether.

Finally, Russia and the United States have made almost no progress in negotiating formal agreements for nuclear stockpile data exchanges, reciprocal monitoring of warhead fissile material storage sites, and other cooperative measures to enhance confidence in reciprocal stockpile declarations. Russia has essentially cut off bilateral talks on these issues, and it is unclear when they will be restored. The 10 May 1995 Joint Statement on Transparency and Irreversibility of the Process of Reducing Nuclear Weapons remains essentially a dead letter.

Notes

1. START II Treaty, Report together with Additional Views, Committee on Foreign Relations, United States Senate, Exec. Report 104-10, 104th Cong., 1st Session, December 15, 1995, pp. 10-11.

2. SASC, DOD FY1996, Hearings, Part 7, p. 366.

3. The "inactive reserve" is reportedly composed of intact warheads stored without the limited-life components, such as plutonium-238 batteries, neutron generators, and deuterium-tritium boost gas reservoirs.

4. Tom Walton, Public Affairs Office, Albuquerque Field Office, DOE, to Robert S. Norris, 9 May 1996.

5. T.B. Cochran, R.S. Norris and O.A. Bukharin, *Making the Russian Bomb: From Stalin to Yeltsin,* Boulder, Co.: Westview Press, 1995, pp. 31-32.

6. Private communication to authors concerning remarks by Viktor Mikhailov. The 45,000 figure was criticized as being too high by a senior official of the Twelfth Main Directorate of the Russian Ministry of Defense (MOD).

7.   "According to Minister Viktor Mikhailov approximately 13,000 nuclear munitions have been dismantled in this time [the last eight to 10 years], 2000 a year on average." Sergei Ovsiyenko, "Weapons-Grade Plutonium Stocks Dwindling," Rossiyskiye Vesti, 19 May 1993, p. 7. Viktor Mikhailov and Evgeni Mikerin, in remarks at the International Symposium on Conversion of Nuclear Warheads for Peaceful Purposes, Rome, Italy, 15-17 June 1992, stated that the stockpile had declined by 20 per cent since it peaked in 1986, which implies that the stockpile was 36,000 in 1992. In an interview with Evgeni Panov, Moscow Rossiyskaya Gazeta, in Russian, 11 December 1992, p. 7 (translated in the Foreign Broadcast Information Service series, FBIS-SOV-92-239, 11 December 1992, p. 3), Mikhailov is quoted as having said, "... if destruction of nuclear weapons in our country is halted as a result of financial and technical difficulties, by the year 2000 the Americans will be scrapping their own weapons but we will be unable to. They will have 10,000 charges left, we will have 35,000." See also, Trip Report, Senate Armed Services Committee Delegation's Visit to Russia, Kazakhstan and Ukraine, 15-20 January 1992, p. 4. "According to officials of the Ministry and other informed sources, some 8-10 thousand warheads have been disassembled in Russia since 1985."

8.   Lawrence K. Gershwin, National Intelligence Officer for Strategic Programs, Central Intelligence Agency, Hearings before the House Committee on Appropriations, DOD Appropriations for 1993, Part 5, 6 May 1992, p. 499.

9.   Mikhailov and Mikerin, International Symposium, Rome, 15-17 June 1992.

10.   Gershwin in HAC, DOD FY 1993, Part 5, p. 499.

11.   V. Mikhailov, I. Andryushin, and A. Chernyshov, "NATO's Expansion and Russia's Security," *Vek*, 20 September 1996.

12.   D. Shambaugh, "China's Military: Real or Paper Tiger?" *The Washington Quarterly*, Spring 1996, p. 24.

13.   K.W. Allen, G. Krumel and J.D. Pollack, *China's Air Force Enters the 21st Century*, Santa Monica, CA: RAND, 1995.

Appendix A

Joint Statement on Parameters on Future Reductions
in Nuclear Forces
White House text, Helsinki, 21 March 1997

Presidents Clinton and Yeltsin underscore that, with the end of the Cold War, major progress has been achieved with regard to strengthening strategic stability and nuclear security. Both the United States and Russia are significantly reducing their nuclear forces. Important steps have been taken to detarget strategic missiles. The START I Treaty has entered into force, and its implementation is ahead of schedule. Belarus, Kazakhstan and Ukraine are nuclear-weapon free. The Nuclear Non-Proliferation Treaty was indefinitely extended on 11 May 1995 and the Comprehensive Nuclear Test Ban Treaty was signed by both the United States and Russia on 24 September 1996.

In another historic step to promote international peace and security, President Clinton and President Yeltsin hereby reaffirm their commitment to take further concrete steps to reduce the nuclear danger and strengthen strategic stability and nuclear security. The Presidents have reached an understanding on further reductions in and limitations on strategic offensive arms that will substantially reduce the roles and risks of nuclear weapons as we move forward into the next century. Recognizing the fundamental significance of the ABM Treaty for these objectives, the Presidents have, in a separate joint statement, given instructions on demarcation between ABM systems and theater missile defense systems, which will allow for deployment of effective theater missile defenses and prevent circumvention of the ABM Treaty.

With the foregoing in mind, President Clinton and President Yeltsin have reached the following understandings.

Once START II enters into force, the United States and Russia will immediately begin negotiations on a START III agreement, which will include, among other things, the following basic components:

– Establishment, by 31 December 2007, of lower aggregate levels of 2000-2500 strategic nuclear warheads for each of the parties.
– Measures relating to the transparency of strategic nuclear warhead inventories and the destruction of strategic nuclear warheads and any other jointly agreed technical and organizational measures to promote the irreversibility of deep reductions including prevention of a rapid increase in the number of warheads.
– Resolving issues related to the goal of making the current START treaties unlimited in duration.
– Placement in a deactivated status of all strategic nuclear delivery vehicles which will be eliminated under START II by 31 December 2003, by removing their nuclear warheads or taking other jointly agreed steps. The United States is providing assistance through the Nunn-Lugar program to facilitate early deactivation.

The Presidents have reached an understanding that the deadline for the elimination of strategic nuclear delivery vehicles under the START II Treaty will be extended to 31 December, 2007. The sides will agree on specific language to be submitted to the Duma and, following Duma approval of START II, to be submitted to the United States Senate.

In this context, the Presidents underscore the importance of prompt ratification of the START II Treaty by the State Duma of the Russian Federation.

The Presidents also agreed that in the context of START III negotiations their experts will explore, as separate issues, possible measures relating to nuclear long-range sea-launched cruise missiles and tactical nuclear systems, to include appropriate confidence-building and transparency measures.

Taking into account all the understandings outlined above, and recalling their statement of 10 May 1995, the Presidents agreed the sides will also consider the issues related to transparency in nuclear materials.

Appendix B

Joint Statement on the Transparency and Irreversibility of the Process of Reducing Nuclear Weapons
10 May 1995

The President of the United States of America and the President of the Russian Federation

After examining the exchange of views which took place during the December 1994 meeting of the Gore-Chernomyrdin Commission in regard to the aggregate stockpiles of nuclear warheads, stocks of fissile materials, and their safety and security, as well as a discussion of the Joint Working Group on Nuclear Safeguards, Transparency and Irreversibility of further measures to improve confidence in and increase the transparency and irreversibility of the process of reducing nuclear weapons,

Reaffirm the commitment of the United States of America and the Russian Federation to the goal of nuclear disarmament and their desire to pursue further measures to improve confidence in and increase the transparency and irreversibility of the process of nuclear arms reduction, as they agreed in January and September 1994;

Reaffirm the desire of the States of America and the Russian Federation to exchange detailed information on aggregate stockpiles of nuclear warheads, on stocks of fissile materials and on their safety and security and to develop a process for exchange of this information on a regular basis; and

Express the desire of the United Sates of America and the Russian Federation to establish as soon as possible concrete arrangements for enhancing transparency and irreversibility of the process of nuclear arms reduction.

Taking into account the proposal by President B N Yeltsin for a treaty on nuclear safety and strategic stability among the five nuclear powers, they declare that:

Fissile materials removed from nuclear weapons being eliminated and excess to national security requirements will not be used to manufacture nuclear weapons;

No newly produced fissile materials will be used in nuclear weapons; and

Fissile materials from or within civil nuclear programmes will not be used to manufacture nuclear weapons.

The United States of America and the Russian Federation will negotiate agreements to increase the transparency and irreversibility of nuclear arms reduction that, *inter alia*, establish:

An exchange on a regular basis of detailed information on aggregate stockpiles of nuclear warheads, on stocks of fissile materials and on their safety and security;

A cooperative arrangement for reciprocal monitoring at storage facilities of fissile materials removed from nuclear warheads and declared to be excess to national security requirements to help confirm the transparency and irreversibility of the process of reducing nuclear weapons, recognizing that progress in this area is linked to progress in implementing the joint US-Russian programme for the fissile material storage facility at Mayak; and

Other cooperative measures, as necessary to enhance confidence in the reciprocal declarations on fissile material stockpiles.

The United States of America and the Russian Federation will strive to conclude as soon as possible agreements which are based on these principles.

The United States of America and the Russian Federation will also examine and seek to define further measures to increase the transparency and irreversibility of the process of reducing nuclear weapons, including intergovernmental arrangements to extend cooperation to further phases of the process of eliminating nuclear weapons declared excess to national security requirements as a result of nuclear arms reduction.

The Presidents urged progress in implementing current agreements affecting the irreversibility of the process of reducing nuclear weapons such as the 23 June 1994, agreement concerning the shutdown of plutonium production reactors and the cessation of use of newly produced plutonium for nuclear weapons, in all its interrelated provisions, including, *inter alia*, cooperation in creation of alternative energy sources, shutdown of plutonium production reactors mentioned above, and development of respective compliance procedures.

The United States of America and the Russian Federation will seek to conclude in the shortest possible time an agreement for cooperation between their governments enabling the exchange of information as necessary to implement the arrangements called for above, by providing for the protection of that information. No information will be exchanged until the respective arrangements enter into force.

Table 1. US Nuclear Forces, End-1996

Type	Name	Launchers/ SSBNs	Warhead Type	Yield (kt)	Total Warheads	Total (Mt)
Operational Forces						
Strategic						
ICBMs						
LGM-30G	Minuteman III:					
	Mk-12	200	3 W62 (MIRV)	170	600	102
	Mk-12A	300	3 W78 (MIRV)	335	900	302
LGM-118A	MX/Peacekeeper	50	10 W87-0 (MIRV)	300	500	150
Subtotal (ICBM)		**550**			**2000**	**554**
SLBMs						
UGM-96A	Trident I C-4	192/8	8 W76 (MIRV)	100	1536	154
UGM-113A	Trident II D-5	216/9				
	Mk-4		8 W76 (MIRV)	100	1344	134
	Mk-5		8 W88 (MIRV)	475	384	182
Subtotal (SLBM)		**408/17**			**3264**	**470**
Bomber/Weapons						
B-1B	Lancer	95/48	only bombs			
B-2	Spirit	13/10	only bombs			
B-52H	Stratofortress	71/44	bombs, ALCM, ACM			
			B53	9000	9	81
			B61-7, -11	0.3-300	400	40
			B83-0, -1	1000	600	600
			ALCM/W80-1	5-150	400	40
			ACM/W80-1	5-150	400	40
Subtotal (Bombers)					**1809**	**801**
Subtotal (Operational Strategic)					**7073**	**1825**
Non-strategic						
SLCM			W80-0	5-150	320	32
Air Force Non-strategic Bombs			B61-3, B61-4, B61-10	0.3-170	630	62
Subtotal (Operational Non-strategic)					**950**	**94**
Subtotal (Operational)					**8023**	**1919**
Spares for Operational Forces					**536**	**136**
Subtotal (Operational with Spares)					**8559**	**2055**
Reserves						
SSBN to be delivered mid-1997		24/1	8 W76 (MIRV)	100	200	20
Bomber Weapons			B61-3, B61-4, B61-10	0.3-170	706	69
			B61-7	0.3-300	260	26
			W80-1	5-150	1030	103
GLCM (Inactive)			W84	0.2-150	400	60
Subtotal (Reserves)					**2596**	**278**
Grand Total					**11,155**	**2333**

Notes: First bomber number reflects total inventory. Second number is "primary mission" number which excludes trainers and spares. Bombers are loaded in a variety of ways depending on mission. B1-Bs and B-2s do not carry ALCMs or ACMs. The first 16 B-2s will initially carry only the B53. Eventually, all B2s will carry both B61s and B83s. B53 bombs are being retired and replaced with B-11s.

ACM – advanced cruise missile; ALCM – air-launched cruise missile; ICBM – intercontinental ballistic missile (range greater than 5500 kilometres); MIRV – multiple independently targetable re-entry vehicle; SLBM – submarine-launched ballistic missile; SSBN – nuclear powered ballistic missile submarine.

Table 2. US Nuclear Forces, 2003 (START II)

Type	Name	Launchers/ SSBNs	Warhead Type	Yield (kt)	Total Warheads	Total (Mt)
Operational Forces						
Strategic						
ICBMs						
LGM-30G	Minuteman III	500	1 W87-0	300	500	150
Subtotal (ICBM)		**500**			**500**	**150**
SLBMs						
UGM-113A	Trident II D-5	14/336				
	Mk-4		5 W76 (MIRV)	100	1296	130
	Mk-5		5 W88 (MIRV)	475	384	182
Subtotal (SLBM)		**14/336**			**1680**	**312**
Bomber/Weapons						
B-2A	Spirit	21	bombs, ALCM, ACM			
B-52H	Stratofortress	66	bombs, ALCM, ACM			
			B61-7, B61-11	0.3-200	300	30
			B83	1000	600	600
			ACM/W80-1	5-150	400	40
Subtotal (Bombers)					**1300**	**670**
Subtotal (Operational Strategic)					**3480**	**1132**
Non-strategic						
SLCM			W80-0	5-150	320	48
Air Force Tactical Bombs			B61-3, B61-4, B61-10	0.3-170	630	107
Subtotal (Operational Non-strategic)					**950**	**155**
Subtotal (Operational)					**4430**	**1287**
Spares for Operational Forces					**493**	**108**
Subtotal (Operational with Spares)					**4923**	**1394**
"Hedge"						
ICBM warheads to upload Minuteman III			W78 (MIRV)	335	870	291
SLBM warheads to upload Trident II		336/14	W76 (MIRV)	100	925	93
Bomber weapons for B-1 and B-52H			B61-7, B61-11	0.3-300	200	20
			W80-1	5-150	500	50
Subtotal ("Hedge")					**2495**	**454**
Inactive Reserves						
ICBM			W62	170	600	102
SLBM			W76	100	800	80
Bomber Weapons			B61-3, B61-4, B61-10	0.3-170	600	59
			B61-7, B61-11	0.3-300	135	14
			W80-1	5-150	900	90
GLCM			W84	0.2-150	390	59
Subtotal (Inactive Reserves)					**3425**	**403**
Grand Total					**10,843**	**2251**

ACM – advanced cruise missile; ALCM – air-launched cruise missile; ICBM – intercontinental ballistic missile (range greater than 5500 kilometres); MIRV – multiple independently targetable re-entry vehicle; SLBM–submarine-launched ballistic missile; SSBN – nuclear powered ballistic missile submarine.

Table 3. Russian Nuclear Forces, End-1996

Category/Type	Weapon System	Launchers	Warheads
Strategic Offence			
ICBM	SS-18 (180), SS-19 (160), SS-24 (46), SS-25 (369)	755	3750
SLBM	SS-N-18 (208), SS-N-20 (120), SS-N-23 (112)	440	2350
Bomber	6 Blackjack, 27 Bear-H6, 36 Bear-H16 (AS-15 ALCMs, AS-16 SRAMs, bombs)	69	1400
Subtotal			7500
Strategic Defence			
ABM	SH-08 Gazelle (64), SH-11 Gorgon (36)	100	100
SAM	SA-5B Gammon, SA-10 Grumble	1100	1100
Subtotal			1200
Land-based Non-strategic			
Bomber and fighter	Backfire (80), Blinder (42), Badger (24), Fencer (280)	426	1600
Subtotal			1600
Naval Non-strategic			
Attack aircraft	Backfire (135), Blinder (30), Badger (50), Bear G (25) (AS-4 ASM, bombs)	240	600
SLCM	SS-N-9, SS-N-12, SS-N-19, SS-N-21, SS-N-22	–	500
ASW	SS-N-15, SS-N-16, torpedoes, depth bombs	n/a	500
Subtotal			1600
Grand Total			11,900

ABM: anti-ballistic missile; **ALCM**: air-launched cruise missile; **ASM**: air-to-surface missile; **ASW**: anti-submarine weapons; **ICBM**: intercontinental ballistic missile; **SAM**: surface-to-air missile; **SLBM**: submarine-launched ballistic missile; **SLCM**: submarine-launched cruise missile; **SRAM**: short-range attack missile; **SSBN**: nuclear powered ballistic missile submarine.

Table 4. Russian Nuclear Force Scenarios, 2003-2004

	Without START II				Under START II			
	High Budget		Low Budget		High Budget		Low Budget	
	Launchers	Warheads	Launchers	Warheads	Launchers	Warheads	Launchers	Warheads
Operational Strategic								
ICBMs	666	2040	496	1870	611	611	441	441
SLBMs	256	1520	168	928	256	1520	168	928
Bombers	45	688	30	448	45	688	30	448
Subtotal (Strategic)	**967**	**4248**	**694**	**3246**	**912**	**2819**	**639**	**1817**
Operational Non-strategic								
SLCM		350		350		350		350
Tactical Bombs		1000		1000		1000		1000
Subtotal (Non-strategic)		**1350**		**1350**		**1350**		**1350**
Spares (10%)		**560**		**460**		**417**		**317**
"Hedge" Warheads								
ICBM warheads to upload SS-19 and SS-24					151	939	151	939
Subtotal ("Hedge")					**151**	**939**	**151**	**939**
Possible Inactive Warheads								
ICBM (SS-18, SS-19)		2962		2962		3452		3452
SLBM (SS-N-18, SS-N-20, SS-N-23)		880		1472		880		1272
Strategic Bomber Weapons		612		812		612		812
Subtotal (Inactive)		**4454**		**5246**		**4944**		**5536**
Grand Total		**10,612**		**10,302**		**10,469**		**9959**

Table 5. US Nuclear Warheads and Yield, FY 1945-FY 1996

End-FY	Stockpile	Yield (Mt)
1945	2	0
1946	9	0
1947	13	0
1948	50	1
1949	170	4
1950	299	10
1951	438	35
1952	841	50
1953	1169	73
1954	1703	339
1955	2422	2880
1956	3692	9189
1957	5543	17,546
1958	7345	17,304
1959	12,298	19,055
1960	18,638	20,491
1961	22,229	10,948
1962	26,082	12,825
1963	28,527	15,977
1964	29,571	16,944
1965	31,229	15,153
1966	31,301	14,037
1967	31,345	12,786
1968	29,687	11,838
1969	27,326	11,714
1970	25,739	9695
1971	25,745	8584
1972	26,230	8532
1973	27,607	8452
1974	28,309	8425
1975	27,277	7368
1976	25,773	5936
1977	24,996	5845
1978	23,898	5721
1979	23,769	5696
1980	23,614	5619
1981	22,705	5383
1982	22,500	5359
1983	22,841	5232
1984	23,084	5192
1985	22,950	5217
1986	22,915	5415
1987	23,236	4882
1988	22,958	4790
1989	21,944	4743
1990	21,234	4519
1991	19,034	3796
1992	13,834	3168
1993	11,534	2647
1994	11,302	2375
1995	11,244	2363
1996	11,172	2336

Table 6. USSR/Russian Nuclear Warheads, 1949-1996

End Year	Strategic	Non-Strategic	Stockpiled	Intact Warheads
1949		1	1	?
1950		5	5	?
1951		25	25	?
1952		50	50	?
1953		120	120	?
1954		150	150	?
1955		200	200	?
1956	126	300	426	?
1957	160	500	660	?
1958	269	600	869	?
1959	360	700	1060	?
1960	405	1200	1605	?
1961	471	2000	2471	?
1962	522	2800	3322	?
1963	638	3600	4238	?
1964	821	4400	5221	?
1965	929	5200	6129	?
1966	1089	6000	7089	?
1967	1539	6800	8339	?
1968	1799	7600	9399	?
1969	2138	8400	10,538	?
1970	2443	9200	11,643	?
1971	2592	10,500	13,092	?
1972	2678	11,800	14,478	?
1973	2815	13,100	15,915	?
1974	2985	14,400	17,385	?
1975	3743	15,700	19,443	?
1976	4205	17,000	21,205	?
1977	4744	18,300	23,044	?
1978	5793	19,600	25,393	?
1979	7035	20,900	27,935	?
1980	7862	22,200	30,062	?
1981	8549	23,500	32,049	?
1982	9152	24,800	33,952	?
1983	9704	26,100	35,804	?
1984	10,031	27,400	37,431	?
1985	10,497	28,700	39,197	
1986	10,723	30,000	40,723	45,000
1987	11,159	27,700	38,859	43,000
1988	11,630	25,700	37,330	41,000
1989	12,117	23,700	35,817	39,000
1990	11,815	21,700	33,515	37,000
1991	10,672	18,933	29,606	35,000
1992	10,089	16,167	26,256	33,000
1993	9385	13,400	22,785	31,000
1994	8434	10,633	19,067	29,000
1995	7748	7867	15,615	27,000
1996	7622	5100	12,722	25,000

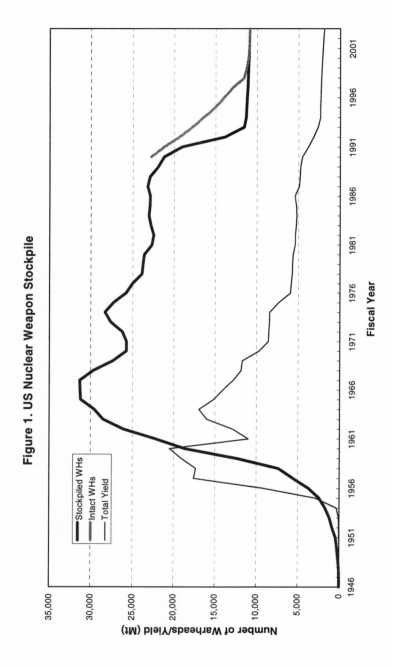

Figure 1. US Nuclear Weapon Stockpile

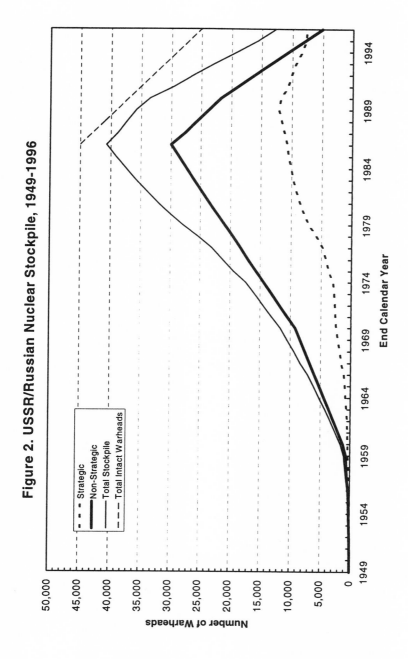

Figure 2. USSR/Russian Nuclear Stockpile, 1949-1996

8

Ballistic Missile Defence:
Enduring Questions

John Pike

Ballistic missile defence remains an enduring national security controversy. The debate over ballistic missile defence retains an intensity approaching that of the Cold War, at least in Washington.

In the summer of 1993 US Secretary of Defense Les Aspin declared an end to the Star Wars debate, and renamed the Strategic Defense Initiative (SDI) the Ballistic Missile Defense Program (BMDP). While a few acronyms were changed, and the staff of the SDI Organization acquired new BMD Organization business cards, little else of substance changed. For the most part the Clinton Administration merely renamed and continued programmes dating from the Reagan or Bush era. In 1995, with the advent of the new Republican Congressional majority, those few Reaganesque programmes that had been curtailed, such as space-based lasers, were projected for revival as part of the Contract With America. And in 1996 the Dole presidential campaign extended the Cold War nostalgia with futile efforts to enact the Defend America Act.

There is, regrettably, little prospect that the BMD debate will follow the test ban debate into final conclusion. The end-game on nuclear testing was a contest between a small and increasingly isolated segment of the nuclear weapons establishment and the rest of the country. In contrast, ballistic missile defence programmes have extensive, pervasive and consolidated ideological and bureaucratic centres of advocacy which continue to propound their solutions as the remedy to the problem of the day, whatever it may be. Ballistic missile defence animates these constituencies with far greater vigour than their nuclear testing counterparts. While the institutional survival of BMD sceptics remains precarious, there is little prospect that the debate over missile defence will end with the demise of BMD proponents. Their institutional consolidation under the Reagan Administration has assured them momentum adequate to retain their suasive powers for years, if not decades, to come.

Throughout the first epoch of the nuclear era, America was continually confronted with a security dilemma for which ballistic missile defence seemed at first an appealing solution. In each instance, closer examination revealed the flaws of BMD, and the availability of more sensible approaches and alternatives. In each instance, the national debate over BMD was a useful framework for examining fundamental national security issues.

There is every reason to anticipate that in this second epoch of the nuclear era continuing debate over BMD will serve to clarify American national security strategy.

We are thus confronted once again with the enduring ballistic missile defence questions: Do we need it? Will it work? How much will it cost? Will it create more problems than it will solve? And, why are we doing this? These are the questions this chapter addresses, ending with a brief comment on the joint statement on ABM issues which resulted from the summit meeting of Presidents Clinton and Yeltsin in March 1997.

Do We Need It?

During the Cold War the apparent need for ballistic missile defence was never wanting in evidence – one need look no further than the Sputniks overhead or the missiles on display in Red Square. Advocates of American strategic supremacy were never reconciled to these developments, contending that mutual deterrence was a strategy which could be changed, rather than a condition that must be accepted.

Thus during the Cold War advocates of strategic defence endlessly rehearsed fears of an implacably hostile Soviet menace, and the necessity for all possible preparations for the final conflict with the forces of evil. In any event, ballistic missile defence remained the missing ingredient in the more comprehensive nuclear warfighting strategies that informed other strategic nuclear programmes. Without ballistic missile defence, these other programmes were clearly deficient in adding more than they subtracted from American security.

Ultimately the case for ballistic missile defence during the Cold War foundered on the presence of a worthy adversary which was clearly prepared to do as much as, if not far more than, would be required to offset whatever advantage might be secured through American anti-missile programmes.

"Limited" Nuclear Wars

With the end of the Cold War the proponents of the military utility of nuclear weapons have gained a new lease on life, with the prospect of limited nuclear wars that are indeed limited, if only by virtue of the modest stockpiles of nuclear weapons which might in the future be held by potential adversaries – the so-called "rogue states," Iran, Iraq, Libya, North Korea and Syria. Visions of splendid first strike and robust damage denial capabilities that proved so elusive in the face of the Evil Empire now seem not implausible in the face of the meagre assets of these so-called "rogue states." Perhaps now at last it will be possible to assert that all the baroque nuclear theology of escalation dominance and nuclear compellance may be given flesh – that nuclear explosive devices may be restored to the armamentarium of "normal" weapons rather than merely relegated to existing to deter their use by others.

These are indeed the issues that are at stake in the present debate. The crystalline clarity of the debates over nuclear theology have become clouded in the more general haze of the post-Cold War strategic confusion. Presently, the case for BMD is couched in broad terms of counter-proliferation and countering the excesses of the "rogue states." Anti-missile systems are deemed a panacea for all manner of advanced missile-delivered weapons that might be employed against American interests.

But the ultimate reality is that the scenario of greatest interest, and ultimate concern, is one in which nuclear tipped missiles are launched, or threaten to be launched, against American citizens. Though the identities of the adversaries may have changed, the major and minor arcana of this moment differ in no ponderable respect from those considerations that entranced generations of nuclear theologians thinking about this unthinkable moment of truth in the contest with the Soviet Union, or with Red China. Apart from the previously noted fact that such a nuclear exchange might indeed be limited by virtue of the relatively modest arsenals of the rogue states, we are presented once again with all the problematic perplexities of fighting and "winning" a limited nuclear war.

The expanded opportunity to realize these nuclear warfighting scenarios is accompanied by the vastly expanded difficulty in defining a problem to which BMD is a solution. That is, the ballistic missile threat must be large enough to be worthy of notice, but not so robust as to merely recapitulate all the conundrums of the Soviet threat. The star warriors and nuclear war-fighters have been not entirely equal to this task.

Scud - The Beginning or the End of the Line?

Advocates of "robust" anti-missile efforts contend that the threat that is posed to the national security of the United States by the proliferation of ballistic missiles is significant and growing, both quantitatively and qualitatively. The reality is that the number of states with active ballistic missile programmes has actually declined in recent years – Argentina, Brazil and South Africa have all abandoned their programmes, and no additional states have entered the lists. Current countries of non-proliferation concern, such as India and Pakistan, are neither current nor plausible adversaries of the United States. In general, the

Missile Technology Control Regime, along with other non-proliferation and export control efforts, have been highly effective in controlling the spread of missile technology

This fundamental premise of the bulk of current BMD programmes – that in the fairly near future the United States and its friends and allies will be confronted with a ballistic missile threat vastly exceeding the current one – is wrong. Essentially all ballistic missiles presently in the hands of potential regional adversaries have ranges in the hundreds, rather than thousands, of kilometres. Currently programmed, treaty-compliant interceptors, such as the PAC-3, will work about as well as can be hoped against these potential threats.

The least controversial and challenging (though non-trivial) threat is that posed by ballistic missiles with ranges of hundreds of kilometres carrying conventional unitary high-explosive warheads. Such missiles, Scuds, Scud-derivatives and the like, have been used in combat on more than one occasion, most recently and memorably by Iraq in the Gulf War. There is little doubt that the rogues have among them hundreds of such missiles, as there are literally thousands of such missiles dispersed among the Earth's nations.

The actual military and operational significance of these weapons has been limited, even in Desert Storm, and anti-missile systems are but one arrow in the quiver of those determined to counter this threat. But in contrast to other notional threats, there is at least little doubt that these missiles exist and that active defences could be deployed to counter them with at least arguable cost-effectiveness.

However, a much broader range of potential missile threats has been conjured with recently to justify continued or expanded BMD programmes. Upon closer examination in turn each is revealed as either too meagre or too daunting a threat to warrant ballistic missile defence as a primary response.

Super-Scud?

BMD advocates contend that the trend in ballistic missile proliferation is towards longer range and increasingly sophisticated missiles. But there is no evident trend towards longer-range ballistic missiles. Apart from the Saudi acquisition of Chinese CSS-2 missiles in the 1980s, and continued Indian development of the intermediate-range Agni, regional missile programmes are focused on missiles with ranges appropriate for attacking regional adversaries, typically with ranges of less than 1000 kilometres.

The rogue states have yet to deploy missiles with ranges of thousands of kilometres. This is no accident. By and large, missiles with ranges of more than a few hundred kilometres would sail harmlessly over the regional rivals of the rogue states. North Korea finds South Korea embarrassingly close, and the bulk of the Japanese home islands are less than a thousand kilometres removed. Deploying ballistic missiles with ranges of thousands of kilometres would bring the Philippines, Vietnam and Outer Mongolia within the North's reach. Although there are reports that North Korea is developing such missiles, this would represent a major technological challenge for no apparent purpose. It is entirely imaginable that the limited photographic intelligence supporting these reports is based on nothing more than imagery of dummy mock-ups of missiles.

Even Iran, often cited as the potential customer for Pyongyang's new and improved missiles, must reach out a mere 1000 kilometres to touch Israeli soil. Indeed, in looking at regional rivalries, there is no plausible pairing of launch site and target that would require missiles with ranges of thousands of kilometres. Thus it should come as no surprise that neither of the rogues with indigenous missile industries – Iraq and North Korea – has devoted great energy to developing such longer-range missiles.

There seems little prospect that such longer-range missiles will be deployed any time soon. The Iraqi missile industrial base has been effectively dismantled in the wake of the Gulf War, with little prospect of its revival in the face of greatly strengthened international controls on access to missile-related technology. The North Korean programme has proceeded at a remarkably leisurely pace, and seems unlikely to produce usable missiles in meaningful numbers in the limited time remaining to the present regime governing that unfortunate land.

In any event, the costs of such longer-range missiles mandate that they be deployed in smaller numbers than the Scud and its kindred, which means that they will be of even less significance if armed with conventional warheads. The potential small inventories of longer-range theatre missiles would primarily be of interest for delivering weapons of mass destruction – most plausibly nuclear weapons. Thus the longer-range theatre missile threat is largely inseparable from the spread of nuclear weapons, which probably accounts in no small measure for the limited interest shown in such missiles. Neither Libya nor Syria have mounted meaningful nuclear weapons efforts, the Iraqi and North Korean programmes are in abeyance, and the Iranian nuclear weapons programme is proceeding rather slowly in the face of heavy international opposition.

Just as there is little reason to anticipate that the North Korean long-range missile programmes will reach fruition prior to the demise of that country's current regime, there is little reason to anticipate that Iran's declining economy and decaying animosity to the West will propel their nuclear weapons programme to culmination.

While it is true that in the late 1980s Saudi Arabia acquired a few dozen CSS-2 missiles, with ranges of about 3000 km, there seems little immediate prospect of these missiles being turned against the friends or forces of the United States. It is equally difficult to envisage the use against American interests of the Indian Agni, with a somewhat shorter range.

There would seem to be no compelling reason for deploying anti-missile systems specifically intended to counter theatre ballistic missiles with ranges of thousands rather than hundreds of kilometres. The case for deploying theatre missile defences with capabilities beyond those of the improved Patriot PAC-3/ ERINT remains unproven. There is little prospect within the foreseeable future that the United States or its allies will be threatened by Third World ballistic missiles that cannot be addressed by such systems.

New Intercontinental Threats?

Finally, BMD advocates claim that several countries that are hostile to the United States (including North Korea, Iran, Libya, and Iraq) have demonstrated an interest in acquiring ballistic missiles capable of reaching the United States.

Apart from a few off-hand comments to reporters, there is no concrete evidence that any of these countries are actively seeking ballistic missiles capable of reaching the continental United States. The Iraqi programme, such as it was, has been dismantled, and Libyan efforts are long in abeyance. At present the only real country of direct concern to the United States is North Korea, which faces substantial technological challenges in developing missiles more capable than the Scud.

Even the most capable North Korean missile for which there is any evidence whatsoever has at most a potential for reaching the furthest tip of the Aleutian islands. Korean intentions concerning development of longer-range ballistic missiles remain uncertain. Intelligence is ambiguous, however, as to whether this Taepo Dong-2 missile represents a serious effort or merely an attempt to deceive the American intelligence community – it may be that the mock-ups and test facilities observed by our intelligence satellites are in fact crafty deception measures. North Korea's capabilities to develop such intermediate-range missiles appear meagre, given the substantial engineering challenges this would pose. It would not be possible to build missiles by simply scaling up technology. Current efforts to contain the North Korean nuclear programme diminished concerns about North Korean missile programmes.

In any event, the profound engineering challenges that in turn confronted America, the Soviet Union, and China in the development of ICBMs has led the US intelligence community to conclude that the emergence of new ICBM threats to the continental United States lies more than a decade in the future. While BMD advocates have quibbled with these conclusions, there is little reason to doubt this fundamental reality.

In light of these daunting challenges posed by indigenous long-range missile development, BMD proponents have asserted that there are ways for determined countries to acquire missiles capable of threatening the United States with little warning by means other than indigenous development. There is simply no evidence for such assertions. The most frequently cited example is the Russian SS-25 ICBM, which forms the basis for the START space launch vehicle. But

Russia is offering space services from Russia, and is not proposing to transfer components of this system to other countries.

The favourite scenario is that a country contracts with Russia to purchase a SS-25 ICBM to use as a space launch vehicle, and when the rocket is delivered, the Russian crew is bound and gagged at gun-point, and the rocket converted into a missile aimed at New York. Even Tom Clancy would have a hard time making this plot believable, and it is difficult to understand basing national policy on such outlandish imaginings.

Russia is a signatory of the Missile Technology Control Regime, and by all accounts is working to ensure its implementation. The Russian aerospace industry has also obtained profitable participation in the international launch services market, and such profits would end with a major violation of the MTCR. Faced with the choice between a sale of a few missiles to a poor country such as North Korea, or continued sales of many launch vehicles to a variety of rich countries, the self-interest of the Russian aerospace industry clearly supports strict compliance with the MTCR.

Although these countries might wish to acquire the means of striking the USA, intercontinental-range ballistic missiles constitute the most expensive and challenging of their options. All of these countries have a demonstrated track record of supporting international terrorist activity, and terrorists would be a far less demanding means of striking America. However, such acts against the United States have been quite rare, and ambiguous in origin, suggesting that it is fear of retaliation, rather than simple inability to reach America, that has stayed the hand of potential adversaries. Ballistic missiles, in contrast, leave the unambiguous return address of their launch site, inviting certain retaliation.

Old Threats in New Bottles

That anti-missile systems remain a solution in search of a problem is most clearly revealed by the extent to which advocates of ballistic missile defence resort to China and Russia as threats of last resort to justify BMD deployment. Implicitly conceding that the rogue states are weak reeds upon which to support ambitious weapons systems, BMD proponents seem disinclined to concede that the demise of the Soviet Union, or the effective collapse of Communism in China, have diminished the case for deploying anti-missile systems against these former adversaries.

The longer-range missile threats posed by the "rogue" states remain no more than future possibilities. But America has now accumulated decades of experience in the face of Russian and Chinese ICBM capabilities. Although die-hard BMD advocates have long insisted that these forces constitute a clear and present danger that can only be countered by anti-missile defences, over time a national consensus has persisted to the contrary, and there seems to be little new in recent years to alter that judgement.

In the immediate aftermath of the collapse of Soviet state power there was heightened concern about the potential for accidental or unauthorized launch of strategic missiles. Over time, this concern has been replaced by the much more tangible and immediate concern about the potential for diversion of Russian nuclear material by terrorists or criminal organizations. The continued disarray of Russian early warning and command and control systems is worrisome, but there are much more direct solutions than BMD, including improvements in joint early warning mechanisms, and further reductions in the alert levels of strategic forces.

As for China, the United States managed to survive the Great Proletarian Cultural Revolution, the Gang of Four, and other alarming excursions by the Chinese polity without the aid of a BMD system. Notwithstanding the continued determination of Beijing to "liberate" Taiwan, there is little prospect that either country would risk burgeoning economic ties in a military confrontation that ran a significant risk of a nuclear exchange.

Will It Work?

A variety of anti-missile systems have been proposed in response to these varied threats. Some are relatively well established and non-controversial, while others remain poorly defined and highly controversial, even among ardent BMD supporters. Some systems have undergone extensive field testing while others have encountered surprisingly poor performance in initial tests, or have yet to leave the laboratory or the drawing board.

Although initially disappointing test results are likely to be improved on in future trials, there is little reason to anticipate that any system will demonstrate perfect performance with perfect confidence. Against some conventional threats one might conclude that something was better than nothing. But against weapons of mass destruction prudent leaders will surely conclude that less than perfect defences of uncertain reliability provide no more comfort than no defence at all.

Lower-Tier Theatre Missile Defences

Near-term anti-missile improvements to existing air defence systems include the deployment of the Army's Patriot PAC-2 Guidance Enhanced Missiles (GEM), which corrected some of the shortcomings identified during Desert Storm, and the Marine Corps' HAWK Upgrades. These radar-guided systems retain their explosive warheads which are detonated near their targets by proximity fuses.

The Patriot PAC-3 is an entirely new missile, derived from the ERINT interceptor, which is intended to counter theatre-class ballistic missile threats using hit-to-kill intercept. The PAC-3 missile is fired from the same launcher as earlier versions of Patriot, although eight of the smaller PAC-3 missiles are carried in each firing unit, versus four each of the earlier versions.

The Navy Area Defense enhancement to the AEGIS/Standard Missile air defence system provides a tactical missile defence capability comparable to that provided by PAC-3. The modified Standard Missile 2 Block IV missiles will be deployed on Ticonderoga-class cruisers and Arleigh Burke-class destroyers equipped with the powerful AEGIS air and missile defence radar. A limited operational capability is planned for 1999 and an initial operational capability is planned for 2001.

Medium Extended Air Defense System (MEADS), formerly known as CorpSAM, is an international effort to develop a replacement for the widely deployed HAWK anti-aircraft system. This highly mobile system, to be deployed with forward ground forces, is intended to provide omni-directional coverage against the full range of air-breathing threats (both aircraft and cruise missiles). The United States, Germany, and Italy are partners in MEADS, following a decision in early 1995 by France to withdraw from the programme.

These programmes are relatively modest in cost, have limited technical risk, and are intended to counter existing threats from ballistic missiles with ranges of hundreds of kilometres. Other more ambitious programmes pose greater challenges in countering potential future emerging theatre threats.

Upper-Tier Theatre Missile Defences

The Army's Theatre High Altitude Area Defense (THAAD) is intended to provide extended coverage, engaging incoming missile at ranges of up to several hundred kilometres, versus the tens of kilometres provided by the previously discussed systems. This hit-to-kill interceptor could thus provide multiple engagement opportunities against missiles with ranges of hundreds of kilometres, and enhanced capabilities against future threats from missiles which might have ranges of thousands of kilometres. Theatre High Altitude Area Defense missiles are intended to actually collide with the target ballistic missile, rather than destroying it by exploding nearby, as fragmentation warheads do. Final guidance to the target is provided by an infra-red seeker on the kill vehicle. The interception of a hostile ballistic missile is intended to occur outside the earth's atmosphere, or high in the atmosphere. The range of the THAAD system is to be approximately 200 km horizontally and 150 km vertically. In order to provide an emergency capability to counter a small number of missiles, plans call for fielding about 40 THAAD missiles and associated radars by 1999. Each THAAD battery would include nine launchers and 150 missiles.

Based on AEGIS-equipped ships, the Navy's theatre wide long-range interceptor system will provide wide area coverage against a wide range of threats, including ascent phase intercepts where the ship's mobility permits such engagements.

Each of these interceptor systems would be supported by associated radars. In addition, other space-based sensors would also be used in theatre (and national) missile defences. Although these programmes were formerly funded as part of the Strategic Defense Initiative programme, more recently they have been funded directly by the Air Force, while retaining their missile defence mission.

The Space-based Infra-red System or SBIRS is an integrated system of global missile warning satellites which will replace the existing Defense Support Program (DSP) satellite constellation in geostationary orbit and the Heritage intelligence sensors in elliptical high earth orbit. In addition to supporting the traditional missile launch detection function of DSP, the SBIRS constellation will provide greatly improved technical intelligence capabilities, and significantly enhanced support to theatre and national missile defences. Deployment of SBIRS will begin in 2002 with the launch of the first of four SBIRS geosynchronous orbit and two highly elliptical orbit satellites. A major block change in the high-altitude satellites to achieve an optimum "high/low" balance is also planned beginning in 2006.

SBIRS also includes deployment of from 21 to 28 low-altitude Space and Missile Tracking System (SMTS) satellites, possibly beginning as early as 2002 and in any event by 2006. SMTS, formerly known as Brilliant Eyes, is the low earth orbit component of the SBIRS architecture, which is able to track missiles following the burnout of the booster motors. This post-boost phase tracking capability enables the system to cue long-range theatre and national missile defence interceptors with precise targeting data.

"Thin" National Missile Defence

The Clinton Administration's NMD deployment programme is referred to as "3 plus 3" – a three year development and planning phase from 1996 through 1999 which, if necessary, could be followed by a three year system acquisition and deployment phase. This system would be intended to counter an ICBM attack consisting of several missiles launched at the United States from a rogue nation, or a very small, accidental launch from more nuclear capable states. If by 1999 it was judged that the ballistic missile threat to the United States warranted the deployment of an NMD system, that system could be deployed three years later, by the year 2003. However, if by 1999 the threat is not judged to warrant NMD deployment, the "3 plus 3" programme would preserve the option to deploy an NMD system within three years of a decision to do so through continued development and testing of system elements.

In the fall of 1995 the Air Force and Army identified alternative deployment options, based on an immediate commitment to deployment, which would require a minimum of approximately four years to achieve an operational capability. These concepts, which were further refined during the course of 1996, use ground-based radars and sensors, and battle management elements similar to those in the baseline 3+3 plan, although they differ in detail. Each plan proposes to provide coverage of the entire United States, including Alaska and Hawaii. Initially using ground-based radars, either option would use target tracking data from advanced space-based sensors – such as the Space-Based Infra-red System and Space and Missile Tracking System – when they become operational.

The primary difference between these plans and the baseline "3+3" programme is that the service proposals envisage an immediate commitment to deployment, while providing a less robust pathway to more extensive future deployment options.

"Defending" America

Deeming these efforts inadequate, Bob Dole's Defend America Act of 1996 required the deployment by the year 2003 of a system to provide a highly effective defence of all 50 states against limited, unauthorized and accidental attacks ... [that would be] augmented over time to provide a layered defence against larger and more sophisticated ballistic missile threats as they emerge. Just what this would entail remains unclear, though the bill specifies that the initial defence must include ground-, sea- or space-based interceptors, ground-based radar, space-based sensors including the Space and Missile Tracking System (SMTS), and a battle management and command and control system to integrate the operations of these various components. The more extensive "augmented" layered defence would follow, adding space-based weapons such as lasers or kinetic energy interceptors (Brilliant Pebbles).

It is difficult to know what to make of this legislation, which was stalled in the Senate and never brought to the floor in the House, since it was essentially a creature of the Dole-for-President effort, largely divorced from concrete military objectives. The putative differences between Dole and Clinton were that Dole was prepared to make an immediate commitment to deployment of an initial national missile defence, and was somewhat more forward leaning in supporting more extensive follow-on deployments. But the Clinton "3+3" plan would achieve the same end, though with a slightly more leisurely decision-making timeline, and the follow-on programmes of the Defend America plan were not unfunded by Clinton.

Gulf War Lessons Learned (and Relearned)

All of these plans stand in the shadow of the Gulf War with Iraq, which imperceptibly accompanied the collapse of Soviet power. The current ballistic missile defence debate is thus not surprisingly framed in terms of lessons learned and mis-learned from Desert Storm. In the wake of that defining event, the broad array of anti-missile systems initiated to counter the Soviet threat from the East were reoriented to counter the impending threat from the South. Today a range of contending proposals are at hand, suggesting a wide range of options as to how these various weapons might be deployed to enhance American security.

The anti-missile debate during the Cold War was mercifully free of combat experience – no nuclear war was fought, and thus no actual combat data were available to leaven the arguments of proponents or sceptics. The end of the Cold War coincided with the first actual combat experience with anti-missile weapons. However, the lessons learned from the Gulf War experience have both illuminated and obscured the subsequent anti-missile debate. It is clear that the Gulf War provided valuable data on key questions such as the importance of intelligence, the workings of deterrence, the effectiveness of counterforce, and actual anti-missile operations. Not surprisingly, the interpretation of these data remains in dispute.

The bare facts are well established. During 40 days of combat operations Iraqi forces fired at least 81 modified Scud missiles, primarily at targets in Israel and Saudi Arabia. All these launches were detected by US early warning satellites, and a total of 157 Patriot interceptor missiles were fired to counter these attacks. The total resulting property damage was subsequently estimated at several hundred million dollars, with a total of numerous injuries, including 28 US soldiers killed by a single Scud that struck a barracks in Saudi Arabia.

The conventional wisdom in the immediate aftermath of Desert Storm focused on the failures of intelligence, arms control, deterrence, and counterforce, and the apparent successes of active defence. Thus were the flagging fortunes of the Strategic Defense Initiative revived. Since then, a more nuanced view has emerged, which stresses the opportunities for improved intelligence collection and dissemination, strengthened arms control measures, the successes of deterrence and counterforce, and the failures of active defence.

The conventional wisdom five years ago was: active defence worked extremely well, counterforce didn't work very well and deterrence failed completely. It is now clear that deterrence, when it was attempted, worked perfectly, counterforce worked extremely well, and active defence worked very poorly, if at all.

The conventional wisdom at the time was that deterrence failed because Iraq grabbed Kuwait while nobody was looking. It has become clear, particularly from various memoirs and recent defectors, that very clear thresholds were laid down in advance of Desert Storm. Saddam Hussein was told: "If you use weapons of mass destruction, it would be better for you if you had never been born." He wanted his regime to survive, and so even though

Iraq had the capability of using weapons of mass destruction, it did not. Saddam was successfully deterred.

At the time, the conventional wisdom was that the great Scud hunt had consumed vast quantities of American air power to no purpose. It is clear that the air campaign against the Scud mobile launchers constituted only about 2 per cent of the total sorties during Desert Storm, and was astonishingly effective in inflicting virtual attrition on the launchers in the sense that Iraq had roughly 500 Scuds that it could have launched. At the maximum launch rate, the Iraqis could have launched all of them, had it not been for the fact that the Scud drivers were far too busy running from the air campaign to worry about trying to perform their mission of firing their missiles. So, in fact, we had about an 85 per cent virtual attrition from the air campaign.

Of course, as is now well known, the Patriot air defence missile, rather than being virtually perfect, failed for precisely the reasons that critics of missile defence have said that active defences will always be leaky. That is, Patriot had a hard time dealing with the inadvertent counter-measures created by the fragments resulting from the Scuds breaking apart, and software reliability proved to be a fatal flaw.

Unfortunately, in future conflicts anti-missile systems might be confronted with adversaries who were deliberately rather than merely inadvertently clever. The next step up the threat ladder is missiles of similar range to the Scud armed with less conventional sub-munitions – cluster-bombs carrying chemical or biological agents. Although it is not believed that such missiles are in the arsenals of potential regional adversaries, Iraq is known to have conducted work on cluster-bomb warheads for its Scud-derivatives prior to the Gulf War. And no great engineering marvel is required to extend the cluster-bomb techniques used for bombs dropped from airplanes to a ballistic missile warhead.

Theatre missiles tipped with cluster bombs recapitulate all the tactical problems posed by nuclear Multiple Independently-Targetable Re-entry Vehicles (MIRVs) during the Cold War, except that nuclear MIRVs were typically limited to a dozen or so warheads per missile, whereas many dozens of chemical-filled cluster bombs might be fitted atop a single Scud-derivative. The task of the defence is greatly complicated by the fact that each cluster bomb is little more than a glorified hand-grenade, too small a target for a million-dollar interceptor. Although there are potentially other means of countering this threat, firing ground-based interceptors at great clouds of incoming cluster bombs seems far from the most promising.

Thus it is clear that all the proposed systems, from improved versions of Patriot to the most ambitious space-based interceptors, cannot plausibly aspire to perfection. While each of these systems might be capable of intercepting some missiles some of the time, the combat experience of Patriot demonstrates that none of these future systems can be relied upon to intercept all their targets all the time.

How Much Will It Cost?

Subsidiary to questions of need or effectiveness, though not entirely unimportant, is the question of what these systems will cost. The costs of currently contemplated anti-missile systems may seem modest compared with the trillion dollar fantasies of a decade ago. But they are nonetheless real money, even by Washington standards. The roughly three billion dollars that the Clinton Administration has proposed for anti-missile systems each year for the remainder of this decade nearly matches the actual level of funding provided by the Congress during the first decade of Star Wars. The billion or so proposed for additional funding by Republicans will certainly match the largess of the Reagan era.

Reviving Reagan and Bush Administration programmes for deployment of National Missile Defense and a Global Protection System could require doubling this budget more or less immediately, with significant further increases thereafter. We have very little to show for the $40 billion spent on Star Wars over the past dozen years. We would have even less to show for spending another $40 billion on Star Wars over the next half-dozen years, should we restore the projects advocated by previous administrations.

Total development costs for the Clinton Administration's "3+3" option are estimated at about $2.5 billion, with total programme deployment costs of about $10 billion. The Air Force estimates that its proposed early deployment option could be fielded at a cost of about $2.5 billion, although other sources have suggested that the total cost could be as high as $4 billion. The Army estimates the cost to develop, test, acquire and deploy its proposed system at about $5.2 billion – a higher risk quick response or emergency capability that would require four years to deploy would encompass less testing, and cost about $4.8 billion.

The Congressional Budget Office (CBO) has estimated that the Dole Defend America Act would cost nearly $10 billion over the next five years – roughly $7 billion more than has been budgeted by the Clinton Administration for national missile defence. Through 2010, CBO estimates that the Defend America plan could cost between $31 billion and $60 billion, depending on what types of systems are deployed. CBO estimated that total recurring costs would be about $2 billion annually for the low-end system and about $4 billion annually for the high-end system.

These are not small amounts of money – the annual recurring costs of the Defend America programme range between the total annual budget of NASA's space station and the annual costs of the space shuttle - roughly equivalent to the entire budget of the National Science Foundation.

Will It Hurt More Than Help?

Unfortunately, these immediate financial costs may be dwarfed by larger strategic and geopolitical costs, which would have far greater though less readily calculated financial implications as well. During the Cold War countering the Soviet strategic arsenal was the abiding focus of anti-missile activities, with in excess of $100 billion expended in the process. With the end of the Cold War the focus has broadened, but Russian strategic forces have not been entirely forgotten.

Some remain concerned that the relatively amicable relations between Russia and the world of the early 1990s were an historical aberration. They fear that the logic of geography and history will inevitably reassert itself in the form of a return to an adversarial stance towards the West, and towards the United States most particularly. Others are concerned that inattention and inadvertence could also lead to a renewal of tensions. That is to say, both contending schools on the origins of the Cold War provide predictions as to how some semblance of Cold War hostilities might resume, though as always they differ as to origins and prescriptions.

Although not prominent in recent debates, those who advocated deployment of large scale anti-missile systems to counter Soviet strategic forces during the Cold War would appear to continue to see utility in such deployments in the event of a resumption of hostilities. The imponderables of such a resumption of adversarial relations have largely precluded speculation on what manner of anti-missile system might be deployed under the circumstances, particularly given the great uncertainties attendant on the state of Russian strategic forces at that future time.

That such a system would extend far beyond the bounds outlined in the 1972 Anti-Ballistic Missile Treaty between the United States and the Soviet Union is without doubt. It is on the question of how far one might go beyond these bounds without invoking an untoward response from Russia that is a key element of the current debate.

As always, there is no prospect that any American anti-missile system could entirely deprive Russia of the capacity to destroy American society in a retaliatory strike. However, neither Russia nor America currently base the strategic calculus simply on such finite deterrence capabilities. Rather, existing and immediately prospective arms control agreements contemplate both sides retaining the capability to rain thousands of nuclear weapons upon the other's territory.

The START-1 and START-2 arms reduction agreements would impose significant reductions in the massive overkill that was accumulated during the Cold War. But these agreements, if implemented, would not entirely eliminate the potential for one side to attack and destroy a substantial proportion of the other side's retaliatory capability. Indeed, some developments, such as large inventories of counterforce-capable submarine-launched missiles, the elimination of mobile land-based missiles, and improved attack submarine capabilities, may have somewhat increased the potential for such a first strike.

Under such worst-case conditions, which have always been the touchstone of the nuclear debate, even relatively modest anti-missile systems might perform relatively well in blunting the resulting ragged retaliation. While certainly not providing a damage-denial capability, they might make the difference between the survival of society and its utter devastation. However, this advantage would accrue only to the side that struck first, increasing the incentives for both sides to pre-empt in a time of crisis. The obvious counter, keeping forces on high levels of alert so that they can be launched before the blow from the other side lands, increases the risk of inadvertent or accidental use of nuclear weapons, particularly in the face of possible failures of command and control systems.

How large a system would provoke such worries is difficult to calculate, which is precisely the heart of the matter. Unlike the duelling-silo calculations of counterforce campaigns, which are a matter of simple arithmetic, calculating the potential effectiveness of an anti-missile system is fraught with profound uncertainties. Inevitably, the conservative attack planner would tend to overestimate the potential effectiveness of the system, and the cautious defender would tend to underestimate its effectiveness. The attacker would wish to add more offensive weapons to be sure of penetrating the defence, and the defender would thicken his shield to add insurance against such penetration.

Guarding against such a futile and potentially open-ended arms race was the central consideration in the signing of the ABM Treaty in 1972. It was agreed at the time that only extremely modest systems would be deployed — 100 interceptors defending a portion of the country's territory from a single site.

It is clear that some of the more robust architectures envisaged for countering accidental or inadvertent launches — as many as 200 warheads — involve architectures that conservative Russian planners might regard as calling into question the viability of their deterrent posture. The hundreds of warheads intercepted by such anti-missile systems might represent a significant fraction of the warheads anticipated to survive an American first strike.

Thus if the United States chose now or in the future to move beyond the long-standing ABM Treaty limits, potential Russian reactions are difficult to gauge. Much would depend on whether the transition to a new regime were done with or without Russian agreement. The Reagan and Bush Administrations sought vainly for years to persuade Moscow of the wisdom of deploying large-scale anti-missile systems. The Clinton Administration has had little more success in persuading Moscow of the merits of far less sweeping revisions to the Treaty.

During the Cold War the achievement of nuclear parity with the United States was one of the signal achievements of the Soviet Union. Shorn of the other trappings of empire, retaining nuclear parity with Washington appears to have high priority in Moscow. Whether the Russian government would mobilize the will and resources to do so, and the forms such an effort might take, remain unclear. Perhaps there would be little or no response. Perhaps the geopolitical evolutions of the past decade have fundamentally severed the nexus between the nuclear genie and great power relations. And perhaps all that remains of the nuclear game is the slow and painful process of dismantling the distended stockpiles that were accumulated with such feverish haste during the Cold War.

But the fact remains that virtually every ballistic missile and nuclear warhead capable of reaching the United States is today under Moscow's control. Thus it would seem only prudent to gauge carefully potential new responses to new or emerging threats in the light of their potential effect in exacerbating this traditional threat.

Why Are We Doing This?

Despite these risks, an impressive array of institutional forces is driving American policy in a direction of ignoring all of the true lessons that we should have learned from Desert Storm.

The Republicans

It continues to be an article of faith within the Republican Party that it was Star Wars and Star Wars alone that led to the demise of the "evil empire." It is certainly the case that Star Wars is a saliva test issue within the Republican Party and that no "true Republican" will say anything against it. It is very important that this should be the case because the Republican Party is otherwise deeply divided between the deficit hawks and the defence hawks. Thus it is no accident that in the Republican Contract on America, Star Wars was about the only plank in the national security component that actually called for spending money. The depth of the divisions in the Republican Party was highlighted by the inability of the House leadership to bring the Defend America Act to the floor in May 1996, once senior Republicans had become aware of the cost estimates of the Act.

Clinton and the Democrats

The Clinton Administration entered office with the watch-word "It's the economy, stupid" – victorious in a campaign predicated on the proposition that it could lose on foreign policy issues but it could not win on foreign policy issues. The keys to denying Republicans effective foreign policy electoral issues have included embracing Republican foreign policies, to the extent that such policies can be discerned.   Although confusion within the ranks of Republicans has complicated this task, as demonstrated by the Defend America Act imbroglio in the House of Representatives, for the most part Clinton Administration tactics have succeeded in denying the Republicans political advantage on foreign policy.

The Military

Each of the military services has its own institutional reasons for advancing the ballistic missile defence agenda, both to satisfy internal political difficulties as well as to advance their interests against the other services.

The Army fears that the possibility of casualties from even a single Scud would stay the hand of politicians contemplating military action.   If this happened, the Army's budget would be at risk.   The Army's answer is THAAD.   But, as with Patriot, THAAD cannot provide a foolproof shield; it might work fairly well at times, but not perfectly all the time.

The Navy says that its interceptor, Upper Tier, will outdo THAAD by intercepting even longer range missiles. Absent this claim, the Navy might lose a skirmish in its eternal battle with the Army.   Upper Tier also solves an internal political problem for the Navy as well.   During the Cold war, a vast armada of cruisers and destroyers were dedicated to protecting the Navy's aircraft carriers from Soviet bombers.   Absent this threat, the rational course would be to load these vessels with Tomahawk cruise missiles.   This would provide a potent strike capability, free of the risk that captured pilots might show up on CNN.   But just as battleship admirals dominated the Navy before Pearl Harbor, today the Navy is dominated by carrier admirals, and Tomahawk-armed cruisers would render aircraft carriers largely superfluous. So another mission, such as carrying Upper Tier, must be found for the Navy's cruisers and destroyers, lest they join the mothballed battleships.

The Air Force has long defined itself as America's "aerospace" champion, and Star Wars and its latter-day descendants have offered an unprecedented opportunity to give operational meaning to doctrinal precepts.   Air Force doctrine has long maintained that air and space are a single indivisible operational medium, and that the full panoply of air power missions and weapons should and will have space counterparts.   Long frustrated in realizing these schemes, which have always foundered on the fundamental and ineradicable physical differences between air and space, the Air Force has embraced ballistic missile defence as the bridge to future glory.   To a far greater extent than the other services, the institutional Air Force is deeply divided between combat and support components, with combat components and their personnel given pride of place and preferment in career advancement. The BMD mission offers the unique opportunity to transform Space Command operators and their supporting development components from second class support units to first-line warfighters, and such opportunities are not to be lightly discarded.

Contractors

Last but certainly not least in this debate is the contractor community, which views ballistic missile defence as one of the few remaining opportunities to get new contracts. Having consumed the better part of $40 billion since 1983 with very little to show as a result, BMD offers ample opportunity for prosperity with little fear of close scrutiny. If one reads the original version of the Missile Defense Act proposed last year in the Senate, and looks at all of the specific programmatic changes that were made, one could very easily call the Missile Defense Act of 1995 the TRW Legislative Relief Act of 1995. For each and every programmatic change that was made in the ballistic missile defence programme there was an identifiable contractor which had an identifiable problem that was being solved. For example, accelerating the deployment of Brilliant Eyes or the Space and Missile Tracking System to the year 2002 ensures that TRW remains in the space-based early warning system business so that its system is being deployed at the same time as those of the other contractors.

Whence the Threat to Peace?

In the closing years of the Cold War, Ronald Reagan finally concluded that "a nuclear war cannot be won and must never be fought." During the Cold War there were both Americans and Russians who contested this proposition in the furtherance of their contending ideological agenda. When, as it seemed at the time, the future freedom or liberation of all humanity for all time was in the balance, it was at least not implausible to conjure with thermonuclear extermination.

If the end of the Cold War has not marked the prematurely heralded "end of history" it has at least marked the end of an era in which there could be any pretence of any correlation between ends and means as regards the use of nuclear weapons.

For the United States, the detonation of even a single nuclear weapon over an American city could easily result in as many dead Americans as in *all* previous wars combined. This is not a risk that any responsible American leader would face lightly. While considerable sacrifice of blood and treasure was expended in the abolition of slavery or the defeat of the forces of fascist tyranny, today the United States and its allies survey a world mercifully free of such weighty concerns.

While the various "rogue" states remain an abiding annoyance to their neighbours, and to American policy-makers, even the most vivid imagination must fail to conflate the declining threats posed by these countries into disputes that would warrant gambling with the lives of hundreds of thousands, if not millions of Americans. Given the modest stakes that are at issue, even a "limited" nuclear war with one of these states in which a single nuclear warhead detonated over an American city would have to be judged as an unparalleled foreign policy catastrophe, regardless of however many weapons were intercepted by an anti-missile system, or whatever vengeance was inflicted upon our adversary.

There is little reason to suspect that the leaders of even the "rogue" states will ultimately make a different calculation. Throughout the first epoch of the nuclear era, the fundamental theological schism was between those who regarded nuclear weapons as ultimately usable, not unlike other weapons, and those who held that these devices existed only to deter their use by others. Over time, the experience of the nuclear powers inexorably dis-confirmed the conjectures of the nuclear war-fighters, as the possessors of these capabilities consistently shied away from situations in which their use might be actually contemplated.

During the Cold War it was often said that the United States needed nuclear weapons to offset the conventional superiority of the Red Army – the semi-mythical "Red Horde." With the end of the Cold War it might not be difficult for some of the rogue states to convince themselves that nuclear weapons might be useful to ward off the "Blue Horde" – the conventional forces of the Sole Remaining Superpower. As Les Aspin observed, the end of the Cold War has fundamentally reversed the *apparent* relationship between nuclear weapons and American security.

While some leaders in Tehran or Pongyang might sleep more soundly at night knowing that their nuclear arsenal would stay the hand of the Blue Horde, there is little reason to anticipate that these or any other leaders would find these capabilities useful for pro-active compellance rather than simple reactive deterrence. Nuclear tipped missiles in the hands of these states might effectively deter the United States from posing clear and immediate existential threats to these regimes – America would be rightly disinclined to wage unlimited war against states possessed of such deadly capabilities. But it is far from apparent that these states would find nuclear weapons any more "usable" than have countries with longer experience and with more abundant arsenals.

And while it is too frequently argued that the leaders of these countries are less rational or calculating than their great-power counterparts, evidence for such assertions is singularly lacking. Documents emerging from Cold War archives demonstrate that Kim Il Sung was exceedingly cautious in planning leading up to the Korean War. Today, the absence of Chinese and Russian support, and the evidence of American commitment to South Korea, would surely stay the hand of his successors from launching another such adventure.

There is too much loose talk about irrational Islamic fanaticism engendering an appetite for martyrdom which would welcome national annihilation as the price of destroying even a single American city. While religious enthusiasm propelled many Iranian soldiers to their deaths in the war with Iraq, the slaughter was no greater than the equally horrendous meat-grinder of the trench warfare of the First World War. While the simulated gushing blood of the Fountain of Martyrs in Tehran was without precedent in European capitals, in the end the "Mad Mullahs" of Tehran proved no less impervious to senseless sacrifice of blood and treasure. While Islam, as all other great religious traditions, provides sanction for personal martyrdom, it in no way compels national suicide.

Fortunately, in contrast to the Soviet Union, it cannot even be *argued* that the "rogue" states, whatever their ideological bent, pose an existential threat to the United States. Thus there can be no case for the United States posing a clear and present threat to the existence of these states, such that the question of the use of nuclear weapons could rationally arise. While it may seem prudent from time to time for America to chastise and rebuke (by judicious force of arms if needed) the leaders of these countries for their excesses, the conclusion of the Cold War is the template for the future of these unhappy lands. Over time, the promise of greater prosperity and personal freedom will lead to an evolution away from their adversarial stance towards the world, and the United States can await and encourage this evolution with the same patience that it awaited this evolution in such other adversaries.

USA and Russia: ABM Negotiations

US research and development of theatre missile defence (TMD) systems has set up a problem for the ABM Treaty. Russia's objective is to preserve the ABM Treaty. It accepts the arguments that were used in the first place, in 1972, when the ABM Treaty was coupled with the SALT 1 agreement: that it would only be possible to agree on limits to the numbers of strategic missiles if there were also strict limits on the deployment of anti-ballistic missile systems.

The USA wants to improve its TMD systems. It also wants eventually to be in a position to develop and deploy an ABM system that could deal with a limited number of incoming long-range ballistic missiles, and has been trying – so far unsuccessfully – to persuade the Russian side to consider amendments to the ABM Treaty. As a consequence, the Russian negotiators have become increasingly concerned about the US research work on high-altitude theatre missile defence, since this could become virtually indistinguishable from research into new ABM systems. This is one of the main stumbling-blocks in the way of START II ratification (see Chapter 11). The Russians are not particularly bothered about lower-velocity systems; an agreement on these was reached in 1996, but was not signed.

At Helsinki in March 1997 the White House announced a "major breakthrough" – a general understanding on a demarcation agreement also for higher-velocity TMD systems. The negotiators on both sides were instructed to reach an agreement as soon as possible in line with an agreed set of general principles and instructions:

–   Both sides declared themselves committed to the ABM Treaty "as a cornerstone of strategic stability." Consequently the deployment of TMD systems "must not lead to violation or circumvention of the ABM Treaty."
–   Theatre missile systems may only be deployed by either side if (i) they will not pose a realistic threat to the strategic nuclear forces of the other side, and (ii) will not be tested to give such systems that capability.
–   To this end, the velocity of the ballistic target missiles will not exceed 5 km/sec, and their range will not exceed 3500 km.
–   Neither side has plans for TMD systems with interceptor missiles faster than 5.5 km/sec for land-based and air-based systems or 4.5 km/sec for sea-based systems, and there will be no flight tests of such missiles before April 1999.
–   It is agreed that space-based interceptors would conflict with the ABM Treaty's ban on such systems, and they will not be developed or deployed.
–   It is agreed that there is considerable scope for cooperation in TMD, and in "resolving the tasks facing them, the parties will act in a spirit of cooperation, mutual openness, and commitment to the ABM Treaty."

In September 1997 two agreements were signed in New York. One was essentially the agreement on lower-velocity TMD systems that had been agreed in 1996 but that had not then been signed. The other was an agreement on higher-velocity systems; this codified the provisions of the Helsinki Summit Joint Statement. In particular, the parties agreed not to develop, test, or deploy space-based TMD interceptor missiles or space-based components based on other physical principles such as lasers that are capable of substituting for space-based TMD interceptor missiles. In addition, it was agreed that there would be a non-legally-binding unilateral statement of plans by each party, and a Joint Statement on the annual exchange of information concerning certain plans. It was also agreed that there could be no amendment or modification to the second agreed statement – that concerning higher-velocity systems – without a consensus among all the parties to the ABM Treaty.

It remains to be seen whether these agreements will get approval in the US Senate, and whether they will be adequate to enable the Russian Duma to ratify START II.

9

Nuclear Weapon Development Without Nuclear Testing?

Richard L. Garwin and Vadim A. Simonenko

Introduction

With the signing of the Comprehensive Test Ban Treaty (CTBT),[1] much of the uncertainty regarding future nuclear explosion testing has been removed. Even though the Treaty will not enter into force for the foreseeable future, the signatories are bound by the Vienna Convention on the Law of Treaties not to conduct nuclear tests. The relevant proscriptions are contained in Article I: Basic Obligations:

1. Each State Party undertakes not to carry out any nuclear weapon test explosion or any other nuclear explosion, and to prohibit and prevent any such nuclear explosion at any place under its jurisdiction or control.

2. Each State Party undertakes, furthermore, to refrain from causing, encouraging, or in any way participating in the carrying out of any nuclear weapon test explosion or any other nuclear explosion.

The negotiating record makes clear that the CTBT permits no yield at all from fission explosions – not one kiloton; not one ton; not one kilogramme; not one milligramme of fission yield. "Peaceful nuclear explosions" (PNEs) are also banned, although they may be considered in a Review Conference [2] normally to be held 10 years after entry into force. PNEs then could take place only if a majority of states voted in favour, with no state casting a negative vote; so it may be expected that no PNEs will occur unless they are judged to provide a compelling benefit for all humankind; any nation (or group of nations) wishing to conduct a PNE will need to convince the international community of the necessity to carry out the particular PNE. The CTBT is discussed more fully in Chapter 12.

In this paper we discuss first the nature of activity compatible with the CTBT that is to be expected in the nuclear weapon states in maintaining a safe and reliable stockpile of nuclear weapons, and then speculate on the types of advances in nuclear weaponry that might possibly be achieved while respecting fully the text of the CTBT. We then discuss the means the nuclear weapon states may use to retain their nuclear weapon expertise both for activities to be conducted under a CTBT and as a precaution against the possibility of collapse of a CTBT regime. Finally, we discuss the degree to which a CTBT would limit the nature of nuclear weaponry that might be achieved by a non-nuclear weapon state – either a State outside the Non-Proliferation Treaty (NPT) but still Party to a CTBT, or one in violation of its NPT obligations.

Perhaps slightly off the main subject of this paper, we treat briefly the utility of PNEs of various types, in order to provide some insight into the discussions that may occur 10 years after the Treaty enters into force.

A Caution

Throughout the long succession of review conferences of the Non-Proliferation Treaty (NPT), the non-nuclear weapon states demanded a CTBT mainly to impede the advancement of nuclear weapon technology in the nuclear weapon states, where the NPT provides no impediment at all. However, in the recent negotiations at Geneva it was clear that a number of the nuclear weapon states regarded a CTBT more as a supplement to the non-proliferation regime. In fact, the CTBT serves both purposes. It certainly would be a tragedy if actions under a CTBT, including irresponsible distribution of information, undermined the barriers to the spread of nuclear weapons so laboriously erected by the NPT and the CTBT.

It is natural for those involved in nuclear weapon development in the nuclear weapon states to consider the designs of 30 to 50 years ago as obsolete, as indeed they are for their own purposes; but "obsolete" does not mean that these designs should be freely discussed or allowed to leak to non-nuclear weapon states. Even if the CTBT persists forever, it does not constitute such an effective barrier to proliferation that weapon designs can be freely communicated; no test is needed for a weapon built according to a certified blueprint. Worse, there is some possibility that the CTBT era will come to an end, and it would be most unfortunate if negligence during its duration facilitated the spread of nuclear weapons.

Activities in Nuclear Weapon States Under a CTBT

A CTBT is only that – a ban on nuclear explosion tests of any yield exceeding zero; it is not a Treaty by which nations agree to give up their nuclear weapons or even to reduce their numbers. Therefore, it is of interest for citizens of the nuclear weapon states as well as of non-nuclear weapon states to understand what activities may lawfully be conducted in the nuclear weapon states under a CTBT and how these activities may be monitored as fully compliant with a CTBT. It may be expected that the weapon establishments in nuclear weapon states will desire to proceed with the following activities:

–   Stockpile maintenance and refabrication. The primary tools are inspection, disassembly, refabrication, with guidance from experts in the engineering and science of nuclear weaponry.
–   Product improvement. The weapon establishments may wish to reduce the mass of a warhead, have the option of increasing the yield, improving safety and reliability, and reducing the cost of maintenance and remanufacture.
–   New product development. Among "new products" might be such audacious developments as the nuclear-explosion pumped X-ray laser, or other nuclear-weapon powered directed-energy weapons, which were under development in the SDI programme of the 1980s.[3] More ordinary development might lead to nuclear explosives with various kinds or amounts of nuclear materials (for instance, without need for tritium), enhanced radiation characteristics, or reduced production of radioactive materials in the PNE environment.[4]

But even though a nuclear weapon state may desire to continue its programmes of nuclear weapon development, the ability to do so will be strongly limited by the CTBT constraints, and the accomplishments of the nuclear weapon states will probably be limited to the maintenance of their weapon stockpiles.

Activities in Non-Nuclear Weapon States Under a CTBT

States party to the NPT are committed not to build or otherwise obtain nuclear weapons or other nuclear explosives, and for them a CTBT adds no new obligation. When it enters into force, the International Monitoring System of the CTBT will provide augmented capability to verify that no nuclear explosion has occurred anywhere under the control of that State or by its citizens or other entities.

Of the eight states which are not parties to the Non-Proliferation Treaty, there are only three which either have, or could soon acquire, a nuclear weapon capability – Israel, India and Pakistan. (Brazil is prevented from testing by its accession to the South American Nuclear-Weapon-Free Zone, and has indicated that it intends to sign the NPT. The other non-signatories are clearly not nuclear-weapon-capable.) Israel has signed the CTBT. India, which tested a nuclear explosive underground in 1974, has said that it will not sign, and Pakistan will only sign if India does so. However, now that the nations of the world have demonstrated their overwhelming support for a CTBT, both states may be deterred from nuclear weapon testing by the obloquy which they would incur if they were to do so.

In discussing the acquisition of nuclear weapons by additional states we must avoid placing too much reliance on history. For example, if we were trying to understand the status of a State towards the acquisition of advanced telecommunications capability, it would be ludicrous to expend much effort in monitoring its production of "vacuum tubes" – that is, hot-cathode radioelectronic valves. For ordinary communications it is now both more effective and simpler technology to use solid-state (transistor-based) electronic devices, and it would be a great mistake to imagine that such capability could emerge only after a State passed through a phase of competence in and widespread use of vacuum tubes.

In the 52 years since the detonation of the first nuclear weapons great progress has been achieved: advances in various fields of basic physics important for implementation of advanced nuclear weapons; sequential revolutions in the ability to model physical systems on computers and an enormous expansion in the population that has access to such tools; enhanced experimental technique and high technology for reliable experimental implementation of various sophisticated nuclear weapon principles. Many other aspects of technology which can be important for nuclear weapon proliferation have evolved over the half century, among them the widespread deployment of nuclear reactors for the production of electrical power, that produce some hundreds of kilogrammes of plutonium a year each (for a reactor powering the nominal million kilowatt generating plant). Furthermore, hundreds of tonnes of "weapon-grade" plutonium have been incorporated into nuclear weapons in the Russian and US inventories, and tens of tonnes of weapon plutonium have been declared excess by the USA. On each side, at least 50 tonnes of plutonium from weapons is expected to be declared excess by the year 2003, as a result of the START I and START II reductions, but there is already more than 100 tonnes of separated "reactor-grade Pu" [5] from commercial reprocessing of spent fuel from power reactors, and more than 1000 tonnes of reactor plutonium is present in spent fuel worldwide. [6]

Some 2000 tonnes of highly-enriched uranium (HEU) – much of it 85-95% U-235 – has been built into the Russian and US weapon stockpiles or produced for use in reactors for propulsion of ships or submarines, and some of this naval HEU would be suitable for use in nuclear weapons.

With the evolution and spread of technology and the enormous amount of weapon material in the world (in comparison with the 6 kg of Pu or 60 kg of HEU used in the first two nuclear explosives in 1945), constraints on the spread of nuclear weapons are more legal and political than technical – although the

NPT's barriers to transfer of weapon-usable material (especially plutonium and highly-enriched uranium) are extremely important.

The world's first two nuclear weapons typify two approaches:

– "Gun assembly," in which two sub-critical masses are brought together in some milliseconds by ordinary propellant such as is used to propel artillery shells.

– Implosion assembly, in which high explosive with similar energy content to propellant but much higher speed of reaction (detonation) is used to propel and to compress fissile materials to exceed a critical mass in a time measured in microseconds rather than milliseconds.

The world-class team assembled at Los Alamos in 1943 actually to design and build the nuclear weapons from the HEU and the plutonium that were to become available from the production facilities, solved the design problems for the gun-type explosive, and then faced the unexpected need for a faster assembly system because of the large spontaneous neutron production from the Pu-240 isotope present as a small percentage in the weapon plutonium. In addition to solving design problems and working with materials that are highly radioactive and chemically reactive, the Los Alamos group avoided such pitfalls as apparently trapped Heisenberg (head of the World War II German nuclear programme) into an estimate that the critical mass would be tonnes of U-235.

Just about one bare-sphere critical mass of HEU was used in the Hiroshima gun-type weapon, and only about 0.6 bare-sphere critical mass of plutonium in the first implosion weapon.[7] In both cases neutron sources were devised that would begin emitting neutrons at the appropriate time, and rapidly enough so that the chain reaction would be initiated with high probability before the material disassembled mechanically at speeds similar to those at which it was assembled.

While it is possible to produce weapons of implosion type without a nuclear explosion test, real organizations of real people would not have much confidence in a stockpile of such untested weapons. The tests to validate an exact copy are different from those that might be required in a native development. But anyone seeing the unclassified pictures of mangled steel tubes that were supposed to be uniformly imploded by early attempts at implosion driven by high explosive begins to get a feeling for the problems inherent in an indigenous nuclear weapon programme. The implosion test work soon graduated to "pin" shots, in which multiple small wires make contact with an advancing metal surface, or to other schemes for diagnosing the motion of material that microseconds earlier was a rigid solid.

Only in the last few years has it been generally accepted, as was briefed by US weapons scientists 20 years ago [8] in support of the NPT, that nuclear weapons can quite readily be made from reactor-grade plutonium. This was published at length by Kankeleit *et al*,[9] and by Carson Mark,[10] and the CISAC (Committee on International Security and Arms Control of the US National Academy of Sciences) study [11] mentions the additional problems of reactor-grade plutonium for weapon use – high neutron background, more highly penetrating gamma rays, and increased heat evolution – and concludes:

> In short, it would be quite possible for a potential proliferator to make a nuclear explosive from reactor-grade plutonium using a simple design that would be assured of having a yield in the range of one to a few kilotons, and more using an advanced design.

This is not to say that making an implosion weapon of reactor-grade plutonium is easy, but that it is not much more difficult than making an implosion weapon from "weapon-grade" plutonium-239, and the difficulties involved are not of a different type.

The fact that there are no national nuclear weapon stockpiles built of reactor-grade plutonium does not in any way reduce the possibility that separated reactor-grade plutonium could be used to make one, a few, or even hundreds of nuclear weapons. So there is a real threat that a potential proliferator will try to use the reactor-grade plutonium for nuclear weapon production.

Nuclear Explosions and Nuclear Weapon Tests

In an unconstrained environment, nuclear explosions were carried out with the following functions:

– Development of new models of nuclear weapons.
– Production verification of a developed design.
– Proof of concept of some new weapon idea.
– Development of peaceful nuclear explosives (PNEs).
– Study and demonstration of PNE effects.
– Study of weapon effects.
– Obtaining physics results related to weapon design.
– Non-weapon basic physics.
– Conduct of PNEs for non-military benefit.
– The use of two nuclear explosives in war.

It is obvious that not every nuclear explosion is a test of a nuclear weapon. A substantial number of the explosions were carried out for peaceful purposes or for basic research.[12] However most of the announced explosions were carried out in relation to military programmes.

The United States typically has used some six nuclear explosion tests in the development of each new model of nuclear weapon, while France is said to have used some 22 per model.[13] The study of a new concept might include all the aspects of traditional nuclear weapon functions, or essentially new design physics research and validation as in the case of exploratory work direc' 1 towards the X-ray laser.

As for weapon physics, such nuclear explosion tests might be used to measure the properties of materials ("equation of state" or opacity) in the relevant range of pressure and temperature that cannot be reached by high explosives, although these ranges are low accessible in part (at very small physical scale) by laser-driven X-ray sources.[14] As for non-weapon physics, this might include such interesting questions as the existence of metallic hydrogen, the properties of metals like iron when squeezed to ten times their normal density (high-pressure, high matter- and energy-density physics), inertial confinement fusion physics, nuclear physics under high neutron flux (high atomic number nuclei study), and the like.

To the extent that all knowledge is valuable and generally has beneficial applications, such experiments have been pursued in the past. Some, such as the US "Halite-Centurion" series of experiments in inertial confinement fusion[15] have provided advanced information at affordable cost. And electron-shell occupation effects on thermodynamic properties of matter were studied in Soviet nuclear explosion experiments,[16] while the laser facilities are still approaching such physics with much more expensive investments.

An additional set of experiments and applications of nuclear explosions is to be found in the "Peaceful Nuclear Explosions," towards which the United States dedicated more than 20 nuclear explosions, and the former Soviet Union more than 100. The United States found no application that was economically competitive with accomplishing these missions by conventional means. And in 1995, the current Minister of Atomic Energy in Russia (Viktor Mikhailov), in a published interview, commented on the US and Soviet PNE programmes, "So far, they have not proven to be economical." However, the 39 deep seismic sounding explosions throughout the Soviet territory provided valuable information that Russian scientists believe well worth the expenditure. Still operating are two underground "fractured collectors" produced by two underground peaceful nuclear explosions, to receive and safely store toxic waste.[17] Mikhailov accedes only reluctantly to the limitation of any tool of scientific progress.

More About Non-nuclear-explosion Testing

Of course, much of the maintenance of stockpile weapons is done without nuclear explosion testing, and indeed very few tests thus far have been for the purpose of verifying that weapons are still all right. In the non-explosion testing realm, a whole panoply of techniques has been created both for weapon development and for the monitoring of weapon condition.[18]

First, there are the various quality control methods used largely in production to verify that the materials of fabrication (or refabrication) are up to standard. To the extent that the individual component can then be fully tested (as is the case of the detonators for the high explosive), additional confidence is available.

The high explosive itself is tested before fabrication and after. A bar can be cut from the fabricated material and its detonation velocity and other characteristics compared with the standard. Similarly for the fabrication of metal parts, pressure vessels, and the like.

Even the flight of a nuclear weapon can be mimicked by dropping a bomb with an inert weapon or launching a missile, so that the "weapon" itself goes through the entire stockpile-to-target sequence (STS), as would a real weapon, right up to the point of firing the high explosive. High-fidelity telemetry can be used, or some of the warheads or bombs could be recovered rather than allowed to impact, in order to verify that unexpected problems have not intervened.

In the development of nuclear weapons, a lot of effort is placed on "pin shots" or other means of determining the performance of the pit – that is, the fissile material surrounded by a metal shell to constitute the "sealed pit" and driven by high explosive.[19]

The designer wants to prescribe the position vs. time of the inner surface of the plutonium shell, and this is measured in multiple experiments by the use of numerous fine "pins" or metal contacts. Laser imaging of the imploding pit is also used, and all of these techniques can be useful to ensure that high explosive in the actual weapons in storage as well as HE for remanufacture is within original production specification.

If actual plutonium needs to be used in experiments, the experiments can be done at reduced scale, so that of the approximately three neutrons from fission, less than one remains within the assembly to cause further fission, and the system will be sub-critical with no energy release. Because of the toxicity of plutonium arising from its natural radioactivity, such experiments must either be done underground or, alternatively, experiments involving tens or even hundreds of pounds of HE could well be done in rugged steel containment, above ground, at Los Alamos, for instance.[20]

Many modern nuclear weapons may have a boosted primary; for it to work properly, the design conditions must be achieved for the boost gas and the fissile material. Uncontrolled mixing under high-explosive impact between them must be avoided, and that mixing may depend upon the surface condition of the plutonium. To detect deterioration not visible on static radiographs, some of the pits taken at random from the stockpile can be cut open and their condition inspected by microscope.[21]

A lot of information can be obtained in an actual nuclear test, and that same information is not available without nuclear explosion testing. Nevertheless, so called "hydrotesting" in which inert material is used, or material at "subscale"[22] so that one does not reach criticality, can allow the gas and the metal to be brought to the stage that in a larger assembly, or with the correct material, would result in the initiation of a nuclear chain reaction. Much use is made of flash radiography by pulsed X-ray systems in order to observe the interior of such hydrotests.[23]

Such measurements provide information in addition to that from static high-resolution radiography and other measurements of the pits in storage, either without disassembly of the weapon or among the eleven of each type disassembled each year.

Since flash radiography plays such an important role, it is natural to want to upgrade it in two ways – by providing a smaller source for the X-rays (and thus better resolution in the photographs) and by allowing multiple temporal and/or spatial views of the imploding assembly. Both DARHT at Los Alamos (Dual Axis Radiographic Hydro Test Facility) and the AHTF (Advanced Hydro Test Facility) at Livermore would move in this direction, with DARHT providing two spatial and two temporal views, while AHTF might provide four to six.[23]

These facilities and their relationship to the Science-Based Stockpile Stewardship Program (SBSS) are described in a report publicly available,[23] and by a more recent review devoted largely to the National Ignition Facility (NIF).[24] These supplement official material available from the Department of Energy (DOE) – for example, at www.doe.gov. Only a portion of the NIF capability is coupled to the stockpile stewardship task, and much of that portion may have more to do with maintaining expertise and developing capability that would be useful in case of a collapse of the CTBT regime rather than for maintaining the enduring stockpile of six existing weapon designs in a safe and reliable state indefinitely.

The major facilities are to be very substantially improved, at a budget that for the next five years in DOE is expected to average almost $4 billion per year. Thus, a primary emphasis for stockpile maintenance has been placed and will be placed on the disassembly and inspection programme, according to which 11 representatives of each type of weapon in the stockpile are brought back for detailed inspection and disassembly. The entire system is radiographed and inspected in fine detail. It is disassembled and each part tested for function. In some cases the high explosive is removed and the detonators and explosive tested. We emphasize that all of the elements of the nuclear weapon can be tested to detect any degradation except the physics package (the primary explosive and the secondary nuclear explosive), although not every element can be tested in the assembled system.

In routine stockpile maintenance, there is a replacement in the field of "limited life components" (LLC), such as batteries, tritium reservoirs, and the like. In the future, every element of the nuclear weapon will need to be regarded as an LLC, to be replaced either on some schedule or on some signal.

So far as the primary and secondary are concerned, even these elements are not inert, and over the years there have been problems with chemical reactions due to volatile components in the high explosive, and the like.

In some cases, these problems have been solved by replacement of components that would certainly not affect the operation of the nuclear weapon (according to analysis and certification by the nuclear weapon laboratories), but in some cases remanufacture of critical elements has been required.

Evidently, a key component of the maintenance of a safe and reliable stockpile is the ability to remanufacture every element of the nuclear weapon, or to certifiably substitute some other component for an existing one.

In addition to the elements in the direct line of operation from detonation of the high explosive, to implosion of the primary, to criticality, to heating of the contained boost gas, to fission chain explosion, to full boosting, and to full primary yield; to emission of large amounts of energy as radiation from the primary to convey the necessary part of the energy to the secondary, to implosion of the secondary, and to thermonuclear reaction and explosion of the secondary,[25] there are many other required functions of the nuclear weapon, with its 4000 parts in a typical unit.

Some of these are the Arming, Firing, and Fusing (AFF) chain, while others simply have to do with the safe transport and carriage of the weapon itself. Most of these can be tested either non-destructively or destructively, and indeed they can be substituted by modern, state-of-the-art elements that can be thoroughly tested for function and that can be proven without suspicion to have no impact on the nuclear explosion itself. However, a high degree of conservatism is necessary in the maintenance of this stockpile, and ultimately there is required the expertise to certify that a substitution in one of these non-critical elements will indeed have no effect on the nuclear explosion.

If the USA Needs Science-Based Stockpile Stewardship, How Will the Other Nuclear Weapon States Manage?

The United States has adopted, with the SBSS, a very aggressive programme for the maintenance of its nuclear arsenal and of its nuclear expertise.[26] This involves several aspects ranging from an Advanced Scientific Computing Initiative, to a greater involvement of weapon designers with the detailed results of the Stockpile Surveillance Program, to the building and operation of major new facilities for improved experimental observation of aspects of nuclear weaponry without nuclear explosion testing. A large part of the SBSS programme has the goal of maintaining nuclear weapon expertise, and also the ability to design, test, manufacture, and certify new nuclear weapons if the CTBT era should come to an end. And, of course, the nuclear weapons that are now in the inventory were designed by use of computers far less powerful than the multi-teraflop systems that will be available in the Science-based Stockpile Stewardship era.[27]

The great demand for computation ("modeling") and for much of the experimental "simulation" (*e.g.*, hydrodynamic test with flash radiography) systems comes from the desire to be able to investigate the effects of flaws that may be found in a stockpile weapon. Examples of such flaws are corrosion, warping of metallic and non-metallic elements, opening of assembly joints, – all problems that may occur within the primary or secondary and that cannot be tested by weapon detonation under a CTBT.[27]

In the earliest days of nuclear weaponry, computational capability was so minimal that only systems of one-dimensional (1-D) spherical or cylindrical symmetry could be considered and diagnostic systems were also extremely limited. With the evolution of computers and of electronics, it became possible to consider systems of axial symmetry (like an orange or an American football) which have some advantages in packaging and also in safety. But a fine-scale computation might have 1000 points along the radius of a spherical system; to do the same job in a system of axial symmetry might require a thousand points in each coordinate, or a million points altogether. Simply cycling through all those points means that the computation is at least a thousand times longer for this 2-dimensional (2-D) than for the 1-D case.

There seems no great benefit in designing weapons without axial symmetry, but if one has a flaw in a 2-D weapon, then the computation becomes 3-dimensional. A full 3-D computation, as is evident, could then require a further factor 1000 in mass points, and a factor 1000 or more growth in computing capability to handle it.

On the experimental side, it can be seen that for a spherical system any orientation of an X-ray picture (or the equivalent) would do to confirm that the assembly in reality moves as predicted, while for a 2-D system one would need specific views. For a 3-D system much more information would have to be gathered, as in the case of the CAT (Computer-Assisted Tomography) scan for medical diagnostic purposes.

But computation does not make a weapon work that would not otherwise have functioned, nor does simulation or static diagnostics. If the weapon would have worked when it was put into the stockpile, then it will assuredly not work after 10,000 years (when a good fraction of the plutonium will have decayed). Nor is it likely to work after 100 years, even if the tritium (of 12.3 year half-life) is replenished on schedule. Clearly, if nuclear weapons are to be reliable and safe for a long time, it will be necessary to remanufacture them or their components, in view of the ageing of plastics, the build up of helium in the solid plutonium, and the accumulated effects of radiation on various elements of the weapon.   A guide to the reliable life is provided by the age of nuclear weapons already in the stockpile.

Although other nations have not indicated how they maintain their nuclear weapons, the USA in recent years has been quite open [28] about its procedures, which involve the dismantling of 11 weapons of each type, taken at random from the stockpile, every year (formerly every two years)[29] with close inspection for potential flaws.   High resolution radiography is used as well. The non-nuclear components such as batteries, valves, fuses and detonators for the high explosive are all tested, and if a flaw is found, a wider inspection for that fault in the inspection may be conducted.

Age-related problems will not affect all weapons of the same type at the same instant, and so there is ordinarily time to remedy the problem by refitting a component of the same or of an improved type.   In some cases, such as a battery or capacitor, the system can be tested initially and frequently after installation, in order to ensure that one has not introduced a new problem.

The fissile materials are an exception, because to subject them to high-explosive, or more severe shock, is to destroy them.   This would be no different from that of testing a valve or power device driven by high explosive, in which one obtains information about the device no longer in existence, but also about the population from which that was drawn.   Worse, to test them in the operational configuration means that one will obtain a nuclear yield of a kiloton, plus or minus a factor 10.   But this means that one must greatly change the environment of the tested fissile "pit," for instance, in order not to violate the CTBT.[30]

One could in this way trephine a sector of the pit and fire it with close observation of its internal surface, but without approaching criticality (because of the smaller mass and reduced symmetry).   Alternatively, when the surface or the dimensions of the pit are no longer well within the variation accepted thus far in the stockpile, one would remanufacture the pit to the original specifications.   One way for a nation to take steps that actually imperil the safety and reliability of their nuclear weapon stockpile would be to make changes in the design or processes by which the untestable items are fabricated. We judge that the most reliable stockpile can be maintained by periodic remanufacture (in addition to remanufacture in case of discovered problems), using processes that from the point of view of the material are within the range defined in initial production.   Changing materials or processes and relying on extensive computation in order to show the equivalence (or improvement!) seems a lot riskier, and with potential benefits that are not worth the risk.[31]

However, a nation might instead try to maintain a safe and reliable stockpile by what has been termed [32] "curatorship" (CS) analogous to the preservation and renewing of precious works of art.   If the USA maintains the capability of remanufacture, the difference between SBSS and CS may involve the decision in SBSS to permit somewhat deteriorated weapons to remain in the stockpile, in view of the SBSS-based confidence that performance would be degraded by no more than 5 per cent on average – to take an arbitrary number. Under CS, weapons would need to be remanufactured at an earlier stage.

That remanufacture is not an inferior option is inherent in the Congressional testimony of the President of the Sandia National Laboratories:[33]

> Ideally, we would like to train our junior weapon design engineers alongside experienced engineers, but this will not be possible during a decades-long hiatus of no weapon development. The Russian laboratories, by contrast, will be able to pass along their critical weapon design skills to a new generation under their announced plans to rebuild thousands of weapons each year.

Of course, the combination of manufacture within initial specifications, with understanding and computation would provide still more assurance of reliability and safety, and that is a reasonable approach if it can be afforded and if strong management prevents changing the design or process of the untestable parts.

We believe that each of the five nuclear states will be able to maintain its stock of nuclear weapons in a reliable and safe state by measures appropriate to those particular weapons.

At this point we note the hazard of focusing on new facilities to the detriment of the task of stockpile maintenance. Expenditures on new facilities and the "less exciting" work of actually surveying and analysing and fixing the enduring stockpile compete for funds and people. Nuclear weapon states would do well to ensure that the tools and conditions afforded to those engaged in this task are upgraded modestly, and that resources are not diverted excessively to new tools that may not be so directly relevant.

Additional material is to be found in two recent Pugwash papers,[34] from which we draw heavily in the following section.

What Fission Experiments Are Banned Under a Zero-yield CTBT?

Compared with fusion, the definition of a "zero yield" fission explosion is considerably more difficult. First, a nominal nuclear power reactor fissions one tonne of heavy nuclei per year, corresponding to an energy release of some 17 megatons of high explosive equivalent. But that is no explosion. In one millisecond (which might be deemed to separate an explosive regime from a steady regime), the fission energy produced corresponds to that of 500 g of HE. It is of interest to note that even for a one microsecond interval, the fission energy produced in a normal reactor is about 0.5 g HE.

The fission energy release from the power reactor is not an explosion, because it operates in a steady state.

Other reactors, however, like the TRIGA, (Training and Research

Inherently-Safe General Atomics) have a very substantial and short-duration energy release, sufficient to raise the temperature of the material by 100 degrees or more within a time determined by the moderation time of the neutrons.

Like water-moderated reactors, normal "fast reactors" are dependent upon the delayed neutrons for their controllability. Only under very special circumstances, such as the "dragon" experiments, initially performed in Los Alamos in 1945 by Robert Frisch, is a system made critical with prompt and fast neutrons. This is achieved by a projectile accelerated by gravity or in some other way, briefly passing through a near-critical assembly, so that the overall reproduction factor exceeds 1.0 on prompt neutrons alone. Even though there is a substantial release of fission energy, there is no disruption, and there is no significant increase in information gained beyond that achieved with sub-critical experiments in which there is a steady neutron multiplication factor $1/(1-k)$, where k is the reproduction factor for prompt neutrons.

The CTBT should not be interpreted as imposing any restrictions on experiments conducted to understand and improve the safety of fast reactors, for instance, where it would be perfectly in order to mock up the core of an energy-producing reactor, and then to suddenly drive out control rods in order to confirm some analysis that the energy release in fission in this simulated accident does not exceed 1 kg of high-explosive, or 100 kg of high-explosive or whatever level the containment is designed safely to withstand. Such experiments contribute nothing to the understanding or advancement of nuclear weapon design, and in our opinion are in no way limited by the CTBT. Of course, they should be done with full transparency.

More relevant to weapon design in the nuclear weapon states are so-called "hydronuclear" experiments and (finally) sub-critical experiments.

During the 1958-1961 moratorium, the USA conducted more than 40 hydronuclear experiments, some in shallow wells [35] in the facilities of the Los Alamos Laboratory, and some at the Nevada Test Site. "Hydronuclear" refers to a system in which the material flow is described by hydrodynamic equations, as in the assembly and compression of fissile material by the use of high explosive; together with a nuclear chain reaction. It is clearly intended to distinguish from a normal nuclear explosion, and various criteria might be invoked for this purpose:

– Fission yield less than the energy of the high explosive used for the assembly.[35]
– Fission yield so small that it does not perturb significantly the hydrodynamic disassembly of the metal "pit."

During the 1958-1961 era, an upper limit was established for the yield of a hydronuclear experiment – 2 kg of HE equivalent. This is related to the standards [36] that the USA set in 1968 for the safety of its nuclear weapons –

given a detonation initiated at any one point in the high explosive system, less than one in a million likelihood of fission energy release exceeding 2 kg; and less than one in a billion probability over the stockpile life of a weapon under normal non-accident circumstances.

Many of the accident scenarios involve the detonation of the high explosive at one point – by a rifle bullet or a fragment from an explosion, so the relevant aspect of the US standard is that the fission yield from the worst-case "one-point" detonation of the primary must be less than 2 kg HE. To determine which US designs were one-point safe, and to take corrective measures for those that were not, was the primary purpose of the hydronuclear experiments. For a design that proves to be one-point safe, the proof is the actual firing of a primary by one-point detonation at the point determined by theory or experiment to be that giving greatest criticality. Because such one-point detonation could in principle give a considerable yield in the range of tons or hundreds of tons of HE, a series of experiments is conducted with gradually increasing amounts of fissile material (or of high explosive). A design found not to be inherently one-point safe might be rendered one-point safe, but still usable, by a mechanism such as inserting removable material in the hollow of the fissile pit.

The important point is that once a design has been demonstrated to be one-point safe, such experiments need never again be done on that weapon design.[37] Banning hydronuclear tests is compatible with the US commitment to retaining a nuclear weapon stockpile that is reliable and safe, based on weapons of types already in the stockpile.

It has been suggested that hydronuclear tests can add significantly to confidence that re-manufactured weapons (for example, pits that needed to be refabricated because of distortion of the metal) will perform within the same yield range as the original weapon. Clearly, a full-yield test of a re-manufactured weapons would give such evidence, but to remain within the "hydronuclear" range for a symmetrical firing of the explosive would require a very big change in the configuration; either the amount of explosive would need to be significantly reduced, or a hollow pit would need to be filled with a dense gas.[38]

In either case, as demonstrated by a close examination by the JASON group of consultants for the US DOE, the necessary modifications are so great that hydronuclear tests would add little to stockpile confidence. The Summary and Conclusions [39] of the JASON study were released by the US Government on 4 August 1996. The study was led by Prof. Sidney Drell, and one of us (Garwin) was a member of the group, together with several other JASONs with nuclear weapons experience, supplemented by four authors who have spent their lives in the nuclear weapon design programme at the US DOE laboratories.

Hydronuclear tests will not be conducted under a CTBT regime. They have no great significance to the military capability in any case, but it would be desirable to be able to verify that they are not being performed. In this regard it would be helpful for all permitted activities to be conducted above ground. Hydrodynamic tests of weapon configurations are permitted under a CTBT, although they are forbidden to non-nuclear weapon states by the NPT. Because such hydrodynamic tests may involve kilogrammes of Pu, they cannot be done in the atmosphere under current standards; as proposed [40] they should be done in a containment vessel, above ground.

A configuration that, assembled, provides two critical masses at the maximum density achieved, will be sub-critical if the mass of every element involved is multiplied by 0.4, and radiography of the system is correspondingly easier, because it is less "thick" at every stage of the assembly. Such model tests are not prohibited and likely will be used, and even smaller scale models can be useful.

Other sub-critical experiments may involve masses of fissile material and configurations that have no chance at all of criticality, such as explosively driven equation-of-state experiments.[41] To provide greatest assurance of compliance with a CTBT, such experiments (which are not prohibited by the CTBT) also should be done above ground, in steel containments, like the hydrodynamic tests described above. If experiments involving plutonium or other fissionable material are nevertheless to take place underground, the planning should include through-pipes into which States could agree to put their measuring equipment to ensure that there is no neutron or gamma-ray output from the test. The stemming must be adequate at least to contain the high explosive and the plutonium dust – a different problem from containing kilotons of nuclear yield.

A Working Definition of Zero-yield Fission Experiments

We would interpret "zero-yield" as satisfied if the prompt reproduction factor for a fissile system $k < 1$ in any experiment – that is, if the static neutron multiplication factor $M = 1/(1-k)$ was bounded. This is in contrast with hydronuclear tests, which are not permitted under a CTBT. M is the more readily measured and more fundamental quantity; k is the fraction of neutrons present after one "generation" or neutron lifetime within the material. Thus k may be two or three in the compressed material of a fission bomb, but $k < 1$ in that same weapon before it is assembled or compressed.

A practical upper limit on k in systems involving high explosives, might be $k = 0.8$ or less.

In contrast, a hydronuclear test that might have involved a yield up to 2 kg of HE, or 8.4 megajoules, must be compared with the energy yield of a single fission, which would contribute promptly about 150 MeV or some 24 picojoules (24 pJ). So the yield of 2 kg HE corresponds to some 3×10^{17} fissions, equivalent to 58 doublings.

A typical nuclear yield of 20 kt is evidently larger by a factor 10^7 than is a yield of 2 kg of HE, corresponding to 23 more doublings.

Does a CTBT Impede Nuclear Proliferation?

A CTBT greatly impedes vertical proliferation – that is, the development of thermonuclear weapons or weapons using a substantially modified design.

It also has a significant effect on horizontal proliferation, in limiting the choice of configuration to those that might be imagined reasonably sure of performance – for example, the U-235 gun weapon which was used at Hiroshima, and was later built in six copies by South Africa before that nation destroyed them and became a non-nuclear weapon state. Or a state might choose a primitive implosion device, with various forms of fissile material.

For the use of plutonium, even the use of some supposedly sure-fire configuration would not provide a lot of confidence without a nuclear explosion test, and to reach for weapons with substantially smaller fissile content (allowing therefore more weapons for a given stock of fissile material) would raise the question as to whether any one of the weapons would work. What about Israel, supposed to have a stock of plutonium weapons from the Dimona reactor of some 60 MW power (and thus 60 g of plutonium created per day)? This would be some 18 kg per year, and these 3-4 nuclear weapons per year would correspond to a stock of some 100 nuclear warheads. This is to be compared with the NRDC estimate of 150 ± 50. The revelations of Vanunu have been interpreted by T.B. Taylor [42] as indicating that the plutonium fission yield may be augmented with fusion fuel containing deuterium, much like the first Soviet experiment with thermonuclear fuel, dubbed by the Americans "Joe-4."[43] This was a single-stage fission system augmented with fusion fuel, rather than having a separate second-stage fusion assembly. Without knowledge of the facts, we imagine that the Israelis have chosen a design that would provide a significant yield without fusion boosting, but that their first detonation in war would confirm whether or not they could count on the higher yield that they have presumably designed into the weapon. Without a test, the designers and the military could not be sure of the performance of such a design – but this would not be the first instance of overconfidence on the part of the Israelis, or of overconfidence on the part of their critics. Presumably they have validated their calculations against known information, such as that regarding the gun-type nuclear weapon used by the United States in 1945 or the first plutonium implosion weapon used in 1945, about which much information has been released. Or they may have received information one way or another from countries with large nuclear stockpiles.

The largest non-proliferation influence of a CTBT, however, is political. As the nuclear weapon states see it in their national security interest to reduce the number of nuclear weapons held by others in the world (and perforce their own), they need the support of the other members of the NPT in order to preserve and universalize the non-proliferation regime. They will not retain that support if they continue nuclear test explosions.

Even without testing, they could squander the good will and political support that might otherwise be theirs (for instance, by not reducing severely the number of nuclear weapons), but there seems no way in which one of the nuclear weapon states could continue to test without provoking the others to do the same, and thereby imperil the NPT regime.

A universal CTBT would put the might and will of the nuclear weapon states on the side of the other NPT adherents, and this could lead to a strong reaction against a state outside the NPT building nuclear weapons or, in particular, having a nuclear test explosion.

Peaceful Nuclear Explosions

In its PNE programme from 1957 to 1973, the USA carried out 12 explosions for applications (6 cratering and 6 contained explosions) and some 15 for development of specialized PNE devices. Of these 15 tests, ten were to develop ultra-low fission explosives for excavation purposes, one was to develop an ultra-low tritium explosive for oil or gas applications, and five were to create heavy elements beyond fermium (which has 100 protons in the nucleus as compared with 92 in the chemical element uranium or 94 in plutonium).

The Soviet programme began in 1965 and ended in 1988. Some 112 explosions were used in applications and many in PNE development work.

In addition to excavation (a proposal to link the Kama and Pechora Rivers in order to feed Siberian water into the Caspian Sea rather than into the Arctic Ocean), work was conducted on oil stimulation, closure of runaway gas wells, and the production of storage cavities. Notably, some 39 PNEs were used in deep seismic sounding across the vast expanse of the Soviet Union. In fact, the primary utility of Soviet PNEs was deep seismic sounding and the excavation of storage cavities (or fragmented reservoirs underground). Some of the cavities were to be used for storing natural gas condensate, and the fragmented reservoirs typically to receive toxic materials instead of liberating them to the environment.

Much technical progress was made in this work. For instance, a 140 kt nuclear explosive in 1965 had some 7 kt of fission yield, while one developed in 1970 had less than 0.3 kt fission yield at 100 kt.[44]

Concepts were developed to reduce the contamination due to the explosive by designs that would "self bury" the radioactive debris (a concept apparently first introduced in the US PNE program), and such devices were tested in 1971 and 1974 and apparently used in mining experiments.[44]

Economic and cost-benefit evaluations of the Soviet programme are not widely available, but for the US programme a substantial study was conducted.[45] One of the authors (Garwin) was a participant in that study and author of an Appendix [46] dealing specifically with a concept for the production of electrical power by use of thermonuclear explosives – Project PACER. (Such concepts have also been explored in Russia, but they are not currently being developed because of the economic situation, among other circumstances.) The other PNE applications in the USA were for production of gas from "tight gas formations," rubblizing of oil shale, production of underground storage cavities, rubblizing copper ore, and general excavation.

A striking result of that study was to recognize the great effectiveness and controllability of non-nuclear means for accomplishing most of the tasks. For instance, for the control of runaway gas or oil wells, precision drilling and the application of sensible non-nuclear technology handles the problem, as was the case with the more than 500 Kuwaiti oil wells set afire in 1991. Even more striking is the substantial scale at which most of the applications would need to be conducted, if nuclear explosives were to be used.

More recently, Soviet nuclear weapon scientists have proposed [47] the use of underground nuclear explosions to destroy toxic chemical agents and chemical weapons, and to render excess nuclear weapons harmless and unavailable. The authors see many obstacles in implementing these proposals.

Regarding the proposal to use underground PNEs to destroy and detoxify chemical agents and munitions, a great deal of the problem of such materials is in the transport to the destruction site, and that would not be eased by the requirement to transport them on the surface and then underground for destruction. Furthermore, there are satisfactory processes for the transformation and destruction of bulk agents, differing according to the nature of the agent and especially as to whether it contains inorganic material, such as arsenic.

Chemists and chemical engineers are perfectly capable of designing and conducting such transformations, and no very large amount of material need be present in the plant at any time. Ultimately, the effluent gas can go through a super-heater and cooler (regenerator) in order to ensure that no organic toxic materials remain. The United States is using incineration to destroy its stock of nerve agents, but it is also possible to use hydrolysis, and such operations would provide employment in Russia in the chemical and related industries.

As for the underground destruction of nuclear warheads, one has to decide whether this means the destruction of intact warheads or of portions of the nuclear warheads. Surely it is not proposed to destroy highly-enriched uranium, which has a substantial value and can be blended down at low cost with natural uranium or depleted uranium to provide valuable fuel for light water reactors or even fast reactors. If the proposal is to destroy the much smaller amount of fissile material in the primaries of two-stage weapons (and it has been discussed to use a single 50 kt explosive to vaporize 5000 such primaries and to mix them with the surrounding melted rock) one has a number of questions about the safety of such an activity – accidents while emplacing 5000 primaries, and the like.[48] This is not really a "disposal" means, and does not even make the material highly inaccessible. According to the rule of thumb of one tonne of melted rock per ton of nuclear yield, each primary would at best be mixed with ten tonnes of rock. So at some later time, anyone who drilled down into the mass underground would need to bring up only ten tonnes of rock in order to be able to extract one primary's worth of plutonium. The radioactivity associated with this plutonium is less by a factor 60,000 or so than that associated with weapon plutonium in spent fuel in a production reactor.

But the primary argument against using underground nuclear explosions to destroy either chemical agents or excess nuclear weapon components is that it is efficient to do this in other ways, without perpetuating the use of nuclear explosives – any one of which could destroy a city and hundreds of thousands of human beings.

Defence of Earth Against an Asteroid or Comet

In recent years it has become accepted that an asteroid or comet of some 5 km diameter struck the Earth some 65 million years ago and the global disruption (dust, smoke, nitric oxide in the atmosphere, *etc.*) led to the extinction of the dinosaurs and 70 per cent of the species on Earth at that time. In the last decade a lot of work has been done to catalogue objects that might strike the Earth, and to consider what might be done about the threat. With very high probability, we have thousands of years before significant damage will be done to a portion of the Earth, and millions of years to an event that could cause extinction.[49] Russian scientists warn that even a modest size asteroid striking the ocean could cause a tsunami along many hundreds of kilometres of shore, and could kill many millions of people with higher probability than if that same asteroid were to land on a city and kill by blast. Since an asteroid weighing two million tonnes has a kinetic energy of 100 megatons at 20 km/s, an asteroid of only a little more than 100 m diameter would provide this energy. One of the options for dealing with such bodies is to meet them at a considerable distance (the greater distance the better), and either to burst them or to gradually deflect them so that they safely miss the Earth. Taking an asteroid of 1 km diameter and 10^9 tonnes mass, moving towards Earth at 20 km/s, one could enforce a miss distance of 20,000 km by giving the asteroid a transverse velocity of some 0.7 m/s one year before impact.[50] The kinetic energy would be a mere 0.05 kilotons. But the efficiency of transferring energy from a nuclear explosion to a massive asteroid is not great.

One of the ways that comes to mind is to use penetrating gamma-rays that would deliver their energy over a depth of some ten grammes per square centimetre and to deliver enough energy that the material to that depth would be heated and vaporized, perhaps to emerge with a kinetic energy corresponding to some 3000 K, or a velocity (for a molecular weight of 20) of some 1 km/s. Since the asteroid needs to be given a momentum of 7×10^{16} gram-cm/s, and the momentum imparted by the departure of a tonne of this overburden is assumed to be 10^{11} g-cm/s per tonne, some 7×10^5 tonnes of materials must be ablated in this way. This really means ablating the entire face of the asteroid to a depth of 70 cm or so, which would require repeated explosions. Since the material at 1 km/s has an energy content of 10^{-4} kt per tonne, only a total of some 70 kt of energy needs to be deposited in such layers to accomplish the job.

Should the task be to similarly divert an asteroid of a mere 100 m diameter, the required momentum transfer is 1000 times less and if repeated explosions are permissible, the job could be done with a deposition of a mere 70 tonnes of radiation energy. On the other hand, with a single blast ablating only 10 cm, the required energy deposition is ten times as large.

Since such considerations have only begun in the last few years, other approaches have been considered as well, such as the focusing of sunlight by mirrors tethered to or near the asteroid, so as to ablate the material in the focused spot and provide a more gentle rocket propulsion for months or years.

Comet-like objects of relatively modest size might be detected only months away from impact, and if they are small enough, the best solution might be to fragment them with a single explosion or with a chain of smaller nuclear explosions laid out in the path of the comet.

On the nuclear side, one could imagine a soft landing on the asteroid, and drilling into its core so that a much smaller nuclear yield would do the job, depending on the strength of the asteroid.

We believe that we ought to take seriously such threats to humanity, and we should work on them together. It would be a tragedy, however, if nuclear explosives kept alive for the purpose were to be used in war, and the mechanism set up in the CTBT to review periodically the prospective benefits of peaceful nuclear explosions seems adequate for the purpose of responding to these threats.

Conclusions

We are confident that compliance with a CTBT will prevent any nation from developing third-generation nuclear weapons such as the nuclear-explosion-pumped x-ray laser.

We believe that the CTBT will prevent states from confidently acquiring new-design two-stage thermonuclear weapons, although a state might design and build weapons within the existing range of experience, in which it would not have full confidence.

Available experience shows that nuclear weapon states will be able to maintain their nuclear weapons stockpiles in a safe and reliable state for some decades at least, by means of appropriate programmes of inspection, analysis, and remanufacture, under a CTBT. Different states may put different emphasis on periodic remanufacture versus science-based stockpile stewardship, versus full funding of the mechanisms that they have used in the past.

Non-nuclear states or sub-state entities building nuclear weapons under a CTBT could with reasonable confidence make gun-type weapons using U-235, and with somewhat lesser confidence could reproduce the first implosion-type weapons using weapon-grade fissile materials. Somewhat greater uncertainty and difficulty would be associated with the use of plutonium metal produced from separated plutonium from reprocessing of commercial reactor-grade spent fuel. Increasing uncertainty would be associated with more advanced implosion system chosen to use less fissile material than the original solid-sphere design.

Still greater uncertainly would be incurred if an organization designed and produced a stockpile of boosted fission weapons without test, and very little confidence would be associated with a stockpile of two-stage thermonuclear weapons that had never been tested.

As for the ban of peaceful nuclear explosions, the world community has chosen the nonproliferation goal over possible benefits to the economy or to basic research. There is even widespread doubt that such net benefits exist. If an acute need occurred the decision to use PNEs should be made on the base of consensus. One potential application of nuclear explosions might be approved unanimously in time, but still requires much study – the use of nuclear explosions to prevent impact on the Earth by space bodies, asteroids and comets. Although the effectiveness of nuclear explosions in this role is far from assured, there is as yet no alternative technology as promising for prevention of large impacts on the Earth. The threat of such impacts must be studied widely before any decision should be made on the technology that might be used. However, the loss caused by such impacts could be so great (even up to global extinction) that it may be desirable to institute a programme (without nuclear explosion testing) to develop the technology or lay the basis for a system of intercept; this should be done at a modest level of effort commensurate with the annual loss to be prevented. Using arbitrary numbers, if the loss is $100 billion, and the interval between such events is anticipated to be 10,000 years, then the expectation of annual loss would be $10 million.

Appendix 1

The Technology of Nuclear Weapons

Inside a Nuclear Weapon

The first design of nuclear weapon in the United States was a "gun assembled" system, by which some 60 kg of HEU [51] was moved by normal artillery propellant in a short gun barrel from a "sub-critical" configuration into a more compact over-critical configuration so that only a relatively small fraction of the neutrons from each fission escaped.[52] A nuclear explosion can take place only when an exponentially growing ("divergent") fission chain reaction can occur, in which a neutron causes fission, liberating two or three neutrons, more than one of which goes on to cause another fission, and so on. This chain breeding of neutrons and, consequently, fission of fissionable materials is terminated by hydrodynamic disassembly (expansion) of the system caused by the rapid energy release or partial burning of fissionable materials. The assembly of a supercritical mass of fissionable materials, the initiation of a chain reaction in it, and the resulting rapid disassembly is the essential sequence in explosive nuclear systems, and the process is called a nuclear explosion.[52]

In the fissionable materials used in nuclear weapons – U-235, Pu-239, and U-233 – the fission is caused mainly by fast neutrons, which go only a distance of 7-10 cm before colliding with a nucleus, so that each doubling of the neutron population occurs in about 0.01 microseconds. The power of compound interest is such that if one begins with a single fission, the time required at this doubling interval to cause fission of 1 kg of fissionable material (approximately 2.5×10^{24} nuclei) is the time required for 80 such doublings, or less than one microsecond. This corresponds to an energy release equivalent to about 17 thousand tonnes of trinitrotoluene (TNT) – a typical high explosive (HE). The explosive termination of the chain reaction produced slightly less than this energy release – about 15 kt (in about 60 kg of fission material) for the case of the Hiroshima bomb.[53]

The result of such rapid energy release (17 kt of HE equivalent per kilogramme of material fissioned) is not only the blast effect that is similar to the actual detonation of an approximately equal but slightly smaller amount of HE, but also the radiation of a substantial fraction of that total as thermal radiation, giving rise to combustion of wood, *etc.*, out to a radius ranging from kilometres to tens of kilometres depending on the yield. In addition, the neutrons that escape from the nuclear explosive, together with the gamma radiation from the fission process itself and the fission products contribute an enormous source of "prompt" radiation which has an additional major damaging weapon effect. Sometimes, special provisions were made to enhance some of these additional effects, *e.g.*, in so-called neutron weapons.[54] For large-yield weapons, the prompt radiation is confined to a region well within that destroyed by blast, and so is less important. However, the fallout from a multi-megaton ground-burst nuclear explosion may deliver a lethal dose of radiation within hours to a region covering 10,000 square kilometres.

The Acquisition of a Nuclear Weapon

The separation of U-235 from the 140-times as abundant U-238 is a costly and difficult process; it was not certain that this would provide fissile material as rapidly as was thought to be needed in the US weapon programme during World War II. Accordingly, with the discovery of the artificial element plutonium, in particular, its 239 isotope, manufacturable in natural-uranium nuclear reactors by the parasitic capture of neutrons in U-238, production reactors were built at Hanford (in the state of Washington, the extreme northwest of the United States) to produce such plutonium. A reactor with a thermal power of 250 megawatts (MW) produces about 250 g of plutonium per day, of which about 6 kg was used in the bomb first tested at Alamagordo (New Mexico) 16 July 1945. An identical weapon was detonated over Nagasaki, three days after the gun-type bomb was used at Hiroshima. However, plutonium cannot be used in a gun-assembled weapon, since the metallic components are moved too slowly[55] by the propellant used in artillery or naval guns.

Thus the implosion method of assembly was mandatory for the plutonium weapon, in which the assembly occurs on a time scale of microseconds or tens of microseconds – so to speak, between the individual stray neutrons. Nevertheless, there was a significant probability for the Nagasaki bomb that a spontaneous neutron would occur at the worst possible time, and even that would have led to a yield no less than 1 kiloton.[56]

In the years following 1945, innovations were made to reduce the amount of costly fissionable material needed for nuclear weapons and to improve the safety. The initial configuration was thus much farther from "criticality" or unbridled neutron multiplication, and was hence safer against undesired nuclear explosion. Nevertheless, one could conceive of accidents in which the high explosive would detonate at one point, for instance by the impact of a rifle bullet on the explosive, or accidental dropping of the nuclear bomb, as happened several times. Thus almost from the beginning it was required that nuclear weapons be safe against such undesired nuclear explosions. For some years this was accomplished by systems in which the fissile core of the weapon would be kept separate from the explosive and inserted only during the flight of the aircraft. This impeded military readiness and flexibility, so later weapons were designed with internal mechanical safety devices [57] or eventually so that they were "inherently" one-point safe.[58]

The Boosted Fission Weapon

In 1951, the USA first tested the "boosting concept" under which a small amount of thermonuclear fuel was added to the ordinary fission bomb. This is currently accomplished by the use of a gas mixture of deuterium (D) and tritium (T) within the hollow "pit" of an implosion weapon. At the temperatures reached in the incipient nuclear explosion, a fraction of the T nuclei react with the D nuclei to form ordinary helium nuclei, plus neutrons of 14 million volt energy, which are extremely effective at causing fission in the now compressed fissionable material in the neighbourhood. Thus the relatively small amount of energy from the thermonuclear reaction produces a substantial number of neutrons and steps up or "boosts" the fission reaction to a higher level. This further increases the safety of such an explosive, since to reach otherwise the yield that can readily be achieved by boosting, a larger amount of fissionable material would need to be used.[59]

However, boosting adds its own problems to nuclear weapon design and maintenance, because hydrogen reacts chemically with plutonium and uranium. Furthermore, the artificial isotope of hydrogen, tritium, has a 12.3 year half-life, so that the tritium supply must be renewed on a scale of some years. This imposes the requirement for production of tritium if nuclear weapon numbers do not fall with time faster than the decay rate of tritium.[60]

Two-stage Thermonuclear Weapons

In 1952, the US MIKE test demonstrated with its ten megaton yield the concept introduced in early 1951 by Edward Teller and Stanislaw Ulam, by which the energy from a "primary" nuclear explosion is used to assemble a "secondary" charge containing thermonuclear fuel. Initially the secondary contained liquid deuterium, and the USA built as well several Emergency Capability Weapons (named "Jughead") deliverable by the B-36 aircraft.[61] These were soon replaced by "solid-fuel" thermonuclear weapons, using deuterium that was solidified by chemical binding to lithium, in particular to the naturally occurring lighter isotope of lithium – Li-6.[62]

It has long been a rule of thumb that many thermonuclear weapons typically produce about half of their total energy from the thermonuclear fuel and half from the fission of uranium in the proximity of that thermonuclear fuel.[63]

The nuclear weapon stockpiles of the nuclear weapon states are probably mostly boosted single-stage weapons or two-stage weapons as described here.[64]

Appendix 2

A Few Comments on Electrical Energy from PNEs (R.L. Garwin)

Having been involved in the study of peaceful nuclear explosions (PNEs) for 35 years or more, I want to emphasize the fact that such proposals for US PNEs, when thoroughly analysed, have not proved to be of economic merit. Certainly some explosions that might be counted as PNEs have had scientific merit, such as the Halite/Centurion series of experiments in which the radiation from a nuclear explosion was used instead of the (thus far unavailable) radiation from lasers in a gold cavity to implode rather large pellets to study inertial confinement fusion. And a Soviet PNE in 1962 quenched a high-pressure gas well that had leaked to a lower pressure reservoir – a task that the conventional technology in the Soviet Union was apparently incapable of performing at that time.

Indeed, one can achieve a useful goal with a PNE, but the cost of doing so turns usually out to be greater than the cost of non-PNE approaches.

I excerpt from a report which I prepared in 1975 for the US Arms Control and Disarmament Agency. This proposed Project Pacer was to build plants equivalent to a nominal nuclear power plant generating 1000 MW(e), by replacing the nuclear-heated steam supply by a steam supply heated by repeated thermonuclear explosions in an underground cavity. Since one tonne of HE contributes 4.2 GJ, and at 30 per cent efficiency a 1000 MWe reactor requires 3.3 GJ/s, about 60 kilotons of nuclear explosive per day is required to provide the necessary heat.

First, one should note that the United States has about 100 nominal reactors, so to replace them (without any further growth) by Pacer-like systems would require some 365 nuclear explosions per year at each plant of some 60 kt energy release – or about 36,000 such nuclear explosions per year in the United States alone.

And this would provide only 17 per cent of the electricity used at present in the United States.

My calculation in 1975 showed that if one assumed that there were no technical problems, the normal nuclear reactor would still be preferred until the cost of natural uranium rose to some $160-220/kg, compared with the present price of around $20/kg. And at higher prices, Pacer (still on the assumption that it is feasible) would need to compete with breeder reactors or with uranium from seawater.

Notes

1. Chairman's Draft Text of the Comprehensive Test Ban Treaty, *Arms Control Today,* August 1996. Also at http://www.acda.gov/

2. Article VIII: Review Of The Treaty, "... On the basis of a request by any State Party, the Review Conference shall consider the possibility of permitting the conduct of underground nuclear explosions for peaceful purposes ... "

3. W.J. Broad, *Star Warriors*, Simon & Schuster, 1985.

4. M.D. Nordyke, *The Soviet Program for Peaceful Uses of Nuclear Explosions*, UCRL-ID-124410, October 1996.

5. Pure Pu-239 is the plutonium isotope of choice for making nuclear weapons, in view of its high fission cross section, long half-life and hence modest heat evolution, relatively small spontaneous neutron emission, and lack of penetrating gamma radiation. The Pu weapons in the US stockpile are made of 94% Pu-239 and about 6% Pu-240 – so-called weapon-grade Pu. The Pu that could be extracted from fully irradiated spent uranium fuel in the normal fuel cycle of the world's some-400 light-water or heavy water reactors contains some 60-65% Pu-239, with most of the remainder being Pu-240. While reactor-grade Pu is often called "civil plutonium" we use the term "reactor-grade" to avoid possible confusion with Pu-238 used in some electrical generators powered by radioactivity, including some pacemakers. Because of its very short half-life of 87 years and the consequent heat evolution of 560 watt per kg, Pu-238 is the only Pu isotope from which one could not make an effective nuclear weapon.

6. J.P. Holdren (Chair), C.M. Kelleher, W.K.H. Panofsky, J.D. Baldeschwieler, P.M. Doty, A.H. Flax, R.L. Garwin, D.C. Jones, S.M. Keeny, J. Lederberg, M.M. May, C.K.N. Patel, J.D. Pollack, J.D. Steinbruner, R.H. Wertheim, and J.B. Wiesner, *Management and Disposition of Excess Weapons Plutonium*, Report of the National Academy of Sciences, Committee on International Security and Arms Control, January 1994.

7. R. Serber, *The Los Alamos Primer*, University of California Press, Berkeley, California, 1992.

8. R.W. Selden, *Reactor Plutonium and Nuclear Explosives*, December 1976.

9. E. Kankeleit, C. Kuppers, and U. Imkelle, *Bericht zur Waffentauglichkeit von Reaktorplutonium*, Institut für Kernphysik Technische Hochschule Darmstadt, December 1989.

10. J.C. Mark, "Explosive Properties of Reactor-Grade Plutonium," *Science and Global Security*, 4:1 (1993), pp. 111-128.

11. *Management and Disposition of Excess Weapons Plutonium*, pp. 32-33.

12. Nordyke, *The Soviet Program ...*

13. R.S. Norris, "French and Chinese Nuclear Weapon Testing," *Security Dialogue*, 27:1 (1996), pp. 39-54.

14. National Ignition Facility documentation from Lawrence Livermore National Laboratory and the Department of Energy.

15. In which pellets of ICF fuel such as deuterium-tritium mixture were driven by nuclear explosions rather than the eventual laser-driven X-ray source.

16. E.N. Avrorin, B.V. Litvinov, V.A. Simonenko, "Nuclear Explosive Experiments for Matter Property Study: Results and Opportunities," I.V. Zababhakin Scientific Talks, Physics of Explosion, Shock and Detonation Waves, Russian Federal Nuclear Center – All-Russian Scientific Research Institute of Technical Physics, Snezhinsk, Russia, 16-20 October 1995.

17. Nordyke, *The Soviet Program ...* (The 'Kama' waste-disposal experiments of 1973 and 1974).

18. S.D. Drell and R. Peurifoy, "Technical Issues of a Nuclear Test Ban," *Annual Review Nucl. Part. Sci.,* 1994, 44, pp. 285-327.

19. R.L. Garwin, "The Maintenance of Nuclear Weapon Stockpiles Without Nuclear Explosion Testing," presented at 24th Pugwash Workshop on Nuclear Forces, "Nuclear Forces in Europe," London, England, 22-24 September 1995. For the text of many Garwin documents, see http://www.fas.org/rlg

20. Garwin, "The Maintenance of Nuclear Weapon Stockpiles ... "

21. Drell and Peurifoy, "Technical Issues ... "

22. S.D. Drell (Chairman), C. Callan, M. Cornwall, D. Eardley, J. Goodman, D. Hammer, W. Happer, J. Kimble, S. Koonin, R. LeLevier, C. Max, W. Panofsky, M. Rosenbluth, J. Sullivan, P. Weinberger, H. York, and F. Zachariasen, *Science Based Stockpile Stewardship*, JASON Report JSR-94-345, November 1994.

23. JASON, *Science Based Stockpile Stewardship*

24. D. Hammer (Chairman), F. Dyson, N. Fortson, R. Novick, W. Panofsky, M. Rosenbluth, S. Treiman, H. York, *Inertial Confinement Fusion (ICF) Review*, JASON Report JSR-96-300, March 1996.

25. R.H. Rhodes, *Dark Sun: The Making of the Hydrogen Bomb*, Simon & Schuster, 1995; Drell and Peurifoy, "Technical Issues ..."; G.A. Goncharov, *Physics Today*, November 1996.

26. In his transmittal letter to the US Senate, seeking the advice and consent of the Senate to ratification of the CTBT, President Clinton sets out "safeguards" including the following:

"The conduct of a Science Based Stockpile Stewardship program to ensure a high level of confidence in the safety and reliability of nuclear weapons in the active stockpile, including the conduct of a broad range of effective and continuing experimental programs.

The maintenance of modern nuclear laboratory facilities and programs in theoretical and exploratory nuclear technology that will attract, retain, and ensure the continued application of our human scientific resources to those programs on which continued progress in nuclear technology depends.

The maintenance of the basic capability to resume nuclear test activities prohibited by the CTBT should the United States cease to be bound to adhere to this Treaty."

27. JASON, *Science Based Stockpile Stewardship*

28. Drell and Peurifoy, "Technical Issues ... "

29. The magic number, 11, is chosen to provide 70% probability of detecting a flaw that affects 10% of the weapons in the stockpile.

30. S.D. Drell (Chairman), J. Cornwall, F. Dyson, D. Eardley, R.L. Garwin, D. Hammer, J. Kammerdiener, R. LeLevier, R. Peurifoy, J. Richter, M. Rosenbluth, S. Sack, J. Sullivan, and F. Zachariasen, *Nuclear Testing – Summary and Conclusions*, JASON Report JSR-95-320, 3 August 1995.

31. R.L. Garwin, "Nuclear Tests Are No Longer Required (to keep a stockpile of weapons in good shape)" (in French), *La Recherche*, December 1995, pp. 70-76.

32. J.I. Katz, "Curatorship, not Stewardship," letter, *Bulletin of the Atomic Scientists*, November/December 1995.

33. C.P. Robinson, Statement to the United States Senate Committee on Armed Services, Hearing of the Subcommittee on Strategic Forces, 12 March 1996.

34. R.L. Garwin, "Monitoring and Verification of a CTBT," presented at 3rd Pugwash Workshop on the Future of the Nuclear-Weapon Complexes of Russia and the USA, Moscow, Russia, 24-26 March 1996; R.L. Garwin, "The Comprehensive Test Ban Treaty in September 1996," presented at the 46th Pugwash Conference on Science and World Affairs, *Security, Cooperation And Disarmament: The Unfinished Agenda For The 1990s*, 2-7 September 1996, Lahti, Finland.

35. Garwin, "Monitoring and Verification ... "

36. Drell and Peurifoy, "Technical Issues ... "

37. JASON, *Nuclear Testing – Summary and Conclusions*

38. Garwin, "Monitoring and Verification ... "

39. JASON, *Nuclear Testing – Summary and Conclusions*

40. Garwin, "Monitoring and Verification ... "

41. Avrorin, Litvinov & Simonenko, "Nuclear Explosive Experiments ... "

42. T.B. Taylor, *Sunday Times*, London, England, 5 October 1986.

43. Goncharov, in *Physics Today*

44. Nordyke, *The Soviet Program* ...

45. F.A. Long, Chairman, L.E. Elkins, R.L. Garwin, T. Greenwood, C. Hocott, H. Jacoby, G.W. Johnson, and R. Morse, *An Analysis of the Economic Feasibility, Technical Significance, and Time Scale for Application of Peaceful Nuclear Explosions in the US, with Special Reference to the GURC Report Thereon*, April 1975.

46. F.A. Long, Chairman, L.E. Elkins, R.L. Garwin, T. Greenwood, C. Hocott, H. Jacoby, G.W. Johnson, and R. Morse, Appendix C: "Comparative Cost Analyses for Electric Power from Project Pacer," from *An Analysis of the Economic Feasibility, Technical Significance, and Time Scale for Application of Peaceful Nuclear Explosions in the US, with Special Reference to the GURC Report Thereon*, April 1975.

47. *e.g.* Y.A. Trutnev and A.K. Chernyschev, presented at the Fourth International Workshop on Nuclear Warhead Elimination and Nonproliferation, Washington D.C., February 1992.

48. *Management and Disposition of Excess Weapons Plutonium* (Appendix C, pp. 272-275).

49. Of course, there is a tiny probability that the cataclysmic event will happen next year or in ten years, but with the improvement in observation systems, we should be able to increase the lead time for errant asteroids. Wayward comets, on the other hand, are more difficult to predict.

50. Although in free space the required velocity is inversely proportional to the travel time, this is not true for orbital dynamics. For short-period asteroids, the maximum deviation for a given velocity is obtained by applying it about one-half of the asteroid "year" before impact. However, spaced multiple impulses can be of use.

51. More than 90% U-235, although HEU is a term used to refer to anything more than 20% U-235.

52. Serber, *The Los Alamos Primer*

53. F.H. Shelton, *Recollections of a Nuclear Weaponeer*, 1988, pp. 1-35.

54. Rhodes, *Dark Sun*; R. Rhodes, *The Making of the Atomic Bomb*, Simon & Schuster, 1987.

55. U-235 is hardly radioactive at all – half-life 700 million years. On the other hand, the most common plutonium isotope in nuclear weapons (Pu-239) has a half-life of 24,000 years – almost 30,000 times shorter than that of U-235. Furthermore, Pu-239 is accompanied to some extent by Pu-240, which has a "spontaneous fission" decay that injects neutrons continuously into any mass of Pu. Thus, the relatively slow (milliseconds) assembly of metallic blocks in a plutonium gun would allow time for such neutrons to start the chain reaction when the assembly is barely supercritical, leading to much reduced yield (Serber, *The Los Alamos Primer*).

56. J.C. Mark, "Explosive Properties of Reactor-Grade Plutonium," in *Science & Global Security*, 4, 1993, pp. 111-128. R.L. Garwin, "Technical Interpretation" and "Explosive Properties of Various Types of Plutonium," in *Managing the Plutonium Surplus: Applications and Technical Options*, ed. R.L. Garwin, M. Grubb, and E. Matanle, NATO ASI Series, 1. Disarmament Technologies – v. 1, November 1994, pp. 1-22.

57. Drell and Peurifoy, "Technical Issues ... "

58. R.E. Kidder, *Report to Congress: Assessment of the Safety of US Nuclear Weapons and Related Nuclear Test Requirements*, UCRL-LR-107454, July 1991; Garwin, "The Maintenance of Nuclear Weapon Stockpiles ... ".

59. H.F. York, *The Advisors: Oppenheimer, Teller, and the Superbomb*, Stanford, Ca: Stanford University Press, 1989.

60. Indeed, the United States is committed to a rate of reduction faster than that, even if by the year 2003 one only has the START I level of some 8000 nuclear warheads. And if one is optimistic about reducing nuclear weapon holdings, it may be that US and Russian warheads could be reduced to 2000 or fewer total warheads on each side by that time. This has significant consequences for the required tritium production or acquisition capability, which we will discuss later.

61.   T.B. Cochran, W.M. Arkin, R.S. Norris, and M.M. Hoenig, *Nuclear Weapons Databook: Vol.II US Nuclear Warhead Production"* Natural Resources Defense Council, 1987, p. 16.

62.   Rhodes, *Dark Sun;* Goncharov, in *Physics Today*.

63.   *Drawing Back the Curtain of Secrecy and Restricted Data Declassification Decisions 1946 to the Present (RDD-3)* 1 January 1996, US Dept of Energy Office of Declassification "Approved for Public Release," p. 81. Also, United Nations Scientific Committee on Effects of Atomic Radiation (UNSCEAR 1993), p. 94, gives full yield of atmospheric tests as 545 megatons, of which 217 are stated to be fission.

64.   Garwin, "The Maintenance of Nuclear Weapon Stockpiles ... "

10

Western Nuclear Doctrine: Changes and Influences

Daniel Plesch

Introduction

The current state of nuclear doctrine and policy in the nuclear-weapon states might be described as besieged. An ambassador of a West European nuclear state likened the weapon states' position to that of the French King just before the French revolution. There was no point in giving any concessions or reforms since it was clear that the mass of countries were demanding complete elimination, would not be satisfied with anything less, and would only be encouraged by concessions.[1]

This chapter analyses current Western nuclear weapon doctrines. Cold war policies of deterrence and indeed of nuclear war-fighting are still there; but in addition there are new rationales for nuclear weapon use in possible conflicts with "rogue states." At the same time, the pressure for nuclear disarmament has intensified.

The 1990-1991 Gulf War and the later discoveries of Iraq's deployment of chemical and biological weapons has reopened the debate on the utility of nuclear weapons against states armed with chemical and biological weapons. This debate has given a new lease of life to proponents of limited nuclear war. On the other side, the diplomacy involved in the indefinite extension of the Nuclear Non-Proliferation Treaty (NPT), the International Court of Justice advisory opinion on the legality of the use or threatened use of nuclear weapons, and the negotiation of the Comprehensive Test Ban Treaty (CTBT), have all brought greater pressure upon all the nuclear weapon states to carry out complete nuclear disarmament.

The five permanent members of the UN Security Council – the nuclear weapon states – have found themselves seeking to defend a common interest – retention of nuclear weapons and options for their use against most other states.

This has led to an unprecedented increase in cooperation between the staffs of different countries' nuclear weapons production complexes; the negotiations on the CTBT helped this process. The doctrinal implications – indeed contradictions – of cooperation on weapons development between potential adversaries, such as Russia, China and the USA, are as yet unexamined.

To the non-specialist, nuclear doctrine and policy are obscure and abstract, with little impact on the real world – since only in the unlikely event of nuclear war would they be relevant. There is even a tendency, as nuclear weapons slip from public view, to regard policies such as "First Use," or the slow pace of new arms reduction talks since 1992, as simply hold-overs from the Cold War, only waiting a little political attention before they are tidied up. Unfortunately, it seems that the nuclear weapon powers are evolving doctrines which are at variance with this picture of how events will evolve – doctrines which imply the continued deployment of nuclear weapons into the indefinite future.

Uses of Nuclear Weapons

For all the nuclear weapon states the use and threat of use of nuclear weapons in response to such policies by a nuclear-armed opponent remains the core justification for the retention of nuclear weapons. For China this so-called second strike deterrence is the only avowed policy. There is little evidence that central logical arguments against nuclear weapons have made an impact on policy-makers. The argument against nuclear weapons is that they can only deter in an error-free and rational world, while the world we live in is often influenced by unpredictable events at all levels. In these circumstances reliance on the "rational" system of deterrence is at best a stop gap. The inability of deterrence theorists to incorporate this consideration into their thinking is one of the most obvious weaknesses in such theories and doctrines. Much of the argument for nuclear arms does indeed rest upon the assumption that the world is a nasty, dangerous and unpredictable place; it follows that deterrence may fail, but this risk does not lead to a serious attempt to eliminate these weapons.

Ever since Ronald Reagan and Mikhail Gorbachev declared that nuclear war cannot be won and should not be fought, public discussion by officials has tended to deny the possibility of the use of nuclear weapons in warfare. However, it is clear from the analysis made below that the nuclear weapon states continue to regard nuclear weapons as a potential means of concluding conflict on favourable terms, that is, winning. In the United States at least this notion is still clearly expressed in doctrine and is even envisaged as applying in a prolonged global nuclear war.

The collapse of the bi-polar nuclear confrontation soon followed by the Gulf War, has caused a renewed interest in the use of nuclear weapons to win regional wars. There are two reasons for this. First, it is now possible to consider a war in which the use of nuclear weapons would not result in a strategic exchange between nuclear weapon states, and second, the experience with Iraq opened up the question of whether nuclear weapons are needed to deter, pre-empt or respond to chemical and biological threats and attacks.

The following analysis focuses upon the USA since it is the world's remaining superpower. However, the main themes of analysis that are developed in relation to the USA are also found in Britain, France and NATO, and these themes are discussed in respect to each of their particulars.

United States

The Nuclear Posture Review and Contemporary Doctrine

The United States Defense Department's Nuclear Posture Review (NPR) of September 1994 sets out current US policy. It broadly reaffirmed the policy inherited from the Bush Administration and recommended no further reductions in the US arsenal before the ratification of START II; it did not look beyond that Treaty. It also appears that the NPR made no examination of the impact of policy options for the reduction and elimination of weapons of mass destruction in enhancing US security and reducing reliance on nuclear arms. For example, the RAND contribution to the NPR contains no exposition of the potential impact of arms control strategies upon US nuclear posture. The intellectual narrowness of what appears to have been the NPR's approach is so self-limiting and self-justifying as to be socially psychotic (psychosis being defined as a state in which a view of the world can only be sustained by the rigid exclusion of commonplace awareness). The complete exclusion of one entire field of thought – arms control – fits this definition precisely. A more organizational critique might say that it was the study of just one government department – Defense – so that it did not include input from sections of the Administration with an arms control mandate. The following exchange in the US Senate illustrates official thinking on force levels – Senator Dale Bumpers:

> I am told that Russia has about 500 cities with 50,000 or more people. START II then will leave us with six or seven operational nuclear warheads for each of those cities. Isn't that enough to deter even a resurgent Russia, regardless of how many strategic nuclear weapons it has?[2]

Secretary William Perry:

> The US START II force is based on the tenet of "rough equivalency." Therefore, a START II force would be insufficient for deterring a resurgent Russia that is non-compliant with its treaty obligations.

Thus the central dynamic of the nuclear arms race remains in place: "enough" is as many as the other guy has, even if there are no rational targets. The US Doctrine for Joint Nuclear Operations issued in December 1995 contains a more detailed exposition of contemporary US policy.[3]

> ... the fundamental purpose of US nuclear forces is to deter the use of weapons of mass destruction (WMD), particularly nuclear weapons, and to serve as a hedge against the emergence of an overwhelming conventional threat ... During World War II, nuclear weapons were instrumental in ending the war on terms favourable to the allies. The US post-war strategy has been one of deterrence.

The document consistently discusses a role for nuclear weapons against non-nuclear threats and attacks. For example:

> WMD used on US forces would cause a significant tactical or operational loss; greatly changing the character of the war, putting the outcome in doubt and threatening escalation; and leave the United States with a difficult choice: to retaliate or not to retaliate. *A selective capability to use lower-yield weapons in retaliation*, without destabilizing the conflict, *is a useful alternative* for the US National Command Authorities (NCA). In respect to conventional warfare, "*The potential employment of nuclear weapons at theater level*, when combined with the means and resolve to use them, *makes the prospects of conflict of any type more dangerous* and the outcome more difficult to assess. They are prescribed as a means of deterring attacks and bolstering the "resolve of allies to resist enemy attempts at political coercion." [emphasis in original]

Heightened readiness is suggested as a means of indicating willingness to use nuclear weapons, in spite of the risk of conveying the message that their use is imminent and so inducing panic.

In war should deterrence fail ."..it is the objective of the United States to repel or defeat a military attack and terminate the conflict on terms favorable to the United States and its allies." This is the same form of words used to describe the unconditional surrender of Japan.

> Terminating a global war involving the use of large numbers of WMD on both sides and the degradation and destruction of their means of control could be vastly more difficult than ending a theatre or regional nuclear conflict involving the relatively constrained use of a limited number of nuclear weapons.
>
> Therefore, US nuclear forces, supporting ... systems, and employment planning must provide the capability to deny enemy war aims, even in a conflict of indefinite duration ... Adequate nuclear reserve forces reduce opportunities for another nation to dominate or coerce behaviour before, during or after the use of WMD. Such forces provide the US with the

capability to continue to deny enemy war aims, to influence other nations, and to exert leverage for war termination.

It seems, therefore, that the Doctrine of Joint Nuclear Operations still states the winning of a nuclear war as one of the objectives of nuclear weapon policy. This is in spite of the fact that ten years earlier Presidents Reagan and Gorbachev had agreed on a statement that "a nuclear war cannot be won and must never be fought." It is surely time for official doctrine to accept that there would be no national interest to serve – indeed no nation to defend – after a prolonged global nuclear war.

Targeting considerations continue to include such concepts as pre-planning, countervalue targeting, counterforce targeting, layering and cross targeting: that is, targeting valuable parts of a nation's infrastructure and military forces – especially nuclear forces – with several nuclear weapons fired from different types of delivery system in order to ensure that the target is destroyed.

A more recent addition, also found in NATO, is the use of adaptive planning against emergent targets. The *New York Times* reported that staff at US Strategic Command (the successor to Strategic Air Command, with the inclusion of control of US ballistic missile submarines) were "in the early stages of b᠁᠁᠁᠁ and testing computer models that could enable Mr Clinton to aim nucl᠁ ᠁pons at Third World nations that threaten the interests of the United States and its allies."[4] Other reports indicated that the capability for "adaptive targeting" existed already in 1992.[5] Adaptive planning enables the political authority to rapidly re-target nuclear weapons.

There is a continuing transition from strategic nuclear targeting to selective nuclear targeting. The Cold War use of strategic nuclear forces would most likely have involved a large-scale launch of weapons against a wide range of targets. The targets were known and analysed months or years in advance, and all formed part of the Single Integrated Operational Plan (SIOP).[6]

As the ex-Soviet target list declines, the number and distribution of aim-points will be much less constant and may occur anywhere in the world, defying pre-planned targeting. An analysis of Third World targeting, and of demands likely to be made by the US National Command Authority (NCA), points out that:

> Some of these targets may warrant, under specific but undefined circumstances, a rapid response with a single low-yield warhead. As the SIOP as we have known it becomes smaller, the recently established US Strategic Command (STRATCOM) may find itself required to generate a similar attack plan quickly – using its precise database of all "potentially strategic targets in the world" – matched to a specific scenario on demand from the NCA or a commander-in-chief. Such a plan might consist of only a few targets, to which the NCA would match the appropriate weapons and delivery systems.[7]

Non-military means are recommended in the US Joint Doctrine as a way of avoiding conflict and include:

> ... nonproliferation, counterproliferation, arms control and verification, and confidence building measures ... These measures make war or conflict less likely by improving communication, reducing opportunities for miscalculation, providing ways to resolve crises, and reducing the destructive capacity of available arsenals.

There is a continuing debate on whether US policy in these areas is adequate, or whether it is given low political and financial priority.

It is, clear, therefore that the USA remains committed to the use of nuclear weapons in a wide variety of situations far beyond the simple concept of retaliatory use in case of a nuclear attack on the homeland. There has been little attempt to reduce the alert status of nuclear missile forces. The requirements of military readiness continue to take precedence over risk reduction measures.

Although the nuclear forces of Britain, Russia and the USA are now no longer targeted, the capability for re-targeting in seconds makes this move cosmetic, since the remaining forces retain a high alert status. No new measures have been taken to reduce the destructive capacity of nuclear weapons under the Clinton Administration. Even though START II was signed before either party had ratified START I, the Clinton Administration policy insists that START III negotiations must wait on START II ratification, although it is prepared to see progress on the "framework" for these talks to assist in the ratification of START II by the Duma (see Chapters 7 and 11). There has been strong and successful military resistance to any intermediate steps.

In the preparation of the NPR the Joint Chiefs of Staff (JCS) and Commander In Chief STRATCOM Admiral Henry Chiles[8] successfully resisted a recommendation that the USA could dispense with the 500 Minuteman IIIs in its arsenal and place greater reliance on its submarine force in accordance with a study by the RAND Corporation commissioned by the US Department of Defense for the NPR.[9] The proposal was also strongly opposed by Republican leaders in the US Senate.

Before the NPT Review and Extension Conference the Arms Control and Disarmament Agency and White House officials recommended that the USA reduce its nuclear weapons by a further 1000 warheads beyond the level of 3500 permitted in START II. This proposal will now not be pursued until START III negotiations begin.

Political and Legal Constraints in US Nuclear Doctrine

In parallel with the military planning outlined above the Doctrine for Joint

Nuclear Operations also contains political and legal guidance which tends to modify to some extent the impression of unsullied military planning. The Joint Doctrine makes clear that international reaction – especially to a state that first uses WMD – will be important and places US policy within the constraints of the "laws of war" and indeed makes reference to "definitions of 'just war.'"

> The tremendous destructive capacity of WMD and the consequences of their use have given rise to a number of arms control agreements restricting deployment and use ... at the same time it is important to recognise that there is no customary or conventional international law to prohibit nations from employing nuclear weapons in armed conflict. Therefore, the use of nuclear weapons against enemy combatants and other military objectives is lawful. The nation that initiates the use of nuclear weapons, however, may find itself the target of world condemnation.

Thus even before the ICJ judgement it is clear that legality was a significant consideration in US doctrine.   It remains to be seen whether the ICJ pronouncement will produce further constraints.

The tension between legal and arms control requirements, on the one hand, and military requirements driven by perceived threats, on the other, is the main theme in contemporary discussions in the US Administration; they are also found in internal debates in the other nuclear weapon states.

The restriction on nuclear use by the NPT and other treaties is of concern to nuclear force commanders.   For example, Admiral Chiles, then CINC STRATCOM, confirmed that the USA had ruled out nuclear use against NPT signatories, but stated in an interview that: "[For] the remaining states of the world who have not signed up with the Non-Proliferation Treaty , I think that we ought not to say whether or not we perceive that we would ever need nuclear weapons in a confrontation with them."[10]   (For all practical purposes, there are now only three states in this category – India, Pakistan and Israel.)

Admiral Chiles noted when discussing the NPT commitments that a policy of studied ambiguity had been used effectively by President Bush in Iraq and President Clinton with respect to North Korea. With respect to the NPT, which both states had signed, the fact that any US action would occur when they were clearly in violation of the Treaty presumably provided the legal room.

These security assurances provided by the United States to non-nuclear weapon state parties to the NPT were first articulated in 1978.

> The United States will not use nuclear weapons against any state party to the Non-Proliferation Treaty (NPT) or any comparable internationally binding commitment not to acquire nuclear explosive devices, except in the case of an attack on the United States, its territories or armed forces, or its allies, by such a state allied to a nuclear-weapons state or associated with a nuclear-weapons state in carrying out or sustaining the attack.[11]

When questioned whether these assurances applied to attacks using chemical or biological weapons, a US official responded:

> The US position on the non-use of nuclear weapons is a broad formulation and is not intended to delineate the specific US response to hypothetical aggression against the United States and its allies, such as attacks by chemical and biological weapons ...[12]

This equivocation can also be found in the UK.

In the run up to the NPT Review and Extension Conference it became clear that a central demand of non-nuclear weapon states, as diverse as Switzerland and Zimbabwe, was for a guarantee that there were no circumstances under which they would be attacked with nuclear weapons. In particular, there was a demand for a legally binding treaty which would give an unqualified guarantee that nuclear weapons would not be used against any non-nuclear weapon state. One of the toughest negotiations in the NPT renewal centred on whether such a treaty should become an agreed objective. In the end it was only agreed that this "could" be done. The final text read:

> "... further steps should be considered to assure non-nuclear-weapon States party to the Treaty against the use or threat of use of nuclear weapons. These steps could take the form of an internationally legally binding instrument."[13]

The topic of nuclear-weapon-free zones (NWFZ) was another policy arena in which the nuclear weapon states were required to reassess their doctrine, since support for such zones requires explicit and unqualified legal undertakings never to use nuclear weapons in a given area.

The South Pacific NWFZ has now been adhered to by all the nuclear weapon states. In reference to the African nuclear-weapon-free zone treaty, while Russia has not agreed to sign up, China, UK, France and the USA have done so. Only the UK submitted the standard equivocation.

However, in the USA the matter became a subject of heated internal debate centred on the fact that Libya, an NPT and African NWFZ signatory, was considered a threat because of its development of chemical weapons. The African NWFZ Protocol unequivocally prohibit nuclear weapons from the Zone and has the force of law. Nevertheless, the USA did not submit any reservations because of the undertakings given to countries such as South Africa in order to obtain their support for the indefinite extension of the NPT. However, a US official stated that the Treaty "will not limit options available to the United States in response to an attack by an African NWFZ party using weapons of mass destruction."[14]

The consideration of the legality of nuclear weapons possession and use by the ICJ has been a renewed challenge to the nuclear weapon states. Again one of the clear arguments for the legality of nuclear weapons rested on the idea that they could be used as weapons of war. The somewhat ambiguous pronouncement of the ICJ seems to be clear in a number of respects; most notably use of nuclear weapons is ruled out in circumstances when national survival is not at stake. As yet there appears to have been no significant inter-agency discussion of the ICJ advisory opinion, partly because it is of limited status. However, it will undoubtedly be raised in the coming period by non-nuclear weapon states in fora such as the NPT review process which started in April 1997.

The diplomatic position of the United States indicates a great reluctance to accept constraints on nuclear weapons employment. This creates a strong impression that the USA is prepared to use them. Whether or not this generates a deterrent effect is hard to say. What is certain is that the USA is seen as giving a high value to nuclear weapons, and in doing so can only encourage others to believe in their utility.

Countering Chemical and Biological Threats

The most frequently used argument to resist further constraints on nuclear weapons relates to CBW threats. In April 1996, a major new report from the Office of the Secretary of Defense publicly confirmed the significance of a perceived threat from chemical and biological weapons:

> We received a wake-up call with Saddam Hussein's use of SCUD missiles during Operation Desert Storm and new information on his ambitious nuclear, biological, and chemical weapons programs. The proliferation of these horrific weapons presents a grave and urgent risk to the United States and our citizens, allies, and troops abroad. Reducing this risk is an absolute priority of the United States.[15]

The Iraqi regime had an unanticipated success in developing and weaponizing chemical and biological weapons. However, these systems are vulnerable to local climate change, they are difficult to deliver, and they should not be put on a par with nuclear weapons for the scale and reliability of the devastation they can cause.

An indication of the new emphasis on CBW threats can be seen in a major simulation exercise conducted at the US Naval War College in July 1995. This involved the development of two major regional crises, one involving North Korea and the other involving a re-armed Iraq. In both cases, the war game extended to the use of chemical weapons by the states concerned. The Korean crisis was subsequently brought under control. This was not the case with the re-worked Gulf crisis, which escalated to the point where Iraq staged substantial biological warfare attacks on Dharan and other targets, leading to massive casualties. It was followed by US nuclear retaliation against Baghdad which terminated the "war."[16]

This perceived need to have the ability to target new threats, especially from biological and chemical weapons in the hands of regional adversaries, became a substantial feature of the nuclear debate in the United States during 1995, with analysts discussing the validity and effectiveness of a nuclear response, especially with low-yield weapons.[17]

A specific concern was with the need to target and destroy heavily protected structures such as deep underground bunkers which contained CBW production facilities or stores. Such targeting, it was said, requires robust penetrating warheads which can produce explosive yields sufficient to completely destroy the contents of the structures, the argument being that only a nuclear charge of around 0.1 kilotons would be adequate for such a purpose.[18] The main reason for US concern over adhering to the African NWFZ centred on concerns over Libya's CW programme. US officials and some media speculated on the possible use of nuclear weapons against Libya. A modified B61 bomb became the focus of attention. Following strong and adverse public reaction the Pentagon publicly ruled out the use of nuclear weapons in any pre-emptive way, leaving open the question of retaliatory use.

The same view was expressed in another debate by then Defense Secretary William Perry. In March 1996, Perry testified in support of US ratification of the Chemical Weapons Convention. He indicated that nuclear weapons could be used in response to a chemical attack:

> The whole range would be considered ... We have conventional weapons, also advanced conventional weapons – precision-guided munitions, Tomahawk land-attack missiles – and then we have nuclear weapons.[19]

This comment goes beyond the studied ambiguity used by previous administrations.

The various "hawkish" approaches can be contrasted both with the constraints of legal commitments and with realities during the Gulf War. It appears from the published memoirs that the Chairman of the Joint Chiefs, Colin Powell, was so reluctant to consider nuclear use that he had to be directly ordered to do so. The exercise was not reassuring:

> The results unnerved me, General Powell wrote. To do serious damage to just one armored division dispersed in the desert would require a considerable number of small tactical nuclear weapons. I showed this analysis to Cheney and then had it destroyed.

It is widely averred that Saddam Hussein was deterred from using weapons of mass destruction by US nuclear weapons. However, he was not deterred from the initial invasion of Kuwait; his weapons of mass destruction, even when dispersed with pre-delegated authority, may have been designed as a response to a US strike. Their existence may indeed have been a factor leading George Bush to terminate the war early, and on terms favourable to Iraq. The veiled US threat to use nuclear weapons, often referred to by advocates of nuclear weapons deterrence, included a threat of their use if oil fields of Kuwait were destroyed. This action did take place and US nuclear weapons were not used.

The tendency to see the lack of utility of nuclear weapons appears to be gaining ground. General Colin Powell, then Chair of the Joint Chiefs of Staff, clearly stated his commitment that "we will eventually see the time when the number of nuclear weapons is down to zero."[20]

The US Debate in 1997

The current climate of hostility to arms control has a long history. During the Cold War, conservatives characterized arms control as tantamount to treason. Ronald Reagan's INF and START agreements gave it a brief consensual popularity but this did not last. One reason for the ascendance of scepticism about arms control is the clear feeling in the United States that with the collapse of communism and the victory in the Gulf the USA stands militarily supreme and, in consequence, does not need arms control.

The United States Senate considered the Chemical Weapons Convention again before the Treaty entered into force at the end of April 1997. Although the Treaty was ratified, the difficulty of the process indicates how even with a treaty crafted by the Reagan and Bush Administrations, Republican opposition has become fierce. It is hard to see other treaties, including the CTBT, the Treaty of Raratonga – South Pacific NWFZ, and the Treaty of Pelindaba – African NWFZ, being ratified easily by the Senate.

Following resistance to START II ratification in the Duma, US Secretaries of Defense Perry and Cohen advanced the idea of an agreed framework on START III as a means of securing Duma ratification (see Chapter 7).

Additional discussions on making reductions irreversible through the bilateral destruction of warheads and controls of fissile materials are also being considered. Some attention is being given to an agreement on tactical weapons, some of which were withdrawn under an agreement on reciprocal unilateral measures to remove thousands of nuclear weapons from armies, navies and air forces at the end of the Cold War (see Chapter 13). These weapons are not subject to any inspection regime. Such an agreement might involve the abolition of such warheads which would necessitate the withdrawal of all US nuclear weapons from Europe.

The debate outside the Administration is discussed elsewhere (Chapter 2). A number of centrist think tanks argue for further cuts. Now a growing number of studies go further, and argue for a move to zero.

France

France maintains a force of nuclear missile submarines supplemented by medium range bombers. For political and financial reasons these programmes have been curtailed and several land-based missile programmes have been scrapped.

In France, there has long been a distinction between a centre and leftist view of nuclear strategy focusing on minimal deterrence, and a concentration on policies to promote non-proliferation, contrasted with a more right-wing Gaullist view which emphasizes the defence of French and allied interests through flexible military capabilities – both offensive and defensive. This includes the development of nuclear forces capable of being used, if necessary, in confrontation with countries of "the South" that may be armed with nuclear, chemical or biological weapons.[21]

Jacques Chirac's victory in the French presidential elections in May 1995 ensured the current pre-eminence of the Gaullist view. This was demonstrated in the decision, shortly after the elections, to resume nuclear testing. The tests were designed both to complete the development of two new warheads and also to ensure that France had a simulation capability if nuclear weapon tests were banned.

The French public opposed the testing program, with polls showing up to 65 per cent against it. On the other hand, support for keeping France's nuclear arsenal was almost as strong as the opposition to testing. This is less of a contradiction than it might appear. The widespread international criticism did cause concern in France and the need for *new* nuclear weapons in the post-Cold War era does not have the support of the French public. However, the more basic desire for an independent French nuclear force remains strong. Nuclear weapons are regarded as essential for France's status in the world, as well as being intended to prevent the disaster of 1940 from recurring.

Today French nuclear strategy is also partially geared towards counter-proliferation. According to one report:

> French officials said the Rafale armed with a long-range standoff missile would be well-suited to deter the growing number of countries in the developing world that have acquired, or are acquiring, nuclear, bacteriological and chemical weapons as well as ballistic missiles.[22]

This "suitability" of such a combination stems from having a low-yield accurate nuclear system appropriate for precision attacks on military installations, a move away from the more traditional French concentration on counter-city targeting.[23] The stretched ASMP missile can fulfil this role.

France is, in some respects, the country with the clearest nuclear doctrine, which has been described in three parts. Only the need to protect vital interests would cause the use of nuclear weapons; only nuclear weapons can assuredly protect vital interests; only the President can decide what are France's vital interests.

This allows the President much discretion, as matters well beyond simple territorial integrity could be considered to be in France's vital interests. French officials under Chirac have pointed out that the use of chemical and biological weapons against French forces could be a threat to France's vital interests.[24]

France has distanced its nuclear weapons from the USA and NATO since 1968. In the mid-1990s, France began to move towards military re-integration. As a result the French defence minister now attends Nuclear Planning Group meetings and their communiques mention the role of French nuclear forces in alliance security.

French nuclear policy is based on the long-held common view that France needs its own nuclear forces because it cannot rely on the United States for a nuclear umbrella. Further, its conventional forces are such that it will rarely be able to respond to a major regional crisis on its own unless it can supplement its conventional forces with a nuclear capability.[25] This latter argument echoes British thinking back to the 1950s.[26] It also has a resonance with the current Russian predicament.

Britain

By the end of the century Britain's nuclear force will consist of four 16 missile Trident submarines. These "D5" missiles are the most modern strategic weapons developed by the United States, and Britain has acquired them in a follow-on agreement to the 1963 Polaris sales agreement. When the decision was made in 1993 to abandon unilaterally the airforce nuclear role it was decided that Trident should take on the sub-strategic tasks.

There continues to be a difference between Britain's declaratory policy on nuclear use and the actual deployment policy. Indeed, one British Secretary of State for Defence declared himself personally dubious about limited nuclear war-fighting, saying:

> [T]here is sometimes speculation that more so-called "usable" nuclear weapons
> – very low-yield devices which could be used to carry out what are
> euphemistically called "surgical strikes" – would allow nuclear deterrence to
> be effective in circumstances where existing weapons would be self-deterring.
> I am thoroughly opposed to this view.[27]

Just as in the Cold War era, the official line is that nuclear weapons are deterrent weapons of last resort, and that their use in a limited nuclear war is virtually inconceivable. In the Cold War years, this went hand in hand with a deployment policy that was linked both to NATO's early first use strategy and to the deployment of nuclear forces in regional crises, such as the Falklands War. In the post-Cold War years, the government points to the withdrawal of Britain's tactical nuclear warheads as an indication that it is moving to minimal deterrence. Yet NATO reports:

> The United Kingdom briefed us on the implementation of its decision to utilize the flexibility of its submarine-launched Trident ballistic missiles to undertake sub-strategic as well as strategic roles and thereby progressively to replace the capability now provided by its air-delivered nuclear weapons.[28]

The British have argued as recently as 1995, while presenting their case for the legality of nuclear weapons at a hearing of the International Court of Justice at the Hague, that use of nuclear weapons at sea is a viable option.

A significant subsidiary thread in British nuclear weapon policy has been the perceived value of nuclear weapons in counterbalancing relative weaknesses in conventional forces in regional confrontations outside NATO. In both the Falklands/Malvinas war of 1982 and the Gulf War in 1991, Britain had the means to escalate to nuclear use, as it apparently had in the confrontation with Indonesia in the early 1960s.[29] This forms part of a continuum in military thinking about nuclear weapons with parallels in the United States, the Soviet Union, and France, as well as being clearly represented in NATO's planning for early first use of nuclear weapons.

With the end of the Cold War, and the diminishing risk of massive Sov nuclear attack or retaliation, the utility of nuclear use against regional threats, especially in the Middle East, is coming to the fore. The second Trident submarine, deployed in January 1996, was reportedly the first to carry Trident missiles armed with one warhead,[30] although British officials would neither confirm nor deny this report.

One analysis saw four levels of possible use of Trident.[31] The most substantial is a response to use of nuclear forces against UK territory or forces. Second, Trident might be used in response to chemical or biological attack. A third possibility would be a demonstration shot to deter an enemy from taking a particular course of action. Finally, a nuclear response might be made to a state that had refused to desist from a specific course of action. Three out of these four cases would involve nuclear first-use. In this way, it is argued:

> the UK will obtain a global, nuclear, sub-strategic strike capability at remarkably low cost. It is also a system that is inherently more flexible and much less vulnerable than using aircraft. Thus, the task of the UK's strategic planners in 1994 is to develop a minimal force that will have strategic – and now sub-strategic – validity in the highly uncertain world through to 2024, and possibly well beyond.[31]

The UK states that it is constrained by the negative security assurances that it has given. Then Defence Secretary Malcolm Rifkind commented:

> These assurances were given in the context of the Cold War, when there was no appreciable risk of our facing a chemical or biological attack from any country outside the Warsaw Pact. They remain in force today and we are prepared (the UK has made it clear to Ukraine) to reiterate them in the same form in respect of any new adherent to the NPT. But the context in which we extend these assurances is one in which we attach ever increasing importance to the Biological and Chemical Weapons Conventions: both to securing universal adherence to these Conventions and to ensuring that they are effectively implemented, with appropriate international action directed against countries which do not abide by their provisions.[32]

There is an alternative view of Britain's sub-strategic capability. Trident is in a number of ways highly unsuitable for a sub-strategic role. It has no visible deployable presence and is, therefore, a poorer means of sending a political signal than moving nuclear-capable aircraft to a regional airbase. Sea-launched ballistic missile accuracy is fine in theory but in operations air-delivered weapons, perhaps with a stand-off weapon, carry less risk of a catastrophic miss.

There are political reasons why the UK may have opted for a single warhead sub-strategic Trident. The Conservative government had invested so much in the ideas of limited nuclear options that, faced with the financially crippling cost of developing a new air delivered missile, the TASM, it opted for a new role for Trident knowing its major limitations. This requirement was particularly important to keep up because of the UK's role in NATO. In NATO, both the USA and the UK deployed sub-strategic warheads. Re-designating Trident is a means for the UK to maintain its nuclear status within the Alliance alongside the USA. In the past the UK has taken decisions on its nuclear forces without telling Parliament. In this context it is also possible that the UK has secretly pursued another option. This might be to retain the option to put a nuclear warhead on the Tomahawk sea-launched cruise missiles that it is buying from the USA for use on British attack submarines.

Britain is completing the deployment of a new nuclear weapon system which is likely to be in place for thirty years. It does not regard this as inconsistent with a policy designed to control the proliferation of nuclear weapons in other states.

Extended Deterrence: The United States, NATO and the EU

The phrase extended deterrence was much in vogue during the Cold War but has been little heard of in recent years. One version of extended deterrence is the concept of using nuclear weapons in retaliation if an ally is attacked with nuclear weapons. The USA offers this guarantee to its NATO allies (as do France and the UK) and to other nations including Japan, South Korea, Australia and New Zealand.

If the US were to reduce and eventually eliminate nuclear weapons, would states such as Japan be tempted to acquire their own? This seems unlikely, since such an arms control process would also involve Russia, China and North Korea – the only states from which Japan might feel threatened.

NATO

The proposed expansion of NATO will extend the footprint of the USA's nuclear weapons over Poland, Hungary and the Czech Republic, when these states join NATO. Poland borders on two states – Belarus and Ukraine – which have become entirely nuclear-weapon-free after strong pressure from the West. Thus the issue of extended deterrence looks set to re-emerge – not least since there are proposals for the creation of a Central European Nuclear-Weapon-Free Zone from the Baltic to the Black Sea.

NATO's present nuclear doctrine is laid out in the November 1991 Strategic Concept. It specifies that:

> A credible Alliance nuclear posture and the demonstration of Alliance solidarity and common commitment to war prevention continue to require widespread participation by European Allies involved in collective defence planning in nuclear roles, in peacetime basing of nuclear forces on their territory and in command, control and consultation arrangements.

This policy is implemented through the allocation of British and US Trident submarines to NATO for targeting purposes and through the presence in Europe of US nuclear weapons for the use of US aircraft and the aircraft of Belgium, Germany, Greece, Italy, Netherlands and Turkey. The physical transfer of the weapons to allied airforces would only take place in wartime, but is exercised in peacetime. There are thought to be some 200 US nuclear weapons in Europe in early 1997.[33]

These sharing arrangements were controversial during the negotiation of the NPT in 1964-1968. In 1995, during the NPT Review, several countries, including Mexico, the Philippines, and Tanzania, raised the question of whether these arrangements were compliant with Articles I and II of the NPT, which prohibit the transfer of weapons or control over them from nuclear weapon states to non-nuclear weapon states.[34]

NATO has specified that new members must be members of the Nuclear Planning Group of Defence Ministers and its subsidiary bodies. However, in

December 1996 the Alliance made a political declaration that it would not forward base nuclear weapons on the territory of new members.

At the 1997 NPT Review PrepCom meeting, the issue of the expansion of NATO nuclear deterrence re-emerged. The representative from South Africa stated:

> We would ... like to place on record our concern about the non-proliferation implications of the plans for the expansion of NATO and the proposals which have been made for a dialogue in Europe on the future role of nuclear deterrence in the context of the European Defence Policy. The planned expansion of NATO would entail an increase in the number of non-nuclear weapon States which participate in nuclear training, planning and decision-making and which have an element of nuclear deterrence in their defence policies.

The "Eurobomb"

Finally, there is France's proposal for "concerted" nuclear deterrence. The idea, a long standing French position, was renewed by President Chirac and Foreign Minister Alain Juppé in August/September 1995. Chirac's offer was made as an attempt to explain the value of France's nuclear testing programme to its EU partners. Although few details have been elaborated publicly, the proposal envisages providing Europe with a French (and perhaps British) "nuclear umbrella."

The reaction of France's allies to the proposal of *"dissuasion concertée"* has been mixed. The two states with the most interest, Germany and the United Kingdom, have responded differently. UK officials have sought to play down the significance of the idea, stressing the continuing strength of the American nuclear commitment. Further, when queried by a non-governmental organization, an official indicated flatly that:

> The Non-Proliferation Treaty (Article I) prohibits nuclear-weapon States Parties from transferring to any recipient whatsoever nuclear weapons, or the control over them ... The establishment of a European nuclear force would therefore entail a breach of the Non-Proliferation Treaty.[35]

Germany's reaction has been more mixed. Foreign Minister Klaus Kinkel, shortly after the idea was broached by Juppé, said that it was "very interesting," but other officials quickly discounted the idea. Opinion polls in Germany show strong opposition to the idea. However, German and French officials are reportedly meeting secretly to discuss it.[36] German adherence to the NPT was accompanied by a note that the NPT should not in anyway prevent the development of a federal Europe.

In other parts of Europe – especially Scandinavia – the prospect of a unified Europe and the development of a common European Foreign and Security Policy has for the first time opened the question of whether or not the European Union will be a nuclear or non-nuclear member of the NPT. Some member states, such as Sweden, are flatly opposed to a nuclear status.

In January 1997 France and Germany initiated a formal discussion on the role of nuclear weapons in the EU Common Foreign and Security Policy following a decision at the Franco-German summit in December 1996.

While nuclear-weapon-free zones spread around the world, in Europe the evidence suggests that an opposite trend might be taking place. New states are about to commit their defence to nuclear weapons and become involved in the nuclear planning process through NATO, while in the EU a similar process is now on the agenda.

British-French-American Cooperation

The various forms of extended deterrence between Western nuclear-weapon states and non-nuclear weapon states described above are underpinned by growing doctrinal and technical cooperation amongst the three Western nuclear powers. The USA and the UK have long enjoyed close collaboration in the design and development of nuclear weapons, dating back at least to the 1958 agreement, and before then to the Manhattan Project itself. Today, areas of technical cooperation, managed by the Joint Atomic Information Exchange Group, include a very wide range of nuclear-weapon-related issues.[37]

British-French Cooperation

Despite British hesitations about France's proposed European nuclear deterrent, British-French cooperation has increased in recent years. In 1992, a Franco-British Joint Commission on Nuclear Policies and Doctrines was established. The Commission brings together senior French and British officials from the foreign and defence ministries to discuss nuclear policy issues. In October 1995, at a UK-French summit it was declared that:

> We do not see situations arising in which the vital interests of either France or the United Kingdom could be threatened without the vital interests of the other also being threatened. We have decided to pursue and deepen nuclear cooperation between our two countries. Our aim is mutually to strengthen deterrence, while retaining the independence of our nuclear forces ... We have instructed our Joint Nuclear Commission to take this forward.[38]

There have been technical discussions between the UK and France on a number of aspects.

The concurrence of "vital interests" implies a strong link between British and French nuclear doctrine. While British nuclear doctrine has not been linked as explicitly as French to protecting "vital interests," there is a clear trend toward the development of similar British and French nuclear policies.

French-American Technical Cooperation

France and the United States reached a new agreement on nuclear cooperation in June 1996. This Memorandum of Agreement (MOA) on Nuclear Safety and Security opened up the range of information which can officially be shared with France. It also paves the way for American, British and French weapons designers to pool data on all aspects of their nuclear weapons programmes, enabling the three countries to work together on stockpile stewardship.

In August 1995 Special Assistant to the President for Defense Policy, Robert Bell, confirmed that the USA was prepared to share computer simulation technology with France so that France would not have to conduct its recent nuclear test programme. In September 1995 Clinton Administration officials indicated that close US-French nuclear cooperation was essential to ensuring French support for the CTB.

The MOA is more explicit than previous agreements between the USA and France. A section on Stockpile Stewardship authorizes cooperation on "theoretical, numerical and experimental simulation methods." A section entitled "Nuclear Safety and Security" covers exchange of information on aspects of nuclear weapons design, including the research, development, testing, fabrication, transportation and disassembly of the nuclear and explosive components.

The MOA also establishes an agreement on "use of facilities" and "long term visits or assignments of technical personnel to participate in joint projects." US and French scientists use each other's laboratories. In the future, the USA is expected to make use of France's *Mégajoule* laser currently under construction near Bordeaux, and France is expected to use facilities such as the proposed National Ignition Facility and the Nevada Test Site. Cooperation under the 1996 MOA will be under the terms of the 1961 US-French Mutual Defense Agreement.

The 1961 Agreement allowed for some cooperation, including on design of delivery systems. The exchange of restricted data concerning nuclear weapons design with France was for a long time illegal under the US Atomic Energy Act. Nevertheless, in the 1970s, covert nuclear cooperation flourished. A system of so-called Negative Guidance (sometimes known as Twenty Questions) circumvented the Atomic Energy Act. US government experts guided their French counterparts towards solutions to their technological problems via nods and winks, headshakes and silences. On occasion this mime show turned into normal conversation.

For domestic political reasons – US Congressional hostility and France's concern for the independence of its *force de frappe* – no formal agreement to share weapon design data was made until 1985, when the 1961 Agreement was amended. The 1985 amendment established according to US law the exchange of classified information concerning atomic weapon design, development and fabrication capability to optimize the safety and security of the recipient's nuclear activities or installations. However, the 1996 MOA goes much further. For the first time the stated aim is cooperation to ensure the safety, security and "reliability" of the nuclear stockpiles.

Work on safety is intended to minimize the risk of nuclear accidents and the possibility of accidental nuclear yield or dispersal of fissile material. Security means assurance that nuclear weapons cannot be stolen, launched or detonated except at the specific order of duly designated commanders. Reliability concerns the weapon's ability to perform as required, detonating at its desired yield. Reliability concerns the main military purpose of the weapon, a distinct concept from weapon safety. Cooperation on reliability greatly extends the range of classified information which may now be shared.

US nuclear cooperation with Britain has been far more extensive than that with France. The 1958 US-UK Mutual Defense Agreement includes British use of the Nevada Test Site, the sale of US Polaris and Trident missiles to Britain, and extensive US assistance with all aspects of the British nuclear weapons programme.

The wording of the 1961 US-French Agreement, as amended, is now remarkably similar to that of the US-UK Agreement. However, whilst cooperation with the French was conducted in the context of improving safety and security, cooperation with the British is conducted with the straightforward aim of improving the recipient's design, development and fabrication capability.

The addition of reliability as an area for cooperation in the 1996 MOA means that US and French labs can now work together on practically the full range of current and future activities. Enhanced nuclear cooperation between the USA and France also opens up new opportunities for cooperation between Britain and France. In the past this was restricted by the 1958 US-UK Mutual Defense Agreement which requires US consent before Britain can communicate any information acquired under the Agreement to a third party and vice versa. With US-French cooperation on a more official footing, it seems likely that US consent has also been given to increased information transfers between Britain and France.

Conclusion and Outlook

The Western nuclear weapon states are putting up a strong resistance to implementing their legal obligations towards disarmament. They have retained doctrines for the use of nuclear weapons in a variety of circumstances.

This paper draws upon P.Rogers, S. Whitby and S. Young, "Nuclear Futures: The Role of Nuclear Weapons in Security Policy," British American Security Information Council Research Report 96.1. I would also like to thank Greenpeace, Otfried Nassauer of the Berlin Information Center on Transatlantic Cooperation and BASIC's staff, especially Nicola Butler, for their assistance.

Notes

1. Conversation with author.

2. US Senate, Appropriations Committee, Defence Appropriations Sub-Committee FY 96, 14 March 1995, p. 97.

3. Joint Pub 3-12 Doctrine for Joint Nuclear Operations 18 December 1995, office of the Chairman, the Joint Chiefs of Staff, Washington D.C.

4. E. Schmitt, "Head of Nuclear Forces Plans for a New World," *New York Times*, 25 February 1993, p. B7.

5. E. Grossman, "DOD Has "Significant" Ability to Alter Nuclear Weapons Targeting on Short Notice," *Inside the Air Force*, 3:32 (7 August 1994), p. 1.

6. C. Giacomo, "U.S. May Use Nuclear Force Against Chemicals," Reuters News Reports, 28 March 1996.

7. J.H. Patton Jr., "New Roles on Horizon for Triad's Last Leg?," *International Defense Review*, 9 (September 1994), pp. 38-42.

8. *Inside the Pentagon,* 29 April 1994.

9. G. Buchan, *U.S. Nuclear Strategy in the Post-Cold war Era,* RAND, 1994.

10. *Inside the Pentagon*, 22 December 1994.

11. Statement by Secretary of State Cyrus Vance, "U.S. Assurances on Non-Use of Nuclear Weapons," 12 June 1978.

12. Letter from Ralph Earle II, Deputy Director, US Arms Control and Disarmament Agency, 24 January 1996.

13. Principles and Objectives for Nuclear Non-Proliferation and Disarmament, NPT Review and Extension Conference, 11 May 1995.

14. Robert Bell, National Security Council staff, White House press conference, 11 April 1996.

15. *Proliferation: Threat and Response*, Office of the Secretary of Dfense, April 1996.

16. Reported in *Defense News*, Washington DC, 28 August 1995.

17. See, for example: K. Bailey, "Responding to the Threat of Biological Weapons," *Security Dialogue*, 26:4 (1995), pp. 383-397.

18. The case for low-yield nuclear weapons to counter protected BW and CW sites is made in: A. Knoth, "Counterproliferation at the Crossroads," *International Defence Review*, 11 (November 1995), pp. 22-24.

19. C. Giacomo, "U.S. May Use Nuclear Force ... "

20. General Colin Powell, Speech at Harvard University, 10 June 1993.

21. D.S. Yost, "Nuclear Debates in France," *Survival*, 36:4 (Winter 1994-95), pp. 113-139.

22. G. de Briganti, "France to Replace Mirage IVP Bomber Fleet by 1997." *Defense News*, Washington DC, 8 January 1996.

23. K. von Stokirch, "Revamping the Rationale for French Nuclear Deterrence," *Newsletter of the Strategic and Defence Studies Centre*, Australian National University, Canberra, Spring 1995, pp. 1-2.

24. Presentation of Dr Bruno Tertrais, French Delegation of Strategic Defence, Ministry of Defence, 27 September, 1995, in Arlington, VA.

25. D.S. Yost, "France's Nuclear Dilemmas," *Foreign Affairs*, 75:1 (1996), pp108-118.

26. P. Rogers, "The Role of British Nuclear Weapons After the Cold War," BASIC Research Report 95.1, British American Security Information Council, Washington and London, November 1995.

27. Malcolm Rifkind, "UK Defence Strategy: A Continuing Role for Nuclear Weapons?," speech delivered as Secretary of State for Defence, 16 November 1994.

28. Press Communique M-DPC/NPG-1(95)57, Paragraph 23, 8 June 1995, NATO Press Service, Brussels.

29. Rogers, "The Role of British Nuclear Weapons ... "

30. D. Fairhall, "Nuclear Deterrent Aimed at Third World Dictators," *The Guardian*, London, 9 January, 1996.

31. D. Miller, "Britain Ponders Single-warhead Option," *International Defence Review*, 9 (September 1994), pp. 38-42.

32. Rifkind, "UK Defence Strategy ... "

33. US Nuclear NATO Arsenals in 1996, BITS-BASIC Research Note.

34. *Extending the Nuclear Umbrella*, BASIC Paper number 20.

35. Letter from Michael Ryder, CFSP Counsellor of the UK Permanent Representation to the European Union, 26 January 1996.

36. M. Hibbs, "Tomorrow a Eurobomb," *The Bulletin of the Atomic Scientists*, Jan/Feb 1996, pp. 16-18.

37. House of Commons, Official Report, HMSO, 27 January 1997, Column 28.

38. "British-French Joint Statement on Nuclear Cooperation," UK-French Summit. 30 October 1995.

11

Russian Nuclear Disarmament Dilemmas

Alexander Nikitin

It was an important achievement in the world politics of the 1970s and 1980s to make disarmament, especially in the nuclear field, to be seen in the USSR as a stable, substantive and publicly appreciated process. Since 1990, with the end of the Cold War, the disintegration of the USSR, and the dissolution of the Warsaw Pact, disarmament issues no longer have the same priority, either with politicians or with the public in Russia. Attitudes to disarmament issues have changed.

Most of the disarmament agreements of the previous decades were essentially bipolar, rooted in mutual perceptions of threat between the USA and USSR, or between NATO and the Warsaw Pact. Now the points of discussion are less about specific threats, and more about general risks not attributed to any particular country. However, under the surface the old ways of thinking still persist. The doctrine of nuclear deterrence has survived the end of open confrontation; both the USA and Russia still adhere to the idea of nuclear parity, that they have to maintain a bilateral nuclear balance.

From Signing to Ratification

The ratification of disarmament agreements almost always leads to controversy. There are many examples where parliamentarians in different countries have delayed the implementation of disarmament agreements, sometimes by linking ratification to other political issues, such as human rights or involvements in regional conflicts; sometimes for financial considerations – the cost of implementing an agreement compared with the benefits to security.

In the previous decades, when treaties were negotiated between the USA and USSR, the ratification process in the two countries was a very long process of lobbying and linkages. In the USSR, where real decisions were made by the central Communist Party authorities, ratification by the Supreme Soviet was automatic: the legislative branch was wholly subservient in the USSR of the 1970s and 1980s. With the new Federal Assembly (Parliament) of the Russian Federation, the situation has changed. One of the important objectives of the democratic reforms in Russia was to ensure a genuine system of checks and balances.

The START II agreement, signed in January 1993, was not submitted to the Parliament for ratification until 1995, more than two years after its signing. The reason was the political conflict between President Yeltsin and the then Supreme Soviet of Russia which ended in the storming of the "White House" in October 1993. The new Parliament, elected in November 1993, did not become fully operational until the end of 1994 and the beginning of 1995. By then it had established a system of committees and subcommittees, with new internal procedural rules and a new system of hearings, and so on.

Over that time the involvement of the Russian Parliament in international relations and security affairs has grown. It is the lower house, the State Duma, which is directly involved in the process of ratification of international agreements on arms control and disarmament.[1] The two committees concerned with this are the Committee on International Affairs and the Committee on Defence. The Committee on Security Affairs mainly concentrates on domestic security issues and considers nuclear policy issues to be outside its direct responsibility and expertise.

START II was brought up for the first time in 1995, not for formal ratification but as part of the discussion of an "international security package" debated in the context of the new Russian military doctrine. Already then, it was clear that ratification would not be automatic. A number of MPs raised the issue of the cost of implementing the Treaty in Russia's strained economic circumstances. The refusal of the US Congress to ratify SALT II, which had previously been criticized, was now referred to as a good precedent for the cautious examination of national interests. A number of civilian and military experts who gave evidence at the hearings commented that the provisions of the Treaty did not fit well with the plans for restructuring Russian nuclear forces.

Russian Military Doctrine and Disarmament Priorities

A new military doctrine for the Russian Federation was adopted in November 1993.[2] This states that nuclear weapons were no longer to be regarded as weapons for war fighting; their purpose was a political one – to deter either nuclear or conventional aggression. Thus Russia now officially accepts the concept of nuclear deterrence; in previous decades this concept was severely criticised. This acceptance of the doctrine of deterrence led to two important doctrinal changes. Supporters of nuclear disarmament consider both these changes to be retrogressive.

First, Russia has now withdrawn its obligation (or rather political promise) of "No First Use." This was a promise given in 1982 at the UN General Assembly Second Special Session on Disarmament. The withdrawal of this promise was explained as a logical consequence of adopting a strategy of deterrence, and also as compensation for the weakness of conventional means of deterrence, compared to those previously available to the undivided Soviet army.

Secondly, very little priority is now given to Gorbachev's declared objective of abolishing all nuclear weapons. This is now seen as something for the far distant future. Neither President Yeltsin, nor his Administration, have included the goal of achieving a NWFW in the list of their foreign policy objectives or priorities.

These changes in official doctrine matched a more general change in political and strategic thinking in the 1990s. This is illustrated in a recent study commissioned by the Russian Parliament. With a certain degree of overstatement, it says:

> Does Russia need nuclear forces today and in the future? There is a nationwide consensus in answer to this question. Everybody – military specialists, academic experts, politicians – unanimously conclude that Russia needs nuclear forces today and in the future.[3]

These are the main arguments presented.

First, Russia is much weaker, militarily, than the former Soviet Union. Six of the former strongest military districts, with all their infrastructure, are now outside Russian territory; missile defence and air defence systems are seriously weakened; the Navy has lost important parts of its shipbuilding and servicing facilities; many new borders are unguarded and indeed even unmarked. As a consequence Russian military planners are relying on nuclear weapons, not only for strategic deterrence, but also for tactical deterrence against possible regional or local non-nuclear threats.

Second, there is a broader political argument. Russia has been weakened not only militarily but economically and politically as well, and it has of course lost its ideological leadership. The only way to support its status as a great power and to "stay in the club" of major international decision-makers is to ensure and then stress its status as a major nuclear weapon power. This is similar to the arguments used both in Britain and in France when they decided to become nuclear weapon powers.

So, although there are still some voices in Russia in favour of the complete elimination of nuclear weapons, in general the debate is no longer about a "non-nuclear future," as it was with Gorbachev in the 1980s. The question is rather: "To what extent would further disarmament serve Russia's interests?" This approach was summarized in a report commissioned by the Russian Parliament in 1996. Disarmament is not necessarily a value in itself. It is valuable if it improves strategic stability and/or if it serves Russian national interests:

> "It is undoubtedly true that disarmament negotiations as such enhance trust among negotiating parties both politically and diplomatically, and are a somewhat stabilizing factor. At the same time negotiated agreements could negatively influence strategic stability. Disarmament, and even a large reduction of weapons, should not be the sole objective of the agreement, especially if it reduces the security of one of the sides."[4]

Such statements are still based on the old "zero-sum game" logic, where one state's gain is the other state's loss, and where stability follows from keeping a numerical balance. These statements fail to take into account the additional safety which follows from a reduction in the number of nuclear devices: fewer weapons to malfunction, to get into the wrong hands, or to be launched by mistake as a consequence of technical or human error.

Further, any failure of prolonged disarmament negotiations creates distrust and mutual suspicions; this results in strategic instability which has to be weighed against any instability which might follow from implementing reductions.

In addition to these doctrinal considerations, there were also more practical matters which influenced the approach of the Russian side to the START negotiations.

The Break-up of the Soviet Union and the START Process

The collapse of the Soviet Union and the creation of new independent states strongly influenced the disarmament process under the START agreements.

The retreat from the Communist system and the division of the USSR into a number of independent states were obviously interconnected: nonetheless, they were two different processes. Nearly all the other Communist countries of Central Europe, as well as the "Socialist-oriented" Third World countries, kept their territorial integrity when they changed their political-economic system; the one exception was Czechoslovakia, which divided into two without any major crisis. The Soviet Union was divided into a number of separate states well before the change in their socio-political systems was complete.

As a result, in the former Soviet Union, the issues of control over nuclear weapons and of the ownership of parts of the nuclear weapon complex came to the fore early on, when the new states were in the process of formation. There were fears that these new states, with inexperienced and possibly strongly nationalistic regimes, might retain strategic and tactical nuclear weapons indefinitely. Then the whole NPT regime, and the "rules of behaviour" of the "nuclear club" would break down. It was because both Moscow and Washington feared that this might happen that they were willing to reach new reduction agreements quickly. Indeed, some critics of START II in Moscow say that this was the main reason why Russia concluded START II and sacrificed its MIRVed missiles: it was to make sure that Ukraine, Belarus and Kazakhstan would be willing to eliminate their strategic nuclear armaments, or transfer them to Russia for elimination. The critics say that since these obligations were secured by the Lisbon protocol, which became part of START I, it was not necessary to make so many concessions in the second Treaty.[5]

So progress in the START process became in a certain sense "hostage" to the denuclearization of Ukraine and other CIS states which inherited parts of the Soviet nuclear weapon complex. Legally START I did not come into force until the last nuclear device left Ukrainian territory. That meant that the formal beginning of the 15 year implementation period of START I was delayed. In fact both sides began to implement the Treaty before it formally came into force.

The supporters of START II argued that even if it was not ratified the process of obsolescence would itself reduce the size of the Russian arsenal to a level comparable with the ceilings negotiated under START II. However, if the Treaty were not implemented, and the Russian reductions would happen anyway, there would be no matching reductions in US numbers.

All in all, up to 50 per cent of the reductions required by START II are reductions of weapon systems which would in any case come to the end of their useful life and service during the period covered by the Treaty.

Concerns and Amendments

START II was signed in January 1993. However, the Treaty stated that it could not enter into force until START I was in force – and this, as already explained, was delayed until Ukraine joined the Non-Proliferation Treaty as a non-nuclear weapon state in December 1994.

A few months earlier, at their September 1994 summit, Presidents Yeltsin and Clinton agreed that once START II was in force, the deactivation of strategic systems intended for further elimination could be accelerated; it was also agreed that experts should begin to consider further strategic arms reductions for a prospective START III.

Once START I was in force, the ratification processes for START II began. In the USA there was some delay because Senator Helms, Chairman of the Foreign Relations Committee, linked Treaty approval with a proposal to reorganize the Administration's foreign affairs agencies. However, after about a year of debates, in January 1996 the US Senate approved a resolution ratifying START II by a vote of 87 to 4.[6] The resolution contains eight conditions which are binding on the President, and twelve declarations which are non-binding expressions of the Senate's intent. None of these amend the Treaty or require any additional action on the Russian side; the Russian Minister of Foreign Affairs, Mr Primakov, welcomed this approval.

One of the US Senate's conditions is that ratification does not obligate the USA to provide financial help to support Russia's implementation of START II. Another says that if the Treaty does not enter into force, the President must consult with the Senate before making any strategic nuclear force reductions below START I levels.

Perhaps the most significant unilateral declaration is the one concerning ballistic missile defence. The declaration argues that defences against ballistic missiles are essential for new deterrent strategies, and urges both states to move forward cooperatively in their development and deployment. This declaration was not welcome on the Russian side, given that the Russian Administration does not want to develop new missile defence systems, and insists that the provisions of the ABM Treaty should be strictly observed.

The preservation of the ABM Treaty is one of the major concerns on the Russian side. There are others: about the strategic balance, and the period of implementation.

–   The Russian critics of the Treaty consider that Russia did not receive adequate concessions from the other side, in exchange for Russia's agreement to give up the heavy multi-warhead SS-18 missiles. The liquidation of these powerful land-based missiles was one of the highest priorities for the US negotiators. The critics argue that the SS-18s were under-used as a bargaining chip.
–   There is an imbalance in the scale and complexity of the reductions required by the two sides. The USA, as required by START I, has already removed all 450 Minutemen II missiles from their silos. The further requirement on the US side is mainly to eliminate 50 MX missiles and deactivate several dozens of heavy bombers. All other reductions are purely downloading of quantities of warheads without changing carriers and without any obligation to destroy stored warheads. No new construction is required to fit into the permitted configuration of the triad.

The Russian side is expected to implement physical destruction of the heavy missiles and their silos in addition to the downloading of certain types of missiles. Further, to fit into the permitted configuration of the triad on the Russian side, Russia, if it still has parity as an objective, needs to invest in building and deploying several hundreds of new missiles – if no new lower ceilings are negotiated.

The following are some of the amendments and modifications of the Treaty which are being discussed on the Russian side:

–   The rearmament potential of the two sides – the "reversible strategic potential" – should be balanced. This concerns the potential reinstallation of warheads that have been removed from carriers but not destroyed. START II allows Russia to have about 650 reversible warheads, while the USA could have as many as 4500-5000. There are different possible methods for dealing with this imbalance. One method would be to allow Russia simply to retain its SS-19 missiles and download them. Another method would be to make it more difficult or costly for the USA to reverse its downloading of Trident SLBMs, and also to make it more difficult to convert conventional bombers back to a nuclear weapon capability.

–   Both sides must comply with the ABM Treaty, narrowly interpreted. It is suggested that Russia should add to the instruments of ratification a resolution which states that Russia would not consider itself bound by the Treaty if the USA violated, left, or prepared to leave the ABM Treaty. The definition of "preparations to leave the Treaty" would include increasing the financing of R&D whose purpose was to create a missile defence system which violated the Treaty, as well as creating, testing or deploying defence systems (and their components) which are prohibited under the Treaty.

–   The methods for liquidating warheads and silos are economically and ecologically more favourable to the USA than to Russia. This inequality should be addressed.

–   Technological aid should be provided for Russia to find safe methods of eliminating the toxic geptil fuel in solid-fuelled missiles.

–   The procedure for the destruction of silos should be modified; the destruction of silos adds to the cost of compliance, and the construction of new silos which might be needed would be even more costly. Critics of the Treaty propose a relaxation of the START II limit of 90 on the number of SS-18 silos that may be converted, and to allow all 154 silos left under START I to be converted for single-warhead ICBMs.

–   Russia might try to negotiate permission to deploy one new type of SLBM at sea, or to deploy an adapted new SLBM, downloaded to a single missile, for silos on land.

–   Some Russian strategists foresee a window of vulnerability at the end of the first seven years of reductions, if MIRVed launchers are, as required by the Treaty, reduced to 120 (with 120 warheads), while there has been only slow deployment of SS-25s; there would then be a widening gap between Russia and the USA. To avoid this, and to meet the time pressure, the Russian side might try to renegotiate the times set for the various stages of implementation or to exclude intermediate ceilings from the treaty.

–   Finally, there is the political linkage between probable NATO enlargement and Russia's readiness to reduce armaments. This is not just a general political argument – as one opponent of the Treaty put it: "It is stupid to

disarm when another military bloc is clearly approaching your borders."
Some Russian strategists are seriously disturbed by the possible effects of
NATO enlargement on the strategic balance. Tactical nuclear weapons, in
time of war, and/or high-precision medium- and long-range conventional
weapons, in time of peace, could be deployed on the territories of Poland
and other new potential NATO members. These could have counterforce
potential against a weakened Russian nuclear arsenal.

These and other concerns and proposed amendments are of varying scales
of importance. The Russian side is ready to accept the basic provisions of the
Treaty. The period of implementation should be negotiable, and some of the
other concerns could be met "on the margins" without endangering the Treaty's
main objectives. The one issue that could bury the Treaty is ABM systems –
if the Russian side insists on full compliance with the ABM Treaty while the US
side insists on pressing ahead with a national missile defence system.

During the summit in Moscow in 1995, the Presidents of Russia and the
USA decided to start consultations at the expert level to clarify distinctions
between "tactical" (permitted) and "strategic" (prohibited) missile defence
systems. A little more than a year after that, in September 1996, US Secretary
of State Christopher and Russian Foreign Minister Primakov signed a joint
statement describing the first results of these Geneva expert consultations.
Unfortunately, these results could not be called either a great success or a
breakthrough. It was agreed that the development and use of low-speed (below
3 km/sec) counter-missile interceptors do not contradict the ABM Treaty of
1972. But low-speed interceptors never were a subject of real disagreement
between Russia and the USA. A deal on demarcation between theatre missile
defence and ABM systems was basically reached only in late 1997.

A series of critical articles in the Russian media appeared soon after the
"demarcation compromise," accusing the Foreign Ministry and Russian
negotiators of "legitimizing" by this agreement the US drive towards tactical
and (prospective) strategic missile defence. It was argued that the very process
of demarcation between tactical and strategic defence is against Russian security
interests, insofar as any new definition of "permitted" research and development
would allow the USA to make several new steps towards strategic defence,
while Russia has neither the resources nor plans to upgrade its existing ABM
systems. (For a summary of the agreements on the ABM Treaty reached at the
Helsinki Summit in March 1997, and in New York in September 1997, see
Chapter 8.)

At the same time it is clear that refusal on the Russian side to ratify
START II could only facilitate the development of strategic defence by the
USA. It is difficult to imagine a better "gift" to the US supporters of the
immediate deployment of strategic defence systems, than a non-ratification of
the signed disarmament treaty by the Russian side.

Scenarios for the World Without START

A new wave of debates in the Russian State Duma concerning START began in the course of the visit of US Defense Secretary William Perry to Russia in October 1996. Mr Perry addressed Russian parliamentarians calling for ratification of START II and received a cold shower of criticism of START II, and especially of NATO enlargement, which was linked by Russian parliamentarians directly to the ratification debate.

The main concern expressed by members of defence and foreign affairs committees was this: USA and NATO could circumvent the START II limitations by deploying tactical nuclear and high precision conventional weapons on the territory of the new NATO member states, and this tactical weaponry would be of strategic concern for Russia insofar as it threatens Russian deterrence arsenals. A real or potential threat to Russian arsenals from US tactical nuclear weapons is not a new factor; it was present and has been taken into consideration during at least the last three decades. It was never before considered to be an obstacle to disarmament agreements. US tactical weapons currently deployed in Europe (at most 700 nuclear air-delivered bombs) are only 10 per cent of the US tactical arsenal in Europe 25 years ago, in a period of intensive disarmament efforts.

One of the suggestions aimed at compromise on this issue is to negotiate a bilateral moratorium on any relocation of US and Russian tactical nuclear weapons during the period until a new START III agreement could provide a more stable solution. The USA, as well as Russia, would benefit from such a moratorium (with the obligation by the USA not to deploy nuclear weapons in future NATO member states). USA and NATO (including new NATO members) are concerned to make sure that Russia does not move nuclear weapons back to Belarus as a reaction to NATO enlargement. Such a move, as the reintroduction of nuclear weapons into Belarus, has become more possible after statements by the Belorussian leadership that it is ready for the return of nuclear weapons onto Belorussian soil if NATO enlargement goes ahead and also after political and legal steps (in January 1997) towards unification of Russia and Belarus into one quasi-state. Both Russia and the West have a great deal to lose if tactical nuclear weapons are brought into juxtaposition in this way, and this makes a compromise (for example, in the form of the suggested moratorium) more vital than ever before.

START II could fail of course if the Russian parliament refused to ratify it; but there could also be other circumstances which could lead to failure. The Treaty might be ratified on the Russian side with several unilateral conditions or amendments, all or some of which could be considered as unacceptable on the American side. Ratification with conditions which were unacceptable to the other side could lead to a long process of renegotiation, with no guarantee of success.

There is also the possibility of a unilateral withdrawal from the Treaty in response to alleged "violations" by the other side. There is no precedent for this in the history of nuclear disarmament; it is a possibility with START II, because of the Russian insistence on preserving the ABM Treaty in its original narrow interpretation.

If for one reason or another START II was not ratified, or the Russian side withdrew after ratification, what would be the outcome? So far as Russia is concerned, the following are some of the arguments used on either side. First, opponents of START II in Russia would claim the following consequences, which they consider favourable:

–   Russia would be able to keep its very effective MIRVed SS-18 missiles (which possess high counterforce potential) as well as solid fuelled SS-24s in railroad and mobile and silo-based modes.
–   SS-19 missiles would no longer have the limit of 105 units and each of them would be able to stay with up to six warheads instead of one.
–   There would be no need to restructure the Russian nuclear triad, so that it would not be necessary to build up to 690 SS-25s in mobile and silo-based modifications to upgrade to the permitted force configuration.
–   Russia would not have to spend large sums on the dismantlement of missiles, the deactivation of toxic fuel, the destruction of silos, and so on, which otherwise it would be obliged to finance during a period when the economy would in all likelihood still be in difficulties.

On the other hand, the failure to ratify START II would have consequences which would not be in Russia's national interest:

–   It would lead to a worsening of the political climate, with serious damage to relations with Western states (not only the USA).
–   It would probably provoke even more rapid NATO enlargement, with the possible deployment of tactical nuclear weapons, or at least high-precision conventional weapons, on the territory of new NATO member states close to Russian borders.
–   Western governments, the World Bank, and other international institutions would probably be much less forthcoming with loans. Currently up to 15 per cent of Russian Government expenditure is financed by international borrowing.
–   If START II were implemented, the number of different types of ICBMs and SLBMs in the Russian arsenal would be reduced from 14 to 7. There would be significant savings in government expenditure from this change – though it is true this would have to be set against the costs of implementation and the construction of the types of launcher still permitted. The withdrawal from START II would leave Russia with an expensive

multiplicity of different missile types and with an obsolete nuclear weapon structure.

- Without START II, the old method of counting air-based warheads would remain in place; this was not favourable to Russia, and gave the USA superiority of 3000-3500 nuclear bombs or cruise missiles.
- Could Russia afford to keep its nuclear forces at a level higher than the START II ceiling? The answer is that it could not. If START II were not implemented, there would be the need to invest in missile defence (or counter-missile defence technologies), the need to cope with US superiority in air-borne nuclear weapons, and the need to replace those Russian nuclear weapon systems that were becoming obsolete. The combined cost of these measures would exceed the costs of implementing START II.

If START II failed, there would of course be broader consequences for the nuclear weapon competition between the USA and Russia, and consequently for international security in general. Let us consider scenarios for the arms race in the world without START.

- The nuclear strategy would remain one of "launch-on-warning." (The Treaty, by shifting emphasis from silo-based to mobile missiles, would have moved nuclear strategies on both sides towards a secure second strike force capability with low vulnerability.) A launch-on-warning system gives deterrence a much higher priority than safety.[7]
- It is now particularly dangerous on the Russian side to follow a "launch-on-warning" strategy, since five out of the eight radar stations which formed the Soviet warning system are now outside Russian territory, which makes the old system of early warning unreliable.
- If, with START failure, it was a question of nuclear rearmament, both US and Russian military planners prefer the idea of mobile missile launchers. As Christopher Bluth has pointed out:

> The sustained but largely fruitless effort to locate and destroy mobile missile launchers in Iraq during the Gulf War of 1991 demonstrated that mobility provides some protection even against modern space-based reconnaissance systems and vastly complicates any first strike plans.[8]

Mobile missiles would certainly, in the first instance, make the idea of a first strike less attractive; but it could lead on to further attempts to improve the penetrability and counterforce of nuclear weapon systems and so set off another stage of a destabilizing arms race.

Even under the constraints of START II Russia would have the right to build and deploy up to 890 additional SS-25 missiles. Russia does not plan to build as many as this. If the START process failed and the USA consequently retained MIRVed counterforce capabilities, Russia might extend its plans for a build-up of SS-25s. Russia might also choose to equip the SS-25 with another platform which would carry up to three warheads; this would be a cheaper way of increasing the number of warheads. The US reaction might well be to accelerate its plans for missile defence.

In any scenario, a world without START would almost certainly reignite the technological nuclear arms race.

START III – After START Two-and-a-Half

If START II is ratified and implemented, this would bring both sides to the threshold of a new disarmament agenda. Some of the possible lines of continuation were already envisaged while START II was being negotiated. Russian experts suggested that immediately after START II both sides should move to lower ceilings. Ambassador U. Nazarkin, a former Russian Security Council official, suggested 2000-2500 warheads;[9] the RAU report to the Parliamentary hearings suggested 1000-2000.[10] One main objective of these proposals was to make it unnecessary to build up the number of Russian single-warhead missiles after the cuts required by START II.

The US side has indicated that it is not interested in setting new ceilings until START II is ratified, enters into force, and is fully implemented. This is the message of the Nuclear Posture Review and is also the position of the US Senate. One formulation is that: "... the United States will deploy the 3500 strategic warheads allowed by START II and does not seek any further reductions for the indefinite future."[11] When US Ambassador to Russia Mr Thomas Pickering explained the new intentions of US Congress in the spring of 1996, he suggested the US side might become ready to proceed to START III negotiations without waiting for the previous Treaty to enter into force.[12] Though Russian parliamentarians remain sceptical about ratification of START II, many Russian negotiators and experts favour beginning START III talks. Such talks could help to cut the Gordian knot of frozen START II ratification.

It could be possible to move ahead without necessarily negotiating a new comprehensive Treaty, by additional protocols or parallel co-ordinating measures. These measures could be called START Two-and-a-Half because they are direct follow-ups, compensating for the dissatisfaction of both sides with some START I and II provisions:

–   A lower warhead ceiling could be set which fitted better with the configuration of the triad after the previous round of reductions.
–   Approaches should be negotiated to reduce the "reversible strategic potential" by:

(a) destroying, instead of storing, excess warheads from formerly-MIRVed missiles;

(b) filling the empty launchers on SLBM submarines with irremovable substances;

(c) introducing measures to make it much more difficult to reintroduce a nuclear weapon capability into bombers which have been converted to a conventional role.

Possibilities for deeper post-START II nuclear reductions are being comprehensively studied by the Deep Cuts Study Group (DCSG)[13] consisting of experts from Princeton and Maryland Universities, MIT, the Brookings Institution and the Union of Concerned Scientists.

The authors of the study agree that on the first post-START II stage an agreement is realizable to proceed to a follow-up ceiling of 2500 total warheads for each side, and suggest adding as the next step de-alerting half the remaining nuclear weapons. This "staircase of dealerting" could then be continued by setting within START-III talks a new limit of 1000 warheads for each side, again with more than half de-alerted and a formal or *de facto* agreement by the middle and threshold nuclear weapon states to verifiably cap their stockpiles of nuclear warheads and unsafeguarded fissile materials. Thus the DCSG also comes to the conclusion that, once the number of warheads in the USA and Russia begin to approach 1000 on each side, START talks must involve other nuclear powers.

An important task is to assure strategic stability at every intermediate level of reductions. In view of this task some calculations were prepared by DCSG showing that there are realistic ways to structure US and Russian arsenals and reductions in such a way that mutual deterrence and relative balance would be preserved at intermediate levels of 2500 warheads for each side (2000 deployed, 500 reserve); 1000 warheads (800 deployed, 200 reserve); 400 warheads (300 deployed, 100 reserve). Each model contains a specific distribution between land-, sea- and air-based components and specifies in detail which carriers and warheads should be eliminated and which should remain.[14] This study is being seriously studied by Russian experts, since they are interested in the idea of complementing START II with immediate follow-up reductions down to the level of 1500-2500 warheads for each side. (For the agreements on STARTs II and III, reached at the Helsinki Summit in March 1997, see Chapter 7.)

Enhancing Strategic Stability

There are a number of measures which could be given priority once the USA and Russia were in a position to move beyond START II.

Further numerical reductions are important, but they are by no means the sole components of the process of disarmament. Reductions should be supplemented by – or indeed led by – measures to diminish the threat of the use of nuclear weapons. Among them:

- Measures which limit the technical possibility of using nuclear weapons in a first strike.
- Measures which increase the survivability of the nuclear arsenals of both sides.
- Abandonment of the strategy of launch-on-warning (a most dangerous and error-prone strategy), with technical measures to ensure that both sides have withdrawn from such a strategy.
- Setting new ceilings for a mutual deterrence posture and negotiating moves towards those ceilings.
- Expanding mutual transparency and confidence-building measures.
- Reaching an agreement to define which systems of armaments, or which communication or space technologies, are most destabilizing, and reaching agreements to limit or indeed eliminate them.
- The prohibition of the development, deployment and use of manoeuvrable warheads.
- The elimination of earth-penetrating warheads (which are useful mainly against underground command posts).
- The limitation of anti-submarine and submarine-detection systems.
- The prohibition of development of space-based anti-missile weapons and devices.
- Limitations on conventional long- or medium-range high-precision weapons and systems that might be used against nuclear launchers or stockpiles.
- Reducing alert level of nuclear forces.

Supplementing START with TACT

START negotiations are of course limited to strategic nuclear weapon systems. However, some action also needs to be taken about tactical nuclear weapons: there are at present no negotiations about them.

The military coup in Moscow in 1991 and the subsequent disintegration of the Soviet Union led both the US and Russian authorities to take quick action on tactical nuclear weapons (TNWs). There was a risk that these weapons would get into the hands of newly independent states, and possibly also into the hands of uncontrolled militarized groups within those states. At the beginning of the 1990s, there were TNWs in all of the 15 new republics: the Russian Federation had 12,320 warheads; Ukraine – 2345; Belarus – 1180; Kazakstan – 330; Armenia – 200; Azerbaijan – 75; Lithuania – 325, and so on.[15] US TNWs were stationed on the territory of seven Western European states.

By 1993 all TNWs had been withdrawn from outside Russia and were under Moscow's full control. The attitude to TNWs then began to change. Some Russian analysts and military planners saw them as a cheaper alternative to conventional weapons and indeed to strategic nuclear weapons as well. In the USA in the same way, after the Gulf War, there was also growing interest in the possible use of TNWs to meet "regional challenges." With the threat of a "big war" declining, more attention was then given to alleged regional threats. The idea of "tactical nuclear deterrence against conventional threats" was developed. It was estimated that after all the TNW reductions initiated in 1991-92 were complete, Russia and the USA would each possess 2500-3000 TNWs.[15]

Tactical weapons began to take a more prominent role in nuclear planning, with potential destabilizing consequences. The threshold for the use of TNWs is much lower than that for strategic weapons, and also much less well defined. The use, or indeed the threat of use, could easily lead to escalation of a conflict to strategic level. That is why it is now important to include TNWs in the nuclear weapon negotiating process.

Widening the Scope of Nuclear Disarmament

If START II is implemented, and if there are further strategic reductions, then it will be the time to bring the arsenals of Britain, France and China into the strategic arms limitation process. (The sensitive issues of the mini-arsenals of threshold states, India, Israel and Pakistan, would come in the next stage thereafter.) Many analysts comment that once the ceilings for Russia and the USA come down towards 1000, then it will be impossible to go further without bringing in the other three of the five major nuclear weapon states. Neither the USA nor Russia would be prepared to accept a situation where their reduced nuclear forces were outnumbered by third parties' combined arsenals.

If START II is implemented, and if Russia does not build up to the permitted ceiling with new weapons, that would bring Russia down to the figure of 2000 operational warheads, which is a figure of the same order of magnitude as the combined nuclear capabilities of the smaller members of the nuclear club. Russian negotiators also take into consideration the consequences of possible missile defence deployment. Also, when NATO enlargement takes place, high-precision conventional weapons might be deployed close to the Russian border. This could reduce Russian second strike capability to a figure of hundreds rather than thousands.

In conclusion, START II will probably be one of the last nuclear disarmament treaties to be based solely on US-Russian comparisons. In the longer term nuclear disarmament will have to become a global, not bipolar, issue.

Notes

1.   The START II treaty was formally submitted for ratification by President Yeltsin to the Federal Assembly on June 22, 1995. Both chambers of the Federal Assembly need to approve the document by a simple majority of votes. It is the Committee on International Affairs in the State Duma (lower chamber) chaired by the former Russian Ambassador to the United States V. Lukin which has been made formally responsible for leading the ratification process; the Committee on Defence, chaired by General Rokhlin, plays a supplementary though important role.

2.   What literally was adopted by the Security Council of Russia on 2 November 1993, and approved by Presidential Decree, were "Foundations for the Military Doctrine" initially announced as a kind of "prolegomena" to the future full version of the doctrine. But the full-scale version has not yet been adopted, and "Foundations for the Military Doctrine" acts as Russian military doctrine.

3.   *Ratification of the START II Treaty: decisions, problems, prospects*, RAU Corporation, Moscow, 1996, p. 32.

4.   "Would the START II treaty influence strategic stability?," in *Ratification of the START II Treaty,* p. 40.

5.   A. Surikov, "How Russian Strategic Nuclear Forces Should be Developed," in *Yaderny Control*, N 12, December 1995.

6.   Senators J. Ashcroft (R-MO), J. Helms (R-NC), J. Inhofe (R-OK) and R. Smith (R-NH) voted against START II ratification.

7.   B. Blair, "Post Cold War Nuclear Strategies," in *Fifty Years of Nuclear Weapons*, Milan: USPID, 1995.

8.   C. Bluth, in *Brassey's Defence Yearbook 1995*, London: Brassey's (UK), 1995, p. 185.

9.   Role and Status of START treaties, in *Issues of Non-proliferation and Disarmament*, Carnegie Endowment for International Peace, Moscow, 1996, p. 30.

10.   *Ratification of the START II Treaty*, p. 70.

11.   Blair, "Post-Cold War Nuclear Strategies," p. 14.

12.   Thomas Pickering, interview in *Krasnay Zvezda*, 22 October 1996.

13.   Core members of the DCSG group are Bruce Blair, Jonathan Dean, Harold Feiveson, Steve Fetter, George Lewis, Theodore Postol and Frank von Hippel. First draft of the study was presented in mid-1996 to be followed by the DCSG book.

14.   F. von Hippel, "The Feasibility of Much Deeper Post-START II Nuclear Reductions," background paper for 18th ISODARCO Course, 25 June 1996.

15.   Figures given in "Tactical Nuclear Weapons in the New Geopolitical Situation," V. Belous, Moscow: PIR Centre, 1996.

12

Prospects for Further Multilateral Nuclear Disarmament Treaties

Rebecca Johnson

The Geneva-based Conference on Disarmament (CD) concluded the principal item on its agenda, a comprehensive test ban treaty (CTBT), in August 1996. The CD, which is the only multilateral negotiating body for disarmament issues under UN auspices,[1] now faces a crisis over what to do. The next item on the agenda would seem to be a ban on the production of fissile materials for weapon purposes ("fissban"), for which the CD agreed a negotiating mandate in March 1995. However, the fissban is in trouble. There is fundamental disagreement over whether to include existing stocks of fissile materials or concentrate only on getting a "cut-off" prohibiting the future production of weapon-grade plutonium and highly-enriched uranium (HEU). Diplomats and observers are now coming to the conclusion that the endgame difficulties of the CTBT show that the CD could not effectively negotiate a fissban at this time. They cite the competing interests of the declared nuclear weapon states (the "P-5" permanent members of the UN Security Council – Britain, China, France, Russia and the United States) and the so-called threshold nuclear weapon states (the "T-3": India, Israel and Pakistan).

The Group of 21 (G-21), which now comprises 30 non-aligned CD members, has repeatedly called for an *ad hoc* Committee on Nuclear Disarmament, finding growing support among some non-nuclear western states and China. To support their argument for a nuclear disarmament committee, 28 members of the G-21 proposed a "Programme of Action for the Elimination of Nuclear Weapons."[2] The idea of setting up such a committee, and indeed any consideration of CD *talks* – let alone negotiations – on nuclear disarmament have so far been dismissed by the three western nuclear powers – Britain, France and the United States. Building on the advisory opinion of the International Court of Justice (ICJ) of 8 July 1996, Malaysia submitted a resolution on nuclear disarmament to the UN General Assembly in December

1996. The resolution, which called for negotiations to begin on a Nuclear Weapons Convention (NWC), received 115 votes in favour, with 22 votes against and 32 abstentions.[3] The opposition consisted mainly of NATO states, which voted *en bloc*. The Malaysian resolution is an important step. It lays the foundation stone for the concept of a Nuclear Weapons Convention. Though no-one imagines that negotiations will begin in 1997, the resolution begins the process of embedding the idea that a Nuclear Weapons Convention is something reasonable and feasible, and that it could be achieved, like the Chemical Weapons Convention (CWC) and the Biological Weapons Convention (BWC).

This chapter looks at the various constraints on the CD and discusses the possibilities for a Nuclear Weapons Convention or other multilateral steps towards nuclear disarmament. Several important questions must be addressed: i) what is the relation between multilateral agreements and the unilateral and bilateral steps already undertaken or underway? ii) will multilateral initiatives complement or conflict with pressure for the P-5 to negotiate deep reductions in their arsenals? iii) is it time for a single all-encompassing convention to ban nuclear weapons or are there other multilateral measures which should be undertaken as steps towards nuclear disarmament? iv) who should negotiate: the CD or some other multilateral body, such as a special conference of interested states? v) would target dates or a time-bound framework be useful? and vi) how can multilateral negotiations reconcile the interests of the P-5, the T-3, and the non-nuclear weapon states?

The chapter concludes that multilateral action has a limited role to play over the next few years. While there is a legitimate role for the CD in negotiating measures such as the CTBT, a fissban and a Nuclear Weapons Convention, it should also work in conjunction with the Non-Proliferation Treaty's (NPT's) enhanced review process to maintain international pressure for irreversible progress in unilateral, bilateral and P-5 reductions of nuclear weapons. The CD and NPT review process both need to develop effective decision-making procedures to address post-Cold War relations. The objective of a Nuclear Weapons Convention and step-by-step progress should be regarded as mutually reinforcing strategies, not competing political demands. As the difficulties of including the T-3 in a first step fissban grow more apparent, the P-5 should conclude an agreement among themselves as soon as possible, with the International Atomic Energy Agency (IAEA) as the verification agency. If the P-5 continue to insist that fissban negotiations have to be multilateral and include the T-3, the CD is unlikely to deliver an effective treaty. One way out would be to establish a nuclear disarmament committee at the same time as a fissban committee, as the non-aligned want. With or without a negotiating mandate, the nuclear disarmament committee would then be able to address the wider context of nuclear disarmament, including existing fissile material stocks. Without this broader context, the basic cut-off is viewed by many non-aligned countries, and especially Pakistan and Egypt, as discriminatory. However,

India's growing belligerence over keeping open its nuclear weapon option means that even if the rest of the non-aligned accept such a deal, there may still be trouble convincing India.

The Conference on Disarmament

There has been recognition for some years that the CD needed to review and update its agenda and institutional arrangements to address the post-Cold War security environment. The First UN Special Session on Disarmament in 1978 had agreed a ten-point programme, known as the decalogue, which covered the whole field of arms control and disarmament in a comprehensive way.

Using this as a broad frame of reference, the CD then attempts to agree its agenda and a work programme (the *ad hoc* committees, special co-ordinators and so on) each year. In 1994, for example, the CD agenda was headed by the nuclear test ban as item one, and "cessation of the nuclear arms race and nuclear disarmament" as item two. In addition to the nuclear test ban committee, three other *ad hoc* committees were convened, but without negotiating mandates: Transparency in Armaments (TIA); Prevention of an Arms Race in Outer Space (PAROS); and Negative Security Assurances (NSA). In 1995 and 1996 the CD was unable to agree any parts of its agenda except the negotiations on a CTBT. The impasse was blamed on "linkage," by which certain delegations or groups refused to let some committees go ahead without agreement on others. The split was particularly between those (primarily in the Western Group) which wanted more emphasis on conventional arms (through the TIA Committee) and those in the G-21 Group of Non-Aligned States which regarded nuclear disarmament as the main priority.

CD decisions are on the basis of consensus. This means that any state can exercise a veto. There is no mechanism for taking majority decisions or a vote. After long consideration, including three years of deadlock caused by the United States' veto of Iraq, the CD accepted 23 new members on 17 June 1996, expanding the participating membership to 60.[4] In order to get round the US veto, the 23 new members agreed not to exercise their veto for a period of two years or, in the case of Iraq, as long as Chapter VII sanctions apply. If sanctions are lifted in less than two years, the condition imposed on the other 22 states can be voided at the same time.

The CD members became organized into three groupings during the Cold War. These groupings have become less relevant to states' real interests and alliances, and the term "non-aligned" has lost its meaning; however, as appointments and consultations are based on the groupings, nothing has yet emerged to replace them for managing decision-making. The three groups are the Group of Western States and Others (21); the Group of East European

States and Others (8); the G-21 Group of Non-Aligned States (30). China is outside all of the groups, and often refers to itself as the "group of one."[5]

Sixteen more countries have applied for CD membership, but were not included in the recent enlargement. Some, such as Ireland and Malaysia, have worked hard in pushing for nuclear disarmament.

The presidency of the CD rotates every four weeks, in accordance with the alphabet. Group co-ordination is rotated at the same time among each group's members. The CD meets in plenary usually once a week, on Thursdays. All members are entitled to attend *ad hoc* committee meetings. Other consultations are often conducted by a special co-ordinator or the CD President on a bilateral or group basis. The President also co-ordinates decisions with a Bureau, which consists of the former and incoming presidents, group leaders and, if appropriate, chairs of *ad hoc* committees. The CD Secretariat provides advice, documentation and continuity.

1996 Comprehensive Test Ban Treaty

After three years of intensive negotiations, the CD finalized the text of a treaty banning nuclear weapons testing in all environments for all time. However, India blocked consensus on adoption of the treaty text and refused to let the CD transmit it to the UN General Assembly for approval. Lack of consensus in the CD meant that the treaty text had no status beyond that of a working paper of the Nuclear Test Ban Committee, as presented by its Chair, Ambassador Jaap Ramaker of The Netherlands. Although several members of the committee said that it was not as strong as they had wanted and contained some significant flaws, the majority in the Committee, including the P-5, were prepared to accept the text. Many feared that the window of opportunity could close if the CTBT was not signed before the end of 1996. There was a widely-held view that further negotiations would not yield a better result. So, rather than lose the CTBT altogether, Australia took a resolution to the General Assembly to endorse the treaty text. This was passed in New York by 158 votes to 3, with 5 abstentions. India, Libya and Bhutan voted against. The CTBT was opened for signature on 24 September and by September 1997, 146 countries had signed, including the P-5 and Israel.

Neither India nor Pakistan have signed. Without them the treaty cannot be fully implemented. Together with Russia, China, Britain and Egypt, Pakistan had pushed for the treaty's Article XIV to specify a list of countries to ensure that the CTBT would not enter into force unless all eight declared and undeclared nuclear weapon states were on board. Despite getting this provision, Pakistan backed away from signing unless India did so. Nationalist sentiment and the recent heated domestic debates on India's nuclear options and international status make New Delhi's accession to the CTBT in the near future extremely unlikely. When the General Assembly adopted the CTBT on 10 September 1996, India's Ambassador to the CD, Arundhati Ghose, declared that India would "never sign this unequal treaty, not now, nor later."[6] India's stated concerns were: i) the treaty did not prohibit further refinement of existing arsenals by simulation, non-fission explosions or other laboratory experiments; ii) the treaty did not commit the P-5 to eliminate their nuclear weapons within a specified timeframe; and iii) Article XIV listed India among the countries required for the treaty to enter into force, thereby violating its sovereignty and subjecting it to coercion and possibly sanctions if it did not join the treaty. India's refusal to sign, coupled with the insistence by certain P-5 countries on India's accession, has profound implications not only for the credibility of the CTBT, but also for the future of multilateral nuclear arms control.[7]

For most of the P-5, agreement to negotiate a CTBT in 1994 had two primary objectives: i) to persuade the non-nuclear weapon states to make the NPT permanent; and ii) to bring the threshold nuclear weapon states into the multilateral non-proliferation regime. As technology advance had increased their ability to monitor nuclear weapon design without nuclear explosive testing, they were prepared to limit their own testing as the price for consolidating non-proliferation. With the first objective achieved in May 1995, it was Russia and Britain that insisted on the second objective. China appeared to signal more flexibility on this issue than over on-site inspections. (It cannot be inferred from this that China *was* more flexible, as a favoured Chinese tactic is to express a "flexible" approach when another state is in front holding down a position that Beijing actually supports.) The United States was more flexible from the beginning, insisting only that the P-5 should join together. France opened with the same position as Britain, but once it had committed itself to close down the South Pacific test site, Paris joined Washington in seeking a flexible provision that would ensure early entry into force. Although Pakistan and Egypt both advocated the "five-plus-three" condition, their objections were not perceived as treaty breakers to the same degree as the intransigence of Russia and Britain.

In addition to specifying the list of 44 countries which have to ratify the Treaty before it comes into force, Article XIV provides for holding a conference of those states which have ratified, if the treaty has not entered into force within three years after its opening for signature.[8] This conference

> shall examine the extent to which the requirement set out in paragraph 1 has been met and shall consider and decide by consensus what measures consistent with international law may be undertaken to accelerate the ratification process in order to facilitate the early entry into force of this Treaty.[9]

Although lawyers will have the final say, the framers of this article claimed at the time that it could not be used to waive the list of 44 countries, but might enable the treaty to be applied provisionally. To allay one of India's objections, Ramaker stated for the record that the provision did not mean sanctions.

The Treaty's implementation was made hostage to the decision of a state which has declared it would not join; this increases the risk that the CTBT will sit in limbo for a long time, perhaps indefinitely. Until the treaty formally takes effect, its parties cannot fully implement the verification system or authorize on-site inspections. If no-one attempts any nuclear explosions, the treaty's norm against testing may be sufficient. However, if there are accusations of low-yield testing or other compliance ambiguities, the treaty regime could be weakened and discredited.

There are unlikely to be serious problems during the first five years, even if India flouts international will by conducting one or more tests.[10] After ten years, it could be a different matter. The USA had initially proposed an easy opt-out provision if testing was required after ten years, and representatives of both the US and British laboratories have claimed that they would not be able to guarantee the safety and reliability of the nuclear arsenals beyond ten years. In a worst case scenario, a Reagan/Thatcher-style combination in the USA and Britain could decide to discard an unratified CTBT in order to test third generation weapons or a follow-on to Trident. While France would be less enthusiastic, after closing down the South Pacific test sites, Russia and China might be glad to resume testing; this time, India would almost certainly follow suit. Most analysts regard this scenario as remote. Making it impossible would require the following: voluntary verification arrangements to increase confidence in the test ban regime regardless of the treaty's legal status; further progress on nuclear disarmament, which would reduce the risk that the nuclear weapon states would want to test modified designs or new weapons – and also would increase pressure on India to join the CTBT; and closure and clean-up of the existing test sites.

Two features of the treaty should concern those who believed that the test ban's contribution "to the process of nuclear disarmament" should be as important as the "prevention of the proliferation of nuclear weapons in all its aspects."[11] Despite strenuous attempts by many non-nuclear weapon states, which had wanted a clear statement on preventing the qualitative improvement or development of new nuclear weapons, the treaty only implies that "constraining the development and qualitative improvement of nuclear weapons and ending the development of advanced new types of nuclear weapons" will be a consequence. When taking his decision that the CTBT would be a "true zero yield" ban, President Clinton, on the insistence of the Pentagon and nuclear laboratories, attached six safeguards to ensure the US stockpile. He also explicitly reserved the right to exercise "our supreme national interest rights under a comprehensive test ban to conduct necessary testing if the safety or reliability of our nuclear deterrent could no longer be certified."[12] Most of the P-5 followed with similar understandings. A CTBT will constrain, but nothing in the treaty prevents those with sufficiently advanced technology from using "stockpile stewardship" programmes or similar to develop new types of warhead or enhance their existing warheads (and see Chapter 9). If the political climate shifts to the right in the future, weapons designed in laboratory conditions could become excuses for exercising the right of withdrawal from the agreement in order to test. However, the United States (and others) would have to weigh the advantages against the very real damage that this could do to the treaty regimes and norms which underpin international law. If the CTBT broke down, the NPT might break down as well.

During 1997 the USA conducted two sub-critical tests. Because these do not generate a self-sustaining fission reaction they are not considered a violation of the CTBT by the US Department of Energy, responsible for the $4 billion-a-year stockpile stewardship programme. However, some officials and nuclear weapon scientists concede that sub-critical tests operate in the treaty's "grey area."[13] Moreover, the tests are to be conducted at underground facilities at the Nevada Test Site, increasing the nervousness of China and Russia about the credibility of verifying US compliance with the CTBT. The USA postponed the sub-critical tests planned to take place in 1996, recognizing that they might derail the talks. John Holum, director of the US Arms Control and Disarmament Agency, sought to allay concerns when he told the CD that the CTBT would mean that the nuclear weapon states:

> will not be able to pursue confidently such technologies as the nuclear explosion pumped X-ray laser, the so-called nuclear shotgun, enhanced electromagnetic pulse weapons, microwave weapons and enhanced radiation weapons ... The true-zero test ban will also place out of reach new "mini-nuke" and "micro-nuke" concepts ... [14]

The determination of the USA, Britain and France to refuse to allow the CTBT's preamble to state that prevention of qualitative development or new nuclear weapons was an aim or objective of the treaty, suggests the desire to maintain as wide a grey area as feasible, for as long as possible.

The history of the CTBT reveals many of the dilemmas of multilateral negotiations. The nuclear weapon states, having come to the decision to constrain or halt a particular activity, are not content with mutual agreement among those who have engaged or benefited most from the activity in question. They want an additional payoff. The most powerful states seek to retain a technological safety net, while arguing that the agreement is void unless it binds the threshold nuclear states. Already this argument has been deployed by the P-5 when insisting on the need for multilateral negotiations on a fissile materials cut-off. Yet the CTBT history shows that multilateral procedures *per se* do not guarantee that all states participating in the negotiations will accede to the treaty.

Ban on Production of Fissile Materials

Like the CTBT, a ban on the production of fissile materials for weapon purposes has long been an objective among nuclear arms control advocates, but successive US and Soviet governments have failed to act. With the end of the Cold War, the USA and Russia are awash with surplus stocks of weapon-usable plutonium and highly-enriched uranium. The USA stopped producing HEU for weapons in 1964 and halted production of plutonium in 1988 when the ageing military production plant was shut because of safety, health and environmental concerns. In 1992, President Bush formally announced the halt, making some political capital out of the fact. Russia ceased HEU production in 1989 and has announced its intention of shutting down its ageing plutonium-producing reactors by the year 2000. In time for the NPT Conference in 1995, the UK and France announced that they too were halting production of fissile material for weapons. France had already ceased production of weapon-grade plutonium at Marcoule in 1992. President Chirac announced in 1996 that this and the uranium enrichment facilities at Pierrelatte would be closed. China has indicated privately that it has, or is about to, stop as well, but has not made a formal statement or announced a moratorium.

After the 1993 UN General Assembly resolution 48/75L, the CD agreed to consider how to ban the production of fissile materials for weapon purposes. In March 1995, pressured by the upcoming NPT Review and Extension Conference, a mandate was agreed, establishing an *ad hoc* "Fissban" Committee. It has never been convened. The core problems concern the existing stockpiles of military plutonium and HEU, and the relation between the envisaged ban or "cut-off" and nuclear disarmament. Pakistan and many non-aligned countries have argued for a fissban that also controls existing stocks. They contend that a fissban should not merely reinforce the nuclear *status quo* but should also address the wider proliferation threat from weapon-usable materials. The P-5 and India have indicated that they would only accept a "cut-off" of future production for weapon purposes. Israel is reluctant to enter into negotiations at all and has signalled that it may refuse the 1995 mandate accepted by the CD before Israel became a member (though the threat is dismissed by US officials).

The March 1995 mandate fudged the issue of stocks but it is now clear that further progress will be impossible unless the purpose and scope of the fissban is clarified. A cut-off has been a priority demand for over forty years; however, its actual significance in 1997 is questionable. Since the P-5 have in effect stopped producing, they could codify this by an agreement among themselves, with appropriate verification through the IAEA. Their motive for insisting on multilateral negotiations is to ensure that the threshold states are halted in producing fissionable material, and that their facilities are placed under full-scope safeguards. France and Britain are particularly vehement on this condition. In addition to excluding consideration of stockpiles, the proposed "cut-off" implies a purpose criterion, and would differentiate between plutonium and HEU produced for civilian and weapon purposes. As far as proliferation is concerned, this distinction is artificial. All separated plutonium and HEU poses a risk. Even reactor-grade plutonium can be used to make nuclear bombs.

From least to greatest scope, the four possible measures for banning fissile materials are the following:

Ban on Future Production of Plutonium and HEU for Weapon Purposes

This is the basic cut-off, covered by the 1993 UN consensus resolution and the Shannon mandate for the CD. It would prevent the nuclear powers and any country which is not a member of the NPT from making more fissile materials for weapon purposes, providing they signed the treaty. It would have no effect on existing arsenals or stockpiles. However, as well as bringing the military nuclear facilities of the P-5 and T-3 into the IAEA verification regime, it could be used to strengthen safeguards provisions and ensure more effective monitoring of nuclear "wannabe" states such as Iraq and North Korea.

Ban on Production and Stockpiling of Plutonium and HEU for Weapon Purposes

In addition to preventing further production, this measure would place controls on existing stockpiles. This could entail just declaration and monitoring, to ensure that no new material is added, or go further with a programme of reduction and disposal. A first step could be to prevent plutonium or HEU from dismantled warheads from being re-used in nuclear weapons, by placing them under IAEA safeguards.

Ban on Production and Stockpiling of Fissile Materials and Tritium for Military Purposes

Tritium is a radioactive gas used in triggering and boosting nuclear weapons. While bombs can be made without tritium, it is necessary for sophisticated designs and missile delivery. Tritium has a half life of 12.3 years, giving it a short shelf life, after which it has to be replaced in the warheads. A ban on tritium production could, therefore, diminish the confidence and utility of nuclear arsenals over time, increasing the likelihood of progressive arms reduction or obsolescence. Extending the fissban to military purposes would include long range nuclear-powered submarines which the USA and Britain fuel with HEU.

Ban on Production and Stockpiling of
Weapon-usable Fissionable Materials

Advocated by a number of non-governmental organizations, the only countries to have shown interest in this fully comprehensive measure are Egypt, Mexico and Indonesia. On the grounds that the possession, trade and transport of the essential material for nuclear bombs carries too great a proliferation or accident risk, this ban would prohibit plutonium separation and uranium enrichment. France, the UK and Russia, as well as non-nuclear weapon states such as Germany, Japan and South Africa, are heavily involved in commercial developments and oppose any measure that would prohibit these activities. While this form of fissban would have the most far-reaching effect in preventing present and future proliferation, there is currently insufficient backing for it to be on the negotiating agenda.

The politically feasible choice at present is between the first two. This may turn out to be short-sighted. China and North Korea have expressed concern about Japan's accumulation of civil plutonium. South Korea, Germany and other, non-NPT, states are also viewed as possessing nuclear "insurance" policies, by having the technology and providing themselves with sufficient fissile materials if they should ever wish to weaponize. Plutonium and HEU are not economically competitive for energy supply. Whether or not there is really a long term security consideration, the plutonium policy of Japan is perceived by neighbouring states as a potential threat and thus undermines regional non-proliferation. The round the world shipments of spent and reprocessed nuclear fuel between the Far East and France and Britain also increase the risk of theft or accident involving plutonium.

A number of CD members are losing enthusiasm for the proposed cut-off, believing that it is no longer worth the time and trouble of multilateral negotiations, and only a minor step now, whose time has passed. While some of the non-nuclear weapon states call for the CD to begin work immediately on a fissban, hoping that the question of stocks will be resolved during the negotiations or in parallel talks, others are concerned that cut-off negotiations will be used to tie up the resources and work of the CD for a long time, thereby delaying progress on nuclear disarmament. Their anxiety could be alleviated if the P-5 were willing to put a target date on a cut-off, in return for agreement that the basic cut-off will be concluded first. This would not rule out discussions on stockpiles and other fissile material issues. They could either be postponed until the basic cut-off has been dealt with or, more appropriately, addressed in the context of wider talks on nuclear disarmament among the P-5 or in an *ad hoc* Committee on Nuclear Disarmament.

A trade-off along these lines might win the support of many non-aligned countries, including Egypt, which is particularly keen to involve Israel in the process of negotiating controls of some kind. However, considerable diplomatic finesse may be required to overcome the opposition of Pakistan to a cut-off without stocks, or the political hostility of India to a cut-off without timebound nuclear disarmament.

In the case of the CTBT, the majority of non-nuclear weapon states perceived a clear interest in achieving a complete halt to all nuclear testing. The limitations of the CTBT as a nuclear disarmament measure became more apparent to the non-nuclear weapon states during negotiations, as the P-5 sought to retain capabilities for maintaining the "safety and reliability" of their arsenals. In the case of a fissile materials ban, the limitations are a source of deep conflict even before negotiations begin. If the P-5 are unwilling to go further than a basic cut-off, they must either decide to make it legally binding among themselves, or consider making a bargain with the non-aligned to convene an *ad hoc* Committee on Nuclear Disarmament in parallel.

The reluctance of some of the nuclear weapon states to entertain the notion of a P-5 cut-off implies that they do not regard such a legally binding agreement among the five most advanced nuclear weapon states to be intrinsically valuable. If it were practical, it is true that a multilateral "cut-off" could build confidence and enable better safeguards to be established across the board. However, a P-5 agreement could also contribute to strengthening the IAEA's "93+2 Programme" of safeguards, and discussions involving the T-3 could be conducted in parallel, both as a confidence-building measure and with a view to opening the treaty for the endorsing signatures of the entire international community. (This was done with the Partial Test Ban Treaty (PTBT) after being concluded by the USA, UK and USSR in 1963.) The likelihood of the T-3 signing this kind of cut-off in the near future may not be very good; but the odds on them acceding to a multilateral cut-off are not very good either. For most of the international community, turning the voluntary moratoria of the major nuclear powers into a legally binding and verified instrument is a valid step with or without the T-3.

At the time of writing, the P-5 are continuing to insist on multilateral fissban negotiations. Their motives are mixed. Despite the CTBT experience, some officials appear to believe that the T-3 can be brought on board if they are involved from the beginning in the negotiations. For others, the CD is a convenient quicksand, a time-consuming process that will ensure there can be little significant progress on this or any other nuclear disarmament measure. For there to be any prospect of successful negotiations, two conditions would have to be fulfilled. The issue of stocks would have to be clarified with either explicit agreement by all concerned to address them within the negotiations (highly unlikely), or with acceptance that they should be considered in parallel. This would be an obvious topic for P-5 talks. If they continue to insist on multilateral deliberations on the control, reduction and elimination of plutonium and HEU stocks, then the obvious place is a nuclear disarmament committee in the CD. Advocates of the nuclear disarmament committee want it to discuss far more than fissile stocks, but as a practical near term step towards the abolition of nuclear weapons, further controls on stockpiles is a central issue that needs to be addressed. The G-21 are unlikely to put their resources into cut-off negotiations in the CD unless there is a disarmament pay-off in the shape of a nuclear disarmament committee. The P-5 cannot reasonably continue to insist that a fissile material cut-off treaty be conducted multilaterally in the CD while refusing to deal with stocks either in fissban negotiations or in the wider nuclear disarmament context. Such an intransigent approach is liable to waste the time of the other CD members and should not be allowed to dominate the multilateral negotiating agenda.

A multilateral cut-off treaty would not need to have a special implementing organization or verification regime, so negotiations need not be as time-consuming as for the CTBT. The IAEA is the obvious verification agency for a fissban treaty, appropriately resourced to strengthen its monitoring procedures and extend them to the unsafeguarded facilities of the P-5 and T-3. Negotiations could be expedited if the USA and Russia would put forward a draft treaty based on their bilateral consultations and work undertaken with the IAEA. If they wanted to guard against open-ended fissban negotiations filling up the CD's sessions, NPT parties could consider putting a target date on the measure, as they did when the Principles and Objectives were agreed in May 1995, with a target date of 1996 for the priority item, then the CTBT. Now that has been achieved, a target date of 1999 could be set for a basic fissile material cut-off.

Nuclear Disarmament

Once dismissed by diplomats and military strategists as the fuzzy idealism of the anti-nuclear lobby, the abolition of nuclear weapons is looking more and more realistic as the best (and most rational) response to the risks from proliferation, and accidental or intentional use of nuclear weapons. The CWC showed that multilateral negotiations could succeed in banning a whole class of weapons of mass destruction. The disintegration of the East-West ideological confrontation rendered a nuclear-weapon-free world feasible, while the increased risks of nuclear theft and terrorism make stringent controls on all nuclear materials and technologies a necessity. Most military specialists now recognize that nuclear weapons have little or no reliable function, while their possession creates an ambition and incentive for others to acquire them. Governments are less and less willing to cover the environmental and economic costs of their production.

The NPT was extended indefinitely in May 1995, carrying with it an obligation on the P-5 to seek nuclear disarmament. In July 1996, the ICJ, in an advisory opinion, endorsed and strengthened this obligation. In December 1996, the UN General Assembly supported the Malaysian-sponsored call for a Nuclear Weapons Convention by 115 votes to 22, with 32 abstentions. Underlining the unanimous conclusion of the Court that "there exists an obligation to pursue in good faith and bring to a conclusion negotiations leading to nuclear disarmament in all its aspects under strict and effective international control" (operative paragraph, OP3) the Malaysian resolution

> calls upon all states to fulfil that obligation immediately by commencing multilateral negotiations in 1997 leading to an early conclusion of a Nuclear Weapons Convention prohibiting the development, production, testing, deployment, stockpiling, transfer, threat or use of nuclear weapons and providing for their elimination (operative paragraph OP4).

If the resolution had not specified that the negotiations should begin in 1997 the vote in favour of OP4 might have been higher.

Few expect that multilateral negotiations on a Nuclear Weapons Convention could be opened before the year 2000, let alone in 1997. But for a first resolution on such a controversial subject the Malaysian initiative did remarkably well. The votes on the two main operative paragraphs, OP3 and OP4, differed in an interesting way. Russia abstained on both paragraphs but voted against the resolution as a whole. The USA, UK and France voted "no" throughout, while China voted "yes" on all parts. The separate vote on OP3 allowed many countries to support the ICJ's opinion on the legal obligation to bring about nuclear disarmament without putting their weight behind the call for an NWC at this point. The unanimous ICJ opinion endorsed here went further than Article VI of the NPT, since the link with general and complete disarmament has been omitted, and states are required to go beyond "pursuit in good faith" and bring the negotiations to conclusion. On OP3 the voting was: 139 for, 7 against, 20 abstentions. Together with the Non-aligned Movement states and China, the following European Union countries voted in favour: Austria, Belgium, Denmark, Finland, Germany, Ireland, Italy, Luxembourg and Sweden. They were joined (among others) by Australia, Canada, Iceland, Japan, New Zealand, Norway and Ukraine. Abstainers included Russia, Israel, The Netherlands, Portugal, Spain and various East European countries, including Belarus and Kazakhstan. In addition to the Western nuclear powers, Latvia, Monaco, Romania and Turkey voted against.[15]

On the call in OP4 for negotiations to begin in 1997, the tally was 110 for, 27 against, and 29 abstentions. Although most of the NAM voted for, a few francophone African states, such as Gabon, Togo and Benin abstained. Among Western states only New Zealand voted in favour. The 27 votes against comprised NATO and would-be NATO countries, including Belgium, Canada, Denmark, Germany, Italy and Norway, who had all voted in favour of OP3.

The 29 abstentions included Australia, Austria, Belarus, Ireland, Israel, Japan, Kazakhstan, Russia, Sweden, and Ukraine.[16]

When the vote was taken on the whole resolution, the following countries which had abstained on OP4 joined the mainly NAM states, China and New Zealand in voting for the resolution: Bosnia-Herzegovina, Gabon, Ireland, and Sweden. However, Argentina, Australia, Austria, Denmark, Israel, Japan, Norway, and the Republic of Korea abstained. Canada joined the mainly NATO and NATO wannabe countries in a vote against.[17] It is noticeable that there were more cracks among Western countries than among the NAM on the parts and the whole of the Malaysian resolution.

It is understood that Malaysia intends to submit a similar resolution each year calling for negotiations towards a Nuclear Weapons Convention. If it does so, the NWC resolution will provide a useful point of pressure and debate in the UN First Committee and General Assembly from now on. This adds to the growing pressure from a number of heavy-weight reports and statements presenting the case for total nuclear disarmament. Together they indicate the growing intellectual credibility of the concept. The CD needs to rise to this challenge, but immediate negotiations are not necessarily the most effective way. Following up the non-aligned states' demand for an *ad hoc* Committee on Nuclear Disarmament, 28 states proposed a three-phase Programme of Action with the goal of achieving the abolition of nuclear weapons by the year 2020.[18] This Programme has some useful ideas, but it would throw up many barriers and problems. The timetable is too mechanistic and the G-21 sacrificed realism for political expediency when it agreed to lump together the

> immediate and concurrent commencement of negotiations and early conclusion of:
> – a multilaterally negotiated legally binding instrument to assure non-nuclear weapon states against the use or threat of use of nuclear weapons;
> – a convention prohibiting the use or threat of use of nuclear weapons;
> – a treaty to eliminate nuclear weapons; and
> – a treaty banning the production of fissile material for nuclear weapons.[19]

Some of the non-aligned countries have suggested that negotiations could be worked out under the "chapeau" of a framework convention, adding in protocols to deal with specific measures, such as a fissban, no first use, a warhead production ban, and so on. However, the framework agreement itself would require long and complex negotiations, before the specific protocols could be worked out. Such an approach could prove counter-productive if attempted prematurely. Deadlock in the CD could become an excuse for no further progress on any aspect of nuclear arms control or disarmament, scuppering hope for a START III and beyond. Those in NATO and Russia opposed to unilateral, US-Russian bilateral, or P-5 measures, could argue that there should be no further reductions in their arsenals, pending multilateral agreement. This approach could revive insistence that the US and Russian arsenals must come down to the hundreds before any P-5 discussions can go forward (a position long promulgated by China, and put forward by the UK at the 1995 NPT Conference). A framework convention might appear attractive as a way of avoiding having to set the priorities now, and could be supported as a mechanism for establishing a timetable for nuclear disarmament. However, it would be very likely to result in an early logjam.

Alternatively, the nuclear disarmament committee, working under a mandate developed from the ICJ ruling and existing treaty obligations, could begin by reinforcing the objective of and commitment to elimination. Instead of starting straight into negotiations it could consider existing studies and perhaps commission its own from independent researchers with a view to gaining better understanding of the processes of dismantlement, verification requirements and limitations, and so on. This would put the CD in a stronger position to identify and push for the next steps to reduce reliance on nuclear weapons and build confidence in nuclear disarmament.

The desire for a hard and fast timetable is understandable but unrealistic. The nuclear weapon states will not get rid of their weapons according to a prearranged schedule, but in response to changing perceptions of their security needs, costs, risks and benefits. International and public pressure, as well as environmental legislation and financial penalties, all have a role to play in creating the conditions for particular steps to be taken. Although a binding timetable is not practical, target dates for specific agreements could be useful. They tend to work best when the measure is already within grasp, such as the 1996 target date established for the CTBT in 1992. There are also good arguments for setting an overall target date for the complete elimination of nuclear weapons, such as the year 2020 in the G-28 Programme. However, attempts to put a linear timetable on an entire framework of nuclear disarmament measures will be doomed to frustration and may impede actual progress. Far better to identify a programme of action in principle and apply a target date only to the short term priorities as they emerge. As each is achieved, momentum can be sustained by setting a realistic date for the next step.

Conclusion

A Nuclear Weapons Convention is a reasonable multilateral objective, but past experience of disarmament negotiations indicates that, with the current level of P-5 and T-3 opposition and distrust, it cannot simply be voted into place. The political demand must be kept at the forefront, but the strategy for achieving it must accept that such abolition conventions are successfully negotiated towards the *end* of a process of political change, after the security conditions have been established. Therefore, the demand for an abolition convention should not be set in contradiction to the step-by-step approach as if they represent either/or approaches to nuclear disarmament. Though moving in the right direction, political developments have not yet established the conditions under which negotiations on a Nuclear Weapons Convention could hope to succeed.

Mobilized public opinion helps to create the right conditions, as does a clear, strong objective. These must be maintained within and outside the multilateral fora, but with the recognition that much more needs to be done by way of unilateral, bilateral and P-5 agreements, verification development and confidence building. This does not absolve the CD of multilateral responsibility for nuclear disarmament. It should address the need to control fissile materials. If the P-5 refuse to codify a cut-off among themselves, and providing there is a limited target date, the CD should clarify the objectives and scope and move forward on the fissban. At the same time, the *ad hoc* Committee on Nuclear Disarmament should be convened to determine the legal, institutional and verification requirements for the elimination of nuclear weapons. The preparatory phase could be done without a negotiating mandate, but the CD could aim for a mandate to negotiate by the year 2000. It would be perfectly possible for the CD to negotiate a fissban agreement in one committee while also discussing existing stockpiles, as well as frameworks and programmes for the elimination of nuclear weapons in an *ad hoc* Committee on Nuclear Disarmament. There is currently a debate over whether the CD should take a more active role in banning landmines and putting teeth into the BWC. Both are important and worthwhile objectives, but if the CD is to take on more conventional or non-nuclear tasks, it should not be at the expense of progress on nuclear disarmament. More resources or alternative negotiating fora would have to be established.

The first PrepCom of the NPT's new review process met in New York in April 1997, and will meet in four out of five years from now on, with full quinquennial Review Conferences. The next will be in the year 2000. When extending the NPT, its states parties adopted two related decisions in May 1995, intending them to be used as a stronger mechanism for reviewing and implementing the Treaty. The enhanced review process should identify and set realistic targets for the nuclear weapon states, to be accomplished by unilateral action and joint agreements. A precedent for this has already been set, in the Programme of Action in the decision on Principles and Objectives of Nuclear Non-Proliferation and Disarmament adopted by NPT parties on 11 May 1995.[20] The CTBT was given the target date of 1996. Now that this has been achieved the second item – the fissban – should either be moved up and given a target date, or it should be reconsidered. If the P-5 were really serious about a fissile materials cut-off they would do it themselves instead of holding it hostage to power struggles with the T-3 in the Conference on Disarmament. If, however, they can get agreement on using the CD to negotiate a basic cut-off, the appropriate target date should be no later than 1999. The NPT has no negotiating powers, but the enhanced review process could take on a stronger monitoring role.

The NPT comprises the P-5, and virtually the whole of the rest of the world as non-nuclear weapon states; the only significant non-signatories are India, Pakistan and Israel. It would be a mistake to redirect multilateral attention on nuclear disarmament issues away from the CD and into the NPT, as suggested recently by some diplomats and US officials. The fora have different functions, strengths and weaknesses, and would accomplish more if they were viewed as complementary. The NPT enhanced review process is barely born, and only time and testing will show whether it can do anything of substance. It is also clear from the experience of negotiating the CTBT that the CD's structures and procedures are in desperate need of an overhaul. Cross-alliances among non-nuclear weapon states should be further developed whereby the Western nuclear powers are not silencing the views of non-nuclear Western states and the non-aligned agenda is not manipulated or obstructed by the demands and interests of threshold states like India and Pakistan.

The mechanism of consensus must be put in context of the CD's responsibilities to the international community represented by the UN General Assembly. Consensus is an important principle of negotiations among parties with an equal interest and responsibility in the outcome. That is not the case in the CD, which makes it vulnerable to manipulation and hostage taking. Ways should be found for bypassing vetoes which are exercised for extraneous political reasons rather than serious objections to the provisions under negotiation. The Australian initiative of taking the vetoed CTBT to the United Nations General Assembly for adoption should not be regarded as a threat to the CD. It is the proper business of the UN to oversee the CD's agenda and priorities. The General Assembly should not be used merely as a rubber stamp once the CD has reached consensus. It should have an acknowledged role if and when the CD becomes badly deadlocked or a completed treaty is vetoed. While all attempts should be made to reach consensus in the CD, the jurisdiction of the wider international community should be available as a recognized mechanism if a blockage is unreasonable or reflects only the interests of one or two states. This should be recognized and incorporated into CD procedures. Any state would still have the sovereign right not to accede to any agreement or treaty; however, individual governments would not be able to veto measures which are sought by the great majority. Even then, an opposition vote by certain powerful states might stymie adoption or implementation of a measure, despite a majority in favour. In such a case, the UN need not be limited to acceptance or rejection; it could send a draft treaty back to the CD for its negotiators to try again.[21]

Over the next three years, in the CD and NPT review Preparatory Committees (PrepComs), the international community should lay the groundwork for eliminating nuclear weapons, while identifying targets and maintaining pressure for continued US-Russian and P-5 nuclear arms control. Thus the demand for a convention and practical step-by-step progress are mutually reinforcing strategies, not competitive or mutually exclusive. Though much can be achieved through programmatic arms control, it is likely that a multilateral convention will be required to make the complete abolition of nuclear weapons legally binding and to create the necessary international norm against clandestine acquisition. When the political conditions are ripe, the CD will probably be the best forum to codify the elimination of nuclear weapons and negotiate the implementation regime in some form of Nuclear Weapons Convention. Setting up an alternative forum would be more time-consuming and fraught with more political minefields than reforming the out-dated decision-making procedures of the CD.

Notes

1. The Conference on Disarmament is formally autonomous of the UN, but holds its meetings on UN premises, is serviced by UN staff and funded by UN members. Traditionally the CD takes account of consensus resolutions by the UN General Assembly and transmits to the General Assembly its annual reports and the texts of any agreements negotiated in the CD.

2. CD/1419, 7 August 1996.

3. UNGA 51, resolution M, 10 December 1996.

4. Officially membership is 61, but Yugoslavia's seat is suspended pending agreement on a successor.

5. The membership of the groups is as follows: Group of Western States and Others: Argentina, Australia, Austria, Belgium, Canada, Finland, France, Germany, Israel, Italy, Japan, The Netherlands, New Zealand, Norway, the Republic of Korea, Spain, Sweden, Switzerland, Turkey, UK and USA (21).

Group of Eastern European States and Others: Belarus, Bulgaria, Hungary, Poland, Romania, Russian Federation, Slovakia, Ukraine (8).

G-21 Group of Non-Aligned States: Algeria, Bangladesh, Brazil, Cameroon, Chile, Colombia, Cuba, The Democratic People's Republic of Korea, Egypt, Ethiopia, India, Indonesia, Iraq, Iran, Kenya, Mexico, Mongolia, Morocco, Myanmar, Nigeria, Pakistan, Peru, Senegal, South Africa, Sri Lanka, Syria, Venezuela, VietNam, Zaire, Zimbabwe (30).

China is outside all of the groups.

6. Arundhati Ghose, Ambassador of India, Statement in explanation of vote, resumed Fiftieth Session of the UN General Assembly, New York, 10 September 1996.

7. See R. Johnson, *A Comprehensive Test Ban Treaty: Signed But Not Sealed*, ACRONYM Report No. 10, May 1997, for a fuller story.

8. There is a simmering dispute over whether Article XIV which in English reads "... three years after the date of the anniversary of its opening for signature ..." means a conference can be held after three years, as its framers insist they intended, or four years, taking the "anniversary" as 24 September 1997.

9. Article XIV, Comprehensive Nuclear Test Ban Treaty, para. 2.

10. In 1996 there were strident calls in the Indian press to test and prove their ability to develop warheads for medium range missile delivery. The danger of this has now receded.

11. Mandate for the ad hoc Committee on a nuclear test ban, adopted by the CD, 25 January 1994, CD/1238, reproduced in preambular paragraph 10 of the CTBT.

12. President Bill Clinton, 11 August 1995. White House Press Release.

13. Off the record conversations with senior US, British and Russian officials and scientists during 1996.

14. John Holum, to the CD Plenary, 23 January 1996, CD/PV.721.

15. General Assembly, Fifty First Session, A/51/566/ADD.11 vote 21, 10 December 1996.

16. General Assembly, Fifty First Session, A/51/566/ADD.11 vote 22, 10 December 1996.

17. General Assembly, Fifty First Session, A/51/566/ADD.11 vote 23, 10 December 1996.

18. CD/1419, 7 August 1996.

19. *Ibid.* Opposition to linking separate measures in this way was cited by South Africa and Chile as the principal reason why they could not support G-21 consensus on the programme of action. It is understood that India had insisted on negotiations on the different measures being "concurrent."

20. NPT/CONF.1995/L.5.

21. R. Johnson, "Making the Conference on Disarmament Accountable to the United Nations," *Disarmament Diplomacy*, 17, July/August 1997.

13

Nuclear Disarmament: Closing the Gaps

Jan Prawitz

Introduction

Approaching the year 2000, the Cold War nuclear arms race has definitely reversed its direction towards disarmament. This process is proceeding along two paths: enhancing the non-proliferation regime and pursuing nuclear disarmament.

The most basic of all attempts to raise barriers against the nuclear arms race, the Non-Proliferation Treaty (NPT),[1] agreed in 1968, has over the years developed into a great success.

- In 1997, almost all states of the world have become parties to the Treaty including the five established nuclear weapon states. Only seven states are non-parties, and four of these are parts of nuclear-weapon-free zones (NWFZs). The remaining three are the well known threshold states of India, Israel, and Pakistan. With the important exception of the five recognized nuclear weapon states, possession of nuclear weapons could thus be considered illegitimate.
- In 1995, after 25 years in force, the NPT parties decided to extend the Treaty's duration indefinitely.[2]
- Almost unnoticed, the NPT parties decided that the Treaty should be implemented "under any circumstances," that is, also in wartime. During the ratification process in the USA, Secretary of State Dean Rusk explained to the US Senate that the NPT "does not deal with arrangements for deployment of nuclear weapons within Allied territory, as these do not involve any transfer of nuclear weapons or control over them unless and until a decision were made to go to war, at which time the treaty would no longer be controlling."[3] This was an interpretation of the Treaty suggesting it would no longer be in force in case of war; it reflected a previously agreed position within the NATO alliance. However, in 1985, the Third

Review Conference of the NPT parties unanimously adopted a final declaration stating *inter alia* that

> the Conference agreed that the strict observance of the terms of Articles I and II remains central to achieving the shared objectives of preventing *under any circumstances* [emphasis added] the further proliferation of nuclear weapons and preserving the Treaty's vital contribution to peace and security, including the peace and security of non-parties,[4]

thus stating the opposite interpretation. While Mr Rusk's statement primarily referred to the East-West conflict dominating at the time, the end of the Cold War and the prospects for local wars in the future now makes the more restrictive 1985 interpretation the only reasonable one. In 1991, the UN Security Council did indeed confirm the 1985 approach in its resolution on Iraq.[5] The opposite interpretation – that Iraq's involvement in the Gulf war would have entitled her to acquire nuclear weapons – would be beyond reason.

– On the other hand, the NPT permits the stationing and deployment of nuclear weapons controlled by the five nuclear weapon states in the territories of NPT parties and at sea. In large areas of the world, however, included in NWFZs, such stationing and deployment is prohibited. Today, five NWFZs have been established, covering 99 per cent of the Southern Hemisphere land areas and some parts of the Northern Hemisphere, while excluding most sea areas.

– At long last, dramatic nuclear disarmament has been agreed; it began in 1987. Today, the measures include the INF (1987), START I (1991) and START II (1993) agreements[6] (see Chapter 7). The three smaller nuclear weapon powers have not joined in these disarmament projects. Most important is the withdrawal of sub-strategic nuclear weapons from theatres of deployment and from ships, unilaterally declared in the fall of 1991 by the USA and by the USSR, later confirmed by the Russian Federation. Many of those are now being dismantled, particularly in the USA; others will be stored.

These developments now point in the general direction of a nuclear-weapon-free world (NWFW). There are now various documents that suggest that the move to an NWFW could be completed in about twenty years.[7]

However, the disarmament processes initiated so far have left lacunae where nuclear weapons may hide, emerge again, or escape the disarmament process. It is important to close these gaps. Such gap-closing measures could include:

– pursuing the NWFZ concept by enhancing the entry into force processes of existing nuclear-weapon-free zones, strengthening the provisions of existing zonal regimes, and establishing new zones, until the whole globe becomes such a zone;

– strengthening and expanding existing nuclear security assurances; and

– strengthening the legal status of softly defined measures; the most important of these concerns sub-strategic nuclear weapons.

Developing the zone concept would be a powerful measure towards an NWFW. There are for instance a number of zone projects proposed but not established that could be pursued further. When the parties to the NPT in May 1995 extended the duration of the Treaty, they also agreed to adopt a document *Principles and Objectives for Nuclear Non-Proliferation and Disarmament*, which encourages the establishment of NWFZs as a matter of priority.[8] As recently as 10 December 1996, the UN General Assembly adopted a resolution requesting a nuclear-weapon-free Southern Hemisphere.[9] On the same day, the UN General Assembly decided that its Disarmament Commission should start considering "the establishment of nuclear-weapon-free zones on the basis of arrangements freely arrived at among the states of the region concerned."[10] The Commission began discussing the issue in April 1997 and will continue to consider it for more sessions in the next few years.[11]

Nuclear-Weapon-Free Zones

The current NWFZ panorama includes four zones. The Tlatelolco Treaty[12] of 1967, the Rarotonga Treaty[13] of 1985, the Bangkok Treaty[14] of 1995, and the Pelindaba Treaty[15] of 1996, created such zones in Latin America, the South Pacific, South East Asia, and Africa respectively. Denuclearization of the Korean peninsula was declared in 1992 by the two Korean states,[16] but the agreement remains to be implemented. In addition, a demilitarization regime for Antarctica was agreed in 1959.[17]

This chapter discusses an array of proposals for extending the range of NWFZs. There are NWFZ proposals for the Middle East, South Asia, North-East Asia, and Eastern and Central Europe "from the Black Sea to the Baltic Sea." A zone for Nordic Europe was discussed for several decades; it was withdrawn from the political agenda following the end of the Cold War, and is not discussed here. There are proposals for two sea areas, the Indian Ocean and the South Atlantic. This leads on to the idea of making the Southern Hemisphere a unified NWFZ.

The Middle East

The issue of establishing an NWFZ in the Middle East was raised in the UN

General Assembly in 1974 by Iran supported by Egypt.[18] Since then, the UN General Assembly has adopted a resolution every year recommending that such a zone should be established. Since 1980, this has been by consensus, with the support of all Arab states, Iran and Israel.[19]

In 1988, "a study on effective and verifiable measures which would facilitate the establishment of a nuclear-weapon-free zone in the Middle East" was initiated within the United Nations. Its report was adopted by consensus.[20]

The report suggested that geographically the zone could include "all states members of the League of Arab States, the Islamic Republic of Iran, and Israel."

It did not propose explicit language for a zone treaty, but did suggest a list of measures which would serve as confidence-building steps to prepare for a regime that would finally become an NWFZ. These measures included a regional nuclear test ban; the application of IAEA safeguards to those nuclear facilities not at present covered;[21] that states that were not parties to the NPT should accede to it, and that there should be full transparency for all major nuclear projects in the area.

The UN report further suggested that nuclear weapon powers should extend negative nuclear security assurances to prospective zonal states and commit themselves not to station nuclear weapons in the area. Any outside state should declare past, current, and future supplies of nuclear material and equipment to recipients in the prospective zonal area; this should serve to clarify which projects in the area had a military role.

The report also recommended that outside support for peaceful nuclear activities in the area should be multilateral or regional in character. International facilities for nuclear waste disposal would help to ensure against diversion of fissionable material to military purposes.

Current evidence suggests that Israel is the only state in the region that has a nuclear weapon capability, and many experts believe it is already a nuclear weapon power. The Israeli government, however, has frequently said that Israel will not be the first country to introduce nuclear weapons into the Middle East. This policy of deliberate ambiguity, it is suggested, serves Israel's security interests in three ways: first, in times of gloom, it gives hope to the Israelis; second, it may caution Israel's enemies; and third, it relieves other states from the delicate burden of taking an explicit position on the matter.[22] The suspicion – indeed the virtual certainty – that a prospective zonal state is in fact a nuclear weapon state would require that the zonal treaty includes provisions for the disposal of nuclear weapons and for verifying that the zone is positively nuclear-weapon-free.

A further development was the proposal, in 1990, by President Mubarak of Egypt to establish a zone free of weapons of mass destruction[23] in the Middle East.[24] The proposal was not intended to replace the earlier idea of an NWFZ in the area but rather to be pursued in parallel with the earlier proposal.[25]

Today, the expansion of the Middle East zone concept to include all weapons of mass destruction and also their means of delivery seems politically accepted. In May 1995, the Review and Extension Conference of the NPT parties adopted a resolution on the Middle East recognizing that the current peace process contributes to "a Middle East zone free of nuclear weapons as well as other weapons of mass destruction" and calling upon all states in the Middle East to take practical steps towards "the establishment of an effectively verifiable Middle East zone free of weapons of mass destruction, nuclear, chemical and biological, and their delivery systems."[26]

South Asia

The issue of establishing an NWFZ in South Asia has been on the agenda of the UN General Assembly since 1974, following the nuclear explosion test carried out by India on 18 May that year.[27] A resolution endorsing the project, initiated by Pakistan, has been adopted every year since then.[28] But as India has always voted against, the proposed zone has never been precisely defined. India argues that nuclear disarmament should be a global rather than a regional issue. There has been no significant progress with this proposal since 1974. There was a small step forward in 1988 when India and Pakistan agreed not to attack the other's nuclear installations and facilities.[29]

An early idea was that the zone should comprise the seven state members of the South Asian Association for Regional Cooperation – Bangladesh, Bhutan, India, the Maldives, Nepal, Pakistan, and Sri Lanka. All of those states, except Bhutan and India, were in favour of the idea. All of them are parties to the NPT, except India and Pakistan.

An NWFZ in South Asia would formidably strengthen the world non-proliferation regime. India and Pakistan are not parties to the NPT; they are considered to be threshold states, or – as some observers suggest – states which either already possess nuclear weapons or could assembly such weapons at short notice. They have a relatively developed nuclear power industry, have unsettled territorial disputes with each other, and generally pursue competitive policies.

North-East Asia

The establishment of an NWFZ in North-East Asia, with the Korean peninsula as a core element, has been discussed for some time. But there has been no thorough official investigation of it, and no draft treaty text has been prepared (except for the Korean Joint Denuclearization Declaration).

In the 1980s, the establishment of an NWFZ on the Korean peninsula was discussed occasionally. In a series of developments including the withdrawal of US nuclear forces from South Korea and adjacent sea areas – a consequence of denuclearization talks between North Korea, South Korea, and the USA in

1991 – the time became ripe for the signing on 31 December 1991 by the two Koreas of a "Joint Declaration on the Denuclearization of the Korean Peninsula."

The brief declaration, which is not an elaborate nuclear-weapon-free zone treaty, states that the two states shall not test, manufacture, produce, receive, possess, store, deploy, or use nuclear weapons. Their nuclear energy activities shall be used for peaceful purposes only, with the restriction, however, that reprocessing and uranium enrichment would not be permitted at all. A "South–North Joint Nuclear Control Commission" was established for verification and inspection.

The Joint Declaration entered into force on 19 February 1992. But a year later, its implementation, particularly the establishment of its control and inspection regime, was suspended in the shadow of the disputes between North Korea and the IAEA on NPT safeguards.

An unofficial outline of an East Asian NWFZ has recently been published by Andrew Mack. His geographical concept "would be one which encompassed the two Koreas, Japan, and Taiwan." They suggest that an agreement on such a zone should be based on "Three Noes," including first, a prohibition of the acquisition, testing, use, *etc.*, of nuclear weapons by zonal states; second, a ban on the stationing of nuclear weapons within the territories of zonal states; and third, an undertaking by the nuclear weapon states not to use or threaten to use nuclear weapons against zonal states.[30] This proposed geographical scope would touch upon certain disputed territories, such as some Kurile islands, Taiwan, and groups of tiny islands in the South China Sea.

Such a zone would be a "rim" outside two continental nuclear weapon states – China and Russia [31] – making a discussion of possible "thinning-out" measures on their territories both relevant and significant.[32] The military presence of US armed forces in the region, including at sea,[33] underlines the issue of "thinning-out" possibly also at sea. However, nuclear weapons earlier deployed by US forces have been withdrawn according to unilateral declaration. Adjacent and semi-enclosed sea areas might also be included in the zone, together with possible commitments attached to such sea areas. But that would raise several detailed issues of straits and other narrow waters and their relation both to zonal interests and to the international law of the sea.

China, the Russian Federation, North Korea, and South Korea have established territorial waters 12 nautical miles wide. So has Japan, except adjacent to five straits used for international navigation where claims are limited to three nautical miles.[34] The application of law of the sea rules to Taiwan is complicated because of its disputed status.

Consideration of a possible NWFZ in East Asia would also have to address a number of important specific issues, including the following:

– the fact that all relevant states in the area are parties to the Non-

Proliferation Treaty, although Taiwan is not officially considered a state and thus is not a party;[35]
- the fact that all the relevant states in the area except North Korea, and all nuclear weapon states except France, are parties to the Sea-Bed Treaty;
- the Joint Declaration of South and North Korea on the Denuclearization of the Korean Peninsula;
- the "Three Non-Nuclear Principles" unilaterally declared by Japan in 1967:[36] not to produce nuclear weapons, not to possess nuclear weapons, and not to permit the entry into Japan of nuclear weapons;
- the developed nuclear power industry in the region, including Japanese stocks of plutonium;[37]
- the status of Taiwan and its related sea areas; although obviously politically controversial, it might nonetheless be possible to accommodate the issue in some way, as the objective of avoiding nuclear confrontation usually takes priority over local sovereignty issues.[38]

Eastern and Central Europe "from the Black Sea to the Baltic Sea"

Belarus introduced, at the NPT Extension and Review Conference in 1995, a new idea that a NWFZ in "in the centre of Europe" could be established as an option alternative to an eastward expansion by the NATO alliance.[39] Such an expansion, admitting new member states in Central and Eastern Europe, might imply a possible deployment of nuclear weapons in areas where such weapons are currently absent.

Following the dissolution of the Warsaw Pact and the Soviet Union, the former East Germany, now part of unified Germany and of the NATO territory, is denuclearized according to treaty.[40] All remaining Soviet nuclear weapons that used to be stationed in Central and Eastern Europe have been withdrawn to the territory of the Russian Federation. All former Soviet Republics – now independent states – but Russia have become parties to the Non-Proliferation Treaty as non-nuclear weapon states.

According to current rules, new member states of NATO will be legally committed to host nuclear weapons, if need be. It is true that NATO has repeatedly indicated that it has "no intention, no plan, and no reason" to deploy nuclear weapons on the territory of new member states, but it rules out the idea of codifying this view into a legally binding instrument or by an amendment to the North Atlantic Treaty.[41] There will thus be an incompatibility between NATO enlargement and the general process of nuclear disarmament.

Facing this situation, the government of Belarus, later supported by Ukraine, has repeatedly proposed the establishment of an NWFZ in Central and Eastern Europe "from the Black Sea to the Baltic Sea." This could be a measure to avoid renuclearization of the area. The original intention was that such a zone should be an alternative to the NATO enlargement, but considering the flexible nature of the zone concept, it could also be a complement, making the enlargement nuclear-weapon-free.

This proposal has since been repeatedly advanced by the governments of Belarus and Ukraine, including in 1996 at the UN General Assembly.[42]

The Russian government has repeatedly expressed the view that an eastward expansion of NATO may lead to a reconsideration of arms control agreements with the West,[43] primarily the Treaty on Conventional Armed Forces in Europe (CFE) and the unilateral declarations of 1991 on the withdrawal of sub-strategic nuclear weapons from theatres of deployment and from general purpose naval ships. One reason given is that the CFE Treaty would permit NATO to deploy conventional forces four times stronger than those of Russia after an expansion up to the Russian border. Renegotiation of the CFE treaty may lower this figure but the Russian anxiety may remain. According to one distinguished expert, Russia cannot afford, for "geopolitical and economic" reasons, to upgrade its conventional forces to restore the previous East-West balance, leaving a reintroduction of tactical nuclear weapons as its only means to do so. He comments that "today, Russia may borrow NATO's recent thesis that superiority in conventional arms should be countered by a nuclear arsenal."[44]

The Belarus proposal has not been presented in any detail. However, it can be assumed that an agreement would include the standard provisions and measures.

An NWFZ from the Black Sea to the Baltic Sea could comprise the former Warsaw Pact territory west of the Russian Federation and include the three Baltic states of Estonia, Latvia, and Lithuania; the four Visegrad states of Poland, the Czech Republic, Slovakia, and Hungary; the newly independent states Belarus, Ukraine, and Moldova; and Romania and Bulgaria. The territory of the former German Democratic Republic could also be included, since there is already a treaty making it nuclear-weapon-free. The Russian exclave of Kaliningrad Oblast could possibly also be part of the zone.

A number of area specific matters would have to be addressed, including:

– the prospective zone would be surrounded by strong military powers with nuclear weapons, Russia to the east and NATO states to the west; this would invite a discussion of thinning-out measures to be applied in areas neighbouring the zone, including adjacent sea areas;
– nuclear warheads and also their delivery vehicles would have to be banned from the zone as is the case in the former East German territory;
– a number of arms control agreements would apply to the region, primarily the CSBMs agreed within the Organization on Security and Cooperation in Europe (OSCE), the CFE treaty, and the unilateral USA-USSR declaration on the withdrawal of sub-strategic nuclear weapons from theatres of deployment and from naval ships;
– security guarantees already apply to the area, including the positive

guarantees adopted by the UN Security Council,[45] the negative guarantees unilaterally extended by all nuclear weapon powers,[46] and the special security assurances given to Ukraine and Belarus by the Russian Federation, the UK, and the USA;[47]

- the question of military bases of extra-zonal states within zonal territory.

Two Maritime Zones

In 1970, a non-aligned summit meeting[48] proposed establishing the Indian Ocean as a zone of peace. A year later, the UN General Assembly declared the Indian Ocean a zone of peace "within limits to be determined."[49] The objective was to remove from the area any manifestation of great power military presence, including military bases and nuclear and other weapons of mass destruction, and to establish a collective security system, "where warships and military aircraft may not use the Indian Ocean for any threat or use of force against littoral or hinterland states." At the same time, there should be no infringement of the right of navigation according to international law. Geographically and politically, the Indian Ocean zone of peace issue is closely related to the long-time proposal to establish an NWFZ in South Asia. The Indian Ocean issue has been on the UN agenda ever since 1970; a resolution on the matter is adopted by the General Assembly each year.[50] An *Ad Hoc* committee was appointed in 1972 to prepare a conference of states concerned to negotiate a treaty. These deliberations have turned out to be very difficult.

In July 1979, the littoral and hinterland states of the Indian Ocean held a meeting resulting in a substantive final document.[51] A preliminary geographical delimitation was agreed as "the Indian Ocean itself, its natural extensions, the islands thereon, the ocean floor subadjacent thereto, the littoral and hinterland states and the air space above." On denuclearization, "the nuclear-weapon states were called upon to undertake not to establish nuclear bases in the Indian Ocean and to refrain from conducting nuclear test activities in the Indian Ocean," and similarly, "the littoral and hinterland states of the Indian Ocean should agree not to acquire or introduce nuclear weapons in the Indian Ocean themselves or to allow their introduction by an external power."

The same document reaffirmed "the right of all states to use the Indian Ocean for navigation and other peaceful uses, freely and without hindrance, in conformity with international law and custom, provided no threats are posed to the independence, sovereignty and territorial integrity of the littoral and hinterland states." But the document also "reaffirmed" the right of the states of the region "to refuse to grant to the great powers facilities for their warships or military aircraft which are or could be used in the context of great-power rivalries or for any other purpose that may be detrimental to the sovereignty, territorial integrity or security of the states of the Indian Ocean." This proposal would infringe on the general principle of freedom of the sea and has provoked opposition from major maritime powers. Both the geographical scope and the scope of measures of a possible zone in the Indian Ocean are only vaguely indicated in the relevant documents.

On the initiative of Brazil, the UN General Assembly declared in October 1986 the South Atlantic a zone of peace and cooperation.[52] Geographically, the zone was briefly described as "the region situated between Africa and South America."

In September 1994, the third meeting of member states of the zone of peace and cooperation of the South Atlantic adopted a "Declaration on the Denuclearization of the South Atlantic."[53] Zonal states would "prohibit and prevent, in their respective territories and jurisdictional waters, the testing, use, manufacture, production, acquisition, receipt, storage, installation, deployment and possession of any nuclear weapons." The "principles and norms of international law applicable to maritime space, in particular the use of the high seas for peaceful purposes and the freedom of navigation and overflight" would be honoured. All states are urged "to fully respect the status of the zone."

Three months later, the UN General Assembly endorsed the proposed zone.[54] The resolution was not unanimous, however. The zone proposal was criticized as imprecise both in terms of its geographical scope and regarding measures relating to high sea areas. It was understood, however, that the purpose of the resolution was not to open negotiations on a new NWFZ but rather to build on the zones already established in Latin America and Africa.

The Southern Hemisphere

The recent establishment of new NWFZs and other favourable conditions have inspired proposals for declaring the whole Southern Hemisphere a NWFZ. Such a zone would constitute a substantial step towards an NWFW.

All states in the Southern Hemisphere but three are parties to the NPT, and the three are members of NWFZs.[55] South Africa has dismantled her six nuclear explosive devices, adhered to the NPT (1991), and is now a member of the African NWFZ. Argentina and Brazil are today members of the Latin American NWFZ. All nuclear weapon powers are located in the Northern Hemisphere. Only a few of their remaining colonial dependencies are located south of the equator.

All land areas in the Southern Hemisphere with the exception of a few tiny islands in the Indian Ocean and the South Atlantic[56] are today included in NWFZs. While predominantly located in the Southern Hemisphere, all of the zones except Antarctica extend north of the equator as well.

Some of the Southern Hemisphere sea areas fall within NWFZs, although prescribed measures are very limited in these areas. Remaining sea areas are not subject to any nuclear-weapon-free regime. However, if it were possible to develop the ideas of a NWFZ in the South Atlantic and a zone of peace in the Indian Ocean, then eventually all the sea area of the Southern Hemisphere could become part of a NWFZ.

The five established NWFZs in the Southern Hemisphere have similar general objectives but differ is some details. The provisions of the Antarctic Treaty are vague as regards nuclear weapons. Two methods for establishing a nuclear-weapon-free Southern Hemisphere could be considered.

One method would be to negotiate a new "Treaty on Denuclearization of the Whole of the Southern Hemisphere" prescribing uniform objectives and measures for the entire zonal area. After entry into force, such a treaty would replace relevant parts of the five zone treaties of today. If the basic objective is the complete physical absence of nuclear weapons in the entire hemisphere, this method may be the obvious one. It has the disadvantage that such negotiations would probably be difficult to initiate, and would probably take a very long time.

A rather more flexible method would be to adopt an umbrella "Declaration on the Denuclearization of the Southern Hemisphere" outlining the general objectives and referring to existing zone treaties in force. In this way, the partial absence of nuclear weapons in the hemisphere will remain and a step by step extension over time would be possible. Such a declaration should be politically rather than legally binding.[57] The declared objectives could be the traditional ones:

–   the non-possession of nuclear weapons by all states located in the Southern Hemisphere;
–   the non-stationing of nuclear weapons south of the equator; and
–   the non-use and non-threat-of-use of nuclear weapons against targets south of the equator.

To this list could be added a ban on all nuclear testing, on dumping or other disposal of radioactive materials except in accordance with norms adopted by the IAEA, and on attacks on nuclear facilities, to be applied throughout the entire hemisphere.

Four protocols could be linked to the declaration, one for each of the existing NWFZs, to be adopted by the implementing bodies of these zones, and committing them to fulfil the guideline objectives within their zones; to proceed to an early entry into force of the zonal treaties for all their zonal territory;[58] and to encourage zonal states who have not yet done so, to adhere to the NPT, to the Sea-Bed Treaty, and to the Comprehensive Test Ban Treaty.[59]

A fifth protocol with similar content as appropriate could be adopted by the consultative parties to the Antarctic Treaty regarding the "white continent." A sixth legally binding protocol could prescribe the denuclearization of the southern island territories falling outside existing zones to be adopted by the states legally responsible for the islands.

A more difficult problem would be to include the vast sea areas – the major part of the hemisphere – into a denuclearization regime. The difficulty is not so much about military considerations, as about the conflict between arms control restrictions and the tradition of the freedom of the sea, and also the fact that so many parties would be involved in negotiating a measure of this kind.

There is a favourable starting point, however. As a consequence of the USA-USSR unilateral declarations in the fall of 1991, sub-strategic nuclear weapons are as a rule not deployed on naval ships of the US Navy and the Russian Navy. The only vessels carrying nuclear weapons are the submarines armed with strategic nuclear missiles. The other nuclear weapon powers have adopted similar policies. A beginning would be to make this situation permanent by requesting the nuclear weapon powers to negotiate a codification of the 1991 unilateral declarations.[60]

If this category of nuclear weapons could be removed permanently from the seas and oceans of the world, much would have been achieved for the states in the Southern Hemisphere as remaining sea-based strategic nuclear weapons are not primarily targeted on them. The umbrella declaration should, therefore, invite such codification as a first priority, and a seventh protocol could link this new treaty to the Southern Hemisphere NWFZ.

Pending such a codification, an eighth protocol could be adopted recommending enhanced "seaboard security"[61] for southern coastal states by means of confidence-building measures regarding nuclear weapons.[62]

A ninth protocol could encourage relevant states to speed up the negotiations on the establishment of a Zone of Peace in the Indian Ocean and a NWFZ in the South Atlantic. If those zones were established, all seas south of the equator would be zonal waters.

The problem of strategic nuclear weapons on submarines could be one of the most difficult for ordinary states – the verification problem would for instance be hopeless; however, these strategic nuclear warheads are directed against adversary nuclear weapon powers, not against states in the Southern Hemisphere. The solution to this problem would probably be the last to be solved before the Hemisphere could be declared completely free of nuclear weapons. A possible measure could be to link this issue to the continued START negotiations towards a nuclear-weapon-free world, and in the meantime accept that this category of weapon is occasionally present in the hemisphere, and adopt a tenth protocol recognizing a link between the START levels of sea-going nuclear weapons and the objectives of the umbrella declaration.[63]

Nuclear Security Assurances or Guarantees

In the nuclear non-proliferation family of international law, security assurances or guarantees constitute a special category. Reference will be made here only to guarantees directly linked to nuclear weapons arms control and not to the many defence alliances and non-aggression pacts, although some of these have a nuclear aspect with one or several nuclear weapons powers involved.

Existing Assurances

The earliest such guarantee issued by a nuclear weapon state was a unilateral declaration by the People's Republic of China on 16 October 1964, after China became a member of the nuclear club, "that China will never at any time and under any circumstances be the first to use nuclear weapons."[64] At the time, China was neither a member of the UN nor a participant in the Geneva Conference on Disarmament.

When the NPT was negotiated in the 1960s, the original idea was to include in the treaty a commitment by the nuclear weapon states not to use or threaten to use nuclear weapons against any non-nuclear weapon state party to the NPT. Instead, the problem was dealt with by means of separate documents outside the NPT.

In June 1968, the UN Security Council adopted a resolution outlining rules for assisting non-nuclear weapon states parties to the NPT subject to attack or threat of attack by nuclear weapons. The resolution

> welcomes the intention expressed by certain states (USSR, USA, UK) that they will provide or support immediate assistance, in accordance with the Charter, to any non-nuclear weapon State Party to the Treaty on the Non-Proliferation of Nuclear Weapons that is the victim of an act or an object of a threat of aggression in which nuclear weapons are used" (Op. 2).[65]

The value of this guarantee, to be operated by the UN Security Council, was limited, however, as four of the five nuclear weapon states at the time (all but the People's Republic of China) were permanent members of the Security Council with a right of veto.

After 1968, negotiations were undertaken at the Geneva Conference on Disarmament in order to develop the security guarantees into a legally binding and generally applicable treaty. The argument was that the non-nuclear weapon states, having renounced their nuclear weapon option, should not risk attack by such weapons before the long range goal of nuclear disarmament has been completed. Those negotiations have been pursued over many years without success.

In the meantime, however, in 1978 and 1982, all nuclear weapon powers extended unilaterally declared "negative"[66] assurances, slightly different in wording, that non-nuclear weapon states parties to the NPT will not be subject to attack or threat of attack with nuclear weapons. The Chinese guarantee was absolute in nature, while those of the four others were subject to various conditions, primarily in case a non-nuclear weapon state carries out an act of aggression in association or alliance with a nuclear weapon state against the guarantor state.

In addition, on 12 June 1982, the Soviet Union declared unilaterally that it had assumed "an obligation not to be the first to use nuclear weapons,"[67] thus matching China's declaration of 1964. The Western nuclear weapon powers did not make such no-first-use declarations, because during the Cold War they considered themselves to be inferior in conventional forces in Europe and thus felt a need for being able to retaliate with nuclear weapons against conventional attack. With the reversed imbalance of forces in Europe after the Cold War, the Russian Federation has arrived at the similar conclusion, and their new "Basic Provisions of the Military Doctrine of the Russian Federation" (Decree No. 1833), adopted on 2 November 1993, does not include the USSR no-first-use declaration of 1982.

Finally in April 1995, the UN Security Council adopted a modernized resolution taking note of both existing negative nuclear assurances and the positive assurances of 1968 where the five nuclear weapon states (now all members of the UN) undertake to provide "immediate assistance, in accordance with the UN Charter, to any non-nuclear weapon state party to the NPT that is a victim of an act of, or an object of a threat of, aggression in which nuclear weapons are used" (Op. 7).[68] Again, the value of this guarantee is limited as the nuclear weapon states are also permanent members of the Security Council with a right of veto. The "threshold states" are not, however. The declarations by the five nuclear weapon powers accompanying the resolution can be interpreted as *legally* binding following a recent ruling by the International Court of Justice.[69]

All four treaties establishing NWFZs include a separate protocol prescribing negative security guarantees not to use or threaten to use nuclear weapons against the zone. The Tlatelolco Treaty's Protocol II, the Rarotonga Treaty's Protocol 2, the Bangkok Treaty's Protocol, and the Pelindaba Treaty's Protocol I, all include such a provision. The five recognized nuclear weapon powers were invited to adhere to these protocols. In case of the Tlatelolco and Rarotonga treaties, they have all done so, however, with statements of interpretation similar to the reservations connected to the unilateral negative guarantees. When signing Protocol I of the Pelindaba Treaty, the USA and UK expressed similar reservations while France did not. Russia has not yet signed that protocol. No nuclear weapon power has yet signed the Protocol of the Bangkok Treaty, which is currently subject to renegotiation.

Sharpening the Guarantees

Thus, all states parties to the Non-Proliferation Treaty or members of nuclear-weapon-free zones enjoy various nuclear security assurances or guarantees from all five nuclear weapon states. However, there are several shortcomings. The negative guarantees are slightly different in wording, and they are unilateral declarations that can be changed without notice and unilaterally interpreted by the guarantor state. The Security Council positive guarantee would be operated subject to the procedural rules of the Council including the right of veto of its five permanent members.

The beneficiaries of these guarantees are states, leaving out the oceans and seas, occupying about 70 per cent of the world's surface. This fact is becoming increasingly obsolete, with the changing attitudes towards the status of the sea. In earlier analyses, seas areas were considered to belong to no-one, with few constraints therefore on military action at sea. Today, international sea areas are considered to belong to all, implying that states must behave at sea in a way that does not infringe on the rights of all others having the same right to enter and use the sea areas. In particular, the use or threat of use of nuclear weapons against targets in international waters can hardly be accepted, considering the enormous potential consequences for very many users beside the belligerents. The fact that sub-strategic nuclear weapons have been withdrawn from general purpose naval ships makes nuclear attack against targets at sea very unlikely.

Two scholars have recently put forward a proposal for a unified nuclear weapon state declaration and a more far-reaching Security Council resolution to protect non-nuclear weapon states parties to the NPT.[70] Another proposal is that of Joseph Rotblat – the conclusion of a legally binding No-First-Use Treaty, Chinese style, "under which the nuclear weapon states commit themselves not to be the first to use, or threaten to use, nuclear weapons against each other, or – by virtue of simple deterrence doctrine – against any other state.[71]" Such a treaty, if universally adhered to, would supersede and make unnecessary the guarantees instituted so far.

The agenda of measures to be pursued in parallel should thus include:

- a unified negative security assurance declaration by the nuclear weapon states not to use or threaten to use nuclear weapons against non-nuclear weapon states;
- a unified declaration that nuclear weapons will not be used against any targets at sea;
- a far-reaching positive guarantee by the UN Security Council protecting non-nuclear weapon states;
- a No-First-Use Treaty.

The permanent elimination of sub-strategic nuclear weapons is relevant here. If they were eliminated, the security guarantee would be strengthened, since weapons that might be used to violate those guarantees would not exist.

A Treaty on Sub-strategic Nuclear Weapons

The agreements, and prospective agreements, on intermediate and long-range nuclear weapons – INF, STARTs I & II and now START III – have tended to dominate the discussion of nuclear disarmament. However, the co-ordinated unilateral decisions on tactical weapons have also been most important.

The Unilateral Declarations

In the fall of 1991, after the failed 19 August coup in Moscow, with the dissolution of the Soviet Union imminent, and a dangerous possibility that 14 Soviet republics seeking their independence could also become *de facto* nuclear weapon states by taking over the control of tactical nuclear weapons that happened to be stationed on their soil, it became clear that measures to guarantee the central control of tactical nuclear weapons would be immediately necessary.

There was no time to work out an elaborate treaty on tactical nuclear weapons together with adequate verification machinery. Instead, the President of the USA on 27 September 1991 and the President of the USSR a week later, made co-ordinated unilateral declarations that all sub-strategic nuclear weapons would be withdrawn from theatres of deployment and from general purpose naval ships; they were to be dismantled or kept in storage.

The central part of the declaration by President George Bush states that

> The USA [will] eliminate its entire world-wide inventory of ground-launched short-range nuclear weapons, that is, theatre nuclear weapons. We will bring home and destroy all of our nuclear artillery shells and short-range ballistic missile warheads. We will, of course, ensure that we preserve an effective air-delivered nuclear capability in Europe ... Recognizing further the major changes in the international military landscape, the USA will withdraw all tactical nuclear weapons from its surface ships, attack submarines, as well as those nuclear weapons associated with our land-based naval aircraft. This means removing all nuclear Tomahawk cruise missiles from US ships and submarines, as well as nuclear bombs aboard aircraft carriers. The bottom line is that under normal conditions, our ships will not carry tactical nuclear weapons. Many of these land- and sea-based warheads will be dismantled and destroyed. The remaining warheads will be secured in central areas where they would be available if necessary in a future crisis.

The central parts of President Mikhail Gorbachev's matching declaration states:

> All nuclear artillery ammunition and nuclear warheads for tactical missiles will

be destroyed; nuclear warheads of anti-aircraft missiles will be removed from the army and stored in central bases. Part of them will be destroyed. All nuclear mines will be destroyed. All tactical nuclear weapons should be removed from surface ships and multipurpose submarines. These weapons, as well as nuclear weapons on ground-based naval aviation, shall be stored in central storage sites and a portion shall be eliminated.

On 29 January 1992, after the dissolution of the Soviet Union, President Boris Yeltsin of the Russian Federation confirmed the commitment of Mr Gorbachev, declaring that

> During the recent period, production has been stopped of nuclear warheads for land based tactical missiles, and also production of nuclear artillery shells and nuclear mines. Stocks of such nuclear devices will be eliminated. Russia is eliminating one-third of sea-based tactical weapons and one-half of nuclear warheads for anti-aircraft missiles. Measures in this direction have already been taken. We also intend to halve stocks of air-launched tactical nuclear munitions. The remaining tactical air-launched nuclear armaments could, on a reciprocal basis with the United States, be removed from combat units of the frontline tactical air force and placed in centralized storage bases.[72]

Reacting to the US-USSR reductions, the British government later declared that "Royal Navy ships and Royal Air Force maritime patrol aircraft will no longer have the capability to deploy tactical nuclear weapons. The UK weapons previously earmarked for this role will be destroyed."[73] The French government reacted by repeating the willingness of France to participate in nuclear disarmament, but expressed no specific commitments on sea-based weapons. Later, France decommissioned or mothballed all its tactical nuclear weapons. China welcomed the US-USSR announcements but made no commitments.

These measures are now being implemented. Many tactical nuclear weapons have been dismantled, particularly in the USA, but many are stored ready for redeployment if needed.

Hardening of Soft Agreements

These unilateral declarations are fundamentally important for European and indeed for world security. However, since they are not legally-binding treaties, they are "soft" agreements; unilateral changes could be made with no great difficulty. It is time to turn them into legally binding treaties; this would greatly enhance the stability of the current nuclear situation in the world and be a fundamentally important basis for nuclear-weapon-free zones everywhere.[74]

Codification could remove some present weaknesses:

– a verification regime could be designed;
– numbers could be defined for weapons to be dismantled and for inventories in storage;
– the use of released weapon-grade fissionable material could be proscribed; and,
– separate protocols could be negotiated to define matching measures to be undertaken by the other three nuclear weapon powers.

Nuclear disarmament has so far focused on strategic nuclear weapons as the most formidable ones and the central military arm of high politics during the Cold War. Results achieved have been solidly based in binding legal documents and their implementation has been scrupulously verified. Tactical nuclear weapons have been given lower priority. The reasons for this seems obvious from the point of view of the nuclear weapon powers. Tactical nuclear weapons have a warfighting function. They are relatively mobile. Their role is overshadowed by the bigger strategic weapons. Their reduction will thus be more difficult to negotiate.

Still, for the majority of the states of the world, any nuclear threat would more probably be from short-range and tactical nuclear systems rather than from strategic weapons. In any move to a NWFW, most states would be concerned more with the elimination of tactical nuclear weapons than with the elimination of strategic ones, since it is the tacticals which present them with the greater threats. The 1991 unilateral declarations are the obvious point of departure. Transforming these declarations into a permanent legally binding treaty would be the obvious next step in such a process.

Concluding Remark

These, then, are some of the gaps that need to be filled in the progress towards a NWFW. The proposals for filling these gaps could imply the following agenda:

1/ removing nuclear weapons and the nuclear threat from ever increasing areas by pursuing the nuclear-weapon-free zone concept;
2/ a treaty to eliminate sub-strategic nuclear weapons;
3/ completing the success of the NPT by finding a formula for the three threshold states to become parties;
4/ conclusion of a No-First-Use Treaty;
5/ continued negotiation of the reduction of strategic nuclear forces beyond START II;
6/ a declaration not to use nuclear weapons against targets at sea.

The order of items on the list does not reflect the general order of priority for achieving a nuclear-weapon-free world. It does, however, indicate the order of issues in which non-nuclear weapon states interested in working for a nuclear-weapon-free world might be able to exercise an influence, individually or collectively.

Notes

1. The Treaty on the Non-Proliferation of Nuclear Weapons (UN *Treaty Series*, Vol. 729, No. 10485) was opened for signature on 1 July 1968 and entered into force on 5 March 1970.
2. Document NPT/CONF. 1995/32/DEC. 3 (11 May 1995), contained in an annex to document NPT/CONF. 1995/32 (Part I).
3. Documents on Disarmament 1968, p. (478) 495.
4. Document NPT/CONF. III/64/I, Annex I.
5. UN document Res S 687 (1991), 3 April 1991.
6. *The Treaty between the USA and the USSR on the Elimination of their Intermediate-Range and Shorter-Range Missiles* (INF Treaty) signed 8 December 1987 and entered into force 1 June 1988. *Treaty between the USA and the USSR on the Reduction and Limitation of Strategic Offensive Arms (START)* signed 31 July 1991 and entered into force 5 December 1994. *Treaty between the USA and the Russian Federation on Further Reduction and Limitation of Strategic Offensive Arms* (START II) signed 3 January 1993 and not yet in force.
7. The Report of the Commission on Global Governance proposed in 1994 that nuclear and other weapons of mass destruction should be eliminated in ten to fifteen years (*Our Global Neighbourhood*, Oxford University Press, 1995, p. 133, pt14); while the *Report of the Canberra Commission on the Elimination of Nuclear Weapons* did not, in its report August 1996, suggest an explicit date for the completion of the nuclear disarmament process, but was "convinced" of the basic importance of agreed targets and guidelines "*which would drive the process inexorably towards the ultimate objective of final elimination, at the earliest possible time*" (*Executive Summary*, p. 15).
8. Principles and Objectives for Nuclear Non-Proliferation and Disarmament [Document NPT/Conf. 1995/32/DEC. 2 contained in an annex to document NPT/CONF. 1995/32 (Part I), paras 5-7.
9. UN Document A/RES/51/45 B.
10. UN Document A/RES/51/47 B, Op. 9(a).
11. *Cf.* UN Document A/CN.10/1997/CRP.3 and Annex, 9 May 1997.
12. The Treaty for the Prohibition of Nuclear Weapons in Latin America and the Caribbean (*UN Treaty Series*, Vol. 634, No. 9068).
13. The South Pacific Nuclear Free Zone Treaty, *UN Treaty Series* No. 24592.
14. Treaty on the Southeast Asia Nuclear-Weapon-Free Zone signed by the ASEAN member states at a summit meeting in Bangkok on 15 December 1995. For text, see *SIPRI Yearbook 1996*, Oxford University Press, 1996, pp. 601-609.

15. The Pelindaba Text of the African Nuclear-Weapon-Free Zone Treaty was signed in Cairo on 11 April 1996. For text, see *SIPRI Yearbook 1996*, Oxford University Press, 1996, pp. 593-601.

16. North-South Joint Declaration on the Denuclearization of the Korean Peninsula was agreed on 31 December 1991 and entered into force on 19 February 1992. For text, see J. Goldblat, *Arms Control: A Guide to Negotiations and Agreements*, PRIO, London: Sage Publications, 1994, pp. 643-644.

17. The Antarctic Treaty, *UN Treaty Series*, Vol. 402, No. 5778.

18. *Cf* UN Documents A/9693/Add. 1 and A/RES/3263 (XXIX).

19. The issue of establishing a nuclear-weapon-free zone in the Middle East (NWFZME) has been researched and studied by the Egyptian scholar and diplomat Mahmoud Karem, *A Nuclear-Weapon-Free Zone in the Middle East: Problems and Prospects*, New York: Greenwood Press, 1988. The same author has later published *A Nuclear-Weapon-Free Zone in the Middle East: A Historical Overview of the Patterns of Involvement of the United Nations* in T. Rauf ed., *Regional Approaches to Curbing Nuclear Proliferation in the Middle East and South Asia*, Aurora Papers 16. Canadian Centre for Global Security, December 1992. *Cf* also S. Feldman, *Nuclear Weapons and Arms Control in the Middle East*, Cambridge, MA: MIT Press, 1997.

20. UN Document A/RES 45/52, Op.8.

21. International safeguard issues involved were explored at an IAEA workshop in Vienna 4-7 May 1993. See *Proceedings of the Workshop on "Modalities for the Application of Safeguards in a Future Nuclear-Weapon-Free Zone in the Middle East*, Division of External Relations, IAEA.

22. As reported by S. Freier in C. Atterling Wedar, S. Hellman, K. Söder, eds., *Towards a Nuclear-Weapon-Free World*, Stockholm: Swedish Initiatives, 1993, p. 181, (ISBN 91-972128-0-6).

23. The concept of weapons of mass destruction was defined by the UN Commission for Conventional Armaments already 13 August 1948 as "*atomic explosive weapons, radioactive material weapons, lethal chemical and biological weapons, and any weapons developed in the future which have characteristics comparable in destructive effect to those of the atomic bomb or other weapons mentioned above*" (UN Document RES/S/C.3/30) or expressed in modern terminology as nuclear, biological, chemical, and radiological weapons, or weapons with similar effects.

In recent years, long range missiles have frequently been considered related to weapons of mass destruction both as carriers of warheads of mass destruction and as instruments of long distance conventional surprise attacks. In 1987, seven western industrialized states agreed to establish a "Missile Technology Control Regime" (MTCR) focusing on both ballistic and cruise missiles with a range exceeding 300 kilometres and with a payload capability exceeding 500 kilogrammes.

The resolution on Iraq adopted by the UN Security Council (UN Document S/RES/687 (1991)) following the 1991 Gulf war include definition type specifications on weapons of mass destruction. Besides nuclear (Op. 12), chemical and biological weapons (Op. 8a), the resolution also addresses "ballistic missiles with a range greater than 150 kilometres" (Op. 8b).

24. Document CD/989 (20 April 1990).

25. The Mubarak plan has recently been described by Mohamed Shaker in *Prospects for Establishing a Zone Free of Weapons of Mass Destruction in the Middle East*, Director's Series on Proliferation, 6 (October 1994), Lawrence Livermore National Laboratory (UCRL-LR-114070-6). The Mubarak plan concept is further developed in J. Prawitz, J F Leonard, *A Zone Free of Weapons of Mass Destruction in the Middle East*, UNIDIR Document 96/24 (UN Sales No GV.E.96.0.19).

26. Document NPT/CONF. 1995/32/RES/1.

27. UN Documents A/RES/3265 A (XXIX) and A/RES/3265 B (XXIX).

28. The most recent resolution is included in UN Document A/RES/51/42.

29. "Agreement between Pakistan and India on the Prohibition of Attack against Nuclear Installations and Facilities" was signed 31 December 1988 and entered into force on 27 January 1991.

30. A. Mack, *A Northeast Asia Nuclear-Free Zone: Problems and Prospects*, in A. Mack ed., *Nuclear Policies in Northeast Asia*. Research Report UNIDIR/95/16 (UN Sales No. GV.E.95.0.8), pp. 97-126.

31. *Cf* D. Lockwood, *The Status of U.S., Russian, and Chinese Nuclear Forces in Northeast Asia*, Arms Control Today, 24:9 (November 1994), pp. 21-24.

32. The "thinning out" idea was first suggested by A. Thunborg in *Nuclear Weapons and the Nordic Countries Today – A Swedish Commentary*, A Special Issue of Ulkopolitiikka 1975, pp. 34-38.

33. Lockwood, *The Status of U.S., Russian* ... The US declared on 22 January 1992 that all nuclear weapons had been withdrawn. The US unilateral declaration of 27 September 1991 was declared implemented 2 July 1992.

34. Relates to the Soya Strait, the Sugaru Strait, the channels on both sides of the Tsushima Island, and the Osumi Strait. Compare *The Law of the Sea. National Claims to Maritime Jurisdiction.* (UN Sales No.E.91.V.15). 1992. p. 72.

35. It should be noted that Taiwan (Republic of China) did ratify the NPT in 1970. After the People's Republic of China replaced Taiwan (Republic of China) in the United Nations in November 1971, the government of Taiwan has been considered a non-governmental organization by the UN and the IAEA, and Taiwan could not conclude an NPT related safeguards agreement with the IAEA. Taiwan should, however, be considered a non-nuclear-weapon party to the NPT. Its nuclear activities are subject to IAEA safeguards according to a unilateral submission in October 1969 (IAEA Document INFCIRC/133) and to the transfer of a US/Taiwan agreement in December 1971 (IAEA Document INFCIRC/158).

36. For an elaboration of the consequences of the "Three Non-Nuclear Principles," see H. Fujita, *The Three Non-Nuclear Principles of Japan*, Kansai University Review of Law and Politics, 5 March 1984, pp. 27-66.

37. The nuclear programmes of some of the prospective zonal states are much bigger than those of member states of other zones, nuclear power being an essential part of the electric energy supply of South Korea (36.1% of total), Japan (33.4%), and Taiwan (28.8%). South Korea has currently 11 reactor units in operation producing 9120 MW(e), Japan has 51 units producing 39893 MW(e), and Taiwan has 6 units producing 4884 MW(e). In addition, more than 8 new units are under construction in these countries. The current nuclear pwoer programme of North Korea is by comparison minor. Beside two research reactors, one small (50 MW(e)) and one

medium size power reactor (200 MW(e)) were being constructed but are now "frozen." However, according to a recent agreement with the USA, an international consortium would provide North Korea with two light water-moderated nuclear reactors with a total generating capacity of approximately 2000 MW(e) by a target date of 2003 (Power data according to IAEA Reference Data Series No 1-3, *Energy, Electricity and Nuclear Power Estimates for the Period up to 2015*, July 1996 edition; *Nuclear power reactors in the World*, April 1996 Edition; and *Nuclear Research Reactors in the World*, December 1996 Edition).

38.   There are several such precedents in the history of arms control when ratification instruments have included interpretative declarations referring, explicitly or implicitly, to the status of territories and governments considered controversial. Examples include the German Democratic Republic, the city of Berlin, Israel, Southern Rhodesia, South Africa, the Democratic Republic of Viet-Nam and the Republic of South Viet-Nam, the Democratic People's Republic of Korea and the Republic of Korea, and others. A special category are declarations related to sovereignty rights at sea.

39.   Document NPT/CONF. 1995/SR. 3, para 10. Compare also Documents NPT/CONF. 1995/MC. II/1 as contained in NPT/CONF. 1995/32 (Part II), p. 330, paras 12-14; NPT/CONF. 1995/DC/CRP. 1/Rev.4; and NPT/CONF. 1995/MC.II/17.

40.   Treaty on the final settlement with respect to Germany (Art. 5:3), signed in Moscow on 12 September 1990.

41.   The North Atlantic Treaty, signed in Washington D.C. on April 4th, 1949, is the founding legal instrument of the NATO alliance. The mutual positive security guarantee is included in its Article 5.

42.   Foreign Minister Syanko of Belarus and Foreign Minister Udovenko of Ukraine spoke at Plenary Sessions of the 51st UN General Assembly on 2 October and 26 September 1996 respectively.

43.   Compare for instance statements by the Minister of Defence of the Russian Federation, General Pavel S. Grachev, on 4 January 1996, at the Military Academy in Kiev, Ukraine, *International Herald Tribune*, 5 January 1996; and by his successor, General Igor Rodionov, at the North Atlantic Council Defence Ministers Session at NATO Headquarters in Brussels on 18 December 1996, *International Herald Tribune*, 19 December 1996.

44.   Major-General (ret) Vladimir Belous, in *National Security and Nuclear Policy*, Former Soviet Union Fifteen Nations: Policy & Security, October 1995, pp. 2-8; and in *Tactical Nuclear Weapons in the New Geopolitical Situation*, Digest of the Russian Nonproliferation Journal, *Yaderny Kontrol*, 1, Spring 1996, pp. 9-12.

45.   UN Documents Res S 255, 1968 and Res S 984, 1995.

46.   The contents of these unilaterally declared guarantees are summarized in *Compilation of Basic Documents relating to the Question of Effective International Arrangements to Assure Non-Nuclear Weapon States against the Use of Nuclear Weapons* (UN document CD/SA/WP.15, 16 March 1993) and in *Developments with regard to effective arrangements to assure non-nuclear weapon states against the use or threat of use of nuclear weapons* (Document NPT/CONF.1995/PC.III/6, 12 July 1994). Compare also *UN Disarmament Yearbook* v. 14, 1989, pp. 179-180. The new "Basic Provisions of the military Doctrine of the Russian Federation" adopted on 2 Nov. 1993 (Decree No. 1833) does not include the USSR no-first-use declaration of 12 June 1982, however.

47. On the occasion of Ukraine's final adherence to the NPT on 5 December 1994, the three nuclear weapon powers Russia, UK, and USA signed with Ukraine a "Memorandum on Security Assurances in Connection With Ukraine's Accession to the Treaty on the Non-Proliferation of Nuclear Weapons." Similar documents were signed on the same occasion with Belarus and Kasakhstan. The memorandum reaffirms the commitments of the three nuclear weapon powers as included in the CSCE Final Act (1975), the UN Charter, the Security Council positive guarantees, and in their unilaterally extended negative security guarantees, i.e. "*to respect the independence and sovereignty and the existing borders of Ukraine* Belarus)." For text, see *Arms Control Today*, 25:1 (January/February 1995), p. 11.

48. The Third Conference of the Heads of State or Government of Non-Aligned Countries, held at Lusaka 8-10 September 1970.

49. UN Document A/RES 2838 (XXVI).

50. The most recent resolution on the Declaration of the Indian Ocean as a Zone of Peace is A/RES/51/51.

51. Final Document of the Meeting of the Littoral and Hinterland States of the Indian Ocean, held in New York 2-13 July 1979 (UN Document A/34/45 and Corr. 1). For text, see also *e.g.* United Nations DISARMAMENT YEARBOOK, Vol. 4: 1979 (UN Sales No E.80.IX.7), pp. 325-330.

52. UN Document A/RES/41/11.

53. UN Document A/49/467 Annex II.

54. UN Document A/RES/49/84.

55. Southern Hemisphere non-parties to the Non-Proliferation Treaty are Brazil, Cook Islands, and Niue (1 February 1997).

56. Such islands are dependencies of two nuclear weapon states, France and the UK, and two non-nuclear weapon states Australia and Norway.

57. All the arms control agreements of the OSCE are considered politically rather than legally binding. Such agreements were adopted by consensus by the participating states and entered into force without elaborate ratification processes.

58. *Cf* UN Document A/RES/51/45 B, Op. 2.

59. UN Document A/RES/50/245, 10 September 1996.

60. The US-USSR agreement on withdrawal of sub-strategic nuclear weapons has the non-legal form of mutual unilateral declarations and is thus vulnerable to possible spontaneous change of mind. The government of Sweden has proposed the codification into legal treaty form of the agreement (5 February 1996).

61. The concept of "seaboard security" for coastal states was introduced in the 1985 United Nations expert report *Study on The Naval Arms Race*, UN Document A/40/535 (Sales No. E.86.IX.3), para. 264.

62. One possible such measure suggested long ago would be to declare that passage through the territorial waters of foreign states with nuclear weapons onboard would not be considered innocent implying the need for coastal state consent as a condition for the passage. This proposal was advanced both at the first and third UN Conference on the Law of the Sea (UN Documents A/CONF.13/C.1/L.21 (1958) and A/CONF.62/C.2/L.16, 1974).

Another could be to constitute a special legal category of warships having nuclear weapons onboard distinguishing themselves by flying an agreed special flag or bearing another agreed external mark. Such ships could then be subject to both precautionary restrictions and navigational privileges serving security and safety purposes. In addition they could be given additional immunity protection to strengthen the non-proliferation regime. A third possible measure could be a commitment by the nuclear powers to declare the number though not the position of their strategic submarines operating at sea at regular points in time. A fourth could be an understanding among the coastal states of the Southern Hemisphere that access to their ports by ships carrying nuclear weapons on board would be restricted to emergency cases.

63. After implementation of START II in the year 2003, 1750 strategic nuclear warheads would remain onboard about 20 submarines in each of Russia and USA.

64. *Documents on Disarmament 1964*, p. 449.

65. UN Document S/RES/255, 1968.

66. "Negative" guarantees imply that the guarantor abstains from nuclear aggression as different from "positive" guarantees implying that the guarantor actively supports a victim of aggression.

67. UN Document: *Official Records of the General Assembly*, 10th Plenary Session, 12th Plenary meeting.

68. UN Document S/RES/984 (1995), unanimously adopted on 11 April 1995, Op. 7. The basic declarations were made on 5 and 6 April 1995 by the Russian Federation (UN Document S/1995/261), the UK (S/1995/262), the USA (S/1995/263), France (S/1995/264), and China (S/1995/265).

69. International Court of Justice, *Legality of the Threat or Use of Nuclear Weapons*, Advisory Opinion to the UN General Assembly, 8 July 1996, para 105 (D).

70. G. Bunn and R. Timerbaev, *Security Assurances to Non-Nuclear Weapon States: Possible Options for Change*, PPNN Issue Review No. 7, September 1996.

71. J. Rotblat, *Beyond Start 2 – Beyond the NPT*, Bulletin of Arms Control, 17, February 1995, pp. 28-32.

72. For the full text of the Bush, Gorbachev, and Yeltsin-statements, see *e.g. SIPRI Yearbook 1992*, Oxford University Press, 1992, pp. 85-92.

73. Statement in the House of Commons 15 June 1992. For full text, see *e.g.* UN Document CD/1156.

74. Recently, the Government of Sweden proposed such a codification (Statement by Sweden's Minister of Foreign Affairs, Ms Lena Hjelm-Wallén on February 5th, 1996). The government of Norway has made a similar proposition (Minister of Foreign Affairs Bjørn Tore Godal on 23 March 1996).

Index